Richard Perceval Graves was born in 1945. He was educated at Charterhouse and St John's College, Oxford. He became a full-time author in 1973. His books include *Lawrence of Arabia and his World* (1976); *A.E. Housman: The Scholar Poet* (1979); *The Brothers Powys* (1983); *Robert Graves: The Assault Heroic 1895-1926* (1986); *Richard Hughes* (1994); and *Robert Graves and the White Goddess 1940-85* (1995). He lives in Shrewsbury.

ROBERT GRAVES
THE YEARS WITH LAURA RIDING, 1926-40

Richard Perceval Graves

WEIDENFELD AND NICOLSON · LONDON

First published in Great Britain in 1990
by Weidenfeld & Nicolson

This paperback edition first published in Great Britain in 1995
by Weidenfeld & Nicolson

The Orion Publishing Group Ltd
Orion House
5 Upper Saint Martin's Lane
London WC2H 9EA

A CIP catalogue record for this book is available from the
British Library.

ISBN: 0 297 81630 6

Printed and bound in Great Britain at
The Bath Press, Avon

FOR

JEFF AND LORNA CAINE

AND FOR MY COUSIN

ROWAN BROCKHURST

CONTENTS

BOOK THREE   THE SHOUT 1929

BOOK FOUR   ROBERT GRAVES AND LAURA RIDING IN MAJORCA 1929–1936

ILLUSTRATIONS

Unless otherwise acknowledged the pictures reproduced here belong to the author.

ACKNOWLEDGEMENTS

Grateful acknowledgement is made to the Executors of the Estate of Robert Graves for permission to quote from the works of Robert Graves, and to Sam Graves for permission to quote from writings by Nancy Nicholson.

For permission to quote from the following, grateful acknowledgement is made to: the Trustees of the *Seven Pillars of Wisdom* Trust for extracts from the writings of T.E.Lawrence; Anthony Sheil Associates Ltd. for *Robert Graves* by Martin Seymour-Smith, published by Hutchinson & Co. and by Abacus; A.P.Watt Ltd on behalf of Paul O'Prey for *In Broken Images: Selected Letters of Robert Graves 1914–1946* published by Hutchinson & Co.; Cassell plc for *Under the Influence* by T.S.Matthews; George T. Sassoon for extracts from Sassoon's letters; T.S.Matthews for unpublished writings of Norah McGuinness and Bob Casey; Mary Taylor for unpublished writings of Geoffrey Phibbs and for *Geoffrey Taylor: A Portrait 1900–1956*, an unpublished monograph by Terence Brown.

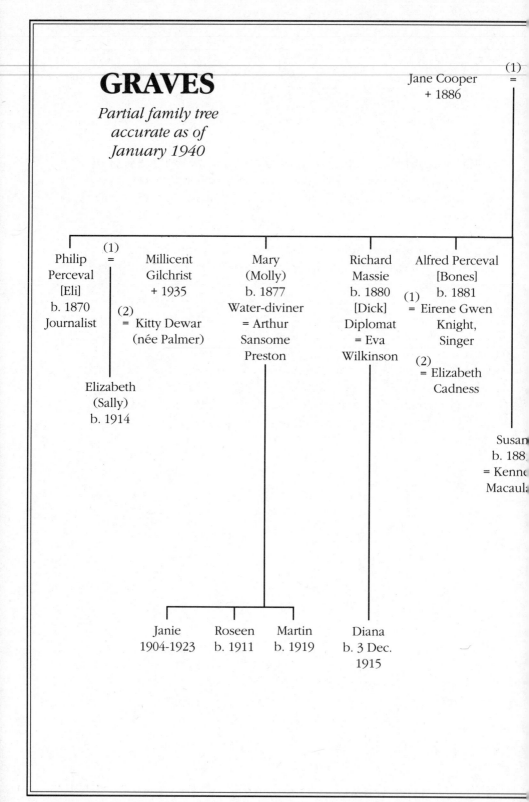

GRAVES

*Partial family tree
accurate as of
January 1940*

(1)
= Jane Cooper
+ 1886

Philip
Perceval
[Eli]
b. 1870
Journalist

(1)
= Millicent
Gilchrist
+ 1935

(2)
= Kitty Dewar
(née Palmer)

Elizabeth
(Sally)
b. 1914

Mary
(Molly)
b. 1877
Water-diviner
= Arthur
Sansome
Preston

Richard
Massie
b. 1880
[Dick]
Diplomat
= Eva
Wilkinson

Alfred Perceval
[Bones]
b. 1881
(1)
= Eirene Gwen
Knight,
Singer

(2)
= Elizabeth
Cadness

Susan
b. 188
= Kenne
Macaula

Janie
1904-1923

Roseen
b. 1911

Martin
b. 1919

Diana
b. 3 Dec.
1915

(2)

lfred Perceval = Amalie Elizabeth
1846-1931   Sophie von Ranke
Poet, HMI   1857-
          d. Heinrich
           von Ranke

Clarissa	Rosaleen	=	James	Robert	=	Annie	Charles
Janie	b. 1894		Francis	von Ranke		Mary	Patrick
b. 1892	Doctor		Cooper	b. 24 July		Nicholson	Ranke
Poet,				1895		(Nancy)	b. 1899
Artist,				Poet,		b. 13 Sept.	Journalist
Christian				Novelist		1899	= Margaret
Science						dr. William	Gordon
actitioner						Nicholson,	(Peggy)
						the artist	

John Tiarks Ranke ——
b. 1903
Scholar of
St John's College,
Oxford,
Working for Oxford
Education Authority
[later to become the father
of the present author]

Jenny Prydie	John David	Catherine	Samuel
(Nicholson)	b. 7 Mar.	(Nicholson)	b. 4 Jan.
b. 6 Jan.	1920	b. 3 Feb.	1924
1919		1922	

Dan	Roger	Paul
b. 1933	b. 1935	b. 1937

INTRODUCTION

Robert Graves and Laura Riding met each other for the first time in January 1926. They rapidly became close friends; and during the period of their association, which lasted some fourteen years until it was finally broken off by Riding in February 1940, each of the two writers produced much of his or her most notable work.

Robert Graves had previously attracted only slight attention as one of the soldier–poets of the 1914–18 War, and (until 1922) as one of the contributors to Edward Marsh's volumes of *Georgian Poetry*. Now he achieved popular fame both with his autobiography *Good-bye to All That* (1929) and with his historical novels *I, Claudius* (1934) and *Claudius the God* (1935); while the appearance of his *Collected Poems* (1938) confirmed his growing reputation as a significant twentieth-century poet.

Laura Riding, briefly a member of that group of American poets who called themselves the 'Fugitives', had attracted still less attention than Graves; but (besides being a formidable critic) she was an original poet of great distinction, and these were the years in which the greater part of her literary work was produced.

The story of the association between Graves and Riding, which forms the principal subject-matter of this book, is not only the story of an important literary partnership, but a highly dramatic saga of personal relationships. Graves's sister Rosaleen, who saw much of Robert and Laura and their circle in the late 1920s, found what happened at that time so extraordinary that she began to feel like a minor character in one of the great Russian novels. All that she could do, she told another member of the family, was to watch helplessly as the principal characters were tossed this way and that by storms of passion.

This book can be read as a separate work; but it also takes its place as the second volume of the trilogy which begins with *Robert Graves: The Assault Heroic, 1895–1926*. In that first volume, Robert Graves's early life was inevitably (for reasons which will become clear in the main body of this work) less dramatic than Robert's own brilliant account of himself in *Good-bye to All That*; and it provided a picture of a very different Graves from that of his middle and later years.

In this second volume the story is a far more dramatic one; and from about 1929 onwards the Graves who is remembered by people who are still alive today comes sharply into focus.

Laura Riding herself appears considerably more complex than in the past; and my account will please neither her small but loyal band of admirers, nor her much larger band of detractors. Within these pages she is (for most of the time) neither saint nor sinner. Instead I found a highly manipulative but also highly vulnerable woman, capable of inspiring both passionate devotion and passionate hatred, who was first Graves's salvation, but ultimately came close to destroying him.

A.E. Housman once asserted that Pride, despite being one of the seven deadly sins, is an efficient substitute for all the cardinal virtues; and from the biographer's point of view the strain of arrogance which runs so strongly through much of the Graves family has had a number of very good effects. Chief of these is the remarkable manner in which so many of them preserved such detailed records of their own lives. In each generation someone with a particular interest in family history acted as unofficial archivist; and when my father John Graves (Robert's brother) died in January 1980 I inherited from him thousands of items dating from the 1790s onwards: chiefly letters, but also diaries, personal memoirs, family trees, portraits and photographs.

These items have provided much important material for the first two volumes of the present biography; but they have not been my only source of original information. Besides studying collections of papers in England, Spain and the United States of America, I have visited eye-witnesses in both England and Spain; and corresponded with those living further afield: in Australia, for example, or Peru.

I am very much in the debt of all those who have given me assistance. In particular I thank my Aunt Beryl, who welcomed me to Deyá in November 1986, in May 1988 and in March 1989, who allowed me once again to comb the Canelluñ archives for information, and who has continued to be unfailingly helpful and encouraging. Others who have supplied me with first-hand information include Doris Ellit (nanny to Robert's children in Egypt and afterwards), the late Mary Ellidge (a close friend of Robert's in the 1930s), Karl Gay (who as Karl Goldschmidt was Robert and Laura's secretary from 1934, and who most generously did some editorial work on the entire text of the present volume), Laura (Riding) Jackson (until the autumn of 1987 when our correspondence sadly came to an end), Eirlys Roberts, Mary Taylor (Geoffrey Phibbs's second wife) and Honor Wyatt. I particularly thank Tom and Pam Matthews for their hospitality, and Tom (who knew Robert and Laura well in the 1930s) for his advice. The late Dr Rosaleen Cooper, Robert's sister also contributed; as did my Aunt Betty Graves,

Perceval's widow; and many of my cousins, especially Catherine Nicholson and Sam Graves (the surviving children of Robert's first marriage), and Sally Chilver, the daughter of Robert's half-brother Philip. I am also grateful to Mr Alan Clark, the friend and bibliographer of Laura (Riding) Jackson, who was an enormous help in supplying me with published material about Mrs Jackson's life.

Others who have kindly given me both advice and information include my friends Jeffrey Caine and Judy Coleridge, Pam Darlow, Justin Evans, Richard Fairbairn of Messrs Thompson Quarrell, Roger Horrocks (the biographer of Len Lye), Elizabeth Inglis (of the MSS section of the University of Sussex library), Ian Jenkin, Lucy McEntee (the literary executor of Richard Hughes), Lady Mancroft, Martin Seymour-Smith, Adrian Sherwood, Saundra Taylor of the Lilly Library at the University of Indiana, James Tyler of the Department of Rare Books at Cornell University, John Vice and Jeremy Wilson (the biographer of T.E. Lawrence). I thank my cousin Lucia Farran (who lent her house in Deyá to me for a while) and William Graves. I also thank my picture-researcher Anne-Marie Ehrlich, and Eric Norris, master-bookseller, for his work in hunting down many of the books which I needed to consult. I also thank Deborah Baker (the biographer of Laura Riding) for help in locating an unpublished journal by Lucie Brown.

I thank my editor at Weidenfeld, Candida Brazil, whose detailed suggestions for the final shaping of the book have once again been most valuable; and my agent Andrew Best, for continuing to look after my interests so effectively.

BOOK ONE

A PASSAGE TO EGYPT
1926

CHAPTER 1

A Backward Glance

London Docks, the morning of Friday 8 January 1926. An easterly breeze. The smell of salt water. Gulls crying. Robert Graves, poet and critic, now halfway through his thirty-first year, says goodbye to his old comrade-in-arms Siegfried Sassoon, and walks up the gang-plank on to the deck of a liner: the P&O *Ranpura*, smoke already pouring from her central funnel, bound for Bombay, via Gibraltar, Marseilles, Malta and Port Said.

Graves is on his way to Egypt where, upon the recommendation of many influential friends and admirers (ranging from Lord Lloyd, High Commissioner of Egypt, to the novelist E.M.Forster), he has been appointed Professor of English Literature at Cairo University. It is the only full-time appointment which he has accepted since he was demobilized from the army in 1919; and although it will provide him (after years of near-destitution) with solid financial security, it may also impose upon him an official and conventional way of life which he knows he would find deeply distasteful. So he views the future with mixed feelings.

There is nobody else but Siegfried Sassoon to see him off. Robert's parents Alfred Perceval Graves, the Irish poet, now in his eightieth year, and Amy, born von Ranke, in her sixty-ninth, are already travelling home to Erinfa, their house on the edge of Harlech, North Wales. Amy, writing a letter in the corner of their railway carriage to her youngest son John, tutoring at St Moritz, declares:

> This is the memorable day upon which Robert & all his family are setting sail for Cairo. We have seen them several times during the last few days but did not see any object in seeing them off at the Docks as they have a lady Secretary to help them & it is always painful to see the people you love slowly receding from the shore & vice versa.[1]

By Robert's side is his wife Nancy, an independent-minded young woman who is nevertheless in a poor mental and physical condition. Her clothes

3

are young and stylish, and her hair is cropped fashionably close under a broad-brimmed hat of the type art students now favour. Appropriate, for her ambition is to become a successful artist. But Nancy seems older than her twenty-six years: she has been suffering badly both from nervous depression and from a pituitary imbalance, and has been advised that she must winter in a warm climate if she is to regain her health.

Besides being an artist, Nancy is an ardent feminist, and has insisted on retaining her Nicholson surname (she is the daughter of Sir William and the sister of Ben, both distinguished artists), and on passing it on to her two daughters: Jenny Nicholson, who has only just had her seventh birthday; and Catherine Nicholson, who will be four in February. Only Nancy's two sons, David, who will be six in March, and Sam, who is just two years old, are allowed to be Graveses. All four children are on board, under the care of Doris, their cheerful young nurse. They take a keen interest in the strange sounds and sights. Whistles blow, horns blare, the gang-plank is lowered away, the mooring ropes are cast off, Robert and Nancy wave a final goodbye to their friend Siegfried (sometimes Robert has jealously suspected that Nancy takes too close an interest in his fellow-poet)[2] and tugs begin pulling the *Ranpura* out into mid-channel and then downriver towards the sea.

The eighth member of the party is the 'lady secretary' of whom Amy wrote. But the term 'lady secretary', comforting and conventional, is also wildly inappropriate; for the woman in question is a twenty-four-year-old American poet, the remarkable Laura Riding Gottschalk.

CHAPTER 2
Laura

Among the millions of Europeans who migrated across the Atlantic during the latter part of the nineteenth century to find security and freedom from persecution in the New World was a fifteen-year-old Austrian Jew named Nathan S. Reichenthal. Arriving in New York in 1884 he remained at first within the traditional Jewish community, working as a tailor and marrying (as his second wife) Sadie, a Jewish girl from downtown Manhattan whose parents had been born in Germany.[3] Striving to better himself and his new wife, Nathan then embarked upon a series of ill-conceived business enterprises. Repeated failure led him to question not his own judgement, but the capitalist society in which his enterprises foundered: he became active in the American Labour movement, and Socialism replaced Judaism as the great religion of his life.[4]

It was into this usually impoverished and always intensely idealistic household that Laura Reichenthal was born on 16 January 1901. Her early life was constantly being disturbed as her father lurched from business failure to business failure, and from bad address to worse address. Laura attended almost a dozen different primary schools, and was said by her school-fellows to have developed 'an ungovernable temper'[5] as a child; while her mother 'withdrew into illness and hypochondria';[6] and a measure of stability was attained only when her half-sister Isabel married and moved to a large house in Brooklyn, where she made the rest of her family welcome. Laura was now fortunate enough to spend all four high-school years at the Girls' High School in Brooklyn, where her formidable intelligence had a chance to make itself apparent.

Laura had already replaced her mother as her father's intellectual companion: though when she was fifteen years old she repudiated his left-wing sympathies,[7] later writing crossly that Nathan had wished her to become 'an American Rosa Luxemburg'; and she left the High School at the age of seventeen with no fewer than three scholarships, and a place at the

College of Arts and Sciences at Cornell University.

When Laura arrived at Cornell in the Fall of 1918,[8] she found the provisions there 'luxuriously adequate'[9] for someone, like herself, with a special interest in literature and writing. In addition to studying Latin, Chaucerian English, French and German, she took courses in French and German literature, and studied English literature under Professor Martin Sampson who presided over his field in a way which (in her own words) made Laura 'feel faced with the broad scene and given the opportunity to take in all that suited one's appetite of feeling'. Apparently Professor Sampson often remarked disapprovingly about aspects of her work, and yet her papers were always given the highest possible mark. This left Laura feeling that she was 'free to be and do whatever came naturally'.[10]

During her second year at Cornell, Miss Reichenthal met and fell in love with Louis Gottschalk, a graduate student who also came from Brooklyn and was two years older than she, had taken his BA in the summer of 1919, and was now teaching at Cornell as an Assistant in Ancient History. Laura and Louis were married on 2 November 1920,[11] when Laura was still only nineteen years old, and her husband was twenty-one. He offered her not only sexual excitement – and she threw herself into the relationship with passionate intensity – but also intellectual companionship of a high order, and security of a kind which she had never previously experienced.

On or soon after their marriage Louis had adopted Laura's maiden name as his new middle name; and Laura had also preserved the name of Reichenthal.[12] By 1923 the marriage was already failing,[13] and Laura threw herself into writing, submitting both fiction and poetry to editors, and decided that 'Laura Reichenthal Gottschalk' was too much of a mouthful for her prospective readers to swallow. She replaced Reichenthal with Riding, a name which pleased her because it preserved the first letter of her original name, but was far easier to pronounce. It seemed to her to possess 'a certain identity-weight'.[14]

Laura believed that she had something important to say. One novel was completed, though unpublished; and then from the late summer of 1923 the poems of 'Laura Riding Gottschalk' began to appear in magazines such as *Nomad*, *The Lyric West* and *The Step Ladder*.[15] More important, her poem 'Dimensions' appeared in the August/September issue of *The Fugitive*. This was the 'house magazine' of the Fugitive group of poets, largely composed of students and teachers at Vanderbilt University in Nashville, Tennessee, and including in its number John Crowe Ransom, Allen Tate and Donald Davidson. 'Dimensions', entered for the Nashville prize of one hundred dollars which was in the gift of *The Fugitive*, did not win the prize, but 'received special remark', and was 'commended for its quality of originality'.[16]

The enthusiastic reception given to 'Dimensions' encouraged Laura to send further poems to *The Fugitive*; and in February 1924 four more were published,[17] including 'Starved', based upon memories of her poverty-stricken early years; and 'The Quids', a description of the sub-atomic structure of things, which also manages to convey a series of wry philosophical comments upon human life. At the same time a more profound point is made. Free will is an illusion; we are governed by a kind of fate, since it is the peripatetic movement of the minute 'quids' which determines how we behave.

Shortly before or after the publication of these further poems Allen Tate visited Laura at Louisville. Laura's marriage had been on the rocks for some while: Louis later wrote that, in his view, their marriage had foundered 'because of his lack of sympathy with her poetic career',[18] and now, in Allen Tate, she had found someone for whom, as for herself, poetry had become of prime importance. Before long she and Tate were having an affair. But, although Tate found Miss Gottschalk sexually desirable, he also found her intellectually inflexible. Since he was not prepared to renounce his own intellectual freedom, the affair was therefore brief. The only lasting and tragic consequence is rumoured to have been that Laura became pregnant, and then had a badly managed abortion which led to years of internal troubles.[19]

The affair was over, and later that year Tate married elsewhere; but Laura's friendship with him continued, and her links with the rest of the Fugitives were strengthened. Indeed, she had begun to see a new future for herself as a central member of their group, and during the summer of 1924 Laura corresponded with Davidson and Ransom, and also tried to raise money on their behalf, both in Louisville and (briefly) in New York. Though her efforts were largely unsuccessful, her enthusiasm was more than rewarded when in November they awarded her the Nashville prize for 1924. Years later one of John Crowe Ransom's friends was told by him 'in his urbane and circumspect way' that:

To the astonishment of the Nashville poets, Laura appeared in person to claim her prize. Furthermore she proposed herself for a job: secretary to the board of editors. I gathered from Mr Ransom that they didn't need and couldn't afford a secretary, and moreover that their wives did not take kindly to the idea.[20]

The intensity of her personality and the dedication which Laura expected from her fellow-poets were also frankly alarming; and her visit ended in some confusion, apparently after she had quarrelled with S.M.Hirsch, a wealthy Jew in his late thirties who had been the co-founder and financial backer of *The Fugitive* magazine.[21]

However, there was no doubt about the value of her work; and when in the December issue of *The Fugitive* the editors formally announced Laura's winning of the Nashville prize, they praised her writing in the most glowing terms:

> In the minds of the members of the group, who were the judges of the award, the poetry of Mrs Gottschalk stands out as the discovery of the year, and they deem it a privilege to be first in calling attention to the work of a young writer who is coming forward as a new figure in American poetry. With a diverse play of imagination she combines in her poetry a sound intellectuality and a keen irony which give her work a substance not often found in current American poetry. Her poetry is philosophical in trend, yet not divorced from life, but generally tense with emotion and concerned with profound issues. Furthermore, she has developed her own idiom of expression ... which gives her poetry the stamp of an original personality.[22]

Three months later, in March 1925, a further notice appeared in *The Fugitive*:

> WE EXPECT to receive general felicitations upon the recent acquisition of Mrs Laura Riding Gottschalk, of Louisville, as a regular and participating member of the Fugitive group. It will be unnecessary in the future to introduce her as a foreign contributor in these pages.[23]

Laura, who was shortly to be divorced from her husband, now made a second and much more prolonged visit to Nashville where (despite their earlier quarrel) she had been invited to stay with S.M.Hirsch, then living as a semi-invalid in the house of his sister Rose Frank and her family.[24]

During this visit Laura seems to have made a determined effort to assume a dominant position among the Fugitives; and indeed she had ideas about the central importance of poetry which any poet might have found inspiring. Her stay in Nashville saw the publication in the April number of *The Reviewer* of her moving article 'A Prophecy or a Plea', in which she argues that the poet should not be merely 'a stream of passage between the source that is life and the outlet that is poetry', but should take a more active role in which he 'envisage[s] life not as an influence upon the soul but the soul as an influence upon life.... He will not recollect life ... but life will proceed from him as from a champion.' In Laura's vision, the poet 'is the only premise. He is the potter. He is the maker of beauty, since all form originates in him, and of meaning, since he names the content.' The task of the poet is to 'tak[e] the universe apart ... [and then to] reintegrat[e] it with his own vitality; and it is this reintegrated universe that will in turn possess him and give him rest. If this voyage reveals a futility, it is a futility worth facing.'

Some of the Fugitives were impressed by Mrs Gottschalk's heroic, indeed almost godlike view of the poet; but others bitterly resented the arrogant manner in which she expected everyone else to fall in with her own views. Once again, her visit ended in some confusion. Hoping to weld the Fugitives more closely together in some kind of 'programmatic association', she had only succeeded in causing dissension within their ranks. Eventually it was made clear that she had outstayed her welcome in the Frank household, and she stormed off to New York.[25]

There she lived not far from Allen and Caroline Tate, and became a central figure at the parties given by their circle of friends. At first Laura threw herself happily enough into the drinking and dancing (often in the company of Hart Crane, with whom she is said to have 'cascaded into and out of most of the households in [New York's] small literary community'), and gained something of a reputation as a man-eater; but poetry remained her prime concern, and she gradually became disillusioned both with New York and with her American fellow-poets: none of whom, it seemed, took poetry seriously enough. And then, right at the end of 1925, she received an invitation to go to Europe to collaborate on a book about modern poetry with Robert Graves, who had been an admirer and occasional correspondent since coming across a group of her poems in *The Fugitive*, a magazine to which he himself was a contributor, in the middle of the previous year. Laura wired her acceptance with alacrity. Here was the chance of another fresh start, at the side of a fellow-poet of considerable distinction.

CHAPTER 3

Robert

Born in Wimbledon, a prosperous London suburb, on 24 July 1895, Robert von Ranke Graves had been brought up within a literary family in which it was taken for granted that artistic achievements were of great importance. Writing poetry had always been the 'second career' of his forty-nine-year-old Irish father, a twice-married Inspector of Schools who would regularly send off two or three poems to the papers when there was an inconvenient bill to be paid; while Robert's saintly but ambitious German mother (who came from the distinguished Bavarian family of von Ranke, and was already aged thirty-seven when Robert was born) not only encouraged him to be 'pure and right-minded', but did what she could to develop Robert's natural literary gifts from his earliest childhood.

It was during a particularly unhappy period while he was boarding at Charterhouse School that Robert had found in the writing of poetry an important way of coping with both external pressures and internal conflicts. From the age of fifteen, he wrote later, poetry was his ruling passion; and his poems appeared regularly in the school magazine, *The Carthusian*.

Robert's earliest Carthusian verse though technically imperfect is highly forceful, reflecting as it does the desperately overwrought condition into which he had been plunged by the assiduous bullying of his peers, boys who resented him chiefly because he was trying to live up to the high moral standards of his home.

Much of his later Carthusian verse, though witty and inventive, is more formal, and he would later condemn it as 'Apollonian' and unnecessary. But Robert enjoyed words and the technical challenge of experimenting with new metres and rhyming patterns, and (under the protective tutelage of George Mallory, schoolmaster and defender of the oppressed) poetry became not only an escape, but a positive pleasure. This pleasure was heightened by the close friendship which developed between himself and a much younger boy, 'Peter' Johnstone, which made writing poetry a celebration of the kind of highly charged idealistic relationship which often springs up in single-sex boarding schools, and which Graves later described as 'pseudo-homosexual'.

On leaving Charterhouse in the summer of 1914, Robert Graves had been caught up almost immediately in the Great War. During the next four years almost an entire generation of young men were slaughtered on the battlefields of Flanders and the Somme. Graves, serving as a junior officer in the Royal Welch Fusiliers, was sustained during this terrible ordeal both by his long-standing friendship with Johnstone and by his new friendship with his brother-officer and fellow-poet Siegfried Sassoon, to whom he wrote affectionately as 'Sassons', at one time planning that after the war they should live and work together on a permanent basis.

The stresses of his wartime experiences – at one point Robert was so badly wounded (shot through the lung) that he was left for dead, and was later able to read his own obituary in *The Times* – had a major impact upon him and upon his poetry, especially when combined with the thoroughgoing criticism which he had invited from Edward Marsh, mentor of so many of the younger poets, whose work he had begun to publish in successive volumes of *Georgian Poetry*. Robert's light-hearted Carthusian verses, full of archaic thees and thous, made way for the horrifying realism of lines such as those on the 'Dead Boche', who 'scowled and stunk / With clothes and face a sodden green'; and in 1916 an impressive first volume of Graves's poems appeared entitled *Over the Brazier*.

Later in the war Graves befriended the poet Wilfred Owen, whose personal favourite among Graves's war poems was 'The Legion', which appeared in his 1917 collection, *Fairies and Fusiliers*, and which runs as follows:

THE LEGION

'Is that the Three-and-Twentieth, Strabo mine,
Marching below, and we still gulping wine?'
From the sad magic of his fragrant cup
The red-faced old centurion started up,
Cursed, battered on the table. 'No,' he said,
'Not that! The Three-and-Twentieth Legion's dead,
Dead in the first year of this damned campaign –
The Legion's dead, dead and won't rise again.
Pity? Rome pities her brave lads that die,
But we need pity also, you and I,
Whom Gallic spear and Belgian arrow miss,

Who live to see the Legion come to this,
Unsoldierlike, slovenly, bent on loot,
Grumblers, diseased, unskilled to thrust or shoot.
O brown cheek, muscled shoulder, sturdy thigh!
Where are they now? God! Watch it straggle by,
The sullen pack of ragged ugly swine.
Is that the Legion, Gracchus? Quick, the wine!'
'Strabo,' said Gracchus, 'you are strange to-night.
The Legion is the Legion, it's all right.
If these new men are slovenly, in your thinking,
Hell take it! You'll not better them by drinking.
They all try, Strabo; trust their hearts and hands.
The Legion is the Legion while Rome stands,
And these same men before the autumn's fall
Shall bang old Vercingetorix out of Gaul.'[26]

In one sense this is a poem about the Roman past; and it is immediately evident that Graves's classical education at Charterhouse has borne fruit, and that like so many ex-public schoolboys of the nineteenth and early twentieth centuries he has a sympathetic and even romantic affinity with the ancient world. But the 'Legion' is also the Regiment in the British Army in which Robert was then serving, which had also suffered huge losses, and was full of raw recruits. The poem reveals something of Robert's intense loyalty to the Royal Welch Fusiliers, and of his faith in the qualities of the ordinary soldier. That loyalty and faith survived his own sufferings from shell-shock (for which he was hospitalized), and his growing conviction that the war was a tragic waste of life.

But not everything in Robert's character remained the same; and while he was recovering from his nervous collapse he underwent a major change of emotional direction. The first sign of this, a sick-bed attraction for a pretty nurse, was followed shortly afterwards by a massive revulsion from 'Peter' Johnstone, who had been convicted by an English court of making homosexual advances. Faced with the alarming thought that he himself had been treading down a dangerous 'pseudo-homosexual' road, Robert distanced himself from Johnstone as rapidly and as thoroughly as possible. The affair with the nurse had hardly begun before it was over; but a few months later Robert was in love with the young, likeable, stylish, artistic, devoted but occasionally stubborn and dogmatic Nancy Nicholson; and they were married in January 1918. The following year they moved to Boar's Hill near Oxford, where Robert resumed his academic studies as an undergraduate at St John's; and at first they were happy together. But their happiness was not to last.

Robert's hopes for popular success faded after the poor reception given in 1920 to *Country Sentiment*, his third volume of poems; while a year or two later Nancy's efforts to make money by running a shop on Boar's Hill also ended in failure. They had to contend with the stresses of a marriage in which they seemed unable either to earn much money or (when they had any) to live within their means. In addition, between 1919 and 1924 Nancy gave birth to four children in just under five years; and Robert suffered from recurring bouts of shell-shock.

For a while their retreat to the peaceful village of Islip gave them renewed hope; but Robert had been compelled by the poor state of his nerves to abandon his formal academic work; and for several years he and Nancy were depressingly dependent upon hand-outs from family and friends. Robert's continued failure to support himself by his writing now began to poison his relationship with Nancy, whose word for many years had been Robert's law. She became ill with worry, while Robert himself underwent a kind of personality crisis.

His nervous troubles had turned Robert away from the cheerful arcadianism of his immediate post-war poetry, and sent him delving first into psychology and then into philosophy. These new interests, which at first increased the interest of his poetry, had at one stage threatened to make his writing utterly obscure; and Robert was later to reflect that by the beginning of 1926 a process of personal disintegration was well under way. Who was he, and what was his purpose in life? Once he could have answered those questions with confidence; but recently there had been too many years of failure. Now, as he set sail for Egypt, he was in serious need of a strong and self-reliant person upon whose judgement he could rely, and in whose affection he could feel secure.

CHAPTER 4

The Voyage

The P&O *Ranpura* steamed down the English Channel, across the Bay of Biscay, southwards past Portugal, and then through the straits of Gibraltar into the Mediterranean. Doris read to the children from the 'Grimm's fairy tales, slightly illustrated', which Amy had given them for the voyage.[27] Nancy, Robert and Laura found that the three of them had fallen into what Robert was later to describe as 'friendship at first sight'.

First, between Nancy and Laura. Sally Graves, Robert's eleven-year-old niece, had already 'classif[ied] them as sisters since they both dressed very much alike in long dark coats buttoned down the front and broad-brimmed felt hats one light (N.), one dark (L.). I had never seen such clothes before, they seemed like a uniform.'[28] Later, when she had asked her mother about the mystifying clothes, she had been told: 'It is what art students wear.'[29] Nancy and Laura were both feminists to the extent that they believed that women should pursue their own careers; and for both women it was artistic endeavour which gave fundamental purpose to their lives. In Laura, Nancy could admire the writer; she could also like the cheerful companion who treated her with great kindness and consideration, who appeared ready and willing to share the intellectual and moral burden of looking after her troubled and dissatisfied husband, and who was a great practical help in dealing with ordinary day-to-day family affairs.[30]

Laura in her turn could admire Nancy's determination to achieve artistic success; and indeed Laura was always particularly kind and generous to women who were trying to lead an independent artistic or literary life. Years later she wrote that she had felt an immediate affinity with Nancy,[31] whom she described as vivacious, discriminating and sympathetic; although, as a result of her thyroid imbalance, she could be impatient and indecisive.[32] It must also have been clear to Laura from the first that Nancy was not Robert's intellectual equal, but that Robert was curiously subservient to her slightest whims; and therefore that her own position with Robert would at first depend very much upon the success of her relationship with his wife.

Next, between Robert and Laura. George Mallory's wife had noticed at Charterhouse that Robert always seemed happiest when he had found someone he admired who would give him direction. Since marrying Nancy, Robert had accepted her ideas and attitudes in many important respects; but intellectually there had been a substantial gap in his life since the departure from their circle in 1923 of the Bengali philosopher, Basanta Mallik. Now, in Laura Riding Gottschalk, Robert had found someone of great intelligence and originality, who listened with interest to his ideas, and whose head teemed with ideas of her own. Like him, she was a poet who believed strongly in the importance of poetry. Like him, she distrusted and even despised much of the literary establishment of the day. She was also a striking young woman with astonishingly blue eyes, and dark-brown hair which had been cut fairly short in America, but which she would now allow to grow until it fell attractively to her shoulders.[33]

Laura found in Robert Graves, a tall somewhat ungainly and yet handsome man, with his broken nose (a rugger injury), his quizzical grey eyes, and his large head covered by a shock of unruly hair, a poet of genius who was nevertheless so unsure of himself that he might very well become her intellectual disciple. After her failure with the Fugitives, all of them lesser men than Robert, this was an exciting prospect.

Friendship established, Gibraltar was their first port of call. Going ashore in holiday mood and fine weather, they bought figs and rode around the town in the open carriages which served as taxis even in winter. Robert, enjoying himself hugely, remembered how he had once deliberately avoided an army posting to Gibraltar, 'and thought what a fool I had been to prefer Rhyl'.[34] On past the Balearic islands to Marseilles, where they went ashore again for a few hours, and Nancy, in practical mood, bought herself a sewing-machine.

In North Wales Robert's mother had been scanning the 'Mails and Shipping' column in *The Times* for news of their progress. 'It is very windy here', she wrote on 10 January, 'and I cannot bear to think of them on the sea. I am glad Nancy is a good sailor but I don't think Robert is.'[35] And then, six days later, she was alarmed by news of violent storms in the Mediterranean, with much wreckage being washed up on the shores of the Riviera.[36]

But the P&O *Ranpura* had come to no harm, steaming south-eastward through the storms to Malta.[37] On 16 January Laura celebrated her twenty-fifth birthday on board ship; and, wishing time to stop, began to discover philosophical reasons why time, as usually understood, *had* stopped. Four days later they docked safely at Port Said. Robert, who had been very seasick, was relieved to be ashore; and so, in his own words, they went by train to Cairo, 'looking out of the windows all the way, delighted at summer fields in January'.[38]

CHAPTER 5

Heliopolis

On their arrival in Cairo, Robert and his household moved into an hotel, and were soon being warmly welcomed to Egypt by several of Robert's closest relatives. The most distinguished of these was his half-brother Richard or 'Dick' Graves, who at the age of forty-five was a senior member of the Egyptian Civil Service, and who lived with his highly strung wife Eva and their ten-year-old daughter Diana in a flat in the exclusive Cairo suburb of Gizereh. Dick and Eva had never had much to do with Robert, and having heard of Robert's unconventional ideas and Socialist politics they were understandably anxious that he might behave in a way which would reflect badly upon themselves. Perhaps partly because of this, they treated him and his family with the greatest possible kindness.

Robert was grateful for their welcome; but he was probably much more pleased to see Molly, his favourite half-sister, who had already helped the newcomers by sending one of her friends to Port Said to see them safely through the Customs. Molly, a water-diviner and a fey redheaded Irish beauty, had been like a second mother to Robert during his earliest childhood; and though she was now in her late thirties, and her beauty was fading, her warmth of manner and large violet eyes still attracted admirers among the young men. She and her husband Arthur Preston had lived in Alexandria for many years; but Arthur's work as a judge had now brought him to Cairo; and shortly before Robert's arrival the Prestons had moved with their children – fourteen-year-old Roseen and six-year-old Martin – into a house in Heliopolis, the City of the Sun, a few miles east of Cairo.

Robert's salary as Professor of English Literature at Cairo University had eventually been fixed at £1,140 a year; but, as his mother pointed out, 'with a motor car [paid for by Sassoon[39] and brought over from England in the hold of the *Ranpura*], nurse, Secretary & no house, only a Hotel, it will not go far'.[40] So the hotel was of necessity only a temporary home; and they moved almost at once into a first-floor flat. This was far from convenient, as it had no garden in which the children could play; and after a day or two Laura became unhappy there, and (supported by the two servants who had been engaged to cook and to clean, and who said that the flat had ghosts in it)[41] she declared it to be haunted.[42]

They immediately began looking for somewhere else; and Eva kindly helped them to find a basement flat with a garden, which would be free on 20 February, and which was also situated not far from Molly's house in Heliopolis. Eva may have been relieved at the prospect of keeping them so far from the centre of things, as Nancy's determination to remain 'Miss Nicholson' was already causing embarrassment.

Robert had been warned about this: shortly before he and Nancy left England, his uncle Charles, visiting them to say goodbye, had been shocked to discover that Nancy had obtained a passport in her maiden name, something which would be regarded as a very serious matter in Cairo society. He had said nothing at the time, not liking to raise objections in the presence of the family. But he had written about it to Alfred; and when Robert paid his first visit in Cairo to his bankers, Thomas Cook and Sons, he had found waiting for him a letter from his father 'expressing my feelings at Nancy's folly & enclosing Charlie's letter'.[43]

Despite this, Robert's first letter to his parents was a happy one. He was grateful to them for having partially financed his trip to Egypt, and for having agreed with his bankers that they would be personally responsible for any overdraft on Robert's account, up to the sum of £100; and he told them of the usefulness of his new motor-car; of the kindness of Dick, Eva, Molly and Arthur; of the purchase of cheap furniture; and of the 'nice flat with garden' that had been found.[44]

But they had only been in Egypt for a week or two, and were still in the first-floor flat which Laura disliked so much, when Sam developed measles – an infection which he must have caught on board ship. As his nurse Doris later recalled,

> Advised by Robert's sister ... a Doctor [Garvis] was called who advised that Sam should go into hospital as we were all so new to the climate and conditions of Egypt. Nancy was loathe [*sic*] to let Sam go to hospital until I volunteered to go with him & this was arranged by the Doctor. It was fortunate that I did because four days later the other three children had caught the infection & arrived in hospital. Jenny and Sam were quite ill [Sam's hearing was permanently affected] & I was thankful to

be with them otherwise it would have been a frightening experience for such young children.[45]

By the time Doris and her charges came out of hospital – the children looking to their father 'very thin and wretched-looking', after having been 'fed on all the things that we had been particular since their birth not to give them',[46] Robert and Nancy moved with Laura into their new Heliopolis flat.

Nancy was soon hard at work with her Marseilles sewing-machine, 'making all the children's clothes, also her own & Robert's shirts, & very soon Laura had discarded her American dresses in favour of simple dresses made by Nancy'.[47] While Doris saw to the children, there were two excellent Sudanese servants to do the cooking and cleaning; and at first it seemed queer to Robert 'not to look after the children or do housework, and almost too good to be true to have as much time as I needed for my writing'.[48] Nancy however was 'not very happy dealing with native servants', and so after a while 'Laura took over the task of planning meals with the cook & shopping, which was mainly done at special shops reserved for the British Army.'[49] Food was much cheaper at those shops, and Robert was able to make use of them in his capacity 'as an officer on the pension list'.[50]

When Robert was not at the University, he and Laura would work together on their writing; and, as Doris later recalled,

> Nancy would often take the children & myself out in the car. Nancy drove the car anywhere into Cairo or out into desert beyond Heliopolis or into farming areas. I remember on one occasion we stopped on the empty desert road a few miles out of Heliopolis for the children to play around for a while. When we came to start the car again the back wheels spun around & we could not move it.... we were stuck there for an hour or so until a Bedouin walking into Cairo came to our rescue.

There were also many outings when Robert and Laura came too:

> somehow eight of us managed to pile in, Nancy driving; later she taught Laura to drive. I remember often on the way somewhere the children would say 'Father tell us a story'.... he told them with such ease & could keep the children interested for hours. We visited the Pyramids, the Botanical Gardens & the Bazaars, & on one memorable occasion the Cairo Museum where we saw the beautiful treasures from Tutenkahmun's [*sic*] Tomb.[51]

On the face of it, everything seemed to be going reasonably well: Robert was able to work; the children had apparently made a full recovery from their measles; and Laura had fitted comfortably into their household. 'You need have no qualms', Graves had written to Sassoon as early as 3 February, 'You need have no qualms about Laura G. who in every way confirms our happiest suspicions about her.'[52] In addition, Nancy's health was improving; and she and Robert had made friends with a number of Heliopolis families with whom visits were exchanged; while Molly and Dr Garvis were also regular callers.

However, Robert had rapidly become dissatisfied with his job at the University. By mid-February he was already describing it in a letter to T.S.Eliot as 'a beautifully constructed farce in the best French style and dangerous if taken in the slightest degree seriously'.[53]

CHAPTER 6
Cairo

It was not until he had been in Cairo for more than a fortnight that Robert Graves presented himself to the University; nor did he make an early call on the Residency of Lord Lloyd, the British High Commissioner, as his brother Dick had advised. His delay in visiting the University was unimportant: as he wrote to Sassoon, 'nobody is ever in a hurry here: and indeed expedition is the height of vulgarity'.[54] But it would have been worth taking his brother's advice about calling on the Residency. For, although Egypt was nominally ruled by its own King Fuad, it was also a British Protectorate, and effective power was concentrated in the hands of Lord Lloyd and his staff. Indeed, it was later made clear to Graves (much to his embarrassment) that his task was to 'keep the British flag flying in the faculty of letters',[55] since most of the other professors were either French or Belgian.

The University was housed in a fine building, which had once been a harem-palace, and was 'French in style, with mirrors and gilding';[56] but it was also in an administrative shambles, with 'Staff fighting Consul Generals and Consul Generals fighting [the] Ministry [of Education]'.[57] And to add to the confusion of Robert and his fellow-professors, only one or two of whom were Egyptian, all official University correspondence was conducted in classical Arabic.

When Robert began his teaching, in early February, he found that he was expected to give two lectures a week: a number very soon reduced to one, as it had been decided that the students needed extra time to learn French, of which they knew hardly a word, despite the fact that it was the language in which most of their lectures were delivered. Luckily, Robert was told, they had all learned English for eight years, so he would have no need of an interpreter. Despite this, his first few lectures were 'pandemonium. The students were not hostile, merely excitable and anxious to show their regard for me and liberty ... and the well-being of Egypt, all at the same time. I often had to shout at the top of my loudest barrack-square voice to restore order.'[58]

After this 'false start', as Robert reported to his parents in mid-February, he was soon 'Working well and quietly with class';[59] but he had discovered to his horror that his students knew nothing; that they had no textbooks of any sort; that even when he tried to teach them 'the simpler literary terms' their inadequate grasp of English made progress extremely slow; that there were no English books in the University library, and that despite all these difficulties he was expected to have his students ready for an examination in English Literature in May.[60]

To begin with, Robert took all this in his stride. Perhaps he remembered the letter in which his old friend T.E.Lawrence had written that, even if he hated the work, there would be:

> no harm done. The climate is good, the country beautiful, the things admirable, the beings curious and disgusting; and you are stable enough not to be caught broadside by a mere dislike for your job. Execute it decently, as long as you draw the pay, and enjoy your free hours (plentiful in Egypt) more freely.[61]

Some of those free hours were agreeably spent in the company of one or other of the only two students whom Robert came to know at all well. The first was a Turk, an 'intelligent, good-natured young man, perhaps twenty years old', who was also very rich, and who 'had a motor-car in which he twice took me for a drive to the Pyramids'. The second was a Greek, who once invited Robert to his home, where tea was served by his 'three beautiful sisters named Pallas, Aphrodite, and Artemis'.[62]

Robert also lunched in February with 'Chawki Bey, the national poet of Egypt, in his Moorish mansion by the Nile'; and one morning, wearing the pre-war frock-coat which Amy had purchased for him in London, he attended 'a levee at the Abdin Palace, King Fuad's Cairo residence'. Neither event made much impression. The national poet only reminded Graves of Thomas Hardy; and he mistook the King for his own Grand Chamberlain. There were a few other official dinners or soirées to which Robert was invited; but since, as he wrote later, he 'had no intention of mixing with the British official class, joining the golf club, or paying official calls', there was little enough for him to do in Cairo.[63]

Most of Robert's time outside the University was therefore spent not in enjoying his free hours more freely (as Lawrence, knowing of his shell-shock and subsequent mental sufferings, had very sensibly suggested), but in working hard at Laura Gottschalk's side in their Heliopolis flat.

CHAPTER 7
Seeing Ghosts

Under the glare of the Egyptian sun, unfamiliar noises in his ears, unfamiliar smells in his nostrils; hearing the daily dawn-cry of a 'fabulous cross-breed between kite and cat ... kept as a pet in a neighbouring tenement';[64] travelling by tram through streets crowded with camels and donkeys; visiting beautiful sisters with the names of ancient Greek goddesses: almost anything began to seem possible to Robert, as everything was so strange. And not only strange, but, from the moment when Laura declared that their first Heliopolis flat was haunted, more than a little sinister. Later it was said by members of Graves's family that Laura had 'vampirised him from the first';[65] and if she had deliberately set out to create the right conditions for the successful seduction of her chosen and still somewhat shell-shocked companion, she could hardly have done better than to invoke the presence of the dead. It was in this heavily charged atmosphere that Robert began falling in love.

Friendship had been immediate; and beside his letter to Sassoon about Laura confirming their 'happiest suspicions', Robert had told his parents that 'Miss Gottschalk' was 'a treasure'.[66] But, to begin with, the most important element in their friendship appeared to be their successful working relationship: something which two writers usually find hard to achieve.

Robert was doing a certain amount of individual work on a study of the English ballad, which he had made the subject of his lectures at the University; and he was also preparing a long essay called 'Lars Porsena, or The Future of Swearing and Improper Language'; but he intended to devote his main efforts to his proposed *Untraditional Elements in Poetry*. Graves had originally asked T.S.Eliot, at that time editor of the *Criterion*, to collaborate upon this work; but he had already warned Eliot that 'if I find it's getting on too fast I shall possibly finish it myself';[67] and on 16 February he wrote to Eliot again, to ask:

Have you any objection to her [Laura] collaborating in this business after what you have seen of her work? She is far more in touch with the American side than I am and is anxious to get ahead with it. She suggests that at the end of a year – until which time you could promise nothing – you might come in as arbiter between our contributions. Please tell me how you feel about this. Her list of poets corresponded exactly with yours: and her critical detachment is certainly greater than mine.[68]

Eliot presumably made no objection; and although Graves and his new collaborator did not do a great deal of writing, they had endless discussions in which they began clarifying each other's ideas in preparation for the main work.

These discussions were so fascinating that Robert and Laura felt little need of society; and Robert did not even go into Cairo to call on his brother Charles, the journalist, who unexpectedly arrived in Egypt for ten days or so at the beginning of March. The beautiful and aristocratic 'Peggy' Gordon was staying not far from Dick and Eva in Gizereh; and Charles had sailed all the way to Egypt in another attempt to persuade her to marry him. Once again (and despite a moonlight visit to the Pyramids), Charles was given an enigmatic answer; and when he returned to England he also brought back with him the alarming news, heard from Dick, that Robert was 'seeing ghosts: though he does not give parties'[69] – so something other than excessive drinking, the usual expatriate problem, was troubling him.

Outwardly, all seemed well. Indeed, the bonds between the flat-dwellers at Heliopolis had grown so strong that by the end of March, when Laura had been a member of his household for less than three months, Robert wrote to Sassoon with this astonishing news: 'It is extremely unlikely that Nancy, Laura and I will ever disband, now we've survived this odd meeting and continue to take everything for granted as before.'[70]

But beneath the surface there were considerable tensions. Laura's worries about being haunted had raised the emotional temperature; and when they moved to the new flat, with its garden of 'fruit-trees and flowering shrubs', Robert was already feeling a little unbalanced. On his first walk in the garden, coming upon 'no less than eight lean and mangy cats dozing in the beds', he took their presence as some kind of evil omen, 'and never walked there again'.[71] Three years later, recalling these haunted months, he wrote not only about the links between himself, Nancy and Laura, in the words 'there was thereupon a unity to which you [Laura] and I [Robert] pledged our faith and she [Nancy] her pleasure'; but also about how they had gone together 'to the land where the dead parade the streets [Egypt], and there met with demons . . .'.[72]

The sinister quality of this haunting is fully realized in Robert's most successful short story, 'The Shout', which he did not complete until 1927, but which actually occurred to him 'one day while I was walking in the desert near Heliopolis in Egypt and came upon a stony stretch where I stopped to pick up a few mis-shapen pebbles; what virtue was in them I do not know, but I somehow had the story from them. . . .'.[73]

Two of the main characters in the story, Richard and Rachel, are an unconventional married couple clearly based to a large extent upon Robert and Nancy. Despite some differences, Richard and Rachel have grown so close to each other that they even share the same dreams; and one night they both dream of meeting a sinister stranger among the nearby sand-hills – sand-hills which Robert later wrote were based on those at Harlech, 'with an added Egyptian cruelty'.[74] In Richard's dream, the stranger makes the sand-hills seem both fascinating and alarming, by telling him: 'There is no life and no death in the sand-hills. Anything might happen in sand-hills.'[75]

The dream becomes a most terrifying nightmare, when the dream-stranger appears in Richard's waking life. Introducing himself as Charles, the stranger clearly has magical powers, and says that he has learned the secret of a 'terror-shout' strong enough to kill anyone who hears it. Soon Richard has lost control of events. Charles and Rachel fall in love; Richard is cast out; and he only recovers the situation when, realizing that some mis-shapen pebbles in the sand-hills contain the souls of all the people living in the area, he uses a hammer to smash Charles's soul to pieces.

It was a story which welled up unbidden from Robert's subconscious; and he later realized to his astonishment that it could be interpreted as a kind of prophecy about the events of the next few years of his life.

Internal tensions added to external pressures had now destroyed the happiness of their first weeks in Egypt. Robert was not only 'seeing ghosts', but suffering from what felt like a perpetual stomach upset; and mental and physical ill-health coloured his view of Egypt permanently. The modern town of Heliopolis, which he had liked at first, now seemed a 'dead' place[76] – he probably thought of it as 'godawful', an Americanism which he had picked up from Laura; and the people seemed irredeemably bourgeois: while Nancy, though she had regained her health, was evidently far from happy. Then, as the weather became 'very hot and uncomfortable there was quite a lot of discussion about where to spend the hottest months of the year'.[77]

It had always been understood that the summer months would be spent somewhere cooler; and, to begin with, Cyprus was favoured; but then there was a crisis. The children 'went down with dysentery & no medication seemed to help them'. It now seemed urgent to move to a cooler climate, at least for a while; and Nancy began 'long[ing] to return home'.[78]

In these circumstances Robert found that his patience with University life had worn intolerably thin; and on 31 March he posted a letter to Sassoon in which he described the University as 'a comic-opera', and added:

> I have never been so useless in my life before or with such pomp and circumstance. I had a lecture a week ago and have my next a week hence. 'Shakespeare was a great poet. He lived in England and wrote plays. London is in England. Plays are what you get at the theatre. A poet is a person who … Oh, yes, I'll spell the word on the blackboard. POET. No, Shakespeare is not another word for Byron.'
>
> Anyhow, Nancy is getting on well: main thing.… I am writing; I think readably. Laura is even more Laureate than ever. We intend to return at the end of May if there's any money to return on: which will be seen in due course.[79]

Robert did not admit it at this stage, but he was already determined that once he had left Egypt he would never return.[80] Given his unsettled state of mind this was a sensible decision, though it would mean giving up his salary and probably returning to financial dependence upon family and friends, several of whom had worked hard to secure the Cairo professorship for him. It would also mean breaking his contract with the Foreign Office and the Egyptian Government, an act just as serious in its day as breaking off an engagement to marry, for which Robert was later to condemn his brother Charles as a cad. It was some time, therefore, before Robert could bring himself to tell anyone his plans; but, early in April, Amy realized that something odd was going on. As she wrote to John (then on a temporary tutoring job at the British Legation in Budapest), she had heard from Robert that he was:

> returning on holiday on May 18th but goes back in the autumn. He intends bringing back all his family, which sounds extravagant, the more so as he has to sell his motor to help the starving 'adopted' family of a friend who let them have a lot of money some time ago. I am told no names or circumstances.… I have told him I cannot help him out again, as he has a salary now; and he must not, obviously, give more than he has got. They will miss the motor terribly out there in the heat.[81]

About a week later there was a further highly enigmatic letter from Robert, in which he once again mentioned the sale of the motor-car, saying that it had been 'paid for by one friend [so] why not sell it for that friend's friend?' He added that the professorship was 'a sham', that his integrity was 'hard to keep', and that because the food in Cyprus was suspect they could not spend the summer there, but would be returning to England instead.[82]

Sassoon was the first to whom Robert confessed the truth: towards the end of May he wrote to him with news of his imminent departure for England, and told him that it was:

> most unlikely that I shall return to this job; I may have to for a short time: but it is quite impossible to do any good with the students and my colleagues are bloody. So I am trying to arrange a lecture tour in America for the autumn and hope to hook a job at some University while I'm there.[83]

However, Egypt had 'done its duty': Nancy was now 'capable of doing a day's work without collapsing'; while he himself had 'done more reading in four months than in the last four years', and 'Not much writing, but enough.' In addition, Laura had become 'just a hundred times more to us than we ever hoped (these instinctive decisions are for the best) and we can't remember a time when she wasn't with us'.[84]

BOOK TWO

STRANGE TRINITY
1926–1929

CHAPTER 1

Resignation

When Robert, Nancy and Laura first landed in England on 10 July 1926, they were faced with the immediate problem of finding enough money to live on. Without it, even if Nancy and the children stayed in England, Robert and Laura might still be forced back to Egypt: for it was now a settled thing between them that Robert and Laura should continue to work together. In the past Robert and Nancy had always turned to their families when they were in need. But now that would mean admitting that Robert intended to break his contract. Instead, Robert turned to his friends; and even from them he half expected to receive acid remarks about his folly in proposing to give up a safe job. Several of them, however, were kinder than he had dared to hope.

In particular T.E.Lawrence (then enjoying life under the name of T.E. Shaw as an ordinary aircraftman at Cranwell) came to Graves's rescue with a copy of the first subscribers' edition of *Seven Pillars of Wisdom*. Marked 'Please sell when read', it fetched over three hundred pounds. Robert sold a number of other books too, 'chiefly autographed first editions of modern poets';[1] and the money which he raised gave him the confidence to write a formal letter of resignation from his Professorship at Cairo.

But three or four hundred pounds would not last for ever, and Robert and Laura were soon calling on Robert's literary agent, Eric Pinker, to see what he could arrange for them. It became clear that there was no chance of the American lecture tour for which they had been hoping, and no other very profitable work was to be had. In addition, Pinker had to report that T.S.Eliot had turned down a number of poems and critical essays by Laura, and that he had been unable to place them elsewhere. However, it was possible that a personal visit might help to change Eliot's mind; if that failed, the Hogarth Press might take an interest in Laura's poems; and Pinker also arranged for Robert and Laura to have a meeting with Heinemann to discuss a number of projects.

Eliot was away in the country; but Leonard and Virginia Woolf at the Hogarth Press admired Laura Gottschalk's work, and agreed to publish a collection of her poems, later in 1926, under the title *The Close Chaplet*; while Heinemann suggested that Robert should finish preparing for them the *Collected Poems* which at one time he had been going to do with Secker. Heinemann also agreed to sign a contract for a work by Robert and Laura to be known as *Modernist Poetry Explained to the Plain Man*.

A few days later, Robert, Nancy, Laura, Doris and the four children all travelled down to Oxfordshire, where they set up home once again at the Islip cottage which Robert rented from his mother, and which was known as The World's End. From there, on the last day of June 1926, Robert wrote to his parents that he was 'very happy ... and getting to work'. He was even hoping to be able to travel up to Harlech later in the month to celebrate his father's (APG's) eightieth birthday; though he pointed out that he was very busy, and would have to make it a flying visit[2].

In the event, he never went to Harlech. For, at about the time that he wrote to APG, his letter of resignation had reached Egypt, where it created a considerable stir. Lord Lloyd, the British High Commissioner, could not have been altogether surprised. Shortly before leaving Egypt, Robert had dined with him at the Residency; and later, over a game of bridge, Lloyd had asked him 'how I found Egypt and I said "All right," with an intonation that made him catch me up quickly. "Only all right?"'[3]

Disliking Egypt was bad enough; but breaking a contract was worse, and within a few hours the news was all over Cairo. There seemed little doubt that the matter would have a serious effect upon Dick Graves's career; and Molly and Arthur Preston immediately sat down to write long letters to APG explaining exactly what had happened, and asking whether he could try to change Robert's mind. Erinfa was thrown into a turmoil when the letters arrived on the morning of 10 July; and later that day Alfred and Amy 'both wrote strong letters to Robert to ask him to withdraw his resignation as an honourable man'.[4]

These letters fell on stony ground: four days later Robert's parents received a reply which APG described as 'haughty, ill-advised, contradictory & generally unsatisfactory'.[5] Other members of the family, recalling only too vividly Robert's long years of poverty, and his constant calls upon the family purse, sent letters of commiseration. 'I am terribly sorry to hear that Robert has chucked his job,' wrote his sister Clarissa for example. 'Really it's dreadful.'[6] But the break with Egypt was final and irrevocable; and Robert did his best to put it behind him and get down to some serious work. This was to prove difficult.

CHAPTER 2

Moods of Despair

Soon after arriving back at Islip, Robert Graves had written to T.S.Eliot, to inform him about progress on the proposed *Untraditional Elements in Poetry*. So far he had only managed to complete 'a little work on Isaac Rosenberg', while Laura Gottschalk had worked on 'John Ransom and Marianne Moore; principally a preliminary essay on Regionalism as a critical clue in American poetry (i.e. a false clue)'.[7] There was therefore a great deal more to be done, besides work on their new projects for Heinemann: *Modernist Poetry Explained to the Plain Man* and Robert's *Collected Poems*. In addition, there were a number of works to be seen through the press: including Robert's *Lars Porsena* and Laura's *The Close Chaplet*.

This enormous amount of work needed to be completed very rapidly if it was to bring in sufficient income; but it was very difficult for Robert and Laura to do much serious work together at The World's End, 'owing to the noises and interruptions and responsibilities'. Even by mid-July, Robert only felt 'sort of settled in'; and although Doris was still looking after the children, Nancy was 'making a valiant effort to draw again'; and Robert, who had in any case become accustomed to treating Nancy as a semi-invalid, was left with all the cooking and housekeeping, in addition to his literary work. The result was that several weeks went by without much being achieved; and, in Robert's words, they 'began feeling the financial pressure rather acutely'.[8]

It was an impossible situation; and although Laura and Nancy still appeared to be the best of friends, the tension in the household was increased by Nancy's inevitable feelings of jealousy for the close intellectual and spiritual ties which had sprung up between Robert and Laura, and which must have threatened at any moment to find some physical expression. Before long, Nancy found that she herself was unable to get any work done, and was therefore 'at a loose end'.[9] Rather than wait for the situation to slide into some possibly catastrophic denouement (perhaps she had read one of Laura's recent poems, 'John and I', in which Laura described a man who needed to be rescued from his wife, and added that there was an emptiness in her own life which no one but that man could fill), Nancy proposed a solution which was as sensible and practical as it was unconventional. Robert and Laura should go up to London to do some serious writing. She would be left at Islip looking after a much reduced household; and since three of the four children were now at school for much of the day, and she had Doris to look after Sam, there would be plenty of peace and quiet for her to resume her drawing.

At the beginning of August, Robert therefore took a basement flat for a month at 9, Ladbroke Square, Notting Hill. This was an unfashionable neighbourhood in West London, which was not only cheap, but which had the advantage of being close both to a station on the London Underground and to the open parkland of Kensington Gardens. It was within five minutes' walking distance of Siegfried Sassoon's rooms in Campden Hill Square; and indeed Robert wrote to him saying that 'We chose it because it is so near you.'[10]

To begin with, only one room in the Ladbroke Square flat was habitable, and so for a few days Laura lodged with the landlady. Then, when it was possible for Laura to move in, a veneer of respectability was added to their arrangements by the arrival of Robert's sister Rosaleen (now a qualified doctor) as a kind of chaperone. Even so, it seemed 'strange' to APG 'that Nancy should allow this'. For the time being he was prepared to accept the explanation that 'Robert cannot work with the children at World's End & Nancy prefers running house now herself & Miss G is doing a book of poetry with Robert';[11] but he was becoming more and more disconcerted by snippets of family gossip about Laura. Dick had made it clear that he 'does not think much of Miss Gottschalk's mentality'; Molly, who had been a good friend in Egypt, was now coming round to the view 'that [Laura] had affected Robert too much Americanwards',[12] and was therefore largely responsible for Robert abandoning his professorship; and a few days later John, who had been staying with Charles in London, and who one day shared a railway compartment with Robert and Laura as far as Oxford (where they were visiting Nancy and he was taking his degree), wrote that he 'did not cotton on' to Robert's new associate.[13]

Someone else, with a predictably hostile view of Laura, was Louis Gottschalk, who was visiting England when he called on his ex-wife and her new partner. Meeting Robert for the first time, he is said to have been:

impressed by his intelligence and wide knowledge. Since Riding kept reiterating that her work with Graves was a full collaboration, while Graves insisted on nothing, Gottschalk concluded she protested too much. He was also amused to notice that she had acquired an English accent along with Graves's learning.[14]

Robert would have cared nothing for any of these opinions. What was important to him was that he and Laura at last had each other almost entirely to themselves. By now it is probable that they were sleeping together: but they still felt compelled to keep up appearances; and when, in the last week of August, Rosaleen went abroad for a week, Robert and Laura returned to Islip before their full month was up, saying that they had 'finished what they wanted to do'.[15]

Within a short time all the old problems had reasserted themselves with greater force. Robert later tried to explain the situation to Sassoon by telling him that:

now [Nancy's] well she can't bring herself to resume the responsibility of the house unless we aren't there to force it on her: and that she can't begin to draw again unless she's alone, and she is longing to draw. [Laura and I] find in our turn that we can't get on with our work unless we have her equally busy.[16]

But this was only part of the truth. The real problem was that Robert, who had once been described by his father as wax in Nancy's hands,[17] was now wholly in Laura's power. Nancy could not help realizing this; and the result was that she began suffering from 'sudden & very black moods of despair in which she even hate[d] Robert'.[18] These moods were quite understandable; but she found herself in the position of Llewelyn Powys's wife Alyse, when faced with her husband's infidelities: her own ideals meant that she should show no jealousy; and when Nancy's black moods were over she was openly apologetic. After several of these episodes (during one of which she unsuccessfully appealed to Laura to return to America), Nancy felt that the situation was becoming intolerable; and so, declaring that she wanted 'a time of quiet & loneliness to find herself again', she 'offered to go away'.[19]

Robert and Laura offered to go in their turn, saying that they could look after themselves better than she could; and then, while they were discussing the matter, a smaller problem swam into focus, and helped in the solution of the greater one. They were very short of money, and Robert had learned that unless he were out of the country for six months of the

1926–7 financial year, he would eventually have to pay a heavy amount of income tax on his Egyptian salary.

Suddenly it seemed to all three of them that the sensible thing would be for Robert and Laura to go abroad to work together. Why not Austria? Its healthy climate would be excellent for Robert's lungs, while Laura would have a chance to explore her family antecedents. Looking at a map, they settled on Vienna; and then continued with their plans. Robert and Laura would come home to Islip for Christmas; and in the summer Nancy would take the children abroad to join them for an Austrian holiday. Everything would be done decently and lovingly, and they would all continue to care deeply for each other. If the experiment succeeded, it would be an important proof that it was possible for three people to enjoy a 'modern' relationship without jealousy, and without any regard for the formal conventions of society.

CHAPTER 3

White Heat

Robert Graves and Nancy Nicholson and Laura Gottschalk were now united in adopting a new scale of values, according to which certain actions which were then normally considered to be grossly unprincipled became highly commendable. This makes it all too easy to condemn them, and to ascribe to Robert and Laura the lowest possible motives for both their actions and their beliefs.

Robert, one could say, accepted the new code because it meant that he could remain virtuous, and think well of himself, despite running away from his wife with another woman. Laura's manipulations, one might add, had been entirely successful. She could now have Robert to herself for as long as she liked, without being compelled to abandon Nancy, for whom she had a considerable regard, to whom she was mildly attracted, and to whom Robert could be returned if and when she grew tired of him.

But on another level, and looked at from a different point of view, everything was working extraordinarily well. Laura was a ruthless manipulator not because she was intrinsically evil, but because at the heart of her character was a need for the kind of unselfish loving which had been denied her when she was a child, and which she had ever afterwards been seeking, from both men and women. Robert gave her that love in full measure, and she drank it in greedily.

Robert, dominated throughout his childhood by the moral force of his virtuous and loving mother, could only find happiness when he could love and obey someone else as he had loved and obeyed her – provided that this love and obedience did not bring him too much pain and guilt, and did not clash too uncomfortably with his remarkable intellectual and artistic gifts. Nancy's unthinking iconoclasm had removed much of his guilt; but although she had considerable artistic gifts, she was no intellectual match for Robert, and could never sit very comfortably on the pedestal which he had erected for her. Laura, on the other hand, was a woman of formidable intellect, whom Robert was able wholeheartedly to respect. She directed him, taught him how to be virtuous, and rewarded him for his discipleship by her loving acceptance and close interest in every aspect of his life and work. In Graves's shell-shocked and partially disintegrated state of mind, Miss Gottschalk was all that he could desire.

As for Nancy: having effectively set Robert and Laura free, she was not only free herself (dismarried at last!) but was amply rewarded for her unselfishness by the loving warmth with which they both surrounded her. Feeling really happy for the first time for weeks, Nancy (rather pathetically from another point of view) threw herself into making 'a trousseau for Laura to have suitable dresses to take with her'.[20] But perhaps happiness is too mild a word to describe the feelings of any of them, now that they had decided how to go forward. Joy was in the air; and for a while things were at white-heat between the three of them; and everything beyond the bounds of their narrow world seemed petty and of indifferent value.

However, Robert naturally hoped that his friends would understand and approve; and on 18 September, back in London, he and Laura called upon Siegfried Sassoon to explain what they intended to do. Finding him out, Robert wrote that:

> What we came to tell you was quite casually that we are going off to Austria together for a bit: unconventional but necessary and Nancy's idea .... We are all very happy about it, though we'll miss each other very much of course, and especially we'll miss the children. Funny life, ain't it?[21]

A day or two later, he decided that it was time to inform his parents, and he wrote them a letter telling them that he and Laura were going to Vienna with Nancy's consent until Christmas. When it arrived at Erinfa, on the morning of 21 September 1926, it threw APG and Amy into a state of utter consternation. Luckily Clarissa was at home, and she helped them to 'concoct ... a telegram to Nancy' which ran: 'Earnestly implore interview here or in London before taking irrevocable step Father, Mother, Clarissa.' That afternoon, they had just had tea when they were jolted by the receipt of the following wire from Nancy: 'Robert left [for] Vienna this morning. Please believe all well, Nancy.'[22]

Nancy sent a copy of the Erinfa telegram to Robert, who received it soon after arriving in Vienna with Laura, and immediately wrote a furious reply, condemning his family in the strongest possible terms for their inter-ference in his private affairs. APG sent the letter on to Clarissa, who destroyed it, and told her parents that it had wounded her:

very much when I read it: but I feel on reflection that it is not to be
taken at its face value. It is written in a fit of anger and nerves after
a trying journey and our joint wire may possibly have seemed the last
straw. One gets bitten if one attempts to touch a sick dog when it has
chosen the best feather-bed to lie on – and that is no bad analysis of
the situation.

All the same I don't regret the stand we made. 'No man liveth and
dieth to himself' and if Robert is fool enough to care nothing for what
the world says, but chooses to imagine that he is better than the society
which gave him birth, he must stand the racket when the world rises
and boxes his ears. He can't break the conventions flagrantly and then
be awarded the honours of the game. We shall suffer with him: but
it will be cheap at the price if he learns his lesson.

But I am awfully sorry for his vicious attack and hope Mother,
especially, will not take it too much to heart but will see it in its true
proportion. When he is well again he will himself forget the cruel things
he has said.[23]

Amy did her best to follow Clarissa's advice, but remained extremely upset
until she received a letter from Rosaleen stating 'that Robert & Laura are
still quite innocent'.[24] However unlikely this seemed, Amy was prepared
to believe it. She wrote at once to both Clarissa and John asking them
'to pray for poor Robert in this difficult and dangerous position. He is
like one of the three men in the fire, who yet were preserved unscathed.
May he be so. I shall not let Charles know till I cannot help it. I fear
he will believe the worst.'[25]

The next step was to write to Robert. Amy had no address for him,
but sent 'a soothing letter' for Nancy to read before forwarding it on to
Vienna. Reminding Robert that she and APG had already booked a month's
holiday at Hof Gastein, a health resort some forty miles south of Salzburg,
she invited Robert and Laura to come and stay with them 'for a week
or fortnight', promising to pay their rail fares for the 170-mile journey
from Vienna.[26]

Robert replied at length; and on Sunday 10 October, a few days after
Alfred and Amy had arrived at their Hof Gastein *pension*, the morning
post brought them what APG described in his diary as 'a really wonderful
letter from Robert about this strange Trinity of friendship & love between
him Nancy & Laura'.[27] They responded by confirming their invitation,
saying that they quite accepted the situation as Robert had described it;
and on Wednesday evening Robert and Laura, 'both rather pasty-faced',[28]

arrived at Hof Gastein in time for a late supper. Robert appeared to Amy to be in a 'highly nervous'[29] state, but he and Laura both ate well, and they enjoyed 'no end of talk till 11 o'clock when we all retired'.[30]

For the next few days the four of them spent most of the time in each other's company. On Thursday and Friday mornings they all went over to Friedrichsburg for radium baths, after which they spent a lazy hour or two before lunching in the open air at an hotel, and then walking up into the surrounding hills and woods, where Laura 'tamed a savage dog', and Robert's 'eye for strawberries and bilberries and wild flowers [was] well rewarded'. On Saturday they decided to do without their baths, to give them a longer day on the hills; Robert carried their lunch in a borrowed rucksack; and the eighty-year-old Alfred managed a ten-mile mountain walk, which would have exhausted many men half his age.

All the time, Amy was carefully observing her son, and the relationship between him and his former 'lady-secretary'; and on Sunday morning, when Robert and Laura had taken the train back to Vienna, Amy sat down to write a long letter to John about what she had seen. Laura she believed to be:

> very unselfish & she is more brain than body & has Robert well in hand. They are like a very intimate brother & sister together. She tells him plainly when he is at fault or she does not agree with him. She wears a picture of Nancy hanging round her neck & falling to her chest & speaks of her just as naturally as a sister might.

Amy admired Laura's strength and intelligence, and warmed to her because she was evidently so 'very kind to Robert'. She also noted Laura's sensitivity, and sympathized with her when 'Robert told me, rather brutally, in conversation one evening that Laura was a Jewess & she shrank as if struck, feeling I should dislike her for it. So, when we all went to bed soon after, I kissed her in sisterly sympathy, to show that it made no difference to me'. Robert, who had been in such a nervous state to begin with, had visibly improved during the brief holiday: 'the beautiful place & I hope also the love & consideration shown him did him good,' wrote Amy, '& he seemed still pale but normal when we saw them off this morning'. She added:

> Poor Robert is getting grey hairs tho' he has plenty of black curls left. He ate very well while here, at meals & at any time when food was about. I expect he does not always eat enough. Laura said if she could

have a chalet in the mountains here she would be quite happy & Robert actually hopes some day to have one to come to every year.

Amy still had no precise address for Robert and Laura: she had been told that only Nancy had that. Anyone else could write to them c/o Thomas Cook & Son, Wien, Austria. The point was that they wanted 'to be isolated for work & not to have any callers or friends passing through & so on. They only call for their mail two or three times a week, when they go out for coffee.'[31]

Rather like A.E.Housman who, in 1884, told his family not to visit him at his lodgings because he would be 'out or too busy', Graves and Gottschalk had something to hide, or perhaps something to protect. Housman wished nothing to impinge upon his relationship with Moses and Adalbert Jackson; Robert von Ranke Graves had similar feelings about his relationship with Laura Riding Gottschalk. Only a privileged few, including Siegfried Sassoon, were allowed to know that he and she were lodging at 9, Mühlgassen, Tür II, Wien IV. Occasionally, as Robert told Siegfried, he and Laura went out to a cinema or a concert; and on one occasion they much enjoyed hearing Roland Hayes sing spirituals. But most of their time was spent alone in their rooms. 'Laura is sweet to me,' wrote Robert, 'and is gradually teaching me how to ratiocinate clearly.'[32]

They were also writing hard; and by late December 1927, when they were making plans for returning to England, they had completed what Graves described to Sassoon as:

a hell of a lot of work .... The *Anthologies Against Poetry* (60,000) is all but done, so is the *Modernist Poetry* book (60,000) in which we discuss just who is real as a poet of Eliot, the Sitwells, the Imagists and all the advanced gang and why – very clearly and decisively I think. Laura has also written *Contemporaries and Snobs*, about 40,000 words.... And *Why Poe?* about 20,000, showing up the whole unwholesome Poe cult.[33]

Robert had also written a number of articles, including a humorous one about the letter from Wordsworth to his friend Robert Perceval Graves, Robert's uncle; he had completed a book on *The English Ballad*, of which his father thought very highly; and he had sent off to Heinemann 'a very much pruned selection of his poems, pruned by Laura's advice, for re-publication'.[34] This selection was to appear in 1927 as *Poems 1914–1926* by Robert Graves; and it did much to secure his somewhat shaky position in the literary world. But, of the critical works, by far the most interesting remains *A Survey of Modernist Poetry* by Laura Riding (who had now dropped the 'Gottschalk') and Robert Graves, a 'word-by-word collaboration'[35] which was published by Heinemann in 1927.

CHAPTER 4
A Survey of
Modernist Poetry

One might at first regard much of *A Survey of Modernist Poetry*[36] as an elaborate piece of special pleading by Laura Riding in favour of the type of poetry written by herself. There certainly seems little doubt that hers was usually the controlling intelligence at work, and that Robert Graves's chief function was to help Laura to clarify her thoughts so far as was necessary in order for them to be expressed in the good, honest prose which he regularly produced.

We are told, for example, that it is necessary for us (as 'plain readers') to 'make certain important alterations' in our critical attitude. We must admit that 'what is called our common intelligence is the mind in its least active state', and that 'poetry obviously demands a more vigorous imaginative effort than the plain reader has been willing to apply to it'. The reading public 'insists that no poetry is clear except what it can understand at a glance'; while:

> the modernist poet insists that the clearness of which the poetic mind is capable demands thought and language of a far greater sensitiveness and complexity than the enlarged reading public will permit it to use. To remain true to his conception of what poetry is, he has therefore to run the risk of seeming obscure or freakish, of having no reading public ....

Indeed, a superior poem 'makes its real meaning clearer and clearer, as it retreats from the average, i.e. as it becomes more and more obscure to the average reader'. This is partly because the most important 'modern' poetry is concerned with a new kind of poetic thought, and the plain reader must enter into it:

> without expecting a cipher-code to the meaning. The ideal modernist poem is its own clearest, fullest and most accurate meaning. Therefore

the modernist poet does not have to talk about the use of images 'to render particulars exactly', since the poem does not give a rendering of a poetical picture or idea existing outside the poem, but presents the literal substance of poetry, a newly created thought-activity: the poem has the character of a creature by itself.

And when a true poem has been written, it stands alone, outside history, because 'all beauty is equally final'.

But the book is more than an explanation or defence of Laura Riding's own poetic practice. It contains a section whose word-by-word investigation of a sonnet by Shakespeare is known to have influenced the poet and critic William Empson in his *Seven Types of Ambiguity*, and is held by some literary historians to mark the birth of the 'New Criticism' based upon close textual analysis. It also contains a detailed and thought-provoking analysis of what was good and bad about the contemporary poetry of the 1920s. Free verse, for example, is praised when it is under proper control, and when its 'irregularity' is part of a process by which the poem is allowed to 'find its own natural size'; but condemned when it means 'not self-government but complete laissez-faire on the part of the poet, a licence to metrical anarchy instead of a harmonious enjoyment of liberty'.

There is also a sharp attack upon 'twentieth-century dead movements' in poetry, by which Riding and Graves understood those movements in which the writers appeared to be seeking novelty for its own sake. The Imagists, for example, are accused of wanting 'to be *new* rather than to be poets; which meant that they could only go so far as to say everything that had already been said before in a slightly different way. "Imagism refers to the manner of presentation, not to the subject."' HD's poetry in particular is decried as thin, poor, empty, insipid and superficial. The Anglo-Irish movement, of which Robert's father had once been a minor luminary, was also 'dead'. So was Georgianism, a movement to which Robert himself had once been outstandingly loyal. His present view was that it had achieved a number of useful things, such as the discarding both of pomposity and of archaic diction; but that it had eventually become 'principally concerned with Nature and love and leisure and old age and childhood and animals and sleep and other uncontroversial subjects'; and that sadly there had been 'no outstanding figure ... capable of writing a new poetry' within its revised form.

Only Robert Frost comes in for unqualified praise, when his nature poems are said to be 'the only real, that is unliterary, ones since Clare's'. Other poets are admired in part: e.e cummings for his technical innovations (though his poems are unfortunately 'too clear', and 'do not present the eternal difficulties that make poems immortal'); Sassoon for his 'aloof moderateness or sensibleness in all directions' (though he 'occasionally yields to the temptation of poeticalness') and Eliot for the 'controlled irregularity' of *The Waste Land* (though the authors imply that in places Eliot's masterpiece is too heavily 'loaded with learned vanities and sophistications').

But most poets, including William Carlos Williams ('a charlatan'), Ezra Pound (with his 'abnormal cultivation of the classics') and W.B. Yeats ('who, observing that his old poetical robes have worn rather shabby, acquires a new outfit'), are dealt with more severely. And in general the authors ask us to distrust any poets who use 'a false idea of "advance" to justify feeble eccentricity'.

Modernism is eventually seen to be an attitude of mind which is not in fact modern at all, but which is the honest response of the finest poets of every age to the poems which are waiting to be written. In an important sense, therefore, 'All poetry that deserves to endure is at once old-fashioned and modernist'; and modernist poetry 'should mean no more than fresh poetry, more poetry, poetry based on honest intention'.

CHAPTER 5

A Sick Household

When Robert Graves and Laura Riding returned to England in January 1927, they went first to Appletree Yard in London; and there they were reunited with the third member of their 'strange Trinity', Nancy Nicholson. A few days later the three of them travelled down to Islip, where Doris had been left in charge of Robert and Nancy's four children. It was a cheerful home-coming. The children had been flourishing in Robert's absence, while Nancy had not only kept the house looking 'as neat as a new pin';[37] but was also in excellent health and had been 'getting on finely' both with her drawing and with her 'new cretonne designs'.[38] Robert and Laura told her that they were tired of writing for the time being, and were now hoping to find paid employment in Oxford.[39]

They recognized that The World's End was not really large enough for all of them, and that this had caused problems in the past; and so it was decided to ask Robert's mother if she would pay for an extension, to provide them with a study for Robert, and a visitor's bedroom. Amy felt that this was asking too much, and she was supported by Clarissa, who pointed out that if Robert secured a job in Oxford he would be out all day: there would then be 'no such urgent need of a study for him, & the want of a visitor's room until money is more plentiful can only be a saving'.[40]

However, despite all their efforts, neither Robert nor Laura could find work, and the situation was made worse by Nancy's father, William Nicholson, who decided that it was time to put a stop to the *ménage-à-trois* at Islip, and announced that so long as Laura formed part of the household he would drop even Nancy's much reduced allowance. Amy came to the rescue early in February, with a cheque for £20 'to tide them thro' till April', Robert earned a little money from a lecture in Cambridge, and both Robert and Laura may have received small fees for talking to a newly formed English Society in Oxford; but as usual it was not enough; and in any case Robert had now added to their expenditure by renting a small two-roomed cottage in Islip, where he and Laura worked together during the day, and Doris slept at night.

Then towards the end of February Jenny, David, Catherine and Sam all went down with influenza, and with the need to pay for doctors' bills and medicines the financial problem became acute. An appeal was made to Amy, who immediately sent them a further £5; and Laura left The World's End to stay with friends in Norfolk, so that William Nicholson could also be approached for help. In the meantime, Robert and Nancy had both become ill; and Nancy's influenza was followed by a severe attack of jaundice. Doris struggled on virtually single-handed, and had nursed three of the four children back to health when the burden became too much: she broke down with heart trouble, and was told by the doctor that she must have a complete change as soon as she was fit enough to travel.

Robert struggled to his feet – he told his parents that he was 'taking Easton's syrup & getting back to life' – and tried to look after the household himself.[41] It was a hard task, and his bout of influenza had left him feeling unusually gloomy about his prospects. His uncle Charles, of *Punch*, was trying to find work for him; and Robert was also writing a novel, and preparing a collection of essays for possible publication. But none of his current projects seemed likely to make much money: 'we are counting on [Nancy] eventually keeping us by her brush,' he wrote bitterly to Sassoon, 'because the pen is played out . . . . I am doing some women-student coaching next term (Eighteenth Century period), the only job I have managed to get & I can't tell you how much I loathe the prospect. And it isn't even decently paid'. He added that they were 'surrounded by floods. Laura says England is a shabby country, but the floods rather impress her'.[42]

Nancy grew more and more anxious. The happy prospects opened up by Laura's arrival, and by Robert's Professorship, had now completely disappeared from view, and they were sinking back into the same morass of poverty and despair which had been so characteristic a feature of their lives ever since the failure of the shop on Boar's Hill. It was true that with Laura's departure they were now once again being given money by Nancy's father; but Laura's absence evidently made Robert miserable, so nothing was really settled or satisfactory. By 11 March, Nancy was in such a distressed state of mind that she suffered from a terrible attack of nerves, after which she could not bear to remain at Islip for another night. Packing her bags, she told Robert that she was going to stay with her brother in Cumberland, and that she would send for the children to follow her, as soon as she was properly established somewhere. Then she set out for the station.

Doris had already left Islip for a rest cure, looking so ill that her return within less than a month seemed highly unlikely; and Robert, who was himself feeling far from well, and who was also deeply shocked by Nancy's sudden desertion, sent a distress signal to Laura Riding. She came at once.

Laura and Robert were delighted to be together again, but they were now in a most delicate position. Their liaison in Vienna had been scandalous enough; but it was hardly an open scandal. Now they were living together in an English cottage, for all the world to see. Not sure what the future held for them, and knowing that news of their relationship would soon be common knowledge, they decided to protect themselves to some extent by convincing Amy Graves that their life together was still an innocent one. Amy had already shown that she wanted to believe the best of them; and so moral and virtuous a woman would be a powerful advocate on their behalf.

So Laura wrote a long letter to Amy, explaining that Nancy had gone to Cumberland and that Doris was also away, and saying (as Amy reported to APG, who was on a lecture tour) that she had:

> found Robert very weak and ill, and unable to get sufficient help in the village. It is not for want of money as the Nicholsons have made him a present .... Laura is not staying on but only to see Robert over the worst, while he is not well & overworked. Robert added a few words to Laura's letter. He sends his love to you also, but the letter is private. He begs us not to write to Nancy or the Nicholsons. So please bear that in mind.
>
> I am greatly depressed, but still hope Nancy will return ... [43]

To another member of the family, Amy wrote that Laura was 'behaving splendidly ... [and] has satisfied me'. [44]

On 19 March, there was a further reassuring letter from Robert, in which he wrote as though things would soon return to normal. Nancy, he felt, had simply needed a holiday after her influenza and jaundice; and no doubt Doris would be returning soon. [45] But this was wishful thinking. Nancy needed much more than a holiday; and when Robert's next letter arrived at Erinfa, more than a month later, it was to announce some major changes. Nancy was now permanently settled with the children in Cumberland, where she had found work on a farm. Robert would visit them occasionally, but would spend most of his time in London, working with Laura Riding. [46]

CHAPTER 6

St Peter's Square

Hammersmith: not only an unfashionable quarter of London, but in May 1927 positively down-at-heel. Once acceptable in polite society, it retained a certain good-humoured charm. It was lively, also: the Great West Road ran through it, with its cargo of trade and travellers from Buckinghamshire, Berkshire and further afield; and a loop of the River Thames lapped against its southern flank.

St Peter's Square was pleasant-looking; but it too had seen better days, and the large Georgian houses were mostly broken up into flats. Rents were cheap; and partly because of this an informal artists' and writers' colony had sprung up and extended into the neighbouring streets, spilled across the Great West Road towards the Thames, and even colonized the edge of the river, which was lined with brightly painted house-boats, including numerous converted barges.

Many of their family and friends were horrified when Robert and his lover took a flat together at Number 35(A). Robert's half-brother Dick, for example, a pillar of the Egyptian establishment, but with his career prospects severely damaged by Robert's action in throwing up his Cairo professorship, already referred most brutally to Laura Riding as a kind of racial disease, and refused to have her mentioned by her first name in his presence. Robert's brother John had at first adopted a similar point of view, until he received a wise letter from their sister Clarissa, who wrote to him at the time of Robert and Laura's stay in Vienna:

They are queer people & it is almost impossible to judge them by ordinary standards, any of them. Your ungenerous labelling of Laura as a Jewess has nothing to say to the matter. Robert feels he needs her help & she, thinking him a great man, feels it is a privilege to work with him. . . . Anyhow these things straighten themselves out. Folly as well as evil punishes itself. So we have only to sit back, watch what happens, and give them a hand when they ask for it but not before. Eh? After all, Robert is making quite a useful experiment, if you are able to look at it in that light.[47]

And now Clarissa did her best to calm down Amy, who was inclined to blame Nancy for having deserted Robert. 'Don't think too badly of [her],' Clarissa wrote. 'She married when she knew nothing and was no more than a child. I think this present separation is Nature's own protest that Nancy should have had no proper youth.'[48]

Not everyone was prepared to be so philosophical. Early in May, writing to Sassoon to ask whether he could find out the selling price of a copy of T.E.Lawrence's *Seven Pillars of Wisdom*, Robert told him that he refrained from sending him any personal news, 'for fear of destroying your carefully balanced view of life';[49] and later that month, having risked telling Siegfried that he was now living with Laura, Robert added that he and she had 'rather sore heads at the moment because of the breakdown of a number of friends who have not been able to stand the embarrassment of this move; and we are apt to anticipate insults never intended'.[50] Sassoon however remained loyal to his old friend; as did E.M.Forster, who replied to a similar communication with the words:

> This letter contains
> No insults no threats
> No chilblains
> No jets
> of acid.
> It's placid.
> It simply do come
> From the partially dumb
> Partially deaf
> E.M.F.[51]

The best thing about the move to London was that it made it much easier for Robert and Laura to find work. By mid-May, Robert was able to tell his father that his money matters were 'square': he and Laura had a commission to write a *Children's Dictionary*, and they had also managed to sub-let The World's End at £109 a year: so they would be able to pay Amy's rent of £5 a month, and still have £49 left over for themselves and for Nancy. This was little enough on which to live; but Robert's copy of *Seven Pillars of Wisdom* had fetched over £300; and then, at the beginning of June 1927, his friendship with Lawrence once again proved to be his salvation, when he secured what was to be (from the financial point of view) the most important commission of his writing career to date.

CHAPTER 7

Lawrence and the Arabs

Revolt in the Desert, T.E.Lawrence's abridged version of *Seven Pillars of Wisdom*, his classic account of the Arab Revolt, had by the end of May 1927 sold more than twenty thousand copies in England, and one hundred thousand in the USA. Then it became clear that Lawrence (now serving with the RAF in India under the name of T.E.Shaw) would soon wish, for complicated personal reasons, to have the book withdrawn from sale. Jonathan Cape and Doran, who were making a small fortune out of it, had no wish to see other publishers capitalize on this situation by bringing out their own versions of the story, and so (*via* his former mentor D.G. Hogarth) they asked T.E. whether they could commission someone to write 'a popular six shillings worth' about his life. This, they explained, would fill the gap in the market with an authoritative account which would discourage imitations.[52]

T.E. agreed to a new book; but he insisted, knowing of Graves's financial troubles, that Graves should be the author. This was a characteristic act of great generosity; and, so that it should not weigh too heavily upon their friendship, T.E. also insisted that Graves should remain in ignorance of his own part in the 'conspiracy' to give him the work.[53]

Accordingly Graves was offered an advance of £500 for what was at first envisaged as a book for boys; and it must have amused Jonathan Cape when Graves told him that he would only write it if he managed to secure Lawrence's consent. There was, of course, no problem:

> Shaw, as I must call him, for he has now taken that name and definitely discarded 'Lawrence', cabled his permission from India, and followed it up with a letter giving me a list of sources for my writing and saying that since a book was intended about him anyway he would prefer it done by me. [54]

Cape wanted the book ready in time for autumn publication the same year;

so Robert was soon hard at work, cutting *Seven Pillars of Wisdom* down to size, and also sending out letters to anyone who might be able to give him useful supplementary information: friends and acquaintances of Lawrence ranging from Robert's half-brother Philip, who had worked with him in military intelligence, to General Allenby, who had used Lawrence and his Bedouin irregulars as an important strategic element in his Palestine campaign.[55]

But then, as Robert wrote later, when the book was well under way, 'Lowell Thomas anticipated me with a *Boy's Book of Colonel Lawrence*; so I decided to make mine a general book, three times the length of his, working eighteen hours a day at it.'[56] A difficult task had become an almost impossible one; but by sheer determination Robert managed within two months to produce a volume of some 130,000 words. It was more of a popular hagiography than a serious biography (Lawrence was said, for example, to have 'inspired and led the broadest national movement of the Arabs that had taken place since the great times of Mohammed and his early successors, and brought it to a triumphant conclusion')[57] but Robert himself described it accurately as 'a very rich collection of Lawrenciana';[58] and it is lively, spirited and highly readable.

While Robert was working on his *Lawrence and the Arabs*, there was time for little else; but he must have been excited by the excellence of the reviews which appeared in the press after the publication by Heinemann in June of his *Poems 1914–1926*; and he was pleased when Nancy brought David and Sam down from Cumberland to stay at 35(A) for three weeks in July, showing by this act that despite everything the Trinity was still in being.

Laura in the meantime had plenty of work to do, as Graves's contract with Jonathan Cape had stipulated that Cape should in due course publish both the Riding/Graves collaboration, *A Pamphlet Against Anthologies*, and Riding's as yet uncompleted critical works, *Contemporaries and Snobs* and *Anarchism Is Not Enough*. When, at the end of July, Robert had completed his *Lawrence* book, Laura therefore remained in London working while he, feeling 'nearly destroyed'[59] by his efforts, went up to Cumberland to enjoy a good rest and to visit Nancy and their children.

He found Nancy comfortably settled in a cottage in a wood near Walton, a small village which straddles Hadrian's Wall some eight miles to the north-east of Carlisle. Here, according to Robert, she had found 'the true sense of absolute rural quiescence'.[60] To his parents he wrote that Nancy had 'made good':[61] Doris was still with her to look after the children; while Nancy was earning money by part-time work on a farm, and also finding time to do her designs and drawings.

On returning to London there was work to be done on the proofs of *Lawrence and the Arabs*; and Robert also became involved in a tiresome literary controversy which stemmed directly from his loyalty to, or some might say adulation of, Laura Riding. The August issue of Eliot's *Criterion* contained reviews by the same critic, John Gould Fletcher, of both Graves's *Poems 1914–1926* and Riding's *The Close Chaplet*. Graves's poems were treated favourably; but Fletcher was less kind about Riding's work, and stated that he could 'readily distinguish the derivations' not only from Graves himself, but from Marianne Moore, John Crowe Ransom and Gertrude Stein.[62]

Both Graves and Riding were furious about this treatment of Riding's work, and Graves sent Eliot an angry letter which he asked him to publish as an answer to the review. Eliot, reckoning that Graves would be embarrassed to see in print something which had so evidently been written in the heat of the moment, replied, giving him a chance to withdraw. However, he would publish the letter if Graves insisted; and he would also be grateful for any verse contributions.[63]

Robert did not withdraw his letter, but took the opportunity to rewrite it and to make it, if anything, more forceful than before; and, far from responding gratefully to Eliot's request for contributions, he stated very bluntly that he did not feel able to submit any verse to the *Criterion*, as:

> It would seem to be approving a popularistic policy in regard to contemporary poetry observable in the last two or three numbers of the *Criterion* with which, frankly, I do not find myself in sympathy. Commercially necessary, I grant, for a monthly: critically indefensible from my point of view.

Graves added that he had now 'come to the point of always saying exactly what I mean in matters concerning poetry', that he expected 'reciprocal activity' on the part of those who disagreed with him, and that when this inevitably led to the loss of all his literary friends, there would be 'a natural and graceful end' to his literary career. But since both he and Miss Riding had no interest in a 'literary career' as such, Eliot need have 'no misgivings on her behalf any more than on mine'.[64]

When Eliot asked for some elaboration of Graves's views, he was told that Robert could:

> only read your editorial consent to reviews by literary politicians such as Wolfe, Flint and Fletcher as a gesture of complete hopelessness and

bankruptcy; and your editorials and book-notes as a humorous ventrilo-
qual entertainment with a journalistic dummy on your knee.[65]

Two further letters passed between them, in the first of which Eliot denied
Graves's accusation that he had vulgarized the magazine for commercial
ends, and in the second of which Robert replied: 'I do think that you
have compromised about [quality] just as far as was necessary to keep it
afloat and I think poetry has been compromised just to that extent.' Eliot
then published Graves's reply to the Fletcher review; but his amicable
links with Graves had been shattered by this unpleasant correspondence,
and were not to be renewed for almost twenty years.[66]

Teaching Graves to say 'exactly what [he] mean[t]' was part of the
thoroughgoing 'reform' of Robert's character which Laura Riding had
begun in Heliopolis, and of which (as we saw) Robert had written so gratefully from Vienna, saying that she was 'gradually teaching me how to
ratiocinate clearly'.[67] Riding believed that only a good person could write
good poetry, and she succeeded in remoulding Robert's ideas to such a
degree that he had even written to Eliot about having 'realized the extent
of my shortcomings and their bad effect upon my poetry'.[68] Graves
had also penned these evidently autobiographical verses (included in his
Poems 1914–1926 but later dropped from the official canon), in which he
describes the difficulties of throwing off the 'early swaddlings of his
mind':

THE TAINT
Being born of a dishonest mother
Who knew one thing and thought the other,
A father too whose golden touch
Was 'think small, please all, compass much',
He was hard put to it to unwind
The early swaddlings of his mind.

'Agree, it is better to confess
The occasion of my rottenness
Than in a desperation try
To cloak, dismiss or justify
The inward taint: of which I knew
Not much until I came to you
And saw it then, furred on the bone,
With as much horror as your own.

'You were born clean; and for the sake
Of your strict eyes I undertake
(If such disunion be allowed
To speak a sentence, to go proud
Among the miseries of to-day)
No more to let mere doing weigh
As counterbalance in my mind
To being rotten-boned and blind,
Nor leave the honesty and love
Of both only for you to prove.'[69]

There is no doubt that to be loved and directed by someone of Laura's evident brilliance and authority, with her 'strict eyes', was gradually restoring Robert's integrity and calming his nerves. He could even use the telephone which was installed in their flat: the first time he had been able to touch one of those instruments since receiving an electric shock from a telephone twelve years previously in the early days of the war. It was only unfortunate that Laura's ideas about how to behave and how to think were so much at odds with those of contemporary society: as in her eyes Robert became a 'better' person, so in the eyes of many of his friends and acquaintances he became an exceedingly difficult one.

E.M.Forster was one of those who experienced Robert's new and more 'honest' social behaviour towards the end of September when Graves, who had presumably visited him at his home near Dorking, sent him a most unusual letter. Forster replied, very politely one might think in the circumstances: 'I can stand you in your setting though you tell me you cannot stand me in mine, and I am quite willing to come to your house again. We must fix something up later on. Are you quite sure you're a mountain and not a mouse? I'm quite sure I'm not Mohammed'.[70] It was not really Robert who was setting himself up as the immovable mountain to which Forster/Mohammed must come, but Laura, whose feelings about her own importance were being daily fed by Robert's adoring love. Nevertheless, he gained much strength from his association with her, and had Riding been less unbalanced about her own undoubted virtues as a thinker and a poet, Graves might never have embarked upon the slow recovery from his years of shell-shock, which was now well under way.

That recovery was stimulated in November by the enormous success of Robert's *Lawrence and the Arabs*. In the middle of the month, Amy and APG went up to London where they were able to bask in the reflected glory not only of Robert, whose book had sold 15,000 copies in advance;

but of Clarissa, whose book of verse entitled *Seven Days* had been rapturously
received by the critics. Taut, personal, idealistic and idiosyncratic, her
verses showed a disconcerting degree of spiritual self-knowledge, and were
a promise of even better things to come. Her brother Dick told her:

> I think you will want a bit more salt in your next brew, but don't be
> like Robert & exclude all the other ingredients – his work fills me at
> once with intellectual admiration & horror at the squalor & misery of
> his mind. Poor chap! And he thinks all the time that he is greater than
> Tennyson or Bismarck or Marshal Foch. God forgive us![71]

Robert met his parents for lunch in town on 16 November, when he 'looked
well';[72] and two days later he came to see them off at Paddington Station,
where he appeared 'rather like a big Boy Scout in dress' and showed them
some excellent reviews of *Lawrence and the Arabs* in both the *Morning Post*
and the *Express*. Soon afterwards there was an unpleasant review in the
Observer, but that was almost the only dissentient voice; and by the third
week in November Robert was earning something in the region of £350
per day.

With money pouring in (sales eventually climbed to a peak of some 10,000
copies a week) Robert and Laura had bought a printing press, hoping
to make themselves independent of the formal publishing world which they
had come to despise; and they had also bought a barge, the *Avoca*, which
they planned to convert into a house-boat and keep near by on the River
Thames. It would provide a convenient home for Robert's children and
their nurse – there was even a garden near by for the children to play
in – and Nancy, remaining behind in Cumberland, would at last have
a proper chance to draw.

CHAPTER 8
The Avoca

For much of December, Robert Graves divided his time between learning how to print, and working as a carpenter in bitterly cold weather on the *Avoca*. Christmas was spent with Nancy and the children in Cumberland; and then Robert returned to London where he was soon spending the whole of each day working on the barge, and seeing almost no one.

Then, in January 1928, John and Clarissa arrived in London for a few days' holiday before the start of their respective spring terms: John at Copthorne, where he was now an assistant master; and Clarissa at Manchester University. But when John asked Robert to dine with them, Robert refused the invitation, explaining to John that:

> I never go out to dine, now, especially at pubs. I like having meals at home with Laura. Or we go out together. Also Clarissa's a problem ever since she signed her name to a ridiculous telegram ... when Laura & I were just off to Austria. It's difficult enough making allowances (maxima debetur senibus reverentia) for Mother & Father. With the second generation they end.
>
> Yes, all my old school-chums seek me out now, blast them the buggers. Comes of selling 60,000 copies in six weeks.[73]

Clarissa immediately wrote back extending the invitation to Laura; but Robert replied that this was 'merely as an afterthought', and told her that Laura 'was not to come in that way'. Clarissa was hurt by Robert's coldness, and wrote to her parents:

> Well, I've not seen Robert for three years, & I'm his sister, and I think it not unreasonable to wish to see him alone after so long an absence, or at least not under the eyes of the woman friend to whom I am a complete stranger. Robert did not stir a finger to see me or invite me to see him, so I made no further move either. He remembers, of course,

that I joined you in signing the original wire begging him not to make the journey to Austria.

She consoled herself with the idea that he and she represented 'contrary streams of thought – as brother and sister we do not wish to hurt each other, but if we met it would be inevitable'.[74]

Robert, too, had been hurt, and sent his mother what APG described as a 'strange' letter, in which he complained about John and Clarissa's attitude to Laura,[75] and said that he did not intend to see either of them, 'because they do not take Laura for granted as a person as Ros & Philip do, (not to mention the Nicholsons) and people who are not friends of Laura's are not friends of Nancy & mine. A simple rule that saves all sorts of difficulties.'[76] Robert had also heard that APG was writing an autobiography, and demanded to be shown every extract in which he appeared.[77]

However, a soothing reply from APG had some effect; and on 10 January, with Clarissa safely on her way back to Manchester, John was invited to lunch at 35 (A). He found Robert and Laura's flat:

> very clean & neat .... A white cupboard in the kitchen had circles of green paint & varying sizes painted on it, & a door facing it bore the legend:– SEIZIN PRESS with reference to the printing press in the work room next door. A 5 foot tree of coloured paper stood by this. Munching a good red apple I was taken by Robert [after lunch] to look over the flat. His room had a small flat couch & Laura's a large double bed – also a carpet made of squares, designed by Mrs Nicholson [Nancy's stepmother] & executed by 20 Cumberland women.

Then the brothers walked to the Atlanta Wharf, where John was shown the *Avoca*:

> a £30 hulk, on which [Robert] is spending £120 having it double-roofed with planks & the inside turned into rooms. Various workmen hailed him as 'Robert' & were introduced to me & I helped Robert scrape away the 'cheese' off wet boards for half an hour. I was hardly clothed for the part, & went back to the flat to get some turpentine from Laura.

After cleaning himself up, John found that he still had some time to wait until his next appointment, and asked if he could 'hang around'. But when Laura agreed to this, John made the mistake of suggesting that he should:

read up in Robert's study. *Sensation*. It was an insult. The room was their common work room & I could swallow that if I liked. She soon followed me up and continued the squabble. I sat & read for some time & as I rose up to go the whole argument started afresh – rather more amicably this time .... She spoke of the insult to Nancy at Islip & to her in London when people came to see Robert and not her (Ha Ha!) & what an insult it was to be called or thought of as Robert's mistress, when they merely kept house together. The press was hers etc.[78]

They parted on good terms, but Laura still felt that she had not made her position wholly clear. The following day John was surprised to receive a letter in which she explained very succinctly that, in voicing her outrage at John's failure to treat her as Robert's equal partner (had he really seen her as a mere appendage for the provision of physical pleasure?), she had not meant to imply that her relationship with Robert was in any way limited.[79] This was the closest that Laura Riding ever came to admitting the intimate nature of her liaison with Robert Graves. No doubt it was partly to set the record straight; indeed in her letter she declared that this was her only aim, but it may also have been an attempt to invest herself with just enough sexual glamour to draw yet another person within her web.

If so, the effort failed. John, saying nothing to anyone else in the family about Laura's revelation, withdrew to the sidelines, a course of action of which Clarissa would have strongly approved. She advised Amy that it was wisest to make no criticisms, but 'to lie low until a far more favourable opportunity of helping them occurs .... After all, we are, like the chorus in a Greek tragedy, not responsible for the action of the principal figures, an action which must work itself out by its own inherent laws.'[80] And she wrote to John regretting that war 'drives men into premature marriage in the hope of propagating themselves before sudden death ... and when the danger is all over, especially in the case of a man who has a mind, there is bound to be a reaction in favour of a type that is able to offer intellectual companionship'.[81] She added that divorce should be made easier in the case of war marriages; and that she was glad that John was not a poet. She would be 'sorry for you to pay the penalty for being a poet as Robert is paying it, and as Shelley & Byron paid it before him. And look at the women who were thrown under the Juggernaut of their poetry.'[82]

For a while it seemed as though it would not be women alone who were to be sacrificed to the artistic ambitions of the Trinity. By the end of January 1928, nine-year-old Jenny, seven-year-old David, six-year-old Catherine and four-year-old Sam were all installed with their nurse Doris on the *Avoca*.[83] But within a few weeks Clarissa was writing to John:

> Queer & sad & troublesome goings-on at Robert's. So efficiently obvious that you would blame a novelist. David ill, & Nancy unable to sleep in the same house because of Laura & now a Lady barrister who is lodging there – the nurse suddenly dismissed for carelessness & rudeness – Complications unlooked for by the chief actors in the piece, but so likely to occur in a house not run on normal lines. Thank goodness Rosaleen stepped in and has acted strongly in the matter.[84]

What had happened was this: in the damp conditions on the barge, not only had David developed a severe cold, but Sam had gone down with bronchitis, and on the second day his temperature climbed to 102 degrees. No one realized how ill Sam was until a chance visit from Rosaleen, now a fully qualified doctor. Robert and Laura, on hearing the news, seem to have lost their heads. They would not let Rosaleen take Sam to hospital, as she wished, but sacked Doris on the spot, wired for Nancy to come down at once from Cumberland, and also wrote to Amy telling her what had happened. On the evening of 22 February, the letter was followed up by a telephone call from Laura, who told Amy 'that Sam was better & taking his brandy & egg-flipp all right'.[85]

Far from being better, he was now very seriously ill with broncho-pneumonia. Rosaleen, visiting the *Avoca* on the morning of the 23rd, the fourth day of Sam's illness, found that his temperature was now over 102 degrees, and that his pulse was up to 154. This time Rosaleen insisted on his instant removal to Charing Cross Hospital. 'The poor little pulse ... I cannot write of it without crying,' Amy told John on the 24th. 'If he is saved it will be entirely due to Rosaleen's intervention (under God) ... Nancy & David brought him to the hospital & after crying at first, he is now settling in happily .... Oh, the folly of that barge for little children!'[86]

Two weeks later Sam was well enough to leave hospital; but the difficulties which had characterized the previous few months continued. At one point Nancy departed to Cumberland alone, leaving Robert to cope with Jenny, David and Catherine while Sam convalesced at Sutton Veny; not long afterwards, all four children were ill again with suspected diphtheria; and by the first week in May Robert had had enough of domestic problems for the time being, and was on his way with Laura to the south of France.

CHAPTER 9

The Seizin Press

The first news that Robert and Laura were intending to go abroad sent shock-waves through both the Graves and Nicholson families. For a while it was assumed that the Trinity had finally split apart, and that, as both feared and expected, it had ended with Laura taking Robert away with her in triumph. After all, what was there to keep either of them in England? Robert's views on family obligations remained highly coloured by his schoolboy reading of Samuel Butler's *The Way of All Flesh*;[87] and he and Laura had by now quarrelled with most of Robert's friends.

Earlier in the year, they had even fallen out with Sassoon, to whom Robert wrote an ill-judged letter at the time of Thomas Hardy's death in January 1928. Sassoon had been feeling irritated with Graves since the previous October, when he had learned of Robert's attempt to secure a friendly review from Sir Edward Gosse for his *Lawrence and the Arabs*.[88] Now irritation had turned into anger. As Sassoon later explained, he had been feeling deeply upset by Hardy's death, and Robert's letter describing the funeral at Westminster Abbey as 'too anatomical in arrangement',[89] and discussing whether Sassoon or Lawrence should write a Hardy biography, had made Siegfried feel that Robert was:

> part of the vulgar uproar which attended his death. I could not trust myself to answer your letter temperately, and I foresaw that I could not 'have it out with you' without some intervention by L[aura]. R[iding]. (who had previously (and pardonably) failed to understand my loyalty to poor old E[dmund]. G[osse].). Your article on Max Gate [Hardy's house, which Robert had once visited with Nancy] made things worse .... the spectacle of the self-advertising antics of literary men exploiting their acquaintance with T[homas]. H[ardy]. maddened me; and your article made me think that you were making fun of him. There was too much about yourself and too little about his greatness.[90]

Eddie Marsh alone remained loyal to his former protégé. Like Robert's father, he admired Robert's work so much, and had so strong an affection for him, that he refused to engage him in serious argument.

But Eddie Marsh's friendship would hardly be enough to keep Robert and Laura in England. No doubt the two of them would disappear from the scene for good, leaving the Graveses and the Nicholsons to pick up the pieces. Clarissa had already rewritten a well-known Biblical proverb into the words: 'What a man sows, that shall he and his relations reap.'[91]

But, although the likely course of events had been accurately judged, the moment of crisis had not yet arrived. On 11 May, Clarissa wrote to Amy to explain that:

> There seems to be less need for anxiety than we thought about Robert's journey abroad. He said in a letter which I had from him two days ago 'We aren't going to Spain for an indefinite time. Just a fancy. We have the flat and the barge. Tied here, really. We are going to near Toulon for 3 weeks – That's all –'
>
>   He also said that he did not expect to see the children again before September, which looks as if a fresh arrangement would then be made for the winter. There is no suggestion of crisis in this.[92]

No crisis yet; but Robert's answer had been somewhat evasive. If all that tied him down was the flat and the barge, then he was hardly tied down at all.

What was really important to both Robert and Laura was not the flat itself, but what the flat contained: the printing press which had been installed there since the previous autumn. When John visited 35(A) in January 1928, he had noted a door bearing the legend 'SEIZIN PRESS';[93] and that was the chosen name of their new imprint. 'Seizin' is an archaic word for 'possession'; and it meant a great deal to them because it signified their possession of the means of production, and came to be a symbol in their minds for 'a spirit of moral resolve to use it well'.[94] With their own printing press, they could hope to make 35(A), St Peter's Square the heart of a publishing enterprise which would allow them to by-pass much of what they disliked about the literary world.

This idea derived in part from conversations which Graves had once had with T.E.Lawrence. As an Oxford undergraduate, Lawrence and his friend Vyvyan Richards had dreamed of building a mediaeval hall in Epping Forest, where they would produce hand-printed books of exceptional quality; and it was an idea to which both men had returned in 1919. For

Lawrence the idea had remained a dream, although he went as far as buying a field at Chingford on which a suitable building could be erected; but Richards now owned a private press and when, in the autumn of 1927, Lawrence heard that Graves and Riding wished to follow suit, he asked Richards to do what he could to help them.

Vyvyan Richards had found them 'a large Crown Albion of 1872 (patent 2937), weighing some seventeen hundredweight',[95] and after seeing it installed at 35(A) he had given Graves and Riding their first lessons in printing. Great skill and accuracy were required; and when Robert later wrote an account of his activities in 1927 and 1928, he declared succinctly: 'In 1927 I began learning to print on a hand-press. In 1928 I continued learning to print.'[96]

But with Robert's persistence, allied to Laura's perfectionism, they learned quickly; and by the summer of 1928 they were ready to plan their first productions. It was important to them that they should print only work which seemed to them to be 'necessary';[97] and while they were abroad in May they not only enjoyed a holiday in the neighbourhood of Hyères, near Toulon on the Côte d'Azur (chosen because a woman-friend of Laura's from her College days was staying there); but they also spent some time in Paris, where they called upon Gertrude Stein, one of the few authors whose work they had praised in *A Survey of Modernist Poetry*.

Stein, who lived in a lesbian *ménage* in the rue de Fleurus with her companion-secretary Alice B. Toklas, had already corresponded with Laura 'about language and linguistic techniques';[98] and now she warmed to the ambivalent character of Laura's sexuality. For, if people would only love her, Laura could respond just as easily to lesbians as to heterosexuals; indeed, she was almost always most attractive either to slightly masculine women or to slightly feminine men; and Gertrude later wrote that she found this striking young woman 'so poignant and so upright', someone who 'gets into your tenderness as well as your interest'.[99] Stein was also flattered by Robert and Laura's admiration for her work; and agreed to find something of hers which they could publish under their new imprint;[100] though the first production was to be *Love as Love, Death as Death*, a new volume of poems by Laura Riding.

Graves and Riding returned to Hammersmith early in June; and on the evening of 2 July, when Clarissa called on them for the first time, Laura made another conquest. 'I cannot say I went to see Laura,' Clarissa wrote to her mother later that night:

but to say that I was greatly impressed is to put it mildly after the descrip-

tions I had had from other members of the family. One must refuse
to form judgments through the senses and brains of others, that is all
about it – Robert was fine drawn, but did not seem at all nervy or irritable.
He was wearing no coat, but a white silk shirt, very oddly cut. The
flat was spotlessly clean, & full of oddities. The scarlet chairs against
the white walls of the kitchen stand out in my mind. Robert made coffee
& we sat & talked for about an hour on Laura's book & her motives
for writing. And then I returned home . . . .

   I think she was surprised that she did not dislike me either. She is
certainly a thinker, which is a rare thing in a woman, and her power
to think must not be esteemed the less because her subjects of thought
are remote, & difficult to deal with easily, and because when she tackles
the subjects with which we are familiar she reaches different conclusions
from our own.[101]

And a few days later Clarissa told John that she had liked Laura 'infinitely
better than I had expected', and that it was 'quite clear, in spite of the
turgidity of her written work, that she has great mental powers'.[102]
   However, this new friendship was of brief duration. Shortly after their
meeting, Clarissa sent Laura a letter which was intended to be both friendly
and admiring. She said how much she had enjoyed meeting her, what
an evidently good person she was, with intellectual qualities which were
most unusual in a woman; how, with some reservations, she admired her
work as a literary critic, and how she accepted her relationship with Robert
and Nancy as an interesting social experiment. Unfortunately it came across
as morally condescending, and Laura could not let it go unanswered. Writing firmly but kindly, as though administering a friendly reproof to a slightly
dim disciple, Laura explained that there was hardly anything in Clarissa's
letter with which she could agree.
   To begin with, it was mistaken of Clarissa to describe her as such a
good person, and then to have reservations about the quality of her work,
as there could be no discrepancy between the two. Nor, she wrote, should
she be thought of as a literary critic, as she hated literary criticism. Also,
she was positively disgusted by Clarissa's notion that there were certain
intellectual qualities more likely to be found in men that in women. As
for Clarissa's emphasis upon the physical appearance of her relationship
with Robert, and her use of the word 'experiment', there, Laura chided,
she was falling into Nancy's trap of being over-impressed by something
which was highly insignificant. Clarissa must understand that Laura and
Robert had inspired each other with a vision of their potential for good,

an important experience which, Laura suggested, might be similar to Clarissa's recent enlightenment about Laura's own virtues.[103]

Clarissa, well aware of the game which Laura was now playing, sensibly declined to become one of her disciples upon such unequal terms; and she replied to her by writing sadly but firmly: 'I love sincerity & so do you. I love Robert & so do you. These two together have been enough to bring us for a moment face to face, but I must go one way & you another.' She added that, so far as she was concerned, there was no disparity at all between Laura's work and her person, or between her thought and her person, for mind and body were a single whole. Indeed:

Whoever shares all your thoughts shares your body also, whether he knows it or not. To the extent that I am like you mentally I also must share your body – but to the extent that I am unlike you I am free of you & of all the rest. For I never yet met anyone who thought wholly as I did. One touches here & there & finds a little familiarity, but it is treachery to unite with those who are obliged to disagree with one on fundamentals. But you may see from this that I set union on the plane of thought.

Clarissa ended by thanking Laura for her 'recognition in me of a purity of self "that gave fresh authenticity to the particular self," (however unworthy both of us may be to be so singled out). Yours, with some desire to laugh – Clarissa Graves.'[104]

Realizing that she had let Clarissa slip through her fingers, Laura replied only indirectly, through Rosaleen, with whom she and Robert dined at an Italian restaurant in mid-July. 'Laura said, about you,' wrote Rosaleen to Clarissa:

she was determined not to be 'sweet' but just herself – but that she may have overdone it and appeared brusque – what do you think of her? I wonder if you liked & admired her as much as I do.

I've long stopped regarding their trio as a problem or passing any judgment on any or all of them.

I consider them as 3 very lovable individuals, all with principles to which they are faithful – all very intolerant & capable of [inflicting] and indeed afflicted with much suffering – I can find no solution to them & so, now, do not try to.

Rosaleen added that Robert and Laura were 'in great form – in better spirits than I'd known them for months', and that Laura was 'trying to teach Robert to dance'.[105]

After a long day's work printing, Robert and Laura would often be found relaxing in the company of a small circle of artistic friends. It was a circle which now included the charming and unconventional twenty-three-year-old Scottish poet Norman Cameron, whom they had first met in Oxford in 1927 while he was still a student there; and the brilliant twenty-six-year-old New Zealander Len Lye, a pioneer in the art of making animated films who had arrived in London in 1926,[106] and probably met Robert and Laura through their mutual friend Eric Kennington.[107] With these and others they talked (Laura could be a most amusing conversationalist in the company of people she liked), smoked (Laura smoked incessantly), and occasionally held lively parties at 35(A) St Peter's Square.

Later in the summer, Robert's children came down again from Cumberland, and stayed on the *Avoca* with Miss Millard, the children's new nurse. As Robert's niece Sally noticed, Laura was excellent with children; and she kept a special wall at 35(A) on which any visiting children could paint in Indian ink. The children were still on the barge in late September, when APG and Amy arrived in London, en route for another holiday in Austria. Robert agreed that his parents should see their grandchildren, but was exasperated that Amy would no longer consent to meet Laura. In the event, as Amy reported to John:

> We had tea with Robert's children on the barge. He met us in a cab & took us there. But neither he nor Miss Millard would be present, as I did not wish to meet Laura. He wrote me a troublesome letter. Your F[ather] was distressed at the dangers of the barge ['a very cold and uncomfortable place', he described it in his diary that evening],[108] but we can do nothing. The children looked bright & well, but suffer frequently from colds. Robert looked well & clean, & was nicely dressed in blazer & new grey flannel trousers. He promises to come to tea with us on Monday.[109]

When Monday arrived, Robert visited his parents at their hotel, where he also met two of his uncles: one of whom, Charles, was busy choosing specimen chapters of APG's autobiography to send to his publishers.

Robert looked 'a bit pale':[110] he and Laura had been working even harder than usual on their printing press, and they were now almost ready to produce their first major publication. By 10 October, Graves was writing to the literary editors asking if they would like a Seizin Press prospectus:

and, before long, 175 copies of Laura Riding's *Love as Love, Death as Death* had been bound and signed.

Had they depended upon sales of this book for their daily bread, they would have starved; but they had brought out a number of publications in a more conventional manner;[111] and at least one of these, Robert's *Mrs Fisher; or the Future of Honour*, was soon enjoying a great success.[112]

Robert and Laura seemed to be very happily established at 35(A); and, when Nancy came down to join her children on the barge for Christmas, everything seemed so much more settled that she began to feel she could bear to stay there on a permanent basis. By the end of December it had definitely been decided that she and Robert were to sell all their goods and goats in Cumberland.[113] Laura's wish for Nancy to be reconciled both with Robert and with herself appeared to have been granted. The strange Trinity which had now survived for almost three years appeared to be flourishing more strongly than ever; and, as they entered the New Year of 1929, neither Nancy nor Robert could have guessed how short would be its remaining life, or how tragic its end. Laura, however, was becoming bored.

BOOK THREE

THE SHOUT
1929

CHAPTER 1
Geoffrey Phibbs

Late in February 1929, Laura Riding sent a telegram summoning a new admirer from Ireland.[1] His name was Geoffrey Phibbs, and his appearance on the scene precipitated a dramatic series of events leading to a major crisis in the relationship between Robert, Nancy and Laura. An awareness that some such crisis was impending had already begun to filter its way into the consciousness of the shrewder members of the Graves family. Susan Macaulay for example, the sharpest of Robert's half-sisters, wrote to John at about this time:

> I think if Robert had been able to keep Nancy properly from the start the present deplorable ménage might have been avoided. Robert is writing dreadful stuff in the *Evening Standard* & *Express* so this talk about 'Laura' being his inspiration seems nonsense. I'm afraid you know John, from what I hear, that Robert & Nancy are fools and that Laura is just a bad woman. Perhaps it's a good thing tho', as if she is, when she's exploited them long enough she'll be up & off with another![2]

Geoffrey Phibbs was born in Norfolk in 1900; and, although he was five years younger than Robert Graves, the two men had much in common. Phibbs, like Graves, was of Anglo-Irish stock on his father's side of the family. Like Graves, he had been devoted to his mother, an intellectual and artistic woman who both dominated and adored her children;[3] and, like Graves, he had enjoyed a generally happy early childhood, which was then followed by a less agreeable period at an English boarding school from which he emerged, like Graves, as a poet and a rebel.[4]

Unlike Robert, however, Geoffrey still had a physical connection with Ireland: when he was fourteen his father inherited Lisheen, the family home in County Sligo; and on leaving school Geoffrey 'was packed off to an Officer's Training Corps attached to Queen's University Belfast, where he insisted on bringing a copy of Shelley's verses on parade'.[5]

The war was over before he could see any action, and he moved to Dublin, where he mixed in literary and artistic circles: AE (George William Russell) published a number of his earliest poems in the *Irish Statesman*; and for a while Phibbs made ends meet by working as a scientific demonstrator at the Royal College of Science. When that institution closed he found work in County Wicklow, to the south of Dublin, where he 'worked as an organiser for the Carnegie Libraries under Sir Horace Plunkett'; but he maintained his links with Dublin; and still thought of himself primarily as a poet.[6]

He was certainly a brilliant conversationalist, and AE once wrote to him admiringly: 'You have been superior to Yeats, myself and everybody else you talked to, not in any objectionable way, but it is quite innate.' And for his close friend and colleague, Frank O'Connor, he appears to have 'represented the very epitome of the iconoclastic avant-garde poet whose disregard for orthodoxies of all kinds was a necessary condition of true poetic inspiration'.[7] Here O'Connor describes meeting Phibbs:

When he was self-conscious, as he usually was for the first quarter of an hour, particularly if there was someone else in the room, he was stiff, curt and mechanical; but when he relaxed he had all the grace of a thoroughbred. The long lanky hair hung over one eye; the thin lips softened, and you saw the thick, sensual lips of the poet, and he paced round the room with his hands in his trouser pockets, bubbling with a boyish laughter. Later, when I read Proust, I knew exactly what Saint-Loup must have looked like.[8]

In 1924, Phibbs fell in love with Norah McGuinness, a beautiful and ambitious young Northerner who had 'passed out of her Art School with highest honours'.[9] Through Geoffrey she found herself (in her own words) being 'introduced to the world of Yeats and the young Irish poets';[10] and soon, despite lack of parental enthusiasm, Phibbs had married her.

Phibbs and his new wife maintained a bed-sitting-room as a base in Dublin; but they spent most of their time in a cottage at Wicklow, a lonely place on the coast, from which Geoffrey continued to organize Carnegie libraries, often to the fury of the Roman Catholic priesthood. Norah continued to paint; they both read avidly: the cottage was full of books; and Norah listened with interest to Geoffrey's theories about:

how life between two people should be led. His theories were based on the life of Shelley – and 'Freedom' in all matters was what was important. I agreed, because I then agreed with Geoffrey in most things. Alas, too late I found that tho' Geoffrey *talked* with conviction and persuasiveness he in fact could not live up to his theories.[11]

For several years, however, they seemed reasonably happy together: and if Geoffrey was disappointed by Norah's refusal to have children, and to some extent frustrated by her consequent or merely concurrent sexual coldness,[12] he was also proud of her growing success as a book-illustrator. He himself continued to write poems; and at last his work was taken up, as Robert's work had been, by Leonard and Virginia Woolf at the Hogarth Press. In 1928, in their 'Living Poets' series, they published two of Phibbs's collections: *The Withering of the Fig Leaf* and *It was not Jones*. The first of these appeared under his own name, though he tried at one point to have it withdrawn from publication; and the second appeared under the pseudonym of R.Fitzurse.

The reason for this reticence was that Phibbs was beginning to turn against the whole body of his work to date; and he later described these early productions, which he came heartily to dislike, as 'in their way typical of the notorious nineteen-twenties outlook. They were witty and cynical in an undergraduate mode, their symbolism perverse and their technique licentious.'[13] What had caused him to change his outlook was that he had begun reading Laura Riding's poems and critical work (and no doubt also her collaboration with Robert, *A Survey of Modernist Poetry*); and, at some stage in the spring or summer of 1928, Geoffrey Phibbs began corresponding with her, just as Robert had done three years earlier.

By coincidence, it was at about this time that Geoffrey became involved in a public controversy with Robert's father. Early in July 1928 the *Irish Statesman* published a typically iconoclastic attack by Phibbs on the work of Mrs Alexander, the nineteenth-century poet and hymn-writer, best known, perhaps, for her 'All things bright and beautiful'. Her daughter wrote to Alfred Perceval Graves asking him to reply on her behalf, which he did;[14] but the correspondence was eventually terminated by the editor with what APG described in his diary as 'another impudent letter from Phibbs'.[15]

This quarrel did Geoffrey Phibbs no harm with Robert Graves; nor did the news that Geoffrey disliked his own father, a bullying Edwardian landlord of the old school. Now more than ever a devotee of Samuel Butler, believing that family ties were frequently used as an excuse for bullying and interfering, and all kinds of behaviour which would otherwise be regarded as intolerable, Graves was pleased to show impartiality where members of his family were concerned.

In late October 1928, Robert Graves travelled over to Ireland in order to meet Geoffrey Phibbs,[16] who had now become a serious candidate for inclusion in Laura's inner circle. The two men liked each other at once,[17] and had a long conversation in which they appear to have discussed Laura Riding's philosophy, and the extent to which one had to change in order to reach 'her entire position'; and also the psychology of family life. But when Robert began talking about the Oedipus Complex, Geoffrey became, in his own words 'bluddy nervous', and therefore far less articulate than usual.[18]

The following day Geoffrey wrote a letter to Robert in which he apologized for this, hoped that neither Robert nor Laura would think him 'wrong-headed' (as it was 'annoying to the point of suicide to be admired by wrong-headed people'), and added: 'If you hear of a job in England will you let me know . . . . I'm tired of dissembling in Ireland.'[19]

Laura can have had no doubt by now about Phibbs's philosophical abilities; and probably she would have liked him in England at once, for she had a scheme at the back of her mind for which his help would be invaluable. But it was not until four or five months later, in February 1929, when Nancy was safely installed on the *Avoca*, and Robert was lunching with her almost every day, that Laura sent Geoffrey an imperious telegram commanding his presence. She made the occasion of the telegram the appearance in an English magazine of one of Geoffrey's poems which, she said, she particularly admired.[20]

The telegram arrived (from Laura's point of view) at the best possible moment, for Geoffrey Phibbs was in a disturbed and almost despairing state of mind. What had happened was that Norah, who often went to see her publishers in London, had met David Garnett and, in her own words:

we became lovers. He was many years older than Geoffrey and maybe it was a feeling of jealousy about this that made him insist on my telling Geoffrey.

This was quite unnecessary, but it was sufficient to ruin my marriage. It was too much of a blow to Geoffrey and his theories flew out of the window. It coincided with his receiving a telegram from Laura Riding commanding him to come to England . . . . Geoffrey jumped at this invitation and said he would travel to London that night. A night of snow and gales. My world collapsed, because I was in love with Geoffrey, not David Garnett.[21]

Norah insisted on travelling with Geoffrey; so they crossed the Irish Sea together, and arrived the following morning in London.

CHAPTER 2
Three into Four

When Geoffrey Phibbs and his wife knocked on the door of 35(A), St Peter's Square one February morning in 1929, they were given an extraordinary reception. Geoffrey was received 'with open arms'; but Norah was made to feel that she was:

> unimportant, an outsider [who] must be got rid of. Laura, as cold as the cheap sparkling trinkets with which she was covered, accompanied Geoffrey and they brought me to the Regent Palace Hotel – thrust a bottle of Brandy into my hand and said 'Drink this and forget your tears'. Then they left me in the desolate bedroom.[22]

This brutal treatment almost finished Norah. Having 'practically never drunk Brandy in my life', she followed instructions, and gulped down half a bottle. The ensuing drunkenness increased her sense of alienation; and for the next three days she was so dazed and confused that she never left her room. On the third day she forced herself to go down to the hotel lounge; but everything still seemed unreal, and for another fifty years she was to be haunted by a nightmare in which she sat in an unknown place and heard nothing but 'the constant crying of room numbers by the page boys'. At length a memory of the real world surfaced: the telephone number of a woman friend, who came at once.

After some days Norah was fit enough to return to Wicklow; but she could not bear to live in that remote place without Geoffrey. So her brother packed her things, and also sent Geoffrey's large library on to him in London. Then Norah travelled alone to Paris, where she painted in André Lehôte's studio, throwing herself into her work in a desperate effort to forget the terrible things that had happened to her.

Meanwhile Geoffrey was in Laura Riding's hands, and was being thoroughly re-educated. Indeed, as Norah later commented, it was a pity that Geoffrey's library had been sent on from Wicklow, since 'most were burned as were all his clothes because they had been contaminated by me !'[23] Robert supplied Geoffrey with everything from underclothes to a coat, in order to replace what had been destroyed; while Laura gave him three silk scarves and a blue tie-pin.[24] Geoffrey then began working with Laura on her proposed philosophical treatise about the knowledge of good and evil; and for a while the members of the Trinity and their new recruit were all quite extraordinarily happy together.

In Riding's form of words, the 'three-life' had become the 'four-life'.[25] In more straightforward terms, the *ménage-à-trois* (difficult enough to sustain) had turned into a *ménage-à-quatre*: though it was an extended kind of household, for Nancy and her children remained on the *Avoca*. Clearly, the strongest links were now between Riding, Graves and Phibbs; but all the participants in the new 'four-life' were of importance; and the complexity of their relationships was often baffling even to themselves.

There was always plenty of work to be done, both literary and philosophical: 'Laura, I & Geoffrey (who lives at the flat) now are exceptionally busy',[26] Robert told his brother John in March. Some time was also taken up in planning their future together, and especially in arranging their living quarters. Since Nancy was now in charge of the *Avoca*, and Laura was the ultimate authority in the flat, Robert and Geoffrey thought it was only reasonable that they should have a space of their own, even if it was mainly used for putting up their friends. Early in March, therefore, Robert bought the barge alongside the *Avoca*, and he and Geoffrey named it the *Ringrose*. It had previously housed a complete family, and Robert bought it at a bargain price of only £21, including furniture and crockery. Rosaleen described it to John as 'lovely', and added: 'When it's done up it should be even nicer than the *Avoca*.'[27]

The two barges and the flat became the centre of a world which, though dominated by Riding, had strongly Gravesian characteristics: it looked back to holidays in North Wales, and the days when Robert's mother, owning an empire of small cottages, could put up many of Robert's family and friends within walking distance of Erinfa; and forward to the long years spent by Robert at the centre of a similar web of properties in a remote Majorcan village. Work was the chief purpose of the community; but its most important function was to make life pleasurable.

Earlier in 1929, Rosaleen had attended a lively party at 35(A), where there was 'a crowd of artists – and we danced & fooled about till 2 a.m.';[28] and now, on 22 March, she told John that she was:

going down to watch the Boat Race tomorrow from [the *Ringrose*]....

I'm bringing a party of 10 down with me. Robert said 'Bring as many as you like' so I'm taking him at his word. . . .

Later Alas! we've lost again. However it was a very jolly party on the barge – and perfect sunshine – and after, I was given as many bananas to eat as I wanted.[29]

It was a fashionable game then for a man and a woman to start eating the same banana from opposite ends; and APG, who had recently been astonished to learn from Robert about the new addition to the 'Trinity', was now incensed to hear that Rosaleen had '[eaten] "bananas" against that blighter Geoffrey Phibbs'.[30] He calmed down a little when Clarissa, who had also been present at the party, and had taken Phibbs to task for his part in the controversy about Mrs Alexander, wrote to say that in her view Phibbs was a 'crashed idealist', and a soured man for whom one should be sorry.[31]

About a week after the Boat Race, Rosaleen stayed for two days 'with the bargees'; and on Saturday 30 March they all drove down to Oxford, where they 'bathed in the river at Islip and got sunburnt & picnicked there – all very nice'.[32] There were also plans for Robert, Laura, Nancy and Geoffrey to go on a walking tour to Germany later in the summer. In the meantime (according to Geoffrey's subsequent reports to Norah), he and Laura and Robert were all 'living on Shelley's theories' and sharing a bed in the flat.[33]

But Clarissa had been right to feel sorry for Geoffrey, who had begun to find that the emotional pressures of the 'four-life' outweighed its pleasures. One of the problems was Laura's extreme jealousy of his continuing affection for Norah; and on one occasion she is said to have 'locked herself in the lavatory for eight hours because Geoffrey said I [Norah] was taller than she was (as I was). She only came out when Geoffrey lied for peace' sake [*sic*] and said I was much smaller.'[34]

More serious was the fact that Laura had become more than a little unbalanced, and now revealed to Phibbs (as presumably she had already done to Graves) that she was more than human. They could think of her, if they liked, as a goddess: she was certainly a figure of destiny, or (as she herself preferred to say) she embodied 'Finality'. So devoted was Robert to his spiritual guide that he unhesitatingly accepted Laura's estimate of her own significance; and it says much for the force of Riding's personality that Phibbs also began to believe that there was some truth in Laura's pronouncements, and even jotted down some notes about time and history being either 'a projection from Laura', or 'necessitated *by* Laura'.[35]

However, Geoffrey was not such an ardent worshipper as Robert; and although he was fascinated by Laura, he retained a healthy enough instinct for self-preservation and began to turn towards Nancy, who was evidently the most balanced member of the group. Before long Geoffrey's feelings for Nancy would become very loving; and while he continued to write to his friends as though Laura were all-important in his life, he would soon make it clear to Nancy that it was really she upon whom he depended for his happiness; although he left it up to her to make any decisive move.

In the meantime Geoffrey made a perceptive analysis of the way in which relationships were developing between the four of them. Robert clearly placed Laura at the top of his list, followed by Nancy, and then by himself. Laura's feelings were ambivalent. On the one hand she preferred Geoffrey, placing him first, Robert second, and Nancy third; but she also greatly admired Nancy, whom at times she placed above herself. So there was a second order of priority, in which Laura placed Nancy first, and Geoffrey second. As for Nancy: it was becoming clear to Geoffrey that she preferred him to any of the others; that she greatly admired Laura; and that Robert now came at the bottom of her list.[36]

It was all becoming too much of a strain for Geoffrey; and then on 1 April, Easter Monday, he had a conversation with Robert on the *Avoca* while Laura and Nancy were looking over the *Ringrose*, probably discussing what new furnishings or decorations were needed. Robert then confessed 'what I knew, that the only life he could have with [Laura] was when I was away'. Geoffrey was deeply touched by Robert's evident unhappiness, especially when it became clear that he still wanted him to stay; and it seemed to Geoffrey from that moment 'that I must go some time'. Then later that evening he went to dinner with a wealthy aunt of his who lived in London, and who told him that Norah was ill and unhappy.[37]

Suddenly it became clear to him where his duty lay. Norah was isolated and alone, and needed him. Laura, on the other hand, had Robert, and could manage without him. In any case everything at Hammersmith was intolerably complicated. So without a word to anyone he set off for Paris.

CHAPTER 3

The Shout

According to Laura's later fictionalized account, when Geoffrey failed to return from dinner with his aunt, she and Nancy hurried to the aunt's flat. Here the only definite news was of Geoffrey being 'out of England – with the right woman [in other words, his wife]'.[38] It seemed most likely that Geoffrey and Norah would be in Ireland; and Robert was despatched immediately to bring them back.[39]

Geoffrey, however, had reached Paris, although Norah had no idea that he was on his way until:

> a friend ... knocked on my door to tell me that Geoffrey was downstairs and begged me to see him. Eventually I did. He begged me to go with him – he had run away from Laura. I was glad and consented to go off to Rouen for a few days (a second honeymoon).
> We had several days together and I felt all might be well and I was happy about this ....[40]

Geoffrey Phibbs was not so happy. On the contrary, soon after arriving in Rouen he wrote a letter to Laura Riding, explaining that he had left her partly for Robert's sake, and partly for Norah's; and that (although he evidently felt that he had done the right thing) he was now 'terribly terribly unhappy'.[41] The letter contained no return address;[42] but the envelope bore a Rouen postmark, which gave his pursuers their first real lead. The actual address was then tricked out of Geoffrey's aunt by Len Lye, who 'pretend[ed] he had a splendid job for him'.[43]

In the meantime, Norah remained happily unaware that Laura was on their track, until, on the morning of Saturday 6 April, 'after two days our peace and attempt at reconciliation were shattered. A waiter knocked on our door at 8 a.m. to tell us that three people wanted to see us – they had a most important statement to make.' The members of the Trinity had travelled all night, *via* Dieppe, and had come to announce to Norah that 'they must have made a mistake in shutting me out of the Holy Circle ... and their mission now was to gather me in'. Norah, totally astonished by this new development, 'could only suggest we might have breakfast!'[44]

Norah had already noticed to her disgust that Laura, 'I expect to fascinate Geoff ... had every Woolworth ornament on her, even sparkling buckles on her shoes!' And after breakfast 'a long morning' in the hotel was spent 'mostly in symbolic language and signs', presumably part of a cabbalistic ritual designed to draw Norah into the 'five-life'. Norah, however, was unimpressed by these sinister proceedings, and eventually left the others to their own devices while she went for a walk in Rouen. On her return she was told that lunch had been ordered in an hotel in some woods just outside the city; and since she was feeling hungry she agreed to go with them.[45]

On the way, Laura stopped to buy yet another necklace with which to dazzle Geoffrey; and then, after an excellent lunch, Norah recalls that:

Geoff and I were told we must walk for half an hour in the woods and come back and report [my] decision. We walked. Geoff said if I didn't go with them, he wouldn't. I sensed he was torn. However, I said *I* wanted to keep sane, and nothing, not even losing Geoff, would induce me to go to what I thought was the mad house of Hammersmith. Even though I had been told Geoff and I would have our own flat – all physical contact would cease between Laura and Geoff (?) and that they would meet only to continue the great work – a dictionary. So I just said 'No'.[46]

Geoffrey declared again that he intended to stay with Norah; and then they walked back to the hotel to report their decision to the others.

Laura Riding, faced with the apparent wreckage of her plans, and the permanent loss of Geoffrey, lost control; and Norah later wrote a scathing description of how '"God" in the Public Lounge threw herself on the floor, had hysterics, threw her legs in the air and screamed. The manager got two waiters to remove this spectacle from the alarmed eyes of the wealthy French onlookers.'[47] In Robert's more sympathetic version of the story, he describes the hotel as a 'hill-top where you [Laura] seemed to die'; and for him the event had another dimension which made it even more nightmarish: they had chosen to go to this hotel because it was on the site of the Rouen hospital to which Robert had been sent after his near-fatal wound on the Somme in 1916. So it was the very place where he himself 'had seemed to die thirteen years before'. That night, as soon as Laura was well enough to travel, she and Robert and Nancy went 'immediately back' to England,[48] arriving in Hammersmith late the following afternoon.

When Nancy reached the *Avoca*, where she had left a nurse in charge of the children, she was surprised to find that APG, Amy, Clarissa and Rosaleen were all on board, and in a highly anxious state because the children 'were showing off their dare-devil tricks – Jenny & Cath[erine] standing on their heads and Sam hanging head downwards from a rope over the deck 11 feet below'. Nancy mentioned that there had been 'an all-night chase with R & L of Geoffrey Phibbs who had bolted from them to Paris', but declined to comment further.[49]

In the meantime, Geoffrey and Norah Phibbs had returned to Paris to collect Norah's things, and had then set out for Lisheen. But, although Geoffrey had not been lured back to Hammersmith, Norah could see that he was 'clearly very upset'.[50] Laura, as manipulative as ever, had written him a letter from Rouen station, begging him to remain silent about their past together. No doubt it was kind but firm, and, having read it, Geoffrey suddenly felt excluded from everything in the world that was worthwhile; he began carrying the letter around with him 'as my most complete humiliation'.[51] In the circumstances, Norah's 'dream of a second honeymoon became a nightmare .... Geoffrey practically never spoke to me *en route*. Perhaps it was about this time that my ardour for him started to cool.'[52] When they arrived at Lisheen, Geoffrey's mother greeted them warmly, and some peaceful days followed.

Laura, wrongly believing as the result of some ambiguous correspondence[53] that Geoffrey was once again falling under her spell, did her idiosyncratic best to tighten the bonds between them. In Norah's words:

Strange objects started to arrive by post – bus tickets, bits of twisted wire, coins and coloured ribbons – accompanied by symbolic signs, which I didn't understand. Geoffrey was in turn annoyed or proud to feel important again.

However, the magic of Miss Riding didn't work .... So she had the brilliant idea of sending her lover's wife, Nancy Nicholson, over to Sligo to plead her cause![54]

Geoffrey was lying ill in bed, when a telegram arrived announcing Nancy's imminent arrival. His mother opened the telegram, showed it to Norah, told her that they should not mention it to Geoffrey, and then instructed the butler not to let Mrs Nicholson into the house. Instead, when she arrived, Nancy was shown round to the east verandah. There, as Norah later recalled, she and Mrs Phibbs were waiting:

> in a piercing east wind. Nancy said she wanted to speak to Geoffrey – Mrs. Phibbs said she couldn't as he was ill and it was much too cold for him to come out. Nancy suggested it would be wiser to sit indoors, to which Mrs. Phibbs replied she did not wish to receive Mrs. Nicholson in her house. At this point I said Geoff must see the telegram as he was no good to me if he couldn't make up his mind whom he wanted or where he wanted to be. I brought the telegram up to Geoff who dressed and came down. He walked with Nancy along the back avenue until they were stopped by ... Geoffrey's father – who ... pointing at Nancy, shouted 'Get out of my grounds, you scarlet woman!'[55]

As he shouted, Mr Phibbs looked like 'a raging bull'; but Geoffrey held his ground, and told his father bluntly that he was 'so ashamed that, from that moment, he was changing his name from Phibbs to Taylor (his mother's name)'. Soon it was clear that Mr Phibbs's angry intervention had achieved precisely the opposite of what was intended, and had drawn Geoffrey and Nancy closer together than ever. By the time of Nancy's departure on the afternoon train from Sligo, Geoffrey had promised that he would do exactly as she asked, and follow her to London as soon as possible.

In the event he remained with Norah at Lisheen for another week (Norah herself was so unhappy that it later seemed to her like three); and then it was Norah who declared that she could not stand their life together any more, and was going back to Paris. The following day, probably Thursday 25 April, the two of them left Sligo. They journeyed together as far as London; but then Norah went on to France, while Geoffrey, instead of travelling to Hammersmith, caught a train to Cambridge, and then another to Hilton, to call on David Garnett.

The contents of the telegram, which he sent from there, and which arrived in Hammersmith on Friday 26 April, were a considerable shock. Phibbs declared very forcibly that it was impossible for him to rejoin the 'four-life';[56] and Graves was immediately despatched to Hilton to bring him back to London. Norah later heard from David Garnett that, before setting out for Hilton, Robert made a telephone call in which he announced that he would 'kill Geoffrey if he wouldn't return to Laura'.[57] When, in his own words, Graves 'burst in upon' David Garnett, who was 'gulping his vintage port', he had no difficulty in persuading Phibbs to return with him after 'scandalising' Garnett with 'soldier's oaths'.[58]

That evening, Robert, Laura, Geoffrey and Nancy began a debate which raged on inconclusively for most of the night. Why had Geoffrey stayed away from them? What were his precise motives for doing so? Did he not care for Laura? Did he not wish to continue work on the dictionary? Could he not arrive at some 'clear decision' about his future which would also be acceptable to Laura? On and on and on, until they were all utterly exhausted.

In the early hours of Saturday 27 April 1929, they snatched a little sleep, and then the debate was resumed. At length Geoffrey, much emboldened by the knowledge that Nancy was falling in love with him, said quite brutally that he was '*not* going to continue to live with or near Laura'.[59]

Laura could take no more. It was not long since there had been a sensation in the press about the suicide of another young woman poet, Charlotte Mew, who had died after drinking a powerful disinfectant called Lysol; and, in an agony of mind and spirit, Laura Riding decided to emulate her example. She drank some Lysol, but evidently not enough, for it had no immediate effect. Then, while the others watched in horror, she leaped from the window of 35(A).[60] It was a fourth-floor flat, with nothing to break her fall but the 'stone area'[61] far down below, and Laura must have expected to be killed. She herself was later to remember chiefly how dignified she had been: 'sitting on the [window-]ledge ... quite calmly, even smiling a little, and saying, "Goodbye, chaps."'[62] Robert's memories, however, centred on her 'doom-echoing shout'[63] as she hurtled towards almost certain death.

CHAPTER 4

Close in the Sunshine

As soon as Laura Riding had thrown herself from the window, Robert Graves began running downstairs. Perhaps to begin with he was hoping to save Laura somehow; but when he had taken no more than a dozen steps, he realized that she must by now be dead. What remained but to join her in death? Reaching the third floor, he forced open a window overlooking the yard in which Laura's body lay, and flung himself out.[64]

Nancy was already telephoning for help, and the first person she thought of was Rosaleen. Then she called an ambulance; and afterwards she walked downstairs with Geoffrey: a terrifying walk, as they pictured in their minds the broken bodies which awaited them.

To their astonishment both Robert and Laura were alive. Robert, although badly shaken and bruised, and lying winded on the ground, had somehow survived his suicidal leap without any serious injury. But Laura was in great agony and appeared to be dying. After a few moments Geoffrey 'walked away ... saying that he couldn't stand it'.[65] Nancy remained; and within minutes Rosaleen had arrived, and had given Laura a large shot of morphia to dull the pain.

When the ambulance drew up outside 35(A), Laura was still alive. Robert was elated by her survival, and later wrote that 'it was a joke between Harold the stretcher-bearer and myself that you [Laura] did not die, but survived your dying, lucid interval'.[66] Rosaleen, as the most senior medical person on the spot, insisted that Laura should be taken to Charing Cross Hospital, where she had done her medical training, and where she was well known and respected; and she accompanied Laura there in the ambulance.

On arrival, Rosaleen immediately began pulling strings. She made it clear that Laura was a friend of hers; and thus secured the best possible nursing care. Laura had broken four vertebrae, her pelvis was in three pieces; and her spinal cord, though unbroken, was severely bent. Even if she lived, it seemed very unlikely that she would ever walk again.

In the meantime, the Hammersmith police had been called in: quite properly, for in those days attempted suicide was a criminal offence. But before long the investigating officers were deeply suspicious that something still more serious had occurred, and that they were dealing with attempted murder.

The first person to be interviewed by the police, later in the morning of Saturday 27 April 1929,[67] was Geoffrey Phibbs. Assuming that Laura was dead, and that it would be better in that case for the whole truth to come out, Phibbs told the police everything that he knew, from the break-up of his marriage to Laura's jump from the window. He told them how he had come to London and become part of the 'four-life', until, in 'a sort of reversion to normality',[68] he had escaped to France. He told them about Laura's subsequent attempts to win him back, and that he had come to regard her as 'a sort of vampire'. He added, in particular, 'that he, as a student of psychology, [now] considered Laura had been mad and enumerated her delusions'.[69] Finally, he explained how Robert Graves had burst in upon him at Hilton, and demanded his instant attendance upon Laura in London; how he had felt compelled to go; and how he had continued to resist all Laura's entreaties.[70]

Most of what Geoffrey said was believed; but after hearing what he had to say about all the 'sex-complications',[71] the police began to wonder whether he was hiding something from them about the final moments before Laura Riding's fall. Robert Graves was evidently in love with Riding, and he had clearly been in a violent mood when he fetched Phibbs to London. He might have found it hard to bear Riding's preference for Phibbs, and possibly her continual attempts to win Phibbs back had driven him temporarily insane, and he had seized her and pushed her out of the window. His own jump would then be explained by his almost immediate feelings of remorse for what he had done. Murder followed by suicide is after all a well-known pattern of domestic violence.[72]

When Nancy and Robert were brought in for questioning, it was soon evident what the police were trying to prove. Nancy, who 'gave evidence first', did some quick thinking, 'and said that she was alone in the room and Laura did the jump when her back was turned'. This was a lie, but it put Robert in the clear; and when it was Robert's turn to speak he bore out Nancy's statement, 'saying that I went down for an emetic for the Lysol and returned just as L[aura]. made the jump'. Everything else that they told the police was true; but it was not the whole truth. Unaware at this stage of what Geoffrey had told the police, they 'gave a very bare account', and said nothing at all about the complicated sexual and emotional relationships which were at the heart of the problem. However, after a further 'grilling', the police became satisfied about the essential truth of the matter, which was that Laura Riding had tried to commit suicide, and that Robert was innocent of attempted murder. He and Nancy were allowed to go free, and the papers relating to the case were sent to the Home Office until Laura should be ready to stand trial.

It was not until the afternoon of Tuesday 30 April, three days after Laura's fall, that Robert wrote to his parents to tell them what had happened: that Laura had thrown herself from a fourth-floor window on to concrete, 'while in a very overwrought condition'; that Rosaleen's help had been 'wonderful'; and that he himself would be glad of 'a gift or a loan to get through the next month', as he was 'hard up & the Press cannot go on without Laura at present'. APG, who received this alarming letter on Wednesday morning, immediately sent his son '£40 ... & said I should not press him for it'.[73]

When APG's letter reached London on Thursday, Robert's condition had deteriorated. Not only was he still shocked both by Laura's and by his own recent fall; but he had been having violent stomach pains. Intestinal ulcers had been tentatively diagnosed, and he was going that night into the Homeopathic Hospital in Great Ormond Street for treatment. In these circumstances, reading his father's businesslike letter outraged him, and he sat down to write what APG described in his diary on Friday as 'A very excited letter from Robert returning my £40, owing to my not in his opinion having shown sufficient sympathy with him over Laura Riding's attempted suicide.'[74]

Clarissa (who was now working in London for a Speech and Drama Institute) called on Robert in his hospital ward but found communication difficult, and described him in a letter to their parents as 'very long-haired & overwrought'.[75] Possibly he had just seen Nancy and Geoffrey, who appear to have called on him at some time on Friday 3 May,[76] Robert's first full day in hospital. To begin with, Nancy came in alone; and according to Robert's later account,

Miss Nicholson ... informed him that she had accidentally met Mr. Phibbs in the lobby of the Plaza Cinema and that she was living with him on the house-boat *Ringrose*. Mr. Graves, who was very ill at the time, said that he no longer had any faith in Mr. Phibbs as a friend and could not welcome him back.[77]

Nancy and Geoffrey were together at last, clinging to each other amid the wreckage of their past relationships; but at first they seem to have hoped that the 'four-life' could be rebuilt, with a different emphasis. Nancy, instead of being a minor attachment to the Robert/Laura/Geoffrey sexual triangle, would now play a much larger role as Geoffrey's lover. The question was, would this be acceptable to the others?

On Saturday, Nancy and Geoffrey went together to Charing Cross Hospital to make a direct appeal to Laura, who was now conscious enough to speak, though she was still in very poor physical condition, and the lower half of her body was virtually paralysed. Once again Nancy went in first, and she told Laura the same story that she had told Robert:

> that she had met Mr. Phibbs by accident, that he wished to return to the three friends, especially to work with her, that he was full of remorse for the confusion of his conduct and its consequences, and that he would obey whatever feelings she might have in the matter. Miss Riding then saw him and said that if Miss Nicholson and Mr. Graves were satisfied that Mr. Phibbs should return she was too.[78]

But nothing was really settled between Robert, Nancy, Laura and Geoffrey; and on Tuesday, Rosaleen wrote to her brother John asking him to:

> write me a nice ordinary letter about anything at all. I've been through such horrors recently .... I see [Laura] every day in hospital and am holding all their hands as it were. She's going to live – and I think to walk – but their problems are all unsolved – and are like the most incredible Russian novel. I feel as if I were watching 4 people in a nightmare – It's all so bad for the children too – ... Jenny is very jumpy. Oh dear – oh dear – it is a beastly world.[79]

Robert himself, after the initial shock of hearing that Nancy and Geoffrey had become lovers, had rapidly realized that this opened the way for him to re-establish his own relationship with Laura on a far more satisfactory footing. Early in the week, therefore, Nancy received two long letters from Robert, in the first of which he apologized for 'trying to insist that the association between us should continue sentimentally', and declared:

> I approve your action, & that you did not consult me I take as meaning that you & Geoffrey are closer than the old association of you & me. That's right .... With you & Geoffrey together – and, dearest Nancy, I love you greatly & deny nothing of how good we were together once

& the children are there to prove it was good and I do think you are good but a different sort of good from my good – what else is there?

Let's see. You must not ask Geoffrey to put Laura first, that is how I feel. The Laura–Geoffrey intensity ended in the area. He could not make it, as he knew & you knew, & Laura & I tried not to know. His good is different from Laura's good. There remains love between them of the sort that is now between you & me; he must put himself & you first, or all of us first or something. But not Laura first. That would be wrong to her & you & him . . . .

Geoffrey & Laura can be as fond as you & I now are but they cannot think together, for Laura will think alone. Geoffrey can help, but not as identity of mind with her. Geoffrey & Laura cannot be lovers, as you & I now cannot, somehow.

You & Laura, Geoffrey & me, these relationships can be strong & good. Then there is Laura & me. As I told Geoffrey, I have loved Laura clumsily in the past & have been so hurt by myself that I will do anything to be good. I love Laura beyond everything thinkable & that has always been so. Our love has always been strong, human, unquestioned, in spite of my muddles. I do not fear her or worship her or desire to possess her or anything that should not be. In this new orientation I do not wish to pair myself off with her in any crude way, to match you & Geoffrey as a man with a woman.

But if geography has to be considered I can see myself near Laura as her steady ally rather than centred with you as the other arrangement was . . . . If only you agree with me about Laura & Geoffrey.[80]

In the second letter, Robert added that he and Laura would probably 'live in the flat ... as lovers & allies', that he was '*intensely* pleased you are with Geoffrey if he is the chap you wanted when you only had me and I believe he is'; and that he had now burned Nancy's love-letters to him as 'I must not be sentimental about you again.'[81]

On Wednesday or Thursday, Robert was allowed to leave hospital, and from then on he spent as much time as possible at Laura's bedside. Neither Geoffrey nor Nancy bothered to visit Laura any more; and now Robert explained to her that they had 'entered into a relationship the spirit of which overshadowed the friendship of the four'.[82] When Laura also learned that Geoffrey had described her to the police as 'mad', she was finally convinced that he had betrayed her. Some hope may have lingered for a while; but her passionate love for Geoffrey was gradually transformed into an equally passionate hatred: Geoffrey was the Devil himself.

This dramatic new vision of Phibbs's role was fully elaborated by Laura Riding the following year in a preface which is totally baffling to anyone who is unaware of the full story. In it, Riding describes how Phibbs, who is never mentioned by name, but who is characterized as 'the Devil and also Judas and so on' had only been pretending that he had passed beyond the normal world into the realm of 'doom' occupied by herself. Sadly, says Riding, he was clinging on to 'nature', the ordinary historical world which he did not realize had effectively been brought to an end by her own arrival on the scene. The result was that he turned his back on her, taking with him an apparently innocent person who is really capable of the utmost viciousness – this was Riding's new view of Nancy Nicholson – and who is therefore characterized as 'the Virgin Mary who was also Medea and so on'. It was in response to this betrayal that Riding 'left that room, by the window of course'. She, after all, had 'finished' with the natural world. A fourth person present, evidently Robert, was not yet in a state of grace, but was 'about to finish with that kind of thing', and has therefore become her only reliable associate.[83]

Graves was overjoyed by Riding's change of heart. Suddenly he was held in the highest possible regard by a being who was not only the woman he loved, but a manifestation of divine authority and perfection. To others, and especially to members of his family, it seemed that Robert's obsession with Laura had seriously unbalanced him; but, in the glowing warmth which she turned upon him during this critical period of both their lives, he was undergoing a kind of rebirth.

When he could look back calmly at what had occurred, Graves wrote his poem 'The Terraced Valley',[84] in which the moment of Laura's 'doom-echoing shout' clearly marks the end of a desperately unhappy period in his life. Graves has been wandering, he writes, in a 'strange region' in which everything is terribly wrong: the earth and everything in it has been 'turned outside-in', and there are 'no heights, no deeps, no birds of the air'. 'But you, my love,' he goes on, in lines clearly addressed to Laura Riding:

> But you, my love, where had you then your station?
> Seeing that on this common earth together
> We go not distant from each other
> I knew you near me in that strange region,
> So searched for you, in hope to see you stand
> On some near olive-terrace, in the heat,
> The left-hand glove drawn on your right hand,
> The empty snake's egg perfect at your feet –

But found you nowhere in the whole land,
And cried disconsolately, until you spoke
Close in the sunshine by me, and your voice broke
That antique spell with a doom-echoing shout
To once more inside-in and outside-out.

Graves's rebirth was a painful process, which stretched out over many months, and which involved him not only in rewriting his earlier life in a way bound to cause great offence, but in a messy separation from Nancy and his children. But it led him eventually to the sunny olive-terraces of a Majorcan village where he found greater happiness and peace than he had done since he was a child; and both the preceding years of spiritual desolation and the subsequent years of fresh growth must be constantly borne in mind as we review the scenes which were enacted in the spring and summer of 1929, in some of which Robert plays a less than glamorous role.

CHAPTER 5

Breaking with Nancy

Laura Riding was preparing herself for a decisive rejection of both Geoffrey Phibbs and Nancy Nicholson; but, first, Geoffrey must be given one last chance to abandon his special relationship with Nancy. On Sunday 12 May 1929,[85] therefore, Robert Graves, acting as Laura's representative or High Priest, summoned Nancy and Geoffrey to a meeting. Laura had asked for a full report of the proceedings, and so Robert made a careful note of the main points which were made. That note still exists,[86] and it shows that Geoffrey, at least, was still suffering to some extent from divided loyalties, and was still rather pathetically hoping for the 'four-life' to be resumed.

The discussion began with Robert declaring that, in the present circumstances, Laura did not wish to see Geoffrey again. Geoffrey then protested that he 'felt hurt' by Laura's 'complete change-over' in her attitude towards him. She seemed to him to be 'in a complete muddle, demanding a pre-fall intenseness of him that he obviously could not give *because* [she] had had the fall'. The fall had inevitably altered everything, he seems to have been saying, and Laura must recognize the new situation. He himself was prepared to continue with the 'four-life'; but now it seemed to him that it was Laura and not he and Nancy who wanted special consideration of a kind which ran counter to their ideals. So he complained that Laura had 'gone back on [her] statement [that it was all right for him to be living] with N[ancy] at the barge', and also that she was 'being possessive (vulgarly speaking) of him'. It was she who had 'broken the 4, not N[ancy] & him', and he asked Robert what he thought Laura 'meant by it all'.

Robert replied coolly that he would 'make no statement' for Laura, who 'had no desires & wanted them to act in the way that would make them happiest'. If there was to be a new statement of intent, it was not up to her to make it: instead she 'wanted it any moment to come from him'. Nor should Geoffrey feel that she was vulgarly 'trying to detach him from

N[ancy]'. Robert was becoming angry now, and he 'asked suddenly: "Have you any sense of Laura's holiness?"'

Geoffrey replied, with equal warmth: 'Holiness in the sense of lots of holes through which I fall. Muddles yes, holes not holiness. Maggots, rather.'

Then Geoffrey elaborated upon his earlier point about the fall having changed everything, and about Laura's failure to recognize this: 'First,' he said, 'she wants me to think of her as not lying here & then wants me to think of her as lying here.' No doubt it seemed unreasonable to him that Laura should not only demand the adoration due to a divinity, as she had done before the fall when she was not yet 'lying here'; but should also expect him to feel sympathy and guilt and other emotions more properly due towards the very human figure who had lain apparently dying in a concrete backyard.

Nancy then intervened. She must have guessed that her own part in the events of the past weeks was about to be heavily rewritten, and she asked Robert to remind Laura 'that from the start she (N[ancy]), had put G[eoffrey]'s relationship with L[aura] before anything'. But things were different now; and Geoffrey pointed out to Robert that, if the 'four-life' could not be resumed, he and Nancy would 'be only too happy to go off together'. Later, however, Phibbs asked for the last time:

'Don't you think the 4 is possible?'
    I [Robert] said: 'Your relationship with Nancy has defined itself in a way that makes the 4 impossible. If it alters (I don't mean if it grows less strong) in its reference to Laura & me anything is possible. No prejudice.'

Geoffrey responded angrily to this statement, which once again made him and Nancy responsible for the break-up of the 'four-life', and once again showed that Laura wished to weaken the links between them: 'If I thought that Laura was able in any way to alter N[ancy]'s relationship with me as it is now,' he declared, 'I would throw her Laura out of the window & break her neck.'[87]

Although Robert would have been shocked by this outburst, he may not have been altogether displeased, as it was damning evidence to use against his former friend. After noting it down in his report, he added only two further sentences, the first of which was probably intended to be equally damning against his wife: 'Nancy did not protest. Then they went.'[88]

The physical separation between Robert and Laura on the one hand,

and Nancy and Geoffrey on the other, was now an accomplished fact. But there were still many things to be sorted out, including a division of property between Robert and Nancy; arrangements for the maintenance of Jenny, David, Catherine and Sam; and the restitution to Geoffrey of certain books and papers of his which were still in the flat at 35(A). Inevitably, it would take some time to resolve the first two of these problems; but the question of the books and papers could have been settled rapidly. Unfortunately Robert, who had once seemed to be encouraging Geoffrey to fall in love with Nancy, was now so angry with him for his opposition to Laura, and so jealous with him for stealing Nancy's affections, that he was anything but reasonable, and he used Laura's angry dictates against Geoffrey as divine authority for some mean and petty behaviour.

It seems that, when Robert had his meeting with Nancy and Geoffrey on Sunday, he agreed to return Geoffrey's manuscripts to him; because two days later, on Tuesday 14 May, Geoffrey wrote to remind Robert of this, and also to ask him for 'the parcel of my *Withering of the Figleaf* which is somewhere at the flat'. In addition, he pointed out that some of his books which had been set aside for sale were still unsold, and asked if he could have them back. This sounds harmless enough; but unfortunately the letter as a whole was far from tactful. Not only did Geoffrey write from the *Avoca*, which was Nancy's barge, but he made a point of asking for 'Nancy's cutting-out scissors', and he explained that he wanted the books because 'We feel that we ought to have these to sell. You see we don't mean to bother you about money (except for the children) but at the same time we must get some!' Finally, he asked Robert for a letter of introduction to the editor of the *Times Literary Supplement*.[89]

By the standards of the 'new' morality which they had all espoused, Robert should no doubt have acted 'decently' and sent Nancy and Geoffrey on their way with a smile and a good-luck wish; but Robert could not help thinking of Geoffrey in more old-fashioned terms as the man who had stolen his wife; and Geoffrey's assuming the role of Nancy's protector, and talking of himself and Nancy as 'we', would have been extremely hurtful to him. He was supported in his dislike of Geoffrey by Laura, who was already fulminating to Rosaleen about the disgraceful manner in which Geoffrey and Nancy had descended from the 'four-life' to becoming 'a couple' ('as if', Rosaleen commented, 'there were virtue in numbers, in relationships of that kind!');[90] and for Geoffrey Phibbs at this stage to begin asking for his help with editors seemed to Robert Graves to be a piece of outrageous insolence.

In the circumstances Graves appears to have written a very bitter reply, in which he began by talking about his 'trouble and anxiety'[91] over Laura's health. It had been clear for some time that without a major operation, whose outcome would be most uncertain, Laura would be crippled for life. It was hoped that she was now strong enough to withstand the shock; and the operation had been scheduled for Thursday 16 May. After mentioning this, Graves went on to accuse Phibbs of writing ironically. He had ended his letter with 'Sorry to bother you & so on',[92] which certainly might have seemed to Graves to be an ironic response from the man who had just walked off with his wife! Graves also questioned Phibbs's right to the books. Why should he have any more financial help, when his clothes, board and lodging had cost so much? Did Phibbs imagine that Graves was now intending to support both him and Nancy on a permanent basis? Were they going to make no efforts to earn money for themselves?

Phibbs received Graves's letter on Wednesday morning, at the *Ringrose*; and when he had shown it to Nancy Nicholson they both sat down to write immediate replies. Geoffrey took his stand on the 'new morality', and wrote in wounded innocence:

Robert
   Really why that letter?
   I didn't write to you ironically, I simply wrote a friendly letter. I understand your trouble and anxiety and I'm awfully sorry about them. In an ordinary person I suppose they'd be a perfect excuse for any amount of bloodiness. But it would be insulting to excuse you on those grounds. What have I done of which you disapprove? There must be something and I should like to know it. You have agreed with me, even foreseen, the whole development of the situation between me and Nancy, & you said you were glad & that it was good. I just don't understand!!!

He went on to answer Graves's point about 'money & expenditure being so much against me', by stating that during the period from 9 February to 1 April he had contributed over £45 to the joint funds. 'I don't believe', he added, 'that my clothes, board and lodging came to more; and as to clothes which you gave me – they replaced clothes & other things that Laura eliminated.' He ended by mentioning that the half-dozen books in question included 'a quite valuable set of Yeats in 2 volumes, but indeed I don't want them'. The important thing was that all his MSS should be sent on at once.[93]

Nancy's letter was far stronger. 'Dear Robert,' she began:

I know how horrible life is for you. I know how you feel about L[aura].

I know what you feel about us & what you know about us & I know just how much you can't afford to feel about us or acknowledge to yourself or anyone the truth about the whole thing. But it's never going to be accepted by me, your false idea of things. Understanding it all, out of respect to you as I still think of you, I won't recognise your attitude to us. You know how wrong your letter to G[eoffrey] is & you know I know you know. I know you have to – being you. But curse the you that does it from me. And just don't do it – however badly you are tortured – you drop that with us. Because we think of you like that.

About the children. We are naturally going to do our best to make money. With Islip & the barges & drawing & writing we will do it allright. When I can't give the children what they should have I'll ask you for money. When I can I won't. If you'd rather make a definite allowance – do what you like. But I'd still ask you for more if they needed it however much. Jenny will have to go to school in July near her dancing. I'll have to arrange it. The others are still practically costless.

I feel almost as bad as you do about L[aura] curiously enough. Or have you forgotten? And why? You know so do I. So never mind.

   Love N[94]

The letters were posted immediately; and, when later that day there had been no reply from Graves, Phibbs decided to walk over to St Peter's Square to collect the manuscripts for himself. However, he was prevented from doing so. According to Graves's later account, Laura Riding had now instructed him 'not to give Mr. Phibbs access to her papers among which were certain of his own without her consent'; and so when Phibbs 'tried to break into the 35(A) premises to rummage for his papers, Mr. Graves restrained him. He went away threatening a legal injunction.'[95]

No doubt Robert was in a particularly difficult mood because of his worries about Laura; and, on Thursday morning, Geoffrey sent Robert an apology for having lost his temper, told him not to worry about the manuscripts, and said that he too was anxious about Laura's imminent operation.[96]

Later that day, before the operation was due to begin, Robert visited Laura in hospital, where he received 'instructions from Miss Riding as to what papers Mr. Phibbs was entitled to'. Those papers were then passed on; but Robert, in his own words, was 'outraged by Mr. Phibbs's behaviour in view of Miss Riding's still critical condition'.[97]

Fortunately for Laura, Rosaleen had once again been pulling strings; and she had succeeded in persuading a certain Mr Lake to take over Laura's case. Lake, then England's foremost specialist in spinal injuries, had just come back from a working holiday in America where he had been studying the most advanced surgical techniques. Rosaleen, who was present throughout the operation, later commented that without Mr Lake's skill Laura would certainly have been paralysed for life.[98] Lake himself treated the difficult operation with studied nonchalance, remarking coolly at one point that 'It is rarely that one sees the spinal-cord exposed to view – especially at right-angles to itself.'[99] One of the most complicated parts of the operation involved removing a smashed piece of bone from the spine, and replacing it with a piece of bone taken from Laura's shin-bone. It was a wonderful piece of work; Rosaleen was never to forget the thrilling moment when the first piece of bone was removed, and Laura's spinal cord, almost miraculously it seemed, slid back into place; and when Laura was wheeled back into the ward, still deeply unconscious, there seemed at least a chance that she would one day be able to walk again.

Robert was still furious with Nancy, for having 'apparently condoned [Mr. Phibbs's] attitude [to Miss Riding]';[100] and on the morning of Friday 17 May, while Laura's recovery from her lengthy operation was still in some doubt, Robert and Nancy met to make 'a practical separation of interests'.[101] Their first arrangement was that Robert should pay Nancy's rent on the cottage at Islip; and that Robert should also contribute towards the cost of keeping the children – he paid her an immediate twelve guineas for this purpose; but that Nancy should hand over the *Avoca* to Robert and Laura. Geoffrey was present, and Robert also mentioned that he would like some of the underclothes which he had lent Geoffrey to be returned; and he agreed that Geoffrey should buy a typewriter to replace the one which he had been instructed by Laura to give up.

The next day, when it was clear that Laura was making good progress – though she would have to lie on her face for three weeks until her operation wounds healed – Robert began to feel guilty about having driven too hard a bargain with Nancy, and he wrote her a letter in which he told her the good news about Laura, and added that Nancy could keep the *Avoca*. But his wife was enjoying her new independence, and she replied:

Dear Robert,
    It's good about Laura.
    You and I decided yesterday that the barge was yours & L[aura]'s. We won't alter that please. Also you shall not pay the equivalent of rent or anything to me. You are in no way responsible for me. It was a muddled idea of mine yesterday resulting from a feeling of resentment about the

whole money business. I have worked as hard as anyone for over ten years and have had far less money than either you or L[aura]. My laziness about money has been taken advantage of and been the means of you and L[aura] getting the attitude that all assets were yours and L[aura]'s, and anything I had was given me from you two. That's ended. Now it will make a cleaner business all round if I spend some necessary money getting the *Ringrose* habitable now...and leave the *Avoca* complete...& ready for you and L[aura] ... and that's finished. In fact spend on the *Ringrose* now some of the money I didn't spend when there was (or should have been) a sharing of money. Then no more.

That fair? Fairer anyhow!

    Love

      N[102]

Robert replied generously that he really did not want the *Avoca*, and offered to pay £200 a year for the children, saying that if necessary he would undertake 'hack work' to fulfil his obligations.[103] But, although he had softened towards Nancy, he was still angry with Phibbs, and the exchanges between the two men became steadily more and more farcical. At about this time, Graves had returned some twenty-five books, including the Yeats volumes, determined that 'Mr. Phibbs should [no longer] have any ground for personal communication with [him or Laura]';[104] but, sad to say, some ground still remained. Phibbs had sent Graves the bill for a new typewriter, and declared that the underpants were nowhere to be found; to which Graves now replied that Phibbs should have bought a second-hand machine – he could not be expected to pay for a new one – and he still wanted his underpants returned![105]

On 20 May, Whit Monday, Nancy gratefully accepted Robert's offer of the *Avoca*, and said that the money he was offering for the children's upkeep would be 'ample', though it would not cover the cost of Jenny's schooling. Jenny's dancing teacher, a Miss de Vos, was 'going to have a school for her dancers in October which will be fairly economical because dancers aren't rich – but she is anxious Jenny shouldn't wait till then to continue dancing as what she has already learnt will be sheer loss.' Nancy also said that she needed £50 to make the *Ringrose* habitable; and pointed out that there were still £30 worth of payments outstanding on her car, and that she could then clean it up and sell it. She would try to be economical, and also to earn money by drawing: 'God forbid', Nancy added, that 'anyone should [do] hack work unless absolutely necessary'. As for the pants, that was all a mistake; she had 'found them now & will send them unless you really don't want them'. But Robert must not accuse them of being mean about the typewriter – they had 'quite innocently believed what you said ... & tried for a second-hand one'.[106]

By the same post Geoffrey asked Robert to:

Please thank Laura for her message. I keep all her letters and messages, but if ever she wants that particular one back she has only to ask for it.

About the typewriter – I said to Nancy that you would probably not pay for it, so I'm not surprised. I shouldn't even have sent the bill to you, only I had a sort of bet with myself about it. Laura, you know, persuaded me to give up my own typewriter which was a better one than this.

Saw my horoscope yesterday at Roz's – didn't know you'd had it done. I'd rather like it and of course will pay for it if you don't want it. It is ridiculously accurate. [Phibbs was described as 'a fiery, energetic and somewhat restless body ... impulsive, enthusiastic, courageous, frank and enterprising ... [but] sometimes quarrelsome and petulant'.][107] Also saw Laura's, but she must have given wrong hour.

Just read a book on Chaldean magic – it might interest Laura as soon as she can read. If she'd like it she can have it.

The frequently referred-to pants. I don't know. Here are two pair; were there any more? If so please sell some of my books and replace pants.

I do hope this is the last letter I shall have to write to you for some time. Your letters and Laura's message make me alternately cross and sorrowful.[108]

Later that day, when the letters had been posted, Nancy was joined by Clarissa, and the two women took the children up to Hampstead Heath – a 'hot but happy experience', as Clarissa reported to her mother. She added that she had 'seen nothing recently of Robert', and that 'Laura is going on very well'.[109] A few days later APG and Amy also heard that Nancy was planning to take the children to Islip at the beginning of June.

Generally speaking only scraps of not very illuminating information of this kind had reached Erinfa since the first alarming news about Laura's fall; no one had yet dared to tell Amy, in particular, the whole truth. But occasionally something more interesting came their way: on 18 May, for example, writing to thank his parents for the gift of another £20, and to tell them how grateful he was to Rosaleen for having secured the services of such an excellent surgeon, Robert added that he was planning to write a book about his experiences during the Great War.[110]

This was the first mention of the autobiography which became world-famous as *Good-bye to All That*. APG, as helpful as ever, was able to send Robert copies of the first letters which he had written from the Front, some of which had already appeared in a slightly edited form in the *Spectator* in September 1915;[111] and on 25 May 1929 Robert wrote a further very cheerful letter to his parents:

Dearest Mother & Father,

Many thanks for letters. I will write to you fully in a few days when I am less desperately busy. I have had to finish printing my [unknown] book & I spend about 4–5 hours visiting.

Laura is getting on finely & for the matter of that, so am I. Laura's sister from America [Isabel] is here & helps a lot. I am busy writing to make money; at a book which I want to get an advance on, so I want something quickly to interest the publisher.

Please please don't worry about me. I have not for many years been less a subject of worry.

Thank you, father, about Atkins & the letters. I may use them in the book in some form.

The children are very well & very sweet. I shall not be going to Islip myself.

It doesn't look as if I shall be able to leave London & look at the country before mid-August at least – that is, when Laura gets out of hospital. She counts on seeing me every day & vice versa.

Best love to you both
          Robert[112]

Graves was still not at peace with the 'outside' world, and could behave in an apparently surly or even petty fashion towards its members, most of whom he now regarded as 'irrelevant'; but in the dramatic 'inside' world which he now shared with Riding, and which might also come to be shared by other 'proper chaps', everything seemed to have fallen into place.[113] The next stage in his own development was clear: following Riding's example, he must cast off the whole of his 'historical' existence; and what better way to do that, for an author, than to write about it?

CHAPTER 6

The Writing of Good-bye to All That

In the first paragraph of *Good-bye to All That*, his classic autobiography, Robert Graves states that the objects of writing about his own life at the early age of thirty-three are simple enough: 'an opportunity for a formal good-bye to you and to you and to you and to me and to all that; forgetfulness, because once all this has been settled in my mind and written down it need never be thought about again; money'.[114] He adds that biographies are usually written about people who have:

> put themselves on the contemporary map as geographical features; but seldom have reality by themselves as proper chaps....
> And yet even proper chaps have their formal geography, however little it may mean to them. They have birth certificates, passports, relatives, earliest recollections ... like all the irrelevant people, the people with only geographical reality. And the less that all these biographical items mean to them the more particularly and faithfully can they fill them in, if ever they feel so inclined. When loyalties have become negligible and friends have all either deserted in alarm or died, or been dismissed, or happen to be chaps to whom geography is also without significance, the task is easy for them.[115]

Robert knew that his own father, the eighty-two-year-old Alfred Perceval Graves, was now some four-fifths of the way through an autobiography, and he added rather pointedly that 'proper chaps' did not have to 'wait until they are at least ninety before publishing, and even then only tell the truth about characters long dead and without influential descendants'.[116]

Later, when *Good-bye to All That* had been written, and was selling well, Graves wrote that this did not surprise him:

> because I have been able to put into the book all the frank answers to all the inquisitive questions that people like to ask about other people's

lives. And not only that, but I have more or less deliberately mixed in all the ingredients that I know are mixed into other popular books … food and drink … murders … Ghosts … kings …. People also like reading about other people's mothers. I put in mine … T.E.Lawrence … the Prince of Wales … racing motorists and millionaires and pedlars and tramps and adopted children and Arctic explorers …. People like reading about poets. I put in a lot of poets. I have met most of the best-known ones in England … Prime Ministers … foreign travel…. Sport … commerce … school episodes, love affairs (regular and irregular), wounds, weddings, religious doubts, methods of bringing up children, severe illnesses, suicides. But the best bet of all is battles, and I had been in two quite good ones …. So it was easy to write a book that would interest everybody. [117]

Good-bye to All That is indeed a brilliantly impressionistic account of Robert's early life; and it is one of the finest and most vivid records of the trench warfare of the 1914–18 war. Written in a cool, laconic style it addresses the reader simply, directly, clearly, and often most movingly. For the historian and biographer, however, it poses serious problems.

Graves wrote *Good-bye to All That* at the time when Laura Riding's intellectual and moral influence over him was at its height. On a prefatory page he quotes in full some moving lines by Riding, taken from her 1928 *Love as Love, Death as Death* collection, in which, at the heart of the 'World's End' [the title of the poem], two lovers somehow make sense of things merely by resting peacefully with their arms about each other. [118]

Later, Graves's dedication comes in the form of a 'Dedicatory Epilogue to Laura Riding', a very moving love-letter in which he describes why he has not mentioned her in the main body of the book. It is because:

by mentioning you as a character in my autobiography I would seem to be denying you in your true quality of one living invisibly, against kind, as dead, beyond event. And yet the silence is false if it makes the book seem to have been written forward from where I was instead of backward from where you are. [119]

That last sentence is a crucial one. For years Graves had been tormented not only by shell-shock, but by divided loyalties and by irreconcilable beliefs. A decisive new alignment of ideas, thoughts and feelings had given him, for the first time since he was a child, an integrated personality and a clear point of view. It was from this position that he now looked back at his 'historical' past; and, although he wrote with an honesty that was sometimes painful, his loyalty to Riding and to their joint beliefs led him inevitably into a significant reconstruction of the past.

This reconstruction was made more extensive by the speed with which Graves wrote, which left little or no time for checking the facts; by the after-effects of shell-shock, which meant that his memory was often highly unreliable; by his excellence as a story-teller, which meant that over the years he had already 'improved' many stories to a considerable extent, making them somewhat less truthful, but far more artistically satisfying; and by his belief, declared long ago, that literal truth is relatively unimportant, as an artist can tell the truth by a condensation and dramatization of the facts.[120]

When Alfred Perceval Graves added a chapter about Robert to his own autobiography, he wrote that: '*Good-bye to All That* calls for many more corrections than I can here enumerate, having been written largely from memory, sometimes from hearsay, and often long after the events described';[121] and it would be just as tedious nowadays to make a catalogue of Robert's errors as it would have been for APG to do so in 1930. Robert's 1957 revision trimmed the flame a little, but in its original 1929 edition *Good-bye to All That* blazes with genius.

However, studying the differences between the actual events of Robert Graves's early life and the way in which he writes about them in his autobiography throws a very clear light upon many of his 1929 attitudes, in particular those to his family and to traditional Christian morality.

It is hardly necessary to repeat that Graves's view of family connections had been permanently coloured by his early reading of Samuel Butler. Until the early 1920s, despite this, a very significant part of his life had been carried on within the context of an extensive and well-connected family network to which he retained a considerable though at times ambivalent loyalty; until 1926 he remained economically dependent upon his family; and as late as 1929 he still needed occasional help from them, while his sister Rosaleen remained until June that year one of his very closest friends. The 1929 crisis meant that he became emotionally free to jettison as much of his family as he pleased, and in that sense to become a full-scale Butlerian of the kind to which he had previously only aspired. In *Good-bye to All That* this attitude is displaced on to his past life in a most interesting manner.

His saintly mother, to whom he remained passionately attached throughout his life, is teased just a little (Graves explained reasonably enough that this was 'to make her read naturally'),[122] but is treated with evident affection and fundamental respect. She is the one, he says, to whom he owes most of his ability as a writer. It now seems evident that it was Amy's powerful and indeed dominating influence which predisposed Robert to his belief, stated as early as 1924, that society had once been matriarchal; to his worship of Laura Riding; and to his subsequent adherence to a linked set of poetic myths which centre upon the figure of the White Goddess.

His elderly father, on the other hand, receives less friendly treatment. Alfred Perceval Graves himself commented that Robert 'gives me no credit for the interest I always felt and showed in his poetry. During the War I offered poems of his to editor after editor, and even arranged with Harold Munro of the Poetry Book Shop to whom I introduced Robert, for the publication of *Over the Brazier*'.[123] This was a very modest statement of his case. APG could have added that most of what he had done for his son had either been played down, sneered at or even omitted altogether from the pages of Robert's autobiography. In particular, there is no mention of the occasions during the 1920s when it was only Alfred's generosity which had preserved Robert and his wife and children from utter destitution.[124]

By mid-1929 Robert Graves's attitude towards Christianity consisted chiefly of a certain cool cynicism; and in *Good-bye to All That* this cynicism is projected on to his past life in a manner which very much distorts the truth. Thus the ceremony of confirmation, one of the highlights of Graves's second year at Charterhouse, is described so that one chiefly remembers the farcical moment when 'the boy whom the Bishop of Zululand was blessing at the same time as myself slipped off the narrow footstool on which we were both kneeling'.[125] Nothing is said about Graves's pilgrimage to Canterbury in the spring of 1912, just over a year later; his moving 1914 poem 'In the Wilderness', about Christ meeting the scapegoat, is described as 'silly' and 'quaint', and those who have derived spiritual comfort from it are mocked;[126] while Graves says little about the strong religious feelings inspired in him by the Great War. In one of his letters home, he had declared that the services meant much more to him in the war zone than they had done at home; but in *Good-bye to All That* this becomes: 'It would have been difficult to remain religious in the trenches though one had survived the irreligion of the training battalion at home.'[127]

Despite the numerous factual errors, and despite heavy rewriting of many of the supposedly original letters which he includes in the text, Graves's descriptions of life at the Front are vivid and largely authentic. But Graves portrays himself too often as a kind of anti-hero: just as coolly cynical towards almost every aspect of the war as he is towards Christianity. Thus he describes himself as signing up chiefly to delay going to Oxford for a few months;[128] and says that he went out on night patrol in order to secure the minor wound which would send him back to England.[129] Statements of this kind are highly misleading.

Far from being cynical, Graves was strongly motivated by the highest Victorian ideals. In 1914 he writes that France is 'the only place for a gentleman'; and in 1915, after the battle of Loos, that the men are 'splendid', and that it has been a 'great experience'. It is true that in 1916 and 1917, influenced by Sassoon, Graves began to question the continuation of the war;[130] but he was horrified by Sassoon's defiance of military authority in the summer of 1917. In *Good-bye to All That* he correctly describes this as an act of the greatest bravery; but at the time he felt that it was essentially disloyal and dishonourable, an 'awful thing' which Sassoon must be persuaded to abandon.[131]

However, Graves's wholehearted contempt for the conventional values which had once inspired him meant that his memoirs struck an original note, and it was one to which large numbers of those who had survived the war were profoundly sympathetic. Since Graves's account was undistorted by heroic preconceptions or sentimental preoccupations, it seemed to his readers to have captured very precisely the reality of wartime service. This paragraph is taken from Graves's description of his first sight of the battle-front in 1915:

> We marched towards the flashes and could soon see the flare-lights curving over the trenches in the distance. The noise of the guns grew louder and louder. Then we were among the batteries. From behind us on the left of the road a salvo of four shells came suddenly over our heads. The battery was only about two hundred yards away. This broke up *Aberystwyth* in the middle of a verse and set us off our balance for a few seconds; the column of fours tangled up. The shells went hissing away eastward; we could see the red flash and hear the hollow bang where they landed in German territory. Then men picked up their step again and began chaffing. A lance-corporal dictated a letter home: 'Dear auntie, this leaves me in the pink. We are at present wading in blood up to our necks. Send me fags and a life-belt. This war is a booger. Love and kisses.'[132]

In an important sense this is the truth, and most of Graves's readers would recognize it as such.

The fact that Robert Graves was also recreating himself, and offering up a considerably altered personal history as a kind of homage to Laura Riding, does not detract from his achievement. On the contrary, it gave to his writing an incandescent quality which makes the 1929 edition of *Good-bye to All That* one of Graves's most powerful and most enduring works.

CHAPTER 7

Distractions from Worship

By the end of May 1929, it seemed probable that Laura Riding would make an excellent recovery from her fall; but she was in a most peculiar state of mind, and gradually alienated even Rosaleen, who had done so much to help her. 'I have been fond of [Laura],' Rosaleen wrote to her brother John some weeks later,

> and at the time of her accident was overwhelmingly sorry for her – but her behaviour in hospital – screaming for fun and not from pain 'just to have something to do', she said – regardless of the other suffering patients – her self-centredness – & her constant complaints of being neglected (though the nurses gave her any amount of attention & she had privileges in the way of visitors that she'd never have had elsewhere – because I got her into hospital as a friend of mine) all this ... [has] made me regard her more as a borderline mental case than anything else.
>
> Such colossal egotism is not sane.[133]

Rosaleen had now joined the circle of those who were allowed to know of Laura's divinity; and when, for example, Rosaleen commented on the wonderful job that Mr Lake had made of the operation, Laura looked at her fiercely and said in a harsh whisper: 'How do you know that I didn't invent Mr. Lake?'[134]

In these circumstances Rosaleen made one last effort to try to reconcile Robert and Nancy; but she failed completely, explaining to John that the reason for the split between Robert and Laura on the one hand, and Nancy and Geoffrey on the other, was:

> simply because G[eoffrey] and N[ancy] cannot see L[aura] as perfect and say they 'refuse to share her delusions.'
>
> Of course they're all completely insane – but G[eoffrey] & N[ancy]

seem to me to be the saner couple of the two. They see L[aura] as selfish, egotistical & domineering – wishing to possess the entire personality of anyone she likes.... [Laura] calls herself 'Finality' whatever that may mean – and imposes on others (such as Robert) the belief that she can do no wrong. He says he's never known her say or do an unkind thing!! Isn't it unbelievable? So the rock on which they split – & which means permanent deprivation to the children of their father – is Laura's perfection.[135]

Although Robert frequently declared at this time that he never wanted to see his children again, he continued to regard them as his financial responsibility and, on 1 June, he gave Nancy a further £80 towards their upkeep. The following day Nancy and Geoffrey took Jenny, David, Catherine and Sam down to Islip.

There they found that The World's End was in a desolate state; and it was not just that some of the furniture and household goods had been removed to London, leaving them in need of a wide range of things from linen and blankets to kitchen chairs and crockery. To Nancy it seemed that 'the place [was] absolutely falling to pieces'. In particular the floor was rotting, and needed to be heavily restained to limit the damage; the curtains needed replacing; and the garden was completely overgrown. The chief purpose of Nancy's visit was to put the house in good enough order for it to be let; and before long there were a number of prospective tenants. But the children were so happy to be back in their old home, and their health improved so enormously, that Nancy was 'almost persuade[d] ... to stay here for them. Only the past is too horribly active here – & also it's their income.'[136]

Nancy was acting in a manner which was both practical and reasonable; but passions were still running too high for either of these qualities to be greatly valued. Robert remained furious with Geoffrey for having 'stolen' Nancy, and was soon writing him angry letters. Very early in June, for example, he appears to have threatened Geoffrey with an action for slander, on the grounds that he had been spreading rumours that Laura was suffering from venereal disease.[137] Geoffrey, who was still hoping for a reconciliation with Robert, strongly denied this accusation.

In the meantime, APG and Amy had finally heard from Rosaleen, invited up to Erinfa for a rest, the full story about what Alfred described in his diary as 'the dreadful practices of the Quadrilateral arrangement between R.N.L.& P.'.[138] When Amy also learned from Rosaleen that Nancy was now 'living in sin' with Geoffrey Phibbs at Islip, she was so distressed by the thought of what was happening in a house which she owned that she immediately gave Robert notice to quit The World's End.

In passing on this news to Nancy – there was an accompanying letter telling Geoffrey that Laura could not be bothered with his latest request (to buy back some of his books from the communal library) so soon after a serious operation – Robert also wrote savagely about the occasion on which Nancy had left him and the children at Islip, and had gone up to Cumberland. Before that incident, he recalled, she had been 'generous and honourable'; since then, it had been a different story. Robert also appears to have commented about the injustice of his having to support not only Nancy and their children, but Nancy's lover.[139]

Nancy was now so much in love with Geoffrey Phibbs that Rosaleen almost came to believe that she had never really been in love with Robert. Nancy's happiness made it easier for her to deal with Robert's latest letter; and in any case, knowing how deeply Amy cared for her grandchildren, she could not take the threat of eviction from The World's End seriously. Instead, in a letter dated 14 June, she told Robert that she had:

> decided yesterday that the children should stay at Islip permanently. We owe them at least that. They are completely happy here with all their friends. It is their home. A pity about your Mother. She's lasted out pretty well I think.... It's a dirty trick when she has been so nice. But she can't suddenly be nasty to the children. For myself there is nothing I'd like better than to leave ....

Nancy added that she believed herself to be:

> just as generous & honourable as I ever was whatever that was. You can persuade other people I'm not. But you can't persuade me, or kid me into thinking you can persuade yourself. And don't go on raking up, as a justification for your own behaviour, the only thing you've got against me. If it was wrong (leaving you here with the children without money while I went to Cumberland) – and you agreed with me I could have done nothing better under the circumstances – I paid for that long ago & you know with what heavy interest.

Nancy also wrote that she did not expect Robert to keep either her or her lover, just to pay for the children; though she might need some support if she found that she had to devote her whole time to them, and was therefore incapable of earning.[140]

Graves must have hoped that Phibbs would start making a financial contribution to the Islip household, because he himself was running short of money, and was facing severe demands from Laura Riding. Well enough to leave hospital, but not yet well enough to return to the flat in St Peter's Square, she wanted to have a further spell of specialist care. Rosaleen, who had been partially reconciled with Laura and Robert, on the strict understanding that she was never to mention Nancy or Geoffrey in their presence, was appalled to learn that Laura insisted on being moved to a private ward in the Homeopathic Hospital. This would cost Robert a minimum of '6 guineas a week for her apart from massage'; but when Rosaleen remonstrated with Laura, and told her:

> that if I were her, I'd go to an Infirmary, on leaving hospital, rather than run up bills I had no money to pay for – She was furious and said: – 'Well, you're not me.'
>
> But really [Rosaleen explained to John], it's simplest not to discuss anything controversial – She gets into such a nervous state – and it does no good.[141]

There was still less point in arguing with Robert. In a recent letter to his mother he had declared that Laura was 'an almost fantastically good woman'; and he had told Rosaleen that 'one cannot talk of there being good in Laura. She is seamless, like the garment of Christ.' Amy replied to Robert, telling him that she 'looked forward to his awakening from his dream', [142] but Rosaleen wisely said nothing further; and on 17 June Laura Riding went into her private ward.

Riding's departure from Charing Cross Hospital had come too late for Rosaleen, who told John on the 19th that:

> My name in my own hospital is mud by now. Everyone knows the story – It has leaked in from outside – & L[aura]'s behaviour in hospital has sickened people .... I hope being related to Robert won't make things hard for you too. The story is all over London and Paris – so there's no hope of concealing things. The only thing is that much is pardoned to literary geniuses.[143]

But worse was almost certainly to come. As soon as Riding was well enough to stand trial, she would be prosecuted on a charge of attempted suicide, and the dramatic story of the 'four-life' would be headline news in the popular press. Laura would probably be deported in a blaze of the most humiliating publicity; Robert had already declared that he would follow her into exile; and, in the moral climate of those days, the open scandal would have serious repercussions not only for the participants in the 'four-life' but for members of their families such as John and Charles.

Graves's most influential friend in Government circles was still Edward Marsh, who was now working as secretary to Winston Churchill at the Exchequer. As early as Monday 13 May, Graves had written to Marsh telling him that he wanted to see him soon because he would 'probably be able to be of great service to me in a way that will cause you no strain';[144] and, when they met for lunch on Sunday 16 June, Graves asked him what could be done to prevent Riding from being brought to trial. Marsh was entirely sympathetic, told Graves that he was a saint (T.E.Lawrence, now back in London, had already described Graves as 'a most excellent and truthful person, drowning in a quagmire'),[145] and asked him to prepare a detailed report. Graves did so later the same day, in the form of a letter which began: 'My dear Eddie, You are, if I may tritely return the compliment, a saint. About all this. A few data for you . . . .'[146]

Marsh took immediate action, and replied on Monday that he had enlisted the support of a private secretary at the Home Office, who had promised to talk to the Director of Public Prosecutions on Laura Riding's behalf. There was therefore a sporting chance of avoiding a prosecution. If, of course, the DPP was determined to take action, such avoidance 'w[oul]d be practically impossible. But I hope that, at any rate when he has had the case explained to him, he will take a humane view – Meanwhile,' Marsh concluded, 'all good wishes & hopes.'[147] The humane view was indeed taken; eleven days later Graves was telling Gertrude Stein: 'I think that (by using influence in Whitehall) we have succeeded in quashing any police nastiness or prosecution for attempted suicide';[148] by the end of June Riding's salvation was an accomplished fact, and Graves was talking of going abroad with her to the Basque provinces of Spain.

First, however, Laura had to be able to travel; and it was not until 12 July 1929 that she was considered fit enough to leave the Homeopathic Hospital. Rosaleen, who two and a half months ago had accompanied Laura in the ambulance which took her to hospital, went with her once again in the ambulance which took Laura back to 35(A) St Peter's Square, and made her comfortable there.

Robert was overjoyed by Laura's return. He was within twelve days of his thirty-fourth birthday, the day on which he was to complete his first draft of *Good-bye to All That*; and he had already begun to feel that, thanks to Laura, he had started to lead a life which was altogether outside the normal course of events.

Unfortunately there were still a number of problems which needed to be dealt with: problems which must have seemed in Robert's exalted state to be almost intolerably mundane, and which included not only how to deal with his wife and children, but also how to come to terms with Geoffrey Phibbs on the question of the books, which was reopened in mid-July.

Phibbs had dropped his earlier offer to buy back one hundred of the books which he had contributed to the joint library at 35(A). Instead he declared, reasonably enough, that he and Nancy were entitled to half the entire collection, since it had become the joint property 'of Nancy and Laura and Robert and me. That was the theory.'[149] However, he would only press for the return of fifteen named books, and a number of other 'dubious' ones which had been put aside for sale. Laura replied to this request in a telegram which read: 'will send books in due course further communications unentertainable'.[150]

However, when the promised books failed to appear, and when Geoffrey also found that a small selection of his books was being openly offered for sale in a local second-hand bookshop, he lost patience and instructed a firm of solicitors to apply to Robert for the return of no fewer than three hundred books. This dispute, which could have been settled in half an hour with the barest modicum of goodwill on both sides, stretched on into August and threatened to become interminable.

Amy, by this time, had been persuaded by Robert not to press for The World's End to be sold: provided that Nancy did not live there with Geoffrey, or Robert with Laura, the house could be kept on and let for the benefit of Nancy and the children, thus giving them the prospect of having at least a small stretch of solid financial ground beneath their feet. For the present, however, Nancy's situation remained serious; and when she wrote to Robert in the third week of August it was to point out that she had only eighteen shillings in hand.

Nancy had enclosed a detailed list of incomings and outgoings for the past three months; but, when Robert replied on 20 August, he declared that he was not satisfied with her statement, which he could not regard as reasonable 'unless supported by fuller details'. He accused her of failing to take into account some money which he believed she had made by letting the barge for a short time; and he asked bitterly whether the £50 of expenditure on The World's End included 'wages for G. Phibbs' unskilled labour'. Robert added that since he was paying Nancy's rent, and since he had only a limited amount of money, it seemed wrong for Nancy to demand as much as £4 a week for the care of the children. She must in any case understand:

that I feel in no way obliged to feel grateful to you for your present
care of the children. I am not only ready but anxious to undertake their
entire custody and to give them every personal care. If you wish to keep
the children and expect me to support them you must no longer behave
in an antagonistic way. That is you must not let any person have free
intercourse with them while he is subjecting me to injurious annoyance
thereby countenancing such annoyance, you must not participate in
slanderous statements with him about me in local shops or elsewhere
or put the children under the custody of persons whom you and I once
agreed to dismiss as undesirable.

Robert added that Nancy must in future give him 'receipts for expenditure
after previous consultation', as he did not wish to feel that he was 'in
any way supporting or by my help enabling you to support persons who
have caused me annoyance, and even supplying them with the wherewithal
to prosecute further annoyances at the expense of my children's proper
maintenance'. If Nancy would agree to Robert's having the custody of the
children, he would keep them at the *Avoca* until the winter, and later take
them to Spain. He wondered whether Nancy found the children 'more
responsibility or pleasure', and concluded formally that:

> whatever your feelings you are not considering mine, and therefore I
> must present my demands in this quasi-legal manner. Recent events
> have alarmed me as to the children's safety (in your car for instance)
> and their proper companionship.
> Robert Graves[51]

Nancy replied that, far from behaving in an antagonistic manner, she was
solely concerned with '*trying to do the best for the children* .... Can't you
too? If our only connection with each other was on that basis we might
do something.' She was surprised by Robert's apparent change of heart
over the children, and said that, if he liked, she would treat his 'repeated
denials of responsibility ... & ... definite statements on two occasions that
[he] never wished to see the children again' as the result of being 'under
strain'; but she was adamant that she would not consider giving the entire
responsibility of any of the children to Robert. It had been his repeated
own choice that she should have them; and she was annoyed by his comments about the children's safety and companionship, writing that it was

'the first time I've heard that our ideas on the children's upbringing differed'. Nancy added that she was 'tired of your attitude of poor good Robert & lucky bloody Nancy'. She had four children to bring up, and a small earning capacity; while Robert had only one adult to look after, and a (comparatively) large earning capacity: in Nancy's view, his life was 'an easy blank', hers 'a very difficult & hard full. In fact you've got exactly what you've been wanting for some time.' She declared that she would 'ask no more from you for the children. It's for you to make the next move. I'm tired of being continually nice to your bloodiness.' If however Robert *did* decide that he would like to help, then he could arrange a meeting with her on Saturday 24 August, by sending a note *via* Rosaleen.[152]

Robert appears to have responded favourably both to this letter and to his immediately subsequent contact with Nancy. Soon he was being informed by Nancy that she was no longer living with Geoffrey Phibbs, and that Phibbs was no longer very concerned about the books. On 3 September, perhaps to test the truth of what he had been told about Phibbs's departure, Robert sent a further sixteen of his books to the *Ringrose*. He must have been delighted when he received in return a note signed by Nancy which read simply: 'Received 16 books belonging to G.B.Phibbs. Kindly deliver in future to him at 49, Shaftesbury Road, W6';[153] and the following morning Nancy received a cheque from her husband for £100 'towards maintenance of four children from September 12'.[154] But although it was true that Phibbs had found a room in the Shaftesbury Road, and that he had decided to let the matter of the books rest for the time being, his apparent separation from Nancy was a hoax: possibly a justifiable one, since its chief purpose was to deceive Robert into doing what was right.

Robert, however, was understandably furious when within a day or two of sending Nancy the cheque, he 'saw Miss Nicholson and Mr. Phibbs together in a car passing through St. Peter's Square',[155] and realized that he had been tricked. Laura (who had now reached the stage of being 'able to walk downstairs leaning on Robert') no doubt shared his fury, and tried to establish the fact that Geoffrey was still living with Nancy by sending a letter to Phibbs at the barge, saying that she had seventeen more books of his which were waiting to be collected. Little was achieved by this tactic. Phibbs simply wrote a letter to Graves 'purporting to come' (or perhaps really coming) 'from Shaftesbury Road', asking for his books to be returned, and, as Graves wrote later, 'complaining that he was being misaddressed'. Laura's letter was returned 'professedly unopened but obviously steamed open and sealed up. Miss Riding replied in a postcard about 9 September, to the effect that she, noted Mr. Phibbs' *minutiae* and *facetiae*,' and that he could have his books if he sent round a messenger who was unknown to her.[156]

Geoffrey was annoyed both by the attempt to trap him and by the stipulation of the 'unknown' intermediary; and on Wednesday 11 September he turned up in person on the doorstep of 35(A). According to Robert's account, 'his manner was threatening and Mr. Graves told the maid to shut the door in his face'. Geoffrey then 'went away'; but on Thursday he went to the West London Police Court, where he took out a summons against Laura Riding. Later that day Laura was visited by a 'Police-Sergeant Bridger of T Division',[157] who handed over the summons, which demanded the return of eighty books, valued at ten pounds; and which was returnable in fourteen days' time, on 26 September 1929.

Riding's first act was to persuade Police-Sergeant Bridger to visit Phibbs at the *Ringrose*,

> to persuade him to stop molesting Miss Riding whose health was suffering from all this annoyance. He informed Sergeant Bridger that he would cease his molestation if he got his books back, and that Miss Riding had sent him an unintelligible postcard half in Latin and half in English.[158]

Next, Laura sent her sister Isabel, together with Mrs Westgate, a friend of hers, 'to protest to Mr. Phibbs about his behaviour'. They found him at the barge with Nancy, and noted further 'evidence' that he was still cohabiting with her. Not only were some of his books arranged on the bookshelves; but he had a work-table there – which Nancy ingenuously pointed out to Mrs Westgate, possibly while she was explaining that Geoffrey was doing what he could to support himself.

Geoffrey Phibbs soon made it clear he meant business, but that he was prepared to be reasonable. He gave Laura's emissaries an application made out to her in which he asked for the return of the books, but he also said that if they were safely delivered to him he would immediately drop any police or civil proceedings against her. Hearing how determined he was, and wishing above all to avoid a court case, Laura at once sent Mrs Westgate back to the barge with some fifty books.

On the following day, Geoffrey wrote a final letter to Laura asking for a further seventeen named volumes, and enclosing a draft form of apology for her to sign. The apology was too much for Laura to stomach; but no doubt she returned a few more books (though not all), and the result was that the police proceedings were dropped. At long last the dispute over the joint library was at an end. The 'four-life', begun with so many high ideals, had finally petered out in a petty squabble. For Graves it had all been an irritating distraction from the serious business of his life; but by the time it was over *Good-bye to All That* had been completed, and he was within five weeks of setting out with his adored mistress to begin a new life somewhere overseas.

CHAPTER 8

Gone Abroad

Robert Graves had thought seriously about living abroad ever since Laura Riding had been in danger of being deported from England for attempted suicide; and, even when that danger had been averted, there seemed to be important advantages in such a move. For one thing, it would be much cheaper to live abroad. Graves certainly hoped that *Good-bye to All That* would be a bestseller; but nothing is certain in a writer's life: the large sums of money which he had made on his *Lawrence and the Arabs* were almost exhausted; and so far the Seizin Press had been a commercial failure. If Graves wished to avoid a return to the humiliating dependence upon family and friends which had been his lot for so many years after the Great War, it made sense for him to find some sunny corner of Europe where food and housing were as cheap as possible. It would also be easier for Graves to live with Riding in a place where no one minded very much that they were not married; and where none of the local people were likely to have come into contact with the malicious gossip about them and their circle which was now going the rounds of society on both sides of the Atlantic.

They would be leaving few friends behind them, and no doubt that made the decision easier. Len Lye and his wife Jane would be a loss: Jane had typed *Good-bye to All That* for Robert, and Len had welcomed Laura back to 35(A) with a composition 'on Laura's bedroom wall in coloured distemper and chalk';[159] but Norman Cameron was comfortably established in his new role as education officer in Southern Nigeria; and there was no one else who mattered very much to them. Besides, in November 1929 Jonathan Cape was due to publish *Good-bye to All That*, a work which on 18 June that year Graves had described in a letter to Gertrude Stein as 'a sort of good-bye to everyone but the very very few people to whom one never says good-bye or has ever said a formal how do you do. Quite ruthless; yet without indignation';[160] and having said good-bye so publicly it would perhaps be prudent to depart.

Gertrude Stein had found Robert's letter highly intriguing, and had written to 'My very dear Laura' telling her that 'I always liked Robert a lot but I have come very close to him lately and am immensely interested in his autobiography, I guess he is going to be better and better as well as you and that means a lot to me.'[161] Later she had commented that she was 'rather selfishly glad' that the outcome of Laura's 'fall' had been that Laura and Robert were:

> more completely together, you do mean that to me the two of you with Len firmly in the background because after all it is hysteria that is vulgar and the complete absence of hysteria is very rare, there is very little absence of hysteria and you two are it and therefore if not for other reasons very dear to me.

Stein added that she and her companion, Alice B. Toklas, were 'here' at Bilignin, their summer residence at Belley in the south-east of France, and that they wanted 'to see the both of you with us'.[162] In another letter she suggested that Laura might 'take treatment at Aix [-les-Bains] or some-where [else] near us'. Laura, she went on, might not necessarily like staying in France, and might even find it a jarring experience; but she must recall that it was 'on the whole a case of the shortest and permanentest cut to liberty'. Gertrude herself found it was 'so uncomplicated that really there is no jar but this is for me and not for you not at all for you and yet I am hoping that we will be seeing you here just the same and for all that'.[163]

While Gertrude Stein found it very exciting to think of her two friends being liberated from English society, Graves's family, as might be expected, took a different view.

Graves's parents, in particular, were horrified to hear that Robert was 'writing a very "truthful" autobiography of himself': as Amy explained to another member of the family, 'we are all nervous of what, in his present mood, he will say. It is sure to cause trouble.'[164] Early in July APG sent Robert a temperate and judiciously phrased letter suggesting that it would be better for him to lay his autobiographical work to one side;[165] and, when this produced no results, both Alfred and Amy became quite ill with worry, and Alfred even began corresponding with a bookseller to find out whether there was any way in which 'the Trade [could] intervene or block' Robert's book. From Rosaleen they heard how completely Robert was 'under Laura';[166] and when, towards the end of August, Nancy wrote a very gloomy

letter to Erinfa with the news that 'Robert is going to Spain in the Autumn
... and there is no guarantee that he will be heard of again,'[167] it seemed
horribly final. Amy, her head 'hot and heavy' with anxiety, wrote to the
family solicitor instructing him to alter her will. Robert was to be cut out
(though he must not be told of this, in case circumstances altered), and
his children were to receive his portion.

After this, Amy's efforts were directed towards lessening the impact of
Robert's forthcoming departure upon his wife and children. In September,
for example, David started at Colet Court, the preparatory school for St
Paul's, at Amy's expense; and efforts were being made to find a suitable
school for Jenny, who could not be taken by Colet Court 'as she cannot
combine the course with dancing'.[168]

In late September, after the end of the long-running books dispute, Robert
was in a more relaxed mood, and he sent his mother two friendly letters:
the first explaining that his autobiography, which had been advertised by
Cape as *Up to Yesterday*, was really to be called *Good-bye to All That*; and
the second telling Amy that the children would write to him when he went
abroad, and that his book would also be published in America and in
Germany. Amy was pleased that Robert wished to maintain some connection
with his family; and news of the German edition came, surprisingly, as
something of a relief: 'After that,' she wrote to Clarissa, 'we need conceal
nothing from my relations. In a way it will be better for me. They know
much more than I told them already.'[169]

Sadly, just when Robert was on the point of leaving England, he was
involved in another major family row which left both Amy and Rosaleen
with severe emotional wounds. Rosaleen had remained a good friend to
Robert throughout the troubles of 1929, though she and Laura had had
one or two serious disagreements: most recently when Laura had 'blazed
out at her' after she described the books dispute as 'sordid'.[170] Robert could
not help noticing that Rosaleen's attitude towards Laura had changed for
the worse; and he also knew that she was still seeing Nancy and Geoffrey.
So, towards the end of September, he presented her with an ultimatum:
she must either 'give up Nancy & Phibbs or forfeit his friendship'.[171]

Rosaleen adored Robert, but she would not be bullied by him; and she
wrote two letters explaining why she could not do as he asked.[172] The result
was an extraordinarily savage reply from Robert, taunting Rosaleen with
her 'dirty, middle-class morality', and saying that Laura was the *only* woman
whom he could love and respect. Rosaleen, utterly wretched, forwarded
the letter to Harlech, where it saddened APG and left Amy feeling even
more wretched than her daughter. A covering letter which APG described

as 'long' and 'rather harrowing' added to their gloom; and a few days later, on 4 October, they heard from Rosaleen that Robert and Laura had at last 'vanished', leaving only a post-office forwarding address and 'a curt p[ost]-c[ard] to Nancy that in case of emergency "Marguerite" (whoever she may be) will help with the children. Roz and I are quite left out,' Amy wrote to her youngest son. '[Robert's] ingratitude & rudeness to Rosaleen are incredible,' she added. '... I can only feel consternation at his attitude & that our dear Robert is dead and gone.'[173]

Meanwhile, Geoffrey Phibbs was doing his best for Nancy. One of the reasons why he had taken a room in the Shaftesbury Road was that his father had refused to pay him an allowance while he was living with someone else's wife; but this was only a temporary manoeuvre, and Geoffrey was determined to earn enough money to support Nancy by his own efforts. After at least one job which he applied for had come to nothing because his prospective employer knew of his part in the 'four-life', Geoffrey turned his attention overseas. Before long he had secured a minor post in Egypt, where he could earn £300 by teaching English for a year; and by the beginning of October he was out in Cairo, apparently looking 'very forlorn', and 'living poorly, so as to send Nancy money every week'.[174]

Rosaleen observed that it was also a very sad and lonely time for Nancy and for her four children: she reported to her parents that Nancy 'misses her absent lover very much';[175] while 'Poor little Sam went to R[obert]'s flat up all the stairs to show him a lemonade powder he had & came back saying "Father gone, Laura gone – all gone."' Amy was terribly saddened by this news, and passed it on to John with the comment: '[Sam] will never forget that.'[176]

The contrast, towards the end of 1929, between the profound misery and even despair which Robert Graves had scattered in his wake, and the profound joy and sense of renewal which were so evident in his own personal life, could hardly have been greater. It is a contrast which would make a fitting introduction to one of those inconclusive discussions about the rights and duties of the artist: inconclusive, because there are no scales in which artistic achievement can be weighed against human suffering. All we know is that the former is often the product of the latter; and the rest is a mystery.

In the eyes of his mother, Robert had committed a series of unforgivable sins, which included most unreasonably deserting his wife and children, and savaging other members of his family. In the eyes of those more generously disposed towards him, he had merely come to the sensible conclusion that life was to be lived rather than endured; and for the sake of his health and strength, both as a human being and as an artist, he had finally broken away not only from a failing marriage but from all kinds of outworn sentiments and convictions whose corrupted remnants had been poisoning both his mind and his spirit. The years of disintegration were finally at an end.

BOOK FOUR

ROBERT GRAVES AND LAURA RIDING IN MAJORCA 1929–1936

CHAPTER 1
Casa Salerosa

On leaving England and the English Channel behind them, Robert Graves and Laura Riding travelled together across France until, very early in October 1929, they reached Bilignin, the home which Gertrude Stein shared with her lover Alice B. Toklas in the small village of Belley. Some twenty miles east of Lyons, it is set in a beautiful area of woods and low hills known as the Savoie. Here the travellers were made welcome, and here they rested for several weeks and gathered their strength for the next stage of their journey. They were staying in an area famed for the health-giving properties both of its climate and of the waters which could be taken at nearby Aix-les-Bains; and Laura, though limping badly, was soon managing short walks in Robert's company. To the east, the hills rose higher and higher into the alps of the Haute Savoie; on a clear day Mont Blanc could be seen towering in the remote distance; and Robert, very much impressed, sent his children long descriptive letters about the beauties of the country-side.

Robert and Laura's next destination was Spain, where, as they had learned, living costs were then only a quarter of what they were in England. At one time, they had been particularly attracted to the Basque provinces in the north-east; but Gertrude Stein suggested that they should try instead the Balearic island of Majorca, telling them that it was 'paradise – if you can stand it!' This last remark was a mild joke at her own expense, since she and Alice Toklas had lived there for almost a year in 1914–15, and had then abandoned it in favour of the more sophisticated cultural and social life which they enjoyed so much in Paris.[1] Since Laura and Robert had both come to despise that kind of sophisticated life, with its artificial literary coteries, its infighting and its insincerities, they need have no similar reservations; and by the end of October they had travelled to Barcelona and boarded an overnight ferry bound for the Majorcan capital of Palma.[2]

Arriving at Majorca by boat for the first time in the early dawn remains an unforgettable experience. After hours of journeying southward across a grey and apparently empty sea, further and further away from the European mainland, an island coastline becomes visible far ahead off the port bow. Gradually cliffs and mountains become apparent, their summits tinged with the rays of the rising sun. Steaming further south, the ferry comes close in to Majorca's western shores, whose cliffs are now glowing with the pink and amber lights of dawn. Everything in that hour seems strange and magical, and it would be easy to imagine that one had stepped out of time into the middle of some ancient legend, and was rediscovering the island where the Cyclops dwelt, or where the Lotus-eaters lived.

The ferry steamed round the southern side of the island, where there are no mountains or cliffs, but flat lands, and a broad bay with the ancient city of Palma at its centre.

Palma was dominated by a magnificent Gothic cathedral standing on the foreshore. Indeed, one of the first impressions a traveller received upon landing in the town was of the almost mediaeval appearance and manner of many of the local inhabitants. Slightly below middle-height, the girls wore dark clothes which accentuated their very waxen features; while the men usually wore dove-grey cotton drill suits; but if you saw them at a local dance, the women wore flounced dresses of a stiff material, which took one back to pictures of the Spanish Inquisition; while the men wore Moorish plus-fours.[3]

Majorca had of course been inhabited long before mediaeval times, having been invaded in turn by Phoenicians, Greeks, Carthaginians, Romans and Arabs. Then in 1229 King James I of Spain had landed a few miles from Palma to begin his conquest of the island; and, when Graves and Riding arrived in Palma exactly seven hundred years later, there were still several Spanish families who owned the same property that had been given to their ancestors on that occasion.

The architecture of Palma was highly individual: it had been strongly influenced by the flourishing trade between Majorca and Italy in the sixteenth, seventeenth and eighteenth centuries; but it was not all Italian Renaissance. There were notable local characteristics like the big rectangular open courtyards with columns at each corner and a grand covered staircase at one side. The façades of these town houses were plain enough despite their arched entrances and double-leaf doors, but indoors there were big chairs upholstered in velvet, with large chests of Gothic design, while the beds were covered in damask; and in many houses the number of paintings, statuary, pottery and lamps, all of them valuable, was a sign of how the leading families had treasured their heirlooms for century after century.

Palma was a fascinating city; but Graves and Riding wanted to be somewhere in the country, where property would be cheap, and where they could grow some of their own food. Using the Grand Hotel in Palma as their base, they began investigating the interior of the island. It was described by Robert's brother Charles, who visited Majorca only a few years later, as being:

an almost exact cross between North Wales and Corfu. It has the blackberries, apples, boulders, pine trees, mountains, and sheep of Snowdonia, and the almonds, pomegranates, peaches, dust, by-roads, corn on the cob, sugar cane, melons and olive trees of the Greek island. Even then to get the exact mixture you must add hundreds upon hundreds of windmills....[4]

It was difficult to decide exactly where to live, until one day Robert and Laura took pity on Clauker, a disabled German café artist, who had burst into tears when Robert refused to be sketched by him. Allowing him to make the drawing after all (though Robert later tore it up), they told him of their problem, and the artist suggested that they should travel northwestward across the plain until they reached the mountains; beyond the mountains they would come to the sea; and some miles along the coast road they would find Deyá, a small fishing and agricultural village, where they could live very cheaply, and which might therefore suit them well.

They took his advice; and their journey took them along a route which was the 'image of Aberglaslyn in North Wales, except for the pure orange-colour of the ploughed land and the groves of olive trees',[5] and which led them up to the mountain village of Valldemosa. Graves and Riding were not the first artistic people to seek a haven from bourgeois respectability in Majorca; and Valldemosa was famous as the village where Chopin and his mistress George Sand had settled for the winter of 1838, living in a deserted Carthusian monastery.

It was not an attractive village, however; and from Valldemosa Robert and Laura took the coast road which leads northward, along a sometimes precipitous route, with the sea hundreds of feet below to the left, and the mountains hundreds of feet above on the right. After several miles of winding through olive groves and clumps of pine, and occasional orchards of lemons and oranges, the road swung sharply round to the right, and the travellers found themselves skirting a broad semi-circular valley. On the west this ran all the way down to the sea, and on the east it settled itself against a tall mountain-range which curved protectively around it from north to south. Some distance below the head of the valley, at the point where the coast road swept round through a cluster of houses, a long ridge of ground extended itself for a quarter of a mile or so towards the sea, climbing first gently and then steeply up to a church and beyond the church to a small, peaceful graveyard.

This was where the centre of the village of Deyá was situated, between the coast road and the church; and with the sea down below, and the mountains up above, and the wild, rocky and seemingly timeless landscape all around, it was the part of the island which most closely resembled Robert Graves's beloved Harlech. He felt instantly at home; but he and Laura Riding wished above all for peace and privacy; and in any case at Harlech Robert had been used to living a little outside the local community. So they did not look for a house in the village itself, charming though that was, with its little main street at the southern end of which was the village wash-place where the local women did their daily washing in the open air.

Instead they rented a small stone cottage known as Casa Salerosa, which stood some distance to the south-west of the village, just above the road to Valldemosa, but still within the broad curve of the valley. The cottage faced north, and outside the front door there was a small rough terrace with a young pine tree, from where the two writers could sit and look out either towards the rocky coast and the sea, or back inland towards the village. To one side of the cottage there was a small garden where Robert could grow vegetables; and to the other there were terraces of olive trees; while at the rear of the building there was a narrow yard with a large hexagonal well-head, and a few rather dilapidated outbuildings.

Casa Salerosa itself was as primitive as its surroundings; but hardly more so than the stone and slate cottage which Robert had once bought from his mother in North Wales and where, before marrying Nancy, he had planned to spend the post-war years writing poetry at his 'darling beechwood table'.[6] Casa Salerosa, like Gwuthdy Bach, was a simple unpretentious cottage, soundly built and pleasant to look at, in a most peaceful and unspoiled setting. Its only serious disadvantage was that on its southern side it backed directly on to the lower slopes of a high mountain, so that during the summer months it received comparatively little sun, and in the winter months none at all.

On entering Casa Salerosa, Robert and Laura found themselves in a large reception area. To the right there was a small kitchen, where cooking could be done over a charcoal stove; and to the left, beyond the foot of a flight of stairs, a doorway led into the best room in the house, with a fire-place across its north-eastern corner, and a large north-facing window. This was immediately chosen by Laura as her workroom; and for the time being Robert shared it with her.

For although it was an enormous relief to arrive at Deyá, and to claim this beautiful place as their own, and to turn their back upon the difficulties of the recent past, that was the only sense in which Graves and Riding could be described as lotus-eaters. Nor did they belong among the eccentrics and vaguely artistic idlers who had made up a small foreign colony in Deyá for many years. Robert and Laura had come to Majorca to work.

As soon as possible, therefore, they had their press transported from London; and while they awaited its arrival they converted an old stable at the back of the house into a combined press-room and study for Robert, with a fireplace in one corner. And to give themselves as much time as possible for literary work, they engaged the services of a spirited seventeen-year-old called Maria, who came from the village each day to cook and to clean. They treated her well, though Maria could not help smiling to herself at the extremity of Laura's passion for cleanliness; and they were a refreshing change from other members of the foreign community, such as the strange American who lived not far away in a white house with a niece she did not like, and far too many dogs. What was impressive about Maria's new employers at Casa Salerosa was their industry. Laura, the Señora, gave the orders, and worked at the front of the house, Robert at the back; and where most of the villagers only went indoors to eat or to sleep, Robert and Laura kept two fires blazing throughout the winter months, while they wrote and wrote and wrote.[7]

Their work was informed by a shared vision of the supreme importance of poetry; and for a while Salerosa was at the centre of a private world which was similar in some respects to the world which Robert had shared with Nancy during the first six months after their wedding. For some time it had seemed that they had escaped from the limitations of the normal world; but reality had kept breaking in. Robert was determined not to let that happen again, as is clear from his poem 'The Next Time', which ends:

> And when we passengers are given two hours,
> When once more the wheels fail at Somewhere Nowhere,
> To climb out, stretch our legs and pick wild flowers –
> Suppose that this time I elect to stay there?[8]

Staying there would of course depend upon earning enough money; but with the publication in November 1929 of *Good-bye to All That* money no longer seemed like a serious problem.

CHAPTER 2
The Publication of Good-bye to All That

Although Robert Graves wished to remain with Laura Riding in the timeless world of 'Somewhere Nowhere', in the rest of the world the seconds ticked by as busily as ever. In London, for example, where his wife Nancy Nicholson was doing rather well with their four children. Eminently practical, she went shopping as late as possible on Saturday nights, when the price of food was at its cheapest; and Clarissa, visiting her on the barge, was impressed by the sight of 'the children ... sitting at tea around their deal table & the lamp shining on each well-brushed head'.[9] Or in North Wales, where Robert's elderly parents worried incessantly about the imminent publication of his autobiography. Charles, as a journalist, was their chief source of information on the subject; and, early in November 1929, they received an encouraging letter from him with the news that the book was 'Fairly harmless & all about Charterhouse & the War'.[10]

Charles himself was in a buoyant mood: after more than four years of courtship, he had a firm date for his wedding to the beautiful and charming Peggy Leigh. They were to be married on 17 December at St Margaret's, the most fashionable church in London. Peggy's parents had been difficult up to the last moment, insisting for example that he should have at least £5,000 worth of life insurance before they would consent to the marriage – 'Romance is certainly dead in 1929,' Robert's half-sister Susan had commented acidly, when hearing of some earlier financial negotiations.[11] But Charles himself was well aware that he had won the most important battle in his life; and even when he saw an advance copy of *Good-bye to All That*, and so learned of the 'dedicatory epilogue' to Laura Riding, he wrote cheerfully to his parents that 'this will not be noticed by the genuine reader'.[12]

Another advance copy had reached Eddie Marsh; and he was horrified by a passage on page 398, in which Robert Graves talked about receiving income from 'the Rupert Brooke fund, of which Edward Marsh was the administrator'. Marsh pointed out to Graves that the paragraph in which this occurred was:

> wrong from beginning to end, and may get me into great trouble. There
> is no such thing as a R.B.Fund . . . and I am not an 'administrator' . . . .
> I tremble to think what will happen if 'needy poets with families' see
> it in print that there is a 'Fund' for their relief. I may be bombarded
> with applications which it will be distressing to refuse.
>
> Further I *may* get into trouble with the Inland Revenue. . . . if they
> see what you have said, they may raise tiresome questions and if they
> *did* insist in arrears [of income tax] I should be broke.[13]

Graves was duly apologetic, and promised that Cape would paste in a suitable
erratum slip. 'I do hope that, apart from all that,' Graves wrote to Marsh,
'you liked the book. Laura and I have a house here on a hill overlooking
the sea towards Spain. It is very good to be here and we intend to stay
a long time. Sun. Olives, figs, oranges, fish, quiet. She is much better
now and can limp two or three miles at a go now.'[14] Graves believed that
the printing and insertion of the *erratum* slip would mean that his autobiography could not appear until the New Year, and that he would therefore
'miss the heavy Christmas sales that we have been counting on. So that
will be my punishment.'[15] However, printing and inserting *erratum* slips
was a comparatively simple task, and Jonathan Cape put it in hand immediately.

A much more serious threat to the early publication of *Good-bye to All
That* came from Siegfried Sassoon. Edmund Blunden had been asked to
review the book, and, on first reading it through, a great many of his earlier
feelings of resentment against Graves surfaced. Deciding that it had been
written in an entirely self-centred manner, but knowing that he could not
attack it convincingly without support from someone who had shared
Graves's wartime experiences, he invited Siegfried Sassoon to examine
it with him page by page.[16]

Sassoon agreed; and by 7 November they had been through the entire
work, and annotated some 250 of Graves's 448 pages.[17] Sassoon, who already
thought of Graves as 'rather impossible',[18] was soon just as angry as Blunden
about the contents of *Good-bye to All That*. He was particularly enraged
by the passage on pages 289–90 in which Graves, though giving no names,
had clearly described his visit to Sassoon's home in September 1916, and
had included details about how Sassoon's mother had been trying to contact
the spirit of her dead elder son. In another place, in a flagrant breach
of copyright, Graves had included Sassoon's long and bitter poem, written

for him in the summer of 1918, which begins: 'I'd timed my death in action to the minute.'

By Tuesday 12 November, five days after he and Blunden had completed their annotations, and only six days before *Good-bye to All That* was due to be published, Sassoon had decided that he could not allow his poem to be printed; nor could he allow the whole of Graves's story about his mother to go into print: she was still alive, and he feared its effect upon her if she read it. So he called on Jonathan Cape, who soon realized that Sassoon was highly wrought up, and that alterations must be made in order to avoid legal action and the almost certain postponement of publication. It was therefore agreed that Cape should print cancel pages, which had the effect of deleting the whole of the poem and eleven lines of Graves's visit to Sassoon, the blank spaces which were left being filled with asterisks. The work had to be done at very high pressure, but it was rushed through just in time. And so *Good-bye to All That* was duly published, complete with *erratum* slip and cancel pages, on Monday 18 November 1929.

On that morning Alfred Perceval Graves, who had been sent a copy of Robert's book by Charles,

went out into the village for *The Times* and found all the papers agog with Robert's *Good-bye to All That*! – a rather severe article in the *Mail*, a friendly one in *The Liverpool Post*, while the front page of the *Daily Herald* was taken up about the most startling war book yet written. I have read up to page 150 with very mixed feelings – distress for what R[obert] went through at Charterhouse & since, & especially for [Robert's sufferings on] the War Front though [I am] only about half way through that.[19]

And when he had finished reading, APG decided that 'if shortened by 50 odd pages and winnowed of all gossip it would be a remarkable book. It left the impression on me that [Robert's] best chance is to become an R[oman] C[atholic] – perhaps through the Osborne Benedictine Monks with whom he was friendly. We'll see!'[20] Amy too was deeply saddened by Robert's painful account of his early experiences. After receiving a letter from him enclosing '2 exquisite views from Deyá', she described the village to Clarissa as 'evidently a beautiful place for [Robert] to rest from his sorrows. His book gives a terrible account of what he has gone through ... and will cause a widespread sensation.'[21] In another letter, to John, she added that 'Poor Robert has suffered terribly & what that led to is not for us to judge of. I do not see what he has to come back to & I fear if Laura failed him he would end his life, having no faith left.'[22]

Concern and sympathy for Robert were paramount to begin with; but within the family these more generous feelings were gradually overshadowed by feelings of considerable irritation over the host of inaccuracies. Even Amy, who had been generally well treated, wrote that it was curious to see an unvarnished portrait of herself in print, and declared to Clarissa that she had been 'far more with you children than he remembers & my social duties came very much second. . . . Robert makes many mistakes of fact.'[23] It was highly disagreeable for APG to read that, according to Robert, he had 'never . . . showed any understanding of my serious work', and 'was always more ready to ask advice about his own work than to offer it for mine';[24] and both APG and his brother CLG of *Punch* were very much upset not only by Robert's criticisms of Charterhouse, but also by his unkind remarks about their father, the Bishop of Limerick, who was described as 'hard' and 'far from generous'.[25]

Nor had Robert's brothers escaped censure: John's conventional outlook was brutally mocked in a passage in which, by constant repetition of the words 'typical', 'good' and 'normal', Robert successfully conveyed the wrong impression that his youngest brother lacked all interest as a human being;[26] and Charles was also treated dismissively. John carried his wounds in silence; but Charles wrote to Robert on 25 November.

Charles could not help admiring his brother's success, and began by congratulating him on the outstanding sales of *Good-bye to All That*, pointing out that '20,000 in five days at half a guinea for an autobiography is pretty hot & easily a record. But then the *D[aily] Herald*, the *Star* & the *Daily Chronicle* all actually led the paper with it. An amazing business. But look Robert,' he added. 'Two things.' He felt that he should have been described as a 'columnist' rather than as a 'society gossip-writer on the middle page of *The Daily Mail*'; and he was angry with Robert for stating that 'I was the only one of my father's five sons of military age who had seen active service.' 'That my dear Sir', complained Charles, 'is rot. Philip did not. Bones enlisted and re-enlisted three times. I managed, with my dead leg, to cheat the Medical exam people and got passed A1 and grade 1 and was going out on Nov 30 1918. I was then still 18 of course. Now you've no right, really, to suggest that I dodged the draft so to speak.'[27] Robert's half-brother Dick was also wounded, though indirectly. Early in 1930, Philip announced that Robert had 'spoilt Dick's career in Egypt by making fun of King Fuad's son. They must find out that Dick is Robert's brother and punish him for the insult.'[28]

Those who were not closely involved, or who were involved but had not been hurt in any way, were able to take a more balanced view of the merits of *Good-bye to All That*. Bernard Rendall, for example, Robert's former Headmaster at Copthorne, told John in January 1930 that he had 'read Robert's book', and that, 'however indiscreet he was, he was certainly brave and modest in very trying times: on the whole a book worth writing & well written though not considerate to parents or careful about the feelings of others. Perhaps Ch'ouse won't be worse for a shaking up!'[29]

However, there were many readers and critics outside the family circle who were deeply offended by Graves's frankness and honesty when describing his experiences. Complaints that it was 'ungentlemanly' of him to attack the public school system were predictable enough; but critics also accused him of speaking unkindly about his own regiment, the Royal Welch Fusiliers, and said that he had libelled the dead by describing how company officers drank large quantities of whisky in the trenches. In the Scottish press there was a further storm of indignation about Graves's comments on the fighting abilities of the Scots, with particular reference to his description of the demoralized state of the Highland Light Infantry during the battle of Loos; and for a while a number of senior officers declared that they intended to take legal action over the matter. The critic of the leading Glasgow daily even called for the book to be suppressed, 'lest a hundred years hence readers may be misled into believing that there is as much as a grain of truth in this whole collection of unmitigated tripe'.[30]

When, in December 1929, Graves was asked by the *Daily Mail* to make a general reply to his critics, he did so in a manner which his father described as 'clever but cynical',[31] claiming that he had 'more or less deliberately mixed in all the ingredients that I know are mixed into other popular books'. He then defended himself against a number of individual accusations, while at the same time adding fresh material, which was certain to give further offence. Thus, on officers being drunk:

all that I had really recorded was that after a long spell their nerves had often got so bad that they had to treat themselves with whisky to stave off a breakdown. It was the only available medicine.

I only once saw officers riotously drunk in trenches, and never any dead drunk. One of the riotously drunk I remember well: it was during a battle. He was a ranker-lieutenant, and he did a very heroic deed which only a drunken man or a fanatic would have attempted. And a bullet went neatly through both nostrils, and he came back sobered and cursing and bleeding like a pig, and everyone laughed, though it was not a laughing day.[32]

In the course of his article, Graves also passed on a few factual corrections which he had received from Dr Dunn, the Regimental Surgeon of the 2nd Royal Welch Fusiliers;[33] and he made a handsome apology for having given the impression that any of his brothers had somehow managed to dodge the draft.

Although many of his most hostile critics clearly showed themselves to be beneath contempt, Graves must have realized that there were more factual errors in his autobiography than he would have liked; and some months after the publication of *Good-bye to All That* he wrote a letter to the editor of the *Times Literary Supplement* in which he suggested that a 'test of historical accuracy' should not be strictly applied to the personal memoirs of a combatant. The more efficient the soldier, the less time he had to write about his experiences at the time; and in any case it was forbidden to keep a diary while at the Front, or to send home letters with detailed accounts of the fighting:

> Great latitude should therefore be allowed to a soldier who has since got his facts or dates mixed. I would even paradoxically say that the memoirs of a man who went through some of the worst experiences are not truthful unless they contain a high proportion of falsities. High-explosive barrages will make a temporary liar or visionary of anyone; the old trench-mind is at work in all over-estimation of casualties, 'unnecessary' dwelling on horrors, mixing of dates and confusion between trench rumours and scenes actually witnessed.[34]

This was an authoritative defence by the author of what had rapidly established itself as both a bestseller and a modern classic.

The commercial success of *Good-bye to All That* had obvious implications for Graves and Riding, whose establishment at Casa Salerosa was now totally secure for many months to come. Not only would there be money for them both to live on, and money to look after Robert's children; but also there would be enough money to begin printing again, or to invest in other artistic projects. And in the medium term it was evident that any publication by or about Robert would be an attractive commercial prospect.

Jonathan Cape, who was a particularly shrewd businessman, immediately showed a renewed interest in Alfred Perceval Graves's autobiography, though he suggested that it should be revised 'with more stress on the latter [i.e. the Robert-related] part of [APG's] life';[35] while to Robert himself he suggested some kind of a sequel to *Good-bye to All That*. Laura Riding, the subject of Robert's mysterious 'Dedicatory Epilogue', might also command rather more public attention than in the past; and Cape promised to publish a volume of her poems. At about the same time, Robert was approached by the leading theatrical producer Maurice Browne, who asked whether he would write a contemporary drama for the stage. Having only recently escaped to their island paradise, and having therefore stepped off the train at 'Somewhere Nowhere', Robert Graves and Laura Riding suddenly found themselves more in demand than either of them had ever been before.

CHAPTER 3
But It Still Goes On

Living at Salerosa Robert Graves and Laura Riding were far enough from the centre of Deyá to be able very easily to lead their lives on their own terms; and gradually they established the kind of relationship both with the villagers and with the rest of the outside world which had already become a characteristic feature of their partnership. It was assumed that their own behaviour was always morally and philosophically correct, and that the intellectual positions which they adopted were impregnable. Riding, as the embodiment of Finality, gave her divine sanction to their shared set of beliefs; and Graves was her champion. Outsiders were to be treated with suspicion until they had proved themselves worthy of joining the select group which centred upon Laura; but once they had been accepted, whether male or female, as 'proper chaps' and provided that they made no serious attempt to challenge Laura's authority, they became part of a charmed circle.

The first 'chaps' to join Graves and Riding in Deyá were Len and Jane Lye, for whom the cottage of C'an Pa Bo was rented some time early in 1930. C'an Pa Bo, or 'the house of good bread', was an extremely attractive cottage on the southern slopes below the church, just across that part of the valley from Casa Salerosa; and no doubt most days the Lyes would walk up to Casa Salerosa to begin a morning of hard work. Jane took up her secretarial duties; while Len's main task was to produce suitable designs for the covers of several books which were to be printed later that year by Nancy Cunard's Hours Press in Paris: a volume of poems by Robert, entitled *Twenty Poems More*; another by Laura, entitled *Ten Poems Less*; and a curious moral tract by Laura entitled *Four Unposted Letters to Catherine*.[36]

Laura Riding was also working on her own *Poems: A Joking Word* for Cape.[37] This was a substantial selection from the best of her work to date, including much of *The Close Chaplet* and *Love as Love, Death as Death*. There were also more than twenty new poems, several of which refer very clearly to what were then recent events. In *To the Devil, Recently Dead*, for example, Riding bids a bitter farewell to Phibbs, whom she now thinks of as a monstrous purveyor of honeyed words, whose hatred of deception in others was far outweighed by his own casual regard for the truth.[38] In other poems she describes her current partner as having finally reached a state of real awareness;[39] and of now being the other self in whose presence she became complete.[40] Graves was particularly impressed by her 'It Is Or Will Be Or Was',[41] the first two lines of which he placed at the head of his *Poems 1926–1930*:[42]

> It is a conversation between angels now,
> Or between who remain when all are gone[.]

Meanwhile, after a brief and unsuccessful stay in Egypt, Phibbs had returned to England and to Nancy.[43] Robert cannot have been pleased to hear about this; and at the beginning of January 1930, after writing a long letter to Jenny, David, Catherine and Sam, he formally renounced his rights over them. He was also angry with his parents, perhaps because they had now accepted Geoffrey's role in Nancy's life; and, on 22 January, his mother received a harshly worded letter in which Robert described her as wrong-headed and wrong-hearted, and added that in future he would only communicate with Nancy through a solicitor.

Graves had not totally abandoned his family: in January 1930 he had sent money to pay for Jenny's dancing lessons, and for a new school uniform for David; but in March he declared that his earnings from *Good-bye to All That*, which had been advertised by Cape as being £4,000, were really no more than £900, of which he had actually received less than £800. He would therefore be compelled, he told Amy, to reduce his monthly allowance to Nancy from £20 to £18. Robert added that Amy's love for him must be a very shadowy thing, because she ignored Laura, who was not only 'a really good, really true & really real person', but also 'the most true and important person in my life'. Under these circumstances, Amy could still write to him about money or about the children's health; but in general he had no further wish 'to be reminded [by her] of my children, or their pretty ways'.[44]

The rift between Robert and his parents widened still further when one of APG's sisters sent Robert an ill-advised letter complaining about the fact that Amy was having to pay for Jenny's and David's education. Robert sent it straight on to Amy, with a covering letter in which he asked her crossly: 'Who has been advertising your bounty and my skinflintedness?'

He added that he would pay nothing for the education of Catherine or Sam either; and (not knowing that she had already arranged this) he asked to be removed from Amy's will in favour of his children.[45]

Laura kept on the sidelines while this correspondence was going on; indeed, Robert took care to tell Amy that he 'Particularly [did] not want [Amy] to think of [Laura] as coming between the children and him; that is the very opposite thing.'[46] However, Laura had evidently taken a special liking to Catherine, and in her *Four Unposted Letters to Catherine* she singled her out as the most interesting of Robert's four children. Although she was 'not clever at carpentering like David or at sewing like Jenny or at drawing like Sam', and although she seemed 'to spend a lot of time dreaming about nothing at all', she was in fact,

> as the few people you really know you recognise, a perfect child. And this is because when you seem to be dreaming about nothing at all you are not being lazy but thinking about yourself. And so you get to be yourself. One doesn't say you are lazy or selfish. If a person is herself she can't be a bad person in any way; she is always a good person in her own way.[47]

Through knowing everything about yourself, says Riding, comes the ability to know everything about everything. Unfortunately, the world is dominated by men, who do not usually realize that most things should be done for comfort or fun, rather than to impress other people: 'it is a world', she tells Catherine, 'not of doing but over-doing.[48]' Writing a poem is also achieved 'with laziness not with busyness'; but it is the one thing which is 'better than fun or comfort', because it is 'like being alive for always'.[49] Since most people do not understand how to live, the world is in a muddle; and all that those with self-knowledge can do is to be true to themselves.[50]

Towards the end of *Four Unposted Letters to Catherine*, Laura Riding added that those with self-knowledge might even find themselves liking people who were wicked and crooked, 'because the wicked crooked people understood about things and, though they were part of the muddle, at any rate knew of the muddle and were what they were quite consciously'.[51] This sounds surprisingly like a reference to the remarkable Juan Marroig Más, known as Gelat, a likeable and life-enhancing rogue who controlled much of what went on in Deyá, and who soon held an important place in the affections of both Laura and Robert.

Water represents considerable power in an island on which no more than nineteen inches of rain fall during an entire year; and on which there is not a single river or stream: just dried-up beds, like the Torrente at Deyá, down which an occasional flood carries off rain-water or melting snow to the sea. And Gelat owed his position in the village very largely to the fact that he controlled some fresh-water springs which fed the cisterns and the reservoirs upon which nearly everyone depended. He was also responsible for generating just enough electricity for an elementary system of electric lighting; and he ran a primitive bus service to Palma: a single bus which he drove himself and which set out and came back only once a day.

Robert was attracted to Gelat for much the same reasons that the young man is attracted to Zorba the Greek in the famous novel of that name by Nikos Kazantzakis. Here was a man who had instinctively achieved what Robert had been aiming at for years, and what most people never manage: to be entirely himself, his scant respect for conventional morality matched by his wholehearted enthusiasm for the simplest and best pleasures of life, such as eating, drinking, making love and enjoying the company of one's friends.

Laura was so strongly attracted to Gelat that when she was asked in 1932 to write an autobiographical sketch for *Authors Today and Yesterday*, she described Juan Marroig as the only person whom she admired. 'He is rarely wrong in his judgments', she explained, 'and when he makes a mistake it does not stay long uncorrected.'[52] She could have added that she was also impressed by her inability to dominate or manipulate him in any way. On the contrary, there were times when he clearly succeeded in dominating her. However, Laura was hardly likely to throw herself at Gelat's feet while her relationship with Robert was still at such a productive stage. In any case, Gelat was a man full of animal spirits, who was not only married but who kept one mistress in the village and another in the nearby town of Sóller; and Laura herself had been so badly injured by her fall that for many years she could not face the prospect of a lover, and even Robert was only invited into her bed to comfort her during thunder-storms. As usual, anything which affected her personally was elevated into something of general significance. Riding had already derided sexual activity in 'The Damned Thing', an essay which had appeared in 1928 in her deliberately provocative collection *Anarchism Is Not Enough*.[53] 'With sex', she had declared, 'there seems to be nothing between masturbation (throwing the damned thing out) and romance (grotesque adaptation)';[54] sexual intercourse was boring in the extreme for women, who, 'to save [themselves] from boredom [were] obliged to enliven the scene with a few gratuitous falsetto turns, which [men wrongly] interpret[ed] as co-operation';[55] and for men she had advocated: 'the relief ... of sexual suicide'.[56] This had not prevented her from taking both Graves and Phibbs as her lovers; but now, when she wrote 'I like men to be men and women to be women; but I think that bodies have had their day,'[57] she was practising what she preached. Nevertheless she admired and respected Gelat, and was later to be drawn by him into some highly ill-advised schemes.

Robert himself was spending much time on the play which he had been asked to write by Maurice Browne, and which he had decided to call *But It Still Goes On*.[58] It is an interesting but not altogether satisfactory mixture of philosophical asides and autobiographical fantasy. Dick Tompion, the central character, clearly based upon Robert himself, is a young poet and ex-soldier who has realized that 'it's finished and ended and over, but it still goes on';[59] or, as he says later in the same scene, 'the bottom of things, after working looser and looser for centuries, has at last fallen out.'[60] This is pure Riding: historical time is effectively over; and, according to this play, the 'catastrophe' happened about two years before the start of the Great War. What went wrong was sheer weight of numbers: there are never more than a few 'proper' people in the world, and when:

> the one unnecessary person too many was born ... the proper people were finally swamped. Once they counted; now they no longer count. So it's impossible for a proper person to feel the world as a necessary world – an intelligible world in which there's any hope or fear for the future – a world worth bothering about – or, if he happens to be a poet, a world worth writing for – a world in which there's any morality left to bother about, but his own personal morality: *that* gets more and more strict, of course.[61]

This, like many of Riding's ideas, remained central to Robert Graves's thinking for the rest of his life.

The autobiographical element is significant and sometimes amusing but largely disagreeable. In *Good-bye to All That* Graves had dismissed the past with laconic maturity; in *But It Still Goes On* he rakes up old grievances and indulges in bitter adolescent fantasies, especially about his father. For if Dick Tompion is Robert, then Cecil Tompion is a savage caricature of Robert's father. Cecil's writing is popular but hopelessly out of date; while Dick's excellent poems are generally unappreciated. Nor is the public likely to have a change of heart. As Dick says: 'There's no reason to expect posterity to be any less turnip-headed. It'll still be reading my father's stuff probably. Or someone equivalently god-awful.'[62] Cecil also subsidizes his son, just as Alfred and Amy had subsidized Robert: but we are told by Dick that the money is only handed over 'because he loathes me and wants me to feel dependent on him and jealous of his literary successes. And he expects me to have feelings of shame about taking the money.'[63] Later in the play, however, the father receives his just deserts: not only does his mistress fall in love with Dick – '*She's* all right,' Dick says, in a characteristically Gravesian comment, when she has recognized that he and not his father is the true 'genius' and 'great man'[64] (one wonders incidentally how on earth those words escaped Laura's blue pencil) – but also the father's unsuccessful attempt to force his attentions on a young woman become known; and the humiliation of this is such that he shoots himself. So much for fathers!

Another important strand in the play is its treatment of homosexuality and lesbianism. Dick Tompion's closest friend, David Casselis, is a homosexual architect who is evidently modelled to a considerable extent upon Robert Graves's friend Siegfried Sassoon. Like Sassoon, Casselis is said to have been 'a good-looking gallant young officer'; but it is made clear that he has 'romantic feelings' for Dick Tompion; that his wartime popularity among his men can best be explained by his acting 'as a sort of military queen-bee'[65] to them; and that he is attractive to women, but only because he has no desire for them, and is therefore 'such a relief from the usual sex-bears'.[66] The sharpness of this portrait no doubt owes much to the fact that it was being penned by Graves while he was simultaneously engaged in an acrimonious correspondence with Sassoon about *Good-bye to All That*.

It was early in February 1930 that Sassoon had written to Graves from Sicily, saying that he had been 'so persistently reminded of you and your book that I am obliged to try and analyse the exasperation it has caused me'. It was an exasperation so intense that 'If I had met you a couple of months ago I should probably have tried to knock you down.' Sassoon felt it best to begin by rehearsing the irritations which had made him avoid Graves's company since November 1927: his hostility towards Gosse; his apparently unsympathetic letter after Hardy's death; his journalistic article about his visit to Hardy's home, Max Gate; and what Sassoon described as the 'needlessly ungracious and egotistical' review which Graves had given to his *Memoirs of a Fox-Hunting Man*.[67]

The appearance of *Good-bye to All That* had apparently come at the very worst time for Sassoon, who was then engaged upon a sequel to *Memoirs*, which was also to cover the war years. 'It was not', wrote Sassoon, 'that you anticipated anything that I wanted to write down, but that you blurted out your hasty version as though you were writing for the *Daily Mail*. . . .

Also I wished that your anecdotal method had been more accurate . . . .
your treatment of me was journalistic and, I think, perfunctory.'[68] Sassoon
then pointed out a number of serious inaccuracies in Graves's account of
the events of July 1917, when Graves had persuaded him to back down
from his confrontation with the military authorities; and also questioned
his story of having been primarily responsible for the cancellation of what
would have been a suicidal raid. He added, to show Robert that despite
everything he remained fundamentally friendly, that he had made a new
will from which Robert would benefit by £300 a year tax paid; and that
no reply was necessary to his letter.[69]

Graves however replied at great length on 20 February, partly to defend
himself ('My egotistical nature: you misunderstand me. I deny any further
interest in great occasions, great men, great emotions, so I can write deta-
chedly'); and partly to launch a counter-attack. Sassoon was said to have
'an inverted vulgarity'; and Robert added that 'The friendship that was
between us was always disturbed by several cross-currents; your homosexual
leanings and I believe your jealousy of Nancy in some way or other; later
Nancy being in love with you (which no doubt you noticed and were afraid
of) for several years (until 1923 or so). . . .'[70] In Sassoon's answering letter
of 2 March, he wrote that he had never been jealous of Nancy; but 'I
would have liked to have seen you independently sometimes. In her presence
I was nervous and uneasy. She didn't give one much assistance, did she?
For *you* I felt affection; but physical attraction never existed.' He added
a number of new complaints, especially about Graves's unkind treatment
of both Wilfred Owen and Robert Ross, and about the passage which he
had compelled Cape to delete, and which he now described as 'a personal
outrage. . . . What you did was to exploit (and betray) something private
in order to add a sensational page to your book.'[71] Not surprisingly, this
exchange of letters was to be the last between Graves and Sassoon for
some three years.

Graves's play *But It Still Goes On* was completed and sent to Maurice
Browne by the end of May 1930; but it was soon returned. The treatment
of homosexuality and lesbianism had been far too candid; and Browne
told Graves that, if produced, the play would 'do definite harm to your
reputation and prejudice your public against your future work'. Graves
shrugged off this criticism, and decided that he would 'tidy it a bit more
and then publish it along with "Papa Johnson", "The Shout", "Avocado
Pears", that journal, parts of "Baal", etc, this autumn in a book called
by the name of the play'.[72]

'The Shout' was of course Robert's Egyptian horror story; and 'Papa

Johnson' and 'Avocado Pears' were two further short stories. In the former, a grimly amusing tale, a man is frozen to death in the Antarctic for failing to heed 'Papa Johnson's' advice; and in the latter there is a depressingly sordid picture of Parisian night-life.

The 'journal' was the diary which Robert had kept for some weeks after completing *Good-bye to All That*, and it is a curious mixture, containing everything from autobiographical scraps, to asides about book publicity, charity appeals, bad writing and the problems of organ music being loudly played in a select residential neighbourhood at three o'clock in the morning. Most interestingly, it includes the synopsis of 'a complete historical romance or interpretative biography' about the Roman emperor Claudius, 'a puzzle to the historians, as indeed he was to his contemporaries'.[73] Graves had a number of ideas about this, and he wrote them down in an attempt 'to lay the ghost of an idea which otherwise might continue to plead for execution'.[74] Luckily for his readers, the attempt failed: for this synopsis was later to become the germ of his brilliant historical novel *I, Claudius*.

One of Graves's last ideas in the 'Journal of Curiosities' was to write as though God had decided to carry on the Journal in his place, and to explain his progress through the centuries as an evolutionary deity.[75] This idea was then followed up in two lengthy chapters called the 'Alpha and Omega of the Autobiography of Baal', which concludes with God declaring that He too has a God which may or may not appear in human shape, and which (in a description which elaborates a little on Graves's previous description of Laura as 'living invisibly, against kind, as dead, beyond event')[76] 'will not be for or of me, or yet even against me. It will be indifferent to me . . . [a] deathless being, no doubt, humanly visible; but without aspects, therefore humanly unknowable; not worshipped, not martyred, left alone, of no kind.'[77]

Len and Jane Lye had recently returned to England to await the birth of their child; but Robert had found in the 'young, shy, fish-faced half-Spanish son of the acting British Consul' a typist to take Jane's place for the time being; and by now Robert and Laura had also learned enough Spanish to be able to converse easily with the villagers. An extract from a letter which Graves wrote to the Lyes at the beginning of June 1930 captures the flavour of the time:

What's new here? Thunder this morning, hot sun this afternoon, heavy rain two days ago, yesterday a very breezy lovely shiny day and we went into Palma; this morning, June 1st, drifts of snow on the hills. I went up the path behind the *Molino* past that Moorish keep and there's a path through the live-oak forest to the top. It took me one hour and twenty minutes to get where I could look down at Valldemosa and across to Palma where I saw six German cruisers anchored that are visiting. It was a good walk, through cloud part of the way, and it was so sticky by the time I had finished with the olive-tree level and got into the oak level that I took off all my clothes except my shoes and stuffed them into my knapsack. But met no one. I am gradually, in streaks, getting the brown egg colour on my skin so highly prized by collectors. But I have toothache, curse it. Must get it fixed tomorrow.

And the shoemaker and his wife sent you their *recuerdos* and asked for your news. And we have just discovered that your bedroom light is on every night since you went! Gelat says it's *nada! nada!* He took us yesterday in the auto, with the *modista* who is making me night-shirts instead of pyjamas for the hot weather, and Maria [their maid] who had lunch with us at the Repla and ate various things for the first time and pretended politely to be bored. . . . Green *pimientos* are in season again. Today I got pebbles by the sea; it was a good beach; I found one pebble with that rich emerald colour that means copper; I hadn't met one before. . . . The flowers in season are lots of poppies and pale-blue chicory.[78]

Riding was shortly to begin making detailed corrections to the material which Graves had assembled for *But It Still Goes On*; and she was also working on proof corrections for *Though Gently*, her series of prose poems which were to be published later in the year as *Seizin Four*. Graves particularly admired a passage in which she wrote with some amusement about the interest which was now being shown in their work: 'I mean to say precisely that we have stopped. We have stopped. And of course the crowd accumulates. . . . My dear crowd, be persuaded that whatever your services in the past nothing more is wanted of you now. Nothing serious, at any rate.'[79] These words appeared as a tribute to Riding at the front of *But It Still Goes On*; while among the new poems which Graves had written for his *1926–1930* collection was this moving recognition of her effect upon his state of mind:[80]

THE AGE OF CERTAINTY
Content in you,
Andromeda alone,
Yet queen of air and ocean
And every fiery dragon,

Chained to no cliff,
Asking no rescue of me.

Content in you,
Mad Atalanta
Stooping unpausing
Ever ahead
Acquitting me of rivalry.

Content in you,
Invariable she-Proteus
Sole unrecordable
Giving my tablets holiday.

Content in you,
Niobe of no children
Sorrow no calamity.

Content in you,
Helen, foiler of beauty.

Robert's contentment was not disturbed when early in June he read a prospectus of his father's autobiography. Despite the highly provocative nature of the title, in which Robert's *Good-bye to All That* was countered with the words *To Return to All That*, Robert felt that it looked 'pretty dreary'.[81] When however a copy reached him, in late July 1930 (it had been published by Cape on the 14th of that month), he found it thoroughly exasperating.

CHAPTER 4

To Return to All That

From the moment in December 1929 that Cape showed renewed interest in his autobiography, Alfred Perceval Graves had been working on little else; but he was now eighty-three, and he soon realized that he needed a good deal of editorial help to knock his narrative into shape. His youngest son John, who was then schoolmastering at Sandroyd in Surrey, volunteered his services, and spent his Christmas holidays working feverishly on the text. John also persuaded his father to write a new chapter devoted entirely to Robert; and successfully urged him to adopt *To Return to All That* as his title.

This was the start of a very trying time for APG. Although he felt that John's cuts were 'on the whole justified', he was also gloomily certain that his son had 'severed ... some of the finest links in my "Life"';[82] and then at the end of January he found that several other members of the family, including his brother CLG and his son Philip, were 'dead against *To Return to All That* in favour of which as you know', APG wrote to John, 'I was overpersuaded by Charles & yourself.'[83] While trying to think of a new title, he was beset by further problems. He had promised that any of his children who wished to do so could revise any passages about themselves; and although Robert did not avail himself of this offer, several of the others, including Philip and Dick, 'insist[ed] on being practically left out'.[84] Philip particularly objected to a passage in which his father had recorded how, as a rebellious child, he had taken to 'saying his prayers & hymns to the devil'.[85] Philip also felt that the end of the book was very weak; and, with John safely out of the way at Sandroyd, he proposed recalling the manuscript from Cape and making a further set of extensive alterations.

When John heard of this he wrote at once to his father, strenuously defending the original title (which APG reluctantly allowed to go forward only when he realized that Cape had already started advertising the book as *To Return to All That*), and begging him not to let Philip 'mutilate the only clean copy'.[86] However Cape insisted on further cuts in any case; and it was Philip who made them. In its revised form, *To Return to All That* was accepted by 14 March, and published only four months later in an edition of two thousand copies. With its fund of good stories, its atmospheric description of an Anglo-Irish past that already seemed utterly remote, its glimpses of Tennyson and the pre-Raphaelites, and its illuminating account of the development of secondary education after the Forster Act of 1870, *To Return to All That* would have been worth reading had it contained nothing at all about Robert. It deservedly received large numbers of favourable reviews, and went into a second and then a third edition before the year was out.

However, a handful of critics did exactly what Philip and CLG had feared: after reading little apart from the title on the dust-jacket, and the chapter devoted to Robert, they reviewed *To Return to All That* as though it were nothing more than a hostile attack on his son by an indignant father. On 21 July 1930, a week after publication, and the day before his eighty-fourth birthday, APG was worried enough by this development to write a long letter to 'My dear Robby', explaining that the title of his autobiography was not his own idea, but had been suggested by John, and then endorsed by others including the Society for the Propagation of Christian Knowledge, and a certain Father Macdonald. He went on to tell Robert (in case he had not yet seen the book for himself) that:

> I speak generally of some inaccurate remarks of yours about my family & my first wife's & in a chapter affectionately devoted to you I write: 'For the change in his outlook I hold the war and recent experiences responsible. To these I impute the bitter and hasty criticism of people who never wished him harm.' – this especially refers to Richard [Dick], who has been the best son I have ever had, in every way, both in his affection for me & your mother, & the way in which he has treated his half-brothers & sisters, even yourself though you would not realize it.[87]

APG pointed out that the Egyptian section of *Good-bye to All That* might seriously undermine Dick's position in Egypt; and told Robert that he should have tried 'to stick it out till you had repaid [your mother and me] the money we lent you or advanced you from the start'. He was also upset by the final chapter which referred cryptically to the events of 1929, and was '"Greek" to all but those likely to be pained by it'. Then, after asking for a number of alterations to any revised edition of *Good-bye to All That*, APG concluded:

> As I have said before & indeed written to *The Daily Herald*, though now they only review my book as a snub to you, very unfairly I think, I regard your book as on the whole a fine piece of writing & certainly showing up the horror of war so convincingly as to make powerfully for peace.
>
> But as you have criticised me, on the whole generously, if in part in a mistaken or forgetful spirit and speak highly of your mother, though not to my mind realising that she kept you pure & right-minded as a child – I say no more about our two books & can only pray as I do daily that your future life may be directed from above so that you may lead an unselfish, honourable and useful life. We shall think a good deal of you, my dear Robby, on the 24th [Robert's thirty-fifth birthday].
>
> Your loving father
>
> Alfred P. Graves[88]

Unfortunately, by the time Robert received this letter he had already had a chance to read the offending passages, and despite the mildness of their tone he was extremely upset. For the first chapter of *But It Still Goes On* he had written a 'Postscript to *Good-bye to All That*' in which he discussed the critical reception which his autobiography had received, and gave a friendly mention to his father's forthcoming autobiography, saying that it was 'likely that his retrospections where they overlap with mine will not differ materially from them'.[89] But on 24 July 1930, after reading what his father had said about him, he added a bitterly sarcastic note about 'the reminiscential title *To Return to All That*'; about the printing of a number of Robert's poems and letters which Robert himself had considered but rejected when writing his autobiography; and about his father's accusation that he had written unkindly about people as the result of his war experiences. 'He is apparently grieved', Robert went on

> that I am not a good Graves – in spite of characteristic talents obviously, to him, inherited from the male line. He cannot, of course, offer excuses on my behalf on the score of my being a genius, because genius does not occur in the best families .... So he has been forced to excuse my behaviour by blaming it on injuries that I incurred while gallantly serving family, God and King in the trenches – and on subsequent enrichments, outside the radius of the decently happy family circle, at which he darkly hints ....

One thing at least is certain; my father has lived his eighty-four years without, so far as I can learn, having ever made a single enemy; and whatever ingratitude he may mentally charge me with ... he will always continue to remain, in all sincerity, ever my affectionate father Alfred Perceval Graves. It would spoil this note to write a single word more.[90]

When APG's explanatory letter arrived, Robert refused to answer it; and later in the year he told Amy that he had decided to apply to his father's autobiography 'the wet blanket of silence'. [91]

However, the pious sentiments with which APG had concluded his letter reminded Robert what it was he had escaped from; and, knowing that his four children now holidayed regularly with their grandparents, and that ten-year-old David has begun a thoroughly traditional education which was being paid for by Amy, he decided that he must return to England to weigh up the situation for himself. There was another reason for his journey: Nancy had finally abandoned both The World's End, Islip, and the barge at Hammersmith, and Robert wanted to see what new arrangements she had made.

In mid-August, therefore, leaving Maria in charge of Salerosa, Graves and Riding set out for England. It is possible that on the way they called in on Gertrude Stein in Paris: there had been some talk of this; and when Laura Riding had completed *Four Unposted Letters to Catherine* earlier in the year, she had prefaced it with a very friendly letter to Gertrude. But, if they did meet, it was to be for the last time, as there was a quarrel of some kind between the two women. Riding never again corresponded with Stein; and Graves only resumed his friendship with her when she wrote to him some months before her death in 1946.[92]

By the time that Graves and Riding arrived in England, careful arrangements had been made so that Robert could see his children as easily as possible, without either Laura Riding or Geoffrey Phibbs having to be involved. Robert had already explained that he was not going to let Laura see the children, 'to save her any nervous shock';[93] and William Nicholson removed Geoffrey Phibbs from the scene for a while by flying with him to Geneva. In the meantime, Nancy's brother Kit and her stepmother Edie had invited Robert and Laura to stay with them at Frome. This had the advantage that it was within easy reach of Sutton Veny, the Wiltshire village about sixteen miles north-west of Salisbury to which Nancy had recently moved with Geoffrey and the four children, though during term-time eleven-year-old Jenny continued to attend dancing classes in London, where she lodged with a family, while David boarded at Colet Court. During

the holidays, the six of them occupied a lovely old building in the heart
of the countryside which had been divided into two semi-detached cottages.
Nancy and Geoffrey had one cottage to themselves, and the children had
the other; while Nancy also had a separate workshop in which she had
begun hand-printing onto fabric. These were the first of a number of beautiful designs in which her early artistic promise would come to a late fruition.
Rosaleen, visiting them early in August, told Clarissa how the children:

> have to keep their house tidy – take turns at the washing-up etc. They
> run about with nothing on most of the time, & look awfully well & brown.
> It's a nice wild garden with a stream flowing by – a dove cot – a stable
> – a shed where the children make hay-houses on wet days – chicken
> & geese in pens – & Cherry the pony wanders about & the children
> ride him bare-backed – sitting, lying, head to tail & anyhow.[94]

When Edie took Robert over to see the children, the visit was a great
success; and when Robert had left Wiltshire, and taken Laura up to London
for the last part of their visit to England, he wrote to his mother agreeing
that Nancy had 'done well with them & *not* alienated them'. There had
been an awkward moment when six-year-old Sam started calling Robert
'Geoffrey', but Robert had been so pleased by the improvement in his
youngest child's speech (impaired to some extent by his continuing deafness)
that he overlooked an incident which a year previously would have enraged
him beyond measure.[95]

Not everything was perfect, however. Nancy had mentioned that David
was being very difficult at home; and had agreed that he should spend
the next Christmas holidays with his father in Majorca. This caused panic
at Erinfa, where feelings had already been ruffled by news of the friendly
manner in which the Nicholsons had treated Robert and Laura. 'Mrs
Nicholson has accepted hospitality in London from Robert & Laura &
walked with them down Bond Street & may go out to Majorca,' Amy complained to John, ' – there seem no standards left.' She thought it most
unlikely that David would be allowed to return to England once he had
reached Deyá. Robert had already made it clear that he was anxious to
educate David himself, and had stressed the financial advantages that would
follow.[96]

However, Laura may have been surprised by Nancy's readiness to part
with David; certainly, she had no wish to have Robert's eldest son staying
in Deyá on a permanent basis; and under her influence Robert suddenly
announced that he was prepared to let David continue at Colet Court for

at least another year. In these circumstances Amy withdrew her objections to David's proposed Christmas visit; and for a while it seemed that Robert's dealings with his family had entered smoother waters.

By the end of September 1930, Robert and Laura were back at Salerosa, which was looking bright and fresh, as Maria had whitewashed the walls in their absence; and a month later Robert wrote a cheerful and amusing letter to his father. The excuse was a letter from the Bishop of Gibraltar, a friend of Robert's half-sister, Molly, who had written to APG, but mistakenly addressed him on the envelope as 'Robert Graves'. The letter had therefore been forwarded to Deyá, and Robert now returned it to APG, together with a covering letter in which he addressed his elderly father in mock-episcopal style as 'My dear son'.[97]

Sad to say, this was the last happy episode in the relationship between father and son. Any remaining sympathy between them was largely destroyed by the publication early in November of Robert's *But It Still Goes On*. The first detailed knowledge which APG and Amy had of its contents came on 7 November, when they received 'a painful letter from Charles about a passage about himself & the girl he was once engaged to, thinly disguised'.[98]

The girl was the highly neurotic Elvira Mullens, to whom Charles had been briefly engaged back in 1924. It was in September that year, when Robert and Nancy were staying at Harlech, that Charles had realized that he was no longer in love with Elvira. Desperately anxious to break off the engagement as soon as possible, he had drafted a letter to Elvira's father, and sent it to his own parents asking them to make whatever revisions they felt necessary. Since they had already formed the view that it would have been a disastrous marriage, they were delighted to help. Robert, however, who was at that time locked into an increasingly unhappy marriage, took the conventional view that Charles was a 'cad' for attempting to escape from his obligations in this manner; and he copied out both Charles's original letter and the redrafted letter for future reference.[99]

Then, in September 1929, when writing what became the 'Journal of Curiosities' section of *But It Still Goes On*, Robert came across the two letters; and despite his own happy escape from a mutually damaging relationship, which might have made him revise his opinion of Charles's actions, he decided to include both of them. The names were changed; but the only other alterations seem to have been designed to place his brother in as bad a light as possible.[100] Charles, now happily married to Peggy, was understandably upset by Robert's unauthorized use of this sensitive material; and although a number of copies of *But It Still Goes On* had already been sold, he forced Cape under threat of legal action to print sets of cancel pages for as much of the edition as remained in stock.

When, on 11 September 1930, a copy of *But It Still Goes On* arrived at Erinfa, it made a devastating impact, and not just because of the malicious attack on Charles. APG had soon found not only several unkind references to himself, but also the chapters in which God's name was 'taken in vain', and the play in which both homosexuality and lesbianism were prominent themes. After wiring to Charles and Philip asking them 'to try & get it boycotted by the Press', APG wrote in his diary that it was 'blasphemous, brutal & even bestial with wrong sex attractions'.[101] Amy, to whom he read out a number of passages, felt 'as though I had been beaten with nettles. It is disgusting', she told John:

> & blasphemous & gives Nancy's adultery fully away. The poor children! I have written to Nancy that it she lets David go out to his Father, even for Xmas, I have finished with his education as it is of no use trying to build up with one hand & pull down with the other.... We are all disgraced if it is read.[102]

Shock gave way to a state of 'the deepest depression', and Amy wrote a second letter to John telling him that 'Robert thinks the bottom has fallen out of everything.... Poor Robert!' she went on:

> I think he must be partly mad, which is some excuse .... I said to Nancy, that she must read every word of this new book before sending David out to Majorca & that I had finished with his education if she did. Robert would be a most dangerous father in his present state of mind.... Poor little boy! I wish him well.[103]

Nancy was always practical enough to know on which side her bread was buttered; and so, recognizing the strength of Amy's feelings, she wrote what APG described as 'a satisfactory letter. . . . she reports well of Sam's improvement at school. . . . She is pleased with reports of David & Jenny. Catherine is not to go to her father: nor David at Christmas.'[104]

APG passed on this news to Robert as part of a letter in which he described *But It Still Goes On* as:

> a powerful book but as you may imagine one of which I largely disapprove. But, thank God, I regard it as only a phase however painful to me in your life & believe you will be brought into the Haven where your Mother

& I desire you should be, if not during our lives at least after we have passed away.[105]

There was nothing much more to be said. Silence fell between father and son, and they both turned to their own work and to their own friends: APG to the writing of some hymns, and to the comforting words of Father Macdonald, with whom he had discussed the possibility of converting Robert to Roman Catholicism; and Robert, after the relative failure of *But It Still Goes On*, to his *No Decency Left* (a book whose title had recently been proposed by Jonathan Cape as that of an undoubted bestseller), and to the prospect of visits to Deyá from his friends John Aldridge and Norman Cameron. Cameron had recently inherited a good deal of money and resigned from the Nigerian Civil Service; and the combination of his legacy, Riding's ambition, Graves's earnings from *Good-bye to All That* and Gelat's greed proved to be formidable.

CHAPTER 5
New Beginnings

By the end of March 1931, after two sunless winters at Casa Salerosa ('so fearfully cold in winter compared with the possibilities of the climate'),[106] Graves and Riding had decided that they would build a new house for themselves on a sunny stretch of land which they could see on the opposite side of the valley. Apart from the extra warmth, it would have the advantage of being within easier walking distance of the village, while allowing them to retain their privacy. They decided to call it simply by its position, 'the house farther on'; and on the advice of one of the villagers, this was translated into the near-Mallorquin of 'Canelluñ'.[107]

Norman Cameron had visited them briefly in March[108] to explain that he now intended to devote himself to literature on a full-time basis; and in April or May he returned with the idea of building a bungalow for himself. Robert and Laura agreed to its being situated just eighty yards to the east of Canelluñ; and Norman decided that it should be called Ca'n Torrent.

While plans were drawn up, and the building work begun, Robert Graves was working hard on *No Decency Left*,[109] a fantasy whose best passages are vividly surreal. The heroine works as a humble shop-assistant in Lion City, the capital of the Kingdom of Lyonesse, and is engaged to someone extremely dull; but when she wakes up on the morning of her twenty-first birthday determined to have 'a really perfect day',[110] it seems that her determination is enough to alter the normal course of events; and by the end of the day she has abandoned her unsuitable fiancé, become owner of the department store in which she used to work; married Maximilian, the heir to the throne; and finally (after a revolution) attained supremacy in her own right, as a kind of benevolent dictator. Although the plot is a fantasy, the heroine has been given much in common with Laura Riding; and, since Riding heavily rewrote *No Decency Left* before it appeared in print, it seems likely that there is an autobiographical element in the story.

It was at about this time that Graves wrote of Riding as Muse:[111]

ON PORTENTS

If strange things happen where she is,
So that men say that graves open,
And the dead walk, or that futurity
Becomes a womb and the unborn are shed,
Such portents are not to be wondered at,
Being tourbillions in Time made
By the strong pulling of her bladed mind
Through that ever-reluctant element.

In *No Decency Left* the heroine's powers are similarly remarkable. After calling for (and thereby creating) a hitherto unknown type of marmalade, she tastes it and announces that 'I intended that slight bitter-orange flavour in it, too'; later she comments: 'I seem to be able to make things not only happen but *have happened*'; and she shares Riding's indifference to anyone outside her own charmed circle, one of whom is ruthlessly stabbed by her, and several of whom are described as being 'quite subsidiary characters in my biography now'. Finally, near the end of the story, the heroine's relationship with Maximilian is described in terms which probably mirror Riding's view at the time of her own relationship with Graves: 'if she developed any further latent powers she would altogether outgrow Max. And Max had to be there to keep things from getting too fantastic. She would become a sort of human Cedar of Lebanon and he would be left cuddling her roots like an ornamental shrub.'[112] Unfortunately the narrative is weighed down with a large number of lengthy and extremely boring asides, and these hold up the plot for long enough to expose its considerable weaknesses. An imaginative editor with a free hand to call for corrections might have guided Graves and Riding towards something both original and memorable; but, as it is, not even Graves's insertion into the plot of an 'auto-giro' with a kind of radar, an idea which he had from T.E. Lawrence, can rescue the work from failure.

While Graves was still working on the first draft of *No Decency Left*, William Heinemann published his *Poems 1926–1930*.[113] It was by far his best collection of poems to date, showing very clearly the influence of Laura Riding's rigorously constructive criticism upon both the style and content of his work. Of the forty-five poems which it contains, no fewer than twenty-five were to survive into Graves's 1975 volume of *Collected Poems*, including not only fine poems like 'Thief', 'Gardener' and 'The Age of Certainty';

but also the pure gold of 'Railway Carriage' (an early title for what is now well known as 'Welsh Incident'), 'O Love In Me' (later, 'Sick Love'), 'Warning to Children', 'In Broken Images' and 'Lost Acres', in which Graves decisively rejects psychological theorizing as a subject for poetry:

LOST ACRES

These acres, always again lost
    By every new Ordnance-survey
And searched for at exhausting cost
    Of time and thought, are still away.

They have their paper-substitute –
    Intercalation of an inch
At the so many thousandth foot:
    And no one parish feels the pinch.

But lost they are, despite all care,
    So perhaps likeliest to be bound
Together in a piece somewhere,
    A plot of undiscovered ground.

Invisible, they have the spite
    To swerve the tautest measuring chain
And the exact theodolite
    Perched every side of them in vain.

Yet there's no scientific need
    To plot these acres of the mind
With prehistoric fern and reed
    And monsters such as heroes find.

They have, no doubt, their flowers, their birds,
    Their trees behind the phantom fence,
But of the substance of mere words:
    To walk there would be loss of sense.[114]

Graves had been a terrible prig when he was a school-boy; and in a handful of poems in this collection he appears to be making up for this, and having some of the adolescent fun he had missed, calling after passers-by with versions of 'rude' words such as 'Copopulation' and 'mansturbantia-tion',[115] and even getting some excitement out of what he admits is:

an old story – f's for s's –
But good enough for them, the suckers.[116]

He also attacked the Christian God, said to be nothing more than 'a necessary superstition';[117] and his own family. One of the anti-family poems is quite good-natured and amusing:

BROTHER

It is odd enough to be alive with others,
But odder yet to have sisters and brothers,
To make one with a characteristic litter –
The sisters vexed and doubtful, the brothers vexed and bitter
That this one wears, through praise and through abuse
His family nose for individual use.[118]

But in 'Front Door',[119] describing himself as 'grandeur's grandson', Graves paints a ferocious picture of a family life in which freedom could only be found once he had decided to:

. . . dung on my grandfather's doorstep,
Which is a reasonable and loving due
To hold no taint of love or vassalage
And understood only to him and me –
But you, you bog-rat-whiskered, mean psalm-griddling
Lame, rotten-livered, this and that canaille,
You, when twin lackeys, with armorial shovels,
Unbolt the bossy gates and bend to the task,
Be off, work out your heads from between the railings,
Lest we unkennel the mastiff and the Dane –
This house is jealous of its nastiness.

Amy Graves, who purchased a copy of *Poems 1926–1930* in mid-March when she was on holiday in Worthing,[120] was frankly appalled. Only the previous month, having heard of her threat to stop paying for David's education if he was allowed to visit Deyá, Robert had written angrily to his mother complaining of her 'fanaticism & [her] soul and mind-withering beliefs', and declaring that whatever happened he would remove David to Majorca at Easter, and forbid him to visit his grandmother ever again. 'So this is the end between us,' Robert had concluded.[121] And now, after reading his poems, Amy wondered despairingly 'how anyone can admire them. They are in parts filthy. He speaks, inter alia, of "dunging on his Grandfather's front doorstep". Your Father', she wrote to John:

> feels inclined to upbraid Heinemann's for publishing such stuff. He is really afraid for Robert's sanity & I also.... It is terrible to think of David going to Robert with his filthy expressions and his blasphemy. I could wish he had died in the war. – Imagine that I have come to that! But I must hope still that he is not really mad, but has no counter-weight to Laura who drags him down.[122]

But, despite Robert's determination, his eldest son was beyond his control; and in April, when it was clear that David would not be coming out for the Easter holidays, Robert wrote an angry letter saying that he was cutting him off absolutely. This was not yet the end of his negotiations with Nancy about David's future; but he was exasperated and upset, and this made him very touchy for a few weeks.

One evening for example, in the presence of a number of villagers, Graves protested against 'the manner in which a foreigner had been speaking about another foreigner, a friend of mine, of a different nationality from either of us who was at that time physically not able to act personally [Laura, perhaps?]. I explained, with apologies, that as the representative of my slan-dered friend I was about to slap the slanderer's face. I then did so.'[123] This roused the feelings of another foreigner, a Swede, who appears to have crossed swords with Graves on a previous occasion. 'Do you remember the tall stinker?' wrote Graves to Aldridge, before going on to explain that at midnight the Swede had come 'shouting past Salerosa waking us all up and wouldn't go away'. Graves eventually came down, and a fight took place on the road. 'He had no science,' Graves told Aldridge, 'all rustic swings, he was. I gave him a straight left and he went over the road onto the next terrace. He wanted more but I had returned to bed.' The following day Graves's assailant tried to put himself in the right by making a formal protest to the Mayor; but this rebounded on his own head: Gelat met the police from Valldemosa who came looking for Graves, and told them that it was the Swede they wanted; and it was therefore the Swede who was warned to keep the peace or face being locked up.[124]

Nothing more happened for the time being; but the incident contributed its own flavour to the stories which had been circulating about Graves and Riding ever since the formation of the 'three-life'. When two formidable literary figures live at such a tangent to the conventional world which bred them, myths and rumours arise as naturally as morning mist, but are much harder to dispel. Most people are disinclined to believe the sober truth if the lie is far more exciting; and the lie will always be the one which is most appropriate for its audience. Disquieting stories therefore began to reach the authorities in Palma about Graves's personal ambition to become master of Deyá;[125] while in New York it was being rumoured that Graves and Riding, 'these two eccentric poets[,] lived in a mountain fastness in Mallorca surrounded by a walled courtyard; [and] that they sometimes invited unsuspecting guests, who were then trapped in the courtyard and set upon by a pack of savage dogs'.[126]

In reality Graves and Riding, together with their close ally Norman Cameron, spent much of the summer of 1931 in long stretches of hard work. The building of Canelluñ was begun in June, and that of Ca'n Torrent about a month later, and both required a good deal of close personal super-vision for the rest of the year; and by mid-July Robert's first unsatisfactory draft of *No Decency Left* had been almost totally rewritten by Laura, and sent off to Cape, with the request that he publish it under the pseudonym of 'Barbara Rich'. Graves loyally declared to John Aldridge (whose first slightly indecent cover for the book was foolishly rejected by Cape in favour of a second and far less exciting design) that the book was now 'what it should have been'; but he seems to have been unhappily aware that despite Laura's alterations it still had serious flaws, and he begged Aldridge to make it clear, whenever necessary, that his own part in the completed work was now negligible.[127]

While Cape considered *No Decency Left*, Graves, aided by both Riding and Cameron, began another new project, also aimed at the popular market: the rewriting of Charles Dickens's *David Copperfield*. This bizarre scheme, possibly the product of a witty but slightly drunken conversation at the café, was founded on sound critical principles. The crucial insight was that Dickens's story, written specifically for serialization in a monthly maga-zine, should have been substantially rewritten to meet the totally different artistic requirements of separate publication as a single work. Graves and his associates, as he explained to Aldridge, were therefore 'taking out all the monthly-part padding and general hysteria and putting what's left into some sort of intelligible order'.[128] After a lapse of nearly sixty years, this can be appreciated as an instructive and valuable exercise, and Graves's version is far more accessible to a modern audience than the original. But, in 1931, it was a sadly misconceived project: Dickens, even at his most sentimental and verbose, was still so popular with ordinary readers that newspapers were to give away tens of thousands of free sets of his works as an inducement to take out a regular subscription; and any attempt to rewrite one of Dickens's novels was bound to be received with critical outrage.[129]

Some hours of relaxation were snatched from the unrelenting demands of both writing and building; in one of the happiest and least complicated relationships of her life, Laura Riding spent much time playing with a pretty six-year-old Mallorquin girl called Francisca, by whom she was so enchanted that she gave her numerous presents, reserved a room for her use,[130] and even wrote a lengthy poem entitled 'Laura and Francisca' in which she described her strong feelings for the child at some length.[131] For their part, Cameron and Graves relaxed by keeping canoes down at the 'Cala', a semi-circle of sandy beach set in an amphitheatre of rock. To one side the bed of the Torrente finds its way down to the sea, a few fishermen's huts cling to a rocky slope, and up-turned boats and drying nets lie waiting in the sun; and ahead, beyond a large rock set in the water close to the shore, lies the clear blue Mediterranean sea. Graves not only swam regularly, but found canoeing 'good fun', and was justifiably proud of having reached 'the Foradada (Miramar) in 15 minutes'; although, as he explained to Aldridge, 'it has to be very calm for that'.[132]

There was at first a friendly rivalry between Graves and Cameron for Riding's attention. Laura, knowing that she could rely upon Robert, seems to have favoured Norman to begin with; but she had considerably complicated their private lives by adding a fourth member to their circle. This was Elfriede, a lusty German girl blazing with a nervous but intense sexual heat which is sometimes found in sufferers (as she was) from tuberculosis. Laura, strongly attracted towards Elfriede, invited her to join the household at Salerosa.

Elfriede later declared that she had been 'procured by Laura for Norman Cameron,' but that 'whilst awaiting Norman's arrival from Nigeria she had fallen in love with Robert'. Laura, according to the same contemporary account, 'explained in a letter to John [Aldridge] that she allowed a relationship between them as denying her own body sexually to Robert. Elfriede's body could be used as an extension of that side of herself which she did not choose to give Robert. However the relationship developed and Elfriede became pregnant'.[133]

Laura's reaction to all this has been variously reported. Outwardly it suited her to remain as calm as possible. Instead of turning against Robert, she drew slightly closer to him. Indeed, she later told a correspondent that such a 'brutal lapse' on Graves's part would be more than 'psychologically interesting',[134] and in time she would convince him that the significance of the episode was slight. Graves, after all, had already penned these lines in which he scorns the lustfulness of the male member:

DOWN, WANTON, DOWN!

Down, wanton, down! Have you no shame
That at the whisper of Love's name
Or Beauty's, presto! up you raise
Your angry head and stand at gaze?

Poor bombard-captain, sworn to reach
The ravelin and effect a breach,
Indifferent what you storm or why
So be that in the breach you die!

Love may be blind, but love at least
Knows what is man and what mere beast:
Or Beauty, wayward, but requires
More delicacy from her squires.

Tell me, my witless, whose one boast
Could be your staunchness at the post,
When were you made a man of parts
To think fine and profess the arts?

Will many-gifted Beauty come
Bowing to your bald rule of thumb,
Or love swear Loyalty to your crown?
Be gone, have done! Down, wanton, down![135]

Inwardly, however, Riding was hurt and angry; and Elfriede's pregnancy was altogether too much. Laura insisted on an immediate abortion, and (according to Elfriede) stood at the bottom of the bed to make sure that this illegal operation was carried out. Afterwards, Elfriede moved from Deyá to a village nearby; but she kept returning to see both Robert and Laura, and to attend the same parties, at which Robert, who seemed to one outsider to be under the most extreme emotional pressure, would talk openly of the 'torment of being deeply in love with Laura who wouldn't sleep with him;' and all three of them were liable to pour out the details of their 'complicated emotions' into any sympathetic ear.[136]

In the meantime, Robert's plans for his eldest son had once again been thwarted: this time by David himself. In July or August he made it clear that his primary loyalty was now to his mother and grandmother. Possibly he felt that Nancy was in particular need of support, because in May Geoffrey had finally been divorced by Norah, and Nancy had been publicly named as the co-respondent. 'It's no good,' Robert wrote angrily to John Aldridge, who had been asked to bring David out to Deyá with him on his next visit. 'He doesn't want to come and I am fed up and am cutting him off without a shilling. If my mother wants to pay for him she can: he cares more for her than me now.'[137] Later in the year Robert wrote his son a letter of final farewell; and at the same time he wrote to Amy making his interest in David over to her. He would no longer pay for David's holidays, he wanted no more news either of him or of Jenny, and he accused his mother of having 'pooled moralities with "NN & GP." This', Amy explained to another member of the family, 'I had to contradict & I told him also he could not give his fatherhood away & signed myself "Ever your Mother."' To David she wrote that his father was 'under a spell & will come back to what we loved in him at Islip'.

The roof of Canelluñ went on some weeks earlier than anticipated, and, in September, it was predicted that both Canelluñ and Cameron's Ca'n Torrent would be ready for occupation by February or March 1932. But Riding had now developed a taste for new developments, especially as they involved her in an agreeable working relationship with both Norman Cameron and Gelat; and before long, with the promise of substantial financial support from Cameron, she had committed herself and her partners to a large-scale and potentially lucrative scheme which sadly, like Graves's rewriting of Dickens, was years ahead of its time, and went so badly wrong that it led both her and Graves to the brink of ruin.

It is obvious that the Gelat was largely responsible. The plot on which Canelluñ was being built had been sold to Riding by a friend of Gelat's who also owned a vast acreage of land between Canelluñ and the sea. When the building of Canelluñ and Ca'n Torrent was well advanced, and it was clear that Riding and her circle had access to a good deal of capital, Gelat allowed them to 'know' that his friend was planning to sell a large part of his property to 'a local German resident who had plans for building a hotel there'. Graves and Riding were understandably horrified by the thought that their 'house farther on' might soon be sitting in the shadow of a new hotel, and that hotel probably crammed with German tourists. But then, no doubt, came a suggestion from Gelat. Why did they not buy the land themselves? As Graves wrote to his old friend Aircraftman T.E. Shaw (formerly Lawrence, and now doing useful work on the development of fast rescue-launches for the RAF), 'Deyá has no hotel and is bound to have one, [so why not] put one up ourselves in a corner of the land far enough removed from our house not to matter.' A road would also be built going right down to the sea; and some of the expense would eventually be recouped by selling building plots alongside the road. In the meantime, a large sum of working capital would be needed. Several people were approached to make contributions, including Tom Matthews, an acquaintance of Robert's from Islip days, and now a journalist on *Time* magazine; and once Norman Cameron had committed himself to investing a large sum of money in the scheme, the land was purchased, and Riding, Graves, Cameron and Gelat began refining their ideas and drawing up plans.

Amid all the work which this involved (quite apart from completing *The Real David Copperfield*, and correcting proofs of *No Decency Left*) came news of a death in the family.

CHAPTER 6
The Passing of Alfred Perceval Graves

Alfred Perceval Graves, whose eighty-fifth birthday fell on 22 July 1931, had borne the trials and indignities of old age with considerable fortitude. Despite attacks of gout and frequent stomach troubles, he had been working on a film-script based on his most popular song, 'Father O'Flynn'; and at the beginning of July, during a visit by his daughter Molly, he recorded proudly in his diary that 'Molly & I danced & I actually danced a few steps of my Irish jig & sang "Father O'Flynn".'[138] But he realized that his health had declined badly during the past twelve months; and later in the visit, on the eve of Molly's departure, he took her aside and told her very quietly: 'Darling, when you pray for me, ask God to take me to him before my brain is dimmed or my body useless.'[139]

Alfred still had enough spirit to assert his independence from time to time; and in August he secretly arranged that Jim Cooper, a young farmer friend of Rosaleen's, should drive him to Bangor for the Eisteddfod. Amy was mildly put out by the secrecy of the arrangements but, as she told their son John, 'when you think what a trial he might be at 85, if he were a *malade imaginaire*, I have every reason to be more than satisfied'. She added proudly that Alfred had 'just earned another guinea by a poem'.[140]

Going to the Eisteddfod was a moving experience for Alfred Graves. After a lifetime of service both to education and to literature, he had been a little disappointed to receive no public honour of any kind. At least once he had been asked if he would allow his name to be put forward; but year after year he had picked up *The Times* eagerly on New Year's Day, or when the King's Birthday Honours were to be announced, only to discover that former friends and colleagues of his had had their work properly recognized, but that he himself had once again been overlooked. But now, in his eighty-sixth year, he entered the Great Hall at Bangor College just as a speaker was praising his work as one of the founders of the Welsh Folk Song Society. And then a sensation. Alfred Perceval Graves was recognized. No one had expected him. First a whisper ran round the Hall; then excited voices broke out; someone began cheering; and the old man, with tears running down his cheeks, received the ovation of his life.

In mid-October, Alfred began a new venture: a volume for Collins provisionally entitled *Stories of the Saints*. He worked at the book with all his usual vigour; but then, on the last Sunday of November, after reading the lesson in an unheated church, he went to bed 'evidently having caught cold'.[141] For the next fortnight he was extremely ill: 'I had practically no sleep at all,' a typical diary entry reads, '& had times of breathless choking.'[142] Despite his illness, he continued work on what had now become *The Lives of the Saints*; and the completed manuscript was posted to Collins on 17 December.

A brief remission followed, during which Alfred recovered both his sleep and his appetite; and John, home for Christmas, found him 'the most cheerful, uncomplaining old man imaginable – sleeping most of the afternoon [and] writing industriously while daylight lasted, though having to crouch more over his papers through failing sight'.[143] Alfred was able to enjoy a 'happy, quietly peaceful Xmas Day';[144] and as usual he made a patriarchal speech, in which he toasted all the members of his extensive family, Robert included. The following day the curate came to Erinfa, and 'gave Amy & myself the Holy Sacrament in the drawing room'.[145] These, appropriately enough, were to be the last words ever written by that devoted husband and most Christian gentleman: my grandfather, whom in the course of writing this biography I have come to know and to love.

After lunch on Sunday 27 December 1931, Alfred Perceval Graves ventured out with his daughter Clarissa for a short walk in the sunshine. Afterwards he went to rest on his bed; and died quietly in his sleep about a quarter of an hour later. As he had hoped, it was before his brain was dimmed or his body useless; and when Molly heard of his death, and of his burial in the little Harlech churchyard, she was 'thankful that Father was laid under the hills he was so fond of towards the "far faint shores [of Ireland] across the Violet deep"'.[146]

Susan recognized that her father had 'made no tiresome demands on his children, & was proud of them whatever they did'; but she was also aware that, compared to Amy, he had sometimes seemed 'a detached parent in many ways',[147] and it is probable that the children of his second family missed him less than he deserved. In reality he had been a better father than Amy had been a mother, in the sense that he had known when to let his children become independent adults in their own right. Amy, loving not wisely but too well, could never let her children go, and this had obvious and important effects upon their emotional development.

It was a personal tragedy for Robert that his father died before the two men could achieve any kind of reconciliation: especially as Robert, like so many rebellious sons, increasingly came to resemble the father whom he had once despised.

Above Alfred's grave his wife and children erected a large Celtic cross; and then they returned to their own pursuits. As had been previously arranged, Alfred's private money had been left to the children of his first family: Philip, Dick, Molly and the needy Perceval each received £900, and Susan twice that amount; while his furniture, chattels and literary earnings were left to his wife.

Amy, whose first reaction on seeing her husband laid to rest had been to declare that her life's work was over, soon realized that she was as firmly enmeshed as ever in a complex pattern of both family and village obligations, and that there was still plenty for her to do in the world; and, although none of her own children had been enriched, a number of ambitions stirred in their minds. Clarissa asked Amy to support her in a new venture and, by the autumn of 1932, was the co-director of a Speech Institute in London. She also organized a 'Family Tea Club' which met once a month, hosted by one or other of Alfred's ten children, and talked over family and other matters. Early in the year, Rosaleen announced that she was to be married on 7 May, to her friend Jim Cooper; and for a while (much to Amy's alarm) John thought of going into publishing, and marrying a girl who was not only a Roman Catholic, but also an actress.

There was, at first, no change in Robert's attitude towards his family. He continued to write angry letters to his mother, one of which was 'fiercely unkind' to David;[48] nor did he subscribe to the fund for setting up the Celtic cross. And yet Robert Graves's entire way of life was later to become centred upon the Celtic myths and legends which had fascinated both his father and his grandfather the Bishop; and which for him came to enshrine the deepest kind of truth.

CHAPTER 7

A Horror of Laura Riding

By the start of 1932, there had been further changes in the quadrilateral relationship between Laura Riding, Robert Graves, Norman Cameron and the beautiful Elfriede. Laura had finally decided to evict Elfriede, who was sent away to the Canary Islands, ostensibly on health grounds. Then, when Elfriede returned unexpectedly, Laura was so furious that she went out hunting for her, 'dead white,' according to an eye-witness account, and with 'a whip in her hand which she kept cracking.' Exactly what happened next remains obscure; but Robert appears to have intervened in time to prevent a whipping, saying that he had seen enough violence in the War; while Norman Cameron, feeling sorry for Elfriede, began falling in love with her.[149]

Towards the end of 1931, the 'tallish, slim [and] good-looking' John Aldridge had also arrived in Deyá, where he was shortly followed by his adoring companion, that 'dark beauty,' Lucie Brown. For a while they stayed at Salerosa where Laura, who was now much more genuinely fond of John than she was of either Robert or Norman, 'insisted that the door of their bedroom remain always open'; and then they had moved to lodgings in the village. Lucie was 'deeply skeptical of Laura, who must have been aware of Lucie's feelings but put up with it because she needed John. He was in her continual service, used as a human brush or pencil to turn out drawings and pictures for which she not only supplied the idea but actively directed the making.'[150]

The growing circle of writers and artists which centred upon Robert and Laura was further extended, during January 1932, by the arrival on the scene of Tom Matthews, now happily married to the 'small, dark, pretty and completely feminine' Julie, his childhood sweetheart. Matthews had obtained a six-months' leave of absence in order to write a novel; and he had decided to write it in Majorca, where he and Julie and their two small sons would live and he would find the 'peace and quiet in which to write my book'.[151] Leaving New York and crossing the Atlantic, Matthews

and his family arrived unannounced in Palma, hired a car and drove out
to Valldemosa and then along the coast road towards Deyá. However, before
reaching the village, they noticed 'a small stone cottage, half-hidden
in trees, above the road', and stopped to ask for directions. Without realizing
it, they had stumbled upon Casa Salerosa. Maria answered the door; and
when Matthews asked if he could tell her where Señor Robert Graves
lived, she replied 'aquí', and showed him into:

> a little room where a table, covered with papers, stood in front of a
> huge, hooded fireplace. A small severe woman, erect behind the table,
> confronted me. She asked me what I wanted. I said that I had called
> to pay my respects to Mr Graves, whom I had had the honor of meeting
> some years before. She said something in Spanish to the maid.
>
> A minute later Robert Graves appeared.
>
> 'Robert,' said the severe little woman [it was of course Laura, who would
> have been exceedingly displeased that it was Robert and not she who was
> being sought out], 'here is a young man who *says* he knows you.'
>
> Robert looked from me to her, rolled his eyes, grinned and shook
> his head. 'Never saw him before in my life.'[152]

This was an unpromising start; but Graves remembered Matthews when
he began describing his visit to Islip in some detail, and promised to help
him to find rooms in the village.

Within a few days, partly as a result of a stranger coincidence than Tom
Matthews's having made Salerosa his first point of enquiry, close links
would be forged between Graves, Riding and the newcomers. Matthews
was visiting Graves to ask for help in filling in a form for the local police,
when Robert noticed Tom's date of birth, and called out: 'Laura! You
and Tom are twins.' Tom felt amazed, and later wrote:

> I would have said she was old enough to be my mother. I came so near
> saying it that I blushed. Laura pursed her lips, gave her slight omniscient
> smile, and nodded, as if she acknowledged the fact, now that it was
> out, but was not yet prepared to commit herself on its significance.[153]

But first Tom and Julie were invited to a picnic, 'the purpose of which
seemed to be to find out whom we knew. Robert summed up the enquiry
by laughing and saying to Laura: "They seem to know all the wrong people."'[154] However, this did not seem to matter. The Matthewses found themselves accepted as 'novitiates' in 'Laura's little group';[155] and although some
things struck them as most unappealing – for example, the way in which
Robert was 'in a constant swivet of anxiety' to please Laura, while she

'treated him – like a dog'; they were so fascinated that they drifted into a close relationship which gave them every opportunity to observe both Robert, whom they came to love, and Laura, whom they came to regard with 'awed respect'.[156] Forty-five years later, Tom Matthews still vividly recalled this extraordinary couple. Robert, who was:

gangly-tall, muscular but shambling; with his broken nose and wildly staring eyes, swarthy colouring and frizzy black hair as unruly as the sun's corona, he looked like a bandit from an earlier century. When he was dressed up he sported a brocaded waistcoat with silver buttons and a stock held in place with an antique pin: then he was a squire; but in the nondescript clothes and straw hat of every day he was a distinguished scarecrow.[157]

And Laura, who hardly came up to Robert's shoulder, and who:

was as primly neat as Robert was gawky. She never had a hair out of place, and her clothes, which were old-fashioned, never seemed odd. When *she* was in full regalia her dignity matched and enhanced her costume, and I can't remember anyone thinking it laughable or even eccentric that on these occasions she was crowned by [a gold band, fastened at the back with gold wire] that [in Greek lettering] spelled LAURA. She could indeed look regal – a Hittite queen.[158]

Graves and Riding had already planned to move out of Casa Salerosa into Ca'n Pa Bo, a much more convenient location from which to supervise the last stages of the building of Canelluñ; and when they did so, some two weeks after Tom and Julie Matthews had arrived in Palma, it was not long before their new friends were allowed to move into Salerosa.

Ca'n Pa Bo, set high up on a terrace about halfway between the low-lying houses of the 'Clot' and the church, could only be reached by such steep paths that Laura, who still needed a stick when she went out walking, must have been a virtual prisoner for the short time that they lived there. However, it was a cheerful, sunny house, with a covered south-facing balcony on the first floor where it was pleasant to sit and write, and occasionally look out across the terraced valley towards the mountains; and the difficult access meant that there would be no casual callers.

Despite having written a 'devastating' review of Tom Matthews's first novel, Laura Riding had begun to take a keen interest in his work:[159] possibly because she had misinterpreted his evident fascination with her.

When she learned that his new novel had become 'bogged down', Laura asked Tom whether he would help her with 'a piece of her own unfinished writing [she described it as "a masque"]: it might get me out of the doldrums'. Flattered by this offer, Tom said that he would be glad to help. Each morning, therefore, he:

> walked the mountain mile from Salerosa to Canpabo, where Laura would be waiting for me. I felt a certain curious aversion to Laura. The texture of her skin was waxy to dead-dull, and her hands were surprisingly large and coarse for a woman's. It may have been partly her eerily brilliant brain, which I felt as an almost tangible force and which seemed to me to render her asexual, sibylline.[160]

Their working sessions lasted from ten in the morning until one in the afternoon. So intense were they, and so adamant was Laura 'in her resolve not to proceed one millimeter further until [Tom] had mastered what she had already put down', that progress was 'almost imperceptible'. Matthews found that Laura was 'a patient but not a sympathetic partner in my struggles: she drove me relentlessly, remorselessly, to the limit of my mental endurance'.[161]

As if this were not enough, Matthews arrived one morning to find that Riding had left a letter for him on their work-table. 'Read that!' she said. 'I'll be back in fifteen minutes.' The gist of the letter, as Tom later recalled, was that:

> she knew the effect she made on me; that if I could master my feelings I was to remain in this room, she would come back and we would go on with our work as before; if, however, I could not be sure of controlling myself I was to get up and go, now; she would understand, she would not hold it against me, but we must not continue to work together.[162]

Matthews stayed, not wanting to give the impression that he was in love and he couldn't trust himself in Laura's presence. But the strain of the collaboration was proving too great, and, when it had been running for only twelve days, Tom felt that he was at the end of his tether, and close to collapse. When he told Laura how he felt, she 'couldn't have been kinder'. She dismissed him 'like a wise and merciful queen'; and the only after-effect was Tom being left impotent for a month.[163]

Tom and Julie Matthews had by now become part of an 'hermetic community':[164] if they wished to remain on speaking terms with Robert and Laura, they were not allowed to be on speaking terms with anyone outside a limited circle, which then included John Aldridge, Lucie Brown and Norman Cameron. And within this circle anything that anyone said or did was immediately reported back to 'headquarters'. For instance Laura, in the light of her own partially disabled state, had concluded that exercise was essentially foolish. Walking, mountain-climbing and swimming were tolerated, 'but only as an occasional aberration, a permitted joke'. Tom, however, liked playing tennis; and surreptitiously slipped away to Palma to have a game every week or ten days. After one such game, he was enjoying a glass of beer in a café when he ran into Norman Cameron and John Aldridge, 'and remarked to them that we were much beholden to Laura and Robert for all they had done for us. Next day at the café in Deyá I was greeted with a grin as Ben Beholden, and for some days [Julie and I] were referred to as "the Beholdens".'[165]

This type of humour, involving nicknames, games with words and other 'mental gambols', is, as Matthews rightly comments, typical of a certain section of the English intelligentsia; it also suited Laura's cliquey and manipulative mind. But these more playful moments could not conceal what was going on in the background. Matthews later commented that, had they appreciated the real situation, he and Julie 'would as soon have cast in our lot with a witches' coven. And', he adds, 'there were some similarities: there was something occult about Laura and her gradually revealed, gradually acknowledged domination over her circle.'[166] However, it was not Matthews who first developed a real horror of Riding, but another of the inner circle.

Sometime in March or April 1932, not long after Robert Graves and Laura Riding had moved into Canelluñ, and with Ca'n Torrent still uncompleted, Norman Cameron began realizing the full extent to which Laura had been calmly manipulating her closest associates. Later he wrote a memorable poem in which he and Robert appear as 'merman' and 'landman', both in love with the same woman. But this 'wanton' cares so little for either of them that she compels them both to risk their lives, ordaining that they should:

> each abandon
> The element in which his suit was fostered
> And undergo this test of transmutation,
> Merman ashore, landman beyond the breakers.[167]

So besotted are the lovers that they obey. This eloquently conveys the extent to which both Cameron and Graves were in thrall to Riding; but it also contains a partial misreading of the situation. Riding did care very much for Norman, and may even have been wondering whether he might take the place of Geoffrey Phibbs in her affections, while Robert reverted to a more subsidiary role in her emotional life. What made this impossible was the fact that Norman Cameron's sympathy for Elfriede, now permanently banished from the inner circle, gradually deepened into love. Caring for Elfriede, he could not fail to see how shamefully Laura had treated her; and a moment came when he suddenly felt that he was aware of Riding's true nature, and the awareness filled him with horror.

At that moment many lesser men would simply have packed their bags and left, without a word of explanation. Norman Cameron, however, was not only a thoroughly decent man, but a very remarkable one, and he was brave enough to confront Laura Riding face to face with his new perceptions. He told her that he had developed 'a kind of horror' of her,[168] and that he would therefore be leaving Deyá. But he was fully aware that the road-building scheme had been begun on the strength of his capital backing; and, in an attempt to even things out between them, he told Riding that she could have Ca'n Torrent; and he also gave her a sum of ten thousand pesetas, saying that she could use it either for furnishings, or to pay off the remaining mortgage on the property. Then Cameron departed for Barcelona, where he and Elfriede lived together for a while. Laura Riding reported Cameron's 'horror' and departure 'gently and sadly' but not desperately.[169] Gelat, seeing a considerable bank-roll departing, was probably more upset than she. Perhaps Laura interpreted the 'horror' as a kind of religious awe; and she seems to have expected that it would not be long before Cameron returned. However, for the time being at least he was gone; and Riding immediately turned her attention elsewhere.

Tom Matthews now became the principal object of her interest. Once again, his novel had become bogged down, and he could 'make no headway with it'. Riding offered to help; and despite unhappy memories of their collaboration on her 'masque', Matthews agreed, fortified by 'some idea that if I could survive the clutch of that octopus brain, the struggle would be worth it'. And a struggle it proved to be. Riding had soon suggested so many new characters that the plot had to be entirely reshaped. In the mornings, therefore, Tom began writing 'what amounted to a first draft', and in the afternoons he 'took what I had written to Canelluñ ... where Laura and Robert were now settling in'.[170]

Canelluñ, set well back from the road in a large terraced garden, was an attractive two-storey house with shuttered windows and walls of hand-hewn limestone whose colour was sometimes grey and sometimes orange, and whose rough-cut exterior made 'the house farther on' appear, even when newly built, as though it had belonged to the landscape for ages past. Canelluñ was built on three sides of a small east-facing courtyard: to the south, on the ground floor, was the kitchen, which looked out across a large square terrace towards the village and the distant mountains; to the south-west the living-room, with a stone fireplace, a few easy chairs and a dining-table; to the west a large hall, from which double-doors opened on to a double-staircase which faced the sea; to the north-west the Press Room, just beyond a doorway which led down into a spacious cellar; and to the north was Robert Graves's study, a cool, quiet, book-lined room with a large desk at which he sat facing the north window, using a sloping writing-board on which to set his blank sheets of paper, and then writing upon them in his distinctive scholarly long-hand for hour after hour.

Having been brought up in a large family, Robert could normally tolerate noise while he was working; but when he was writing a poem silence was his primary demand: in those circumstances the slightest sound would infuriate him; and so it was perhaps unfortunate that Laura Riding's work-room was on the top floor, directly above his. One day, when Tom Matthews was closeted with her, looking on with 'dismay and helpless resentment' while she inexorably revised or rather rewrote his new novel paragraph by paragraph, Robert suddenly:

> fl[ung] open the door, white-faced and shaking, and saying in a furious voice: 'Will you *please* stop shuffling your feet!' We hadn't been conscious of it [writes Matthews], but apparently our mental efforts had been accompanied by tappings and draggings of the feet ('It sounded as though you were *dancing!*' said the indignant Robert), and it had driven him wild. *He* was trying to work too.[71]

Laura accepted the rebuke in good part; but later Tom could not help wondering whether the vehemence of Robert's outburst was the result of jealousy; and indeed it seems most likely that Laura's friendship with Tom, though partly based on her genuine admiration for his intellect, was also partly based upon her wish not simply to make Robert jealous (though that may have been a factor after his involvement with Elfriede) but to provide herself with a new substitute for Geoffrey Phibbs.

Gradually, Laura Riding's plans developed to include Julie Matthews. Inviting herself to supper at Salerosa one evening – Robert was left behind at Canelluñ – Laura attempted to distance Julie from her husband, by 'trying to get [her] to admit that never once in her life, in anything of any importance, had she ever been in the slightest degree influenced or led by [him]'. Tom said nothing, but watched with admiration as Julie stood her ground. Laura, who was now enraged by her inability to make Julie admit that Tom did not matter to her, suddenly became aware of Tom's attitude. Whirling round in her chair to face him, she 'cried, "Stop sitting there saying nothing – and *lying*!"'. A moment later she had rushed out of the door, 'with no light, not even her stick, and it was a dark night on the mountain'. Julie pressed a flashlight into Tom's hands and sent him out to look for her; and he found her in Robert's arms at the foot of a precipitous path some distance away. 'To get there at that speed', as Matthews later recounted, 'she must have half-run, half-fallen. [Robert] had felt that something was wrong and had dashed out headlong into the dark, taking the quickest way.'[72]

There was a sequel to this adventure. In June 1932, when Tom and Julie were due to return to America, Laura invited them to a 'farewell feast' at Canelluñ with her and Robert. During the course of the feast, she gave Tom Matthews a moment of horror similar to that which had been experienced by Norman Cameron. In Tom's own words, Laura made an extraordinary proposition:

> It was couched in such delicate and diplomatic language that I knew Julie didn't understand it – which was just as well, for it would have shocked her profoundly.... I understood all too well what Laura was proposing; but I didn't want a scene, or a quarrel that would end our friendship; I simply wanted, above all, to get away. How I managed to reply without offending Laura or without letting Julie know what was up, I don't know, but somehow I must have. Laura's proposition was that we should not go back to America but stay on in Deyá: she and I would work together, Robert and Julie would live together.[73]

However, it was not long before the Matthewses were back in New York. They were met at the dock by Tom's closest friend, the handsome and dazzlingly brilliant Schuyler Jackson, a poet who had been his classmate at Princeton. In conversation with Laura Riding, Tom Matthews had often said that Schuyler Jackson would have suited her much better as a collaborator; and this was to have consequences later. For the time being, however, as Matthews records, Schuyler's:

> only response to my lengthy descriptions of her was a noncommittal

silence, and when I gave him her poems to read he returned the book with the comment, 'This isn't poetry; its philosophy.' I went to see my old mentor, Edmund Wilson, and after hearing my report on Laura and the life in Deyá he said dryly, 'I think you got away just in time.'[174]

It was Laura Riding's preoccupation first with Norman Cameron and then with Tom Matthews which gave Robert some room to be independent. He made use of his limited independence in two ways: to attempt to sort out some family matters; and to begin work on his famous historical novel *I, Claudius*.

CHAPTER 8
Family Matters

Although Robert had bravely said *Good-bye to All That* as long ago as 1929, he retained a strong affection for his mother, and a powerful interest in several other members of his immediate family. When any of their doings appeared to affect him, he reacted strongly and unequivocally. In the autumn of 1931, for example, his brother John published an extremely popular *Boy's Book of Association Football* which he dedicated to:

MY BROTHER
ROBERT GRAVES
IN MEMORY OF
THE ONE OCCASION ON WHICH WE PURSUED
THE SAME OBJECT TOWARDS THE SAME GOAL
THEREBY GAINING THE VICTORY FOR THE
VILLAGE OF ISLIP IN OXFORDSHIRE
(IN THE YEAR OF GRACE ONE THOUSAND NINE HUNDRED
AND TWENTY-TWO)[175]

Robert heard of the dedication from press-cuttings which reached him in Deyá; and when, in February 1932, Clarissa wrote asking him for a message to be read out at the second of the 'Graves Family Tea Parties'[176] which she was organizing in London, he replied crossly that she should tell the gathering that 'if [John] was sincere over dedicating a book to me he should have sent me a copy. Otherwise it looks so much like a publicity stunt.' News of Robert's displeasure reached John *via* Amy, who suggested that he should write at once to Robert in order to smooth things over.[177]

John wrote as requested, on 21 February; but not to smooth things over. He had been angry with Robert for some time, and now he asked how his brother dared to criticize him, after the inaccurate and wounding remarks which had appeared in *Good-bye to All That*. In particular, John had been hurt by the section in which he had been described as:

> the 'typically normal person', superficially flattering, but containing an unmistakable sneer.
>
> I was at a loss to explain a hit below the belt like this. So far as I know, I have always been friends with you, and have the happiest recollections of Boar's Hill & Islip, especially of Islip and the famous match in which the great Soccer rivals were defeated, & you & I shared 4 goals.
>
> I have seen too much of your painful (to the recipients) correspondence, to wish to have any myself. It might destroy the pleasant memories. So I have kept entirely clear of you. My only interference was to prevent David being sent to Bedales when he was doing well & making friends at Colet Court.[78]

John had also thought it wise for David to continue his education in England, rather than going to join his father in Spain. Why, then, had John dedicated his book to Robert? Because the rest of the family had never taken the slightest interest in his football; but he admitted that if Robert's words about him in *Good-bye to All That* could be 'interpreted in two ways, [then] so can mine [about you]. You sent me no copy. I sent you none.' There followed a strong attack upon Robert's treatment of their mother, whose feelings had been 'so harrowed' that, in John's eyes, 'no "principles" could ever justify your treatment [of her]. . . . She invariably acts after anxious thought and prayer, so that accusations of insincerity or prejudice can only hurt her. They will not convince.' Their differences in outlook were so vast that argument was in any case useless, and both Rosaleen; and Amy 'might have been spared unnecessary pain, if you had grasped the salient point – that no real rapprochement can take place with things as they are. When you met in Austria,' John continued:

> she did not know (and refused ostrich-like to infer) your relations with Laura. As a conventionally moral person, she could never make friends with Laura. So why remind her of 'how well she got on with her' in Austria, before she knew?
>
> I have made no judgment of your acts. I think we should all be free to lead our own lives as we wish. But where your life intersects (or has intersected) with Mother & Rosaleen, pain & unhappiness have followed. For that I must hold you responsible, as you seem to have deliberately selected words that will wound. . . .[79]

Robert was stung by this letter to a reply which combines a bitter attack upon his brother with some exceptionally revealing passages about how Robert perceived his own relationship with their mother:

John,

I don't know that there's a general rule about it anywhere in any particular code, but I have never heard of anyone before you dedicating a book to someone without permission and then not sending a copy.

Writing *about* people without their permission is quite another thing: it raises a different set of moral questionings. Usually it's a frank act of hostility or disrespect. In writing about you in that book I was not being hostile, and not particularly disrespectful, only historical! And this letter of yours justifies all that I said about your normality. It's perfectly normal.

Yes, I now write as nearly as possible what I mean in letters. This is perfectly abnormal, but the usual result is satisfactory: I force the addressee either to silence or to an abnormal expression of what he as nearly as possible means.

The most remarkable instance of normality in your letter is the bit about wanting to retain pleasant memories etc ... which prepares for the admission of a, to you, trifling interference in my affairs – preventing David from coming out here. . . . What the effing jaycee do you expect me to answer to that? 'Thank you, darling'? All right, thank you, darling. And thank you, darling, for not sending him to Bedales. Curiously enough I also objected to that place. Such a weak Classical training the boys get there: the good tone hardly makes up for that.

Oh, did it ever occur to you that there might be English teachers with B. of E. [Board of Education] qualifications on this very island, also organised games, even a quite recognisable game of soccer, and nice boys of quite good family to play with, not to mention useful foreign languages and wholesome food and an excellent climate? No. You'd not make a good detective.

A country policeman, perhaps, good at interfering conscientiously in family matters where a sight of the uniform is such a quieting agent. . . .

Mother's pain. If she adopts a code in which it is possible to try to separate David from me for Christ's sake rather than either his, hers or mine, she must suffer for Christ's sake and rejoice in suffering for Christ's sake. I don't suffer. I am sorry naturally that David has been fooled into going back on his friendship with me. . . .

I also believe in direct contact with people. If I get on well with you, say, and then one day you fling some metaphysical buffer between us like Christ or Corinth or the B. of E. or Established Education, that washes out the friendship. . . . you dodge behind that or this and there's an end. Where are you? I lose interest. . . .

About Mother again. There's a strong bond between us but it is only a human one: and she doesn't want it human. She won't risk her chances of Heaven by behaving towards me as she would humanly like to, which is to come and see me & kiss me and be friends and go for long walks & enjoy the beautiful scenery. . . .

I am not torn with pain about this. Because there is no mental conflict. I recognise the bond as human & I offer unqualified human relationship. She refuses. (It is not my drama.) She tries to beat my defences down with prayer. But I have no defences, so she only beats away at herself: which is called pain.

You have made no judgment of my acts?

Thank you, darling, but you're an awful liar, and this has wasted a lot of time.[180]

John, having made the points he wished to make in his original letter, now sent Robert a copy of *The Boy's Book of Association Football* together with a conciliatory reply; and Robert accepted his brother's friendly overtures, replying briefly: 'It is an extremely good book. Thank you for sending it, and for the dedication.'[181] He was in reality much more hurt by his mother's total hostility than by John's schoolmasterly judgment of his acts: she had written to Robert in January that, since reading as much as she could manage of *But It Still Goes On*, she had 'felt really afraid of your influence on David at an impressionable age', and 'much more afraid of you than of Laura for his spiritual welfare'.[182]

Later in the year Amy wrote a more friendly letter, saying that she could not think that Robert had 'quite torn us from your heart, so must tell you that Rosaleen will be married on May 7th at 2.30 at St. Martin's Trafalgar Square to Mr. Jim Cooper, your Father's nephew by marriage, & that I wish you could have been present'.[183] However by this time there had been a further quarrel between Rosaleen and the household at Canelluñ. On writing to Deyá in order to announce her impending marriage, Rosaleen had tried to make it easier for Robert and Laura to accept that she was entering upon a highly traditional relationship by adopting a slightly flippant tone, telling them for example that she was '*afraid* he'll be very faithful'. She had also offered them her new home, the Stud Farm at Halstead in Kent, as 'neutral territory on which to see the children'.[184]

Laura immediately sent Rosaleen a most ferocious reply (described by

Robert as 'wound[ing]', but 'instructive')[185] in which she conducted a minute examination of their past relationship, and proved to her own satisfaction that Rosaleen had behaved badly throughout, and that her latest letter was the final insult. 'Oh Laura!', Rosaleen replied despairingly. 'Why can't you treat an ordinary letter just as an ordinary letter? Mine contained no deep & hidden meanings or "insults". It was just happy and lighthearted.' She told Laura that it was a waste of time to rake up the past. Things had moved on: 'Yet for you Geoffrey is still the devil – Nancy still base and treacherous – Jenny still a frightened untruthful child – and so on.'[186]

Despite sharing this out-of-date view of Jenny, who was now apparently 'gay, delightful and confident as a dancer',[187] Robert was missing his children dreadfully; in June and then again towards the end of July he wrote to Amy saying that he was now so short of money that he could no longer make any contribution towards their upkeep or education in England, and he wanted them to join him at Canelluñ. As he explained in a letter to another member of the family:

If I had plenty of loose money I naturally would continue but I do not propose to run into debt and nervous breakdowns and things – finding money from *anywhere* to keep them at school. The natural thing would be for them to be here with me for a long time, (Nancy having had them for a long time), where I could afford to keep them and give them a better education and a better life than they get now.[188]

At the beginning of August, thirteen-year-old Jenny, twelve-year-old David, ten-year-old Catherine and eight-year-old Sam arrived at Erinfa to stay with their grandmother and their Aunt Clarissa for part of the summer holidays; and Amy read out to them the relevant parts of the letter in which Robert asked whether they would go to join him at Canelluñ. Clarissa kept a note of the ensuing conversation, which was sent to Robert together with a covering letter from Amy.

According to Clarissa's note, Jenny declared that she wanted to continue her dancing and her education in England, but that she would gladly pay Robert a visit. David agreed that he too would 'like to go for a holiday but not altogether'. The reaction of the younger two children was understandably less constructive. Catherine declared gloomily at one point that her father 'shouldn't have had us children at all, then'; while Sam said that he 'would like to go across the sea', but then burst into tears, and was upset for the rest of the afternoon.[189] 'I am sure,' Amy wrote to Robert in her covering letter, 'you were prepared for the answer that the children definitely prefer the life they know for the unknown life in Majorca, which would be for years to come & not for a short time only.'[190]

Robert, however, was not at all prepared for this, and he immediately wrote to Clarissa begging her to reopen the debate, and adding:

> ... I don't want to let the children have the fantastic idea of Laura's broken-heartedly pleading for their love, begging them to come and think better of her, or of me encouraging this idea. Rather they must think of themselves as having turned down a generous offer with ingratitude and self-deception, and of me having kept my patience with them to the point of hopelessness and disinterest, that is, too long, deceiving myself. Sam is still excepted from this disinterest, but what can Sam do, poor fellow? Let him please realise that I and Laura have not changed our feelings for him at all, because he has not changed towards us and that one day we'll manage to see him again.[191]

Clarissa refused to help: 'I don't think anything would be gained by going over the whole ground again with the children,' she declared. But she agreed with Robert 'that the children regard Laura as having broken up their home', and that this was:

> nonsense. If you were prepared to allow your home to be broken up the first time you met a woman who was mentally more akin to you than your own wife, and if she agreed, then Laura was effect rather than cause. I can see I am writing unjustly, for you did try to keep your home together in patriarchal fashion with a wife and a mistress, but you did not make allowances for the impossible strain, in a modern world, on either of the two women concerned. Geoffrey is merely another effect, foretold by Mother before he appeared.
>
> The rest of us, so far as your story is concerned, are no more than the chorus of mourning women in a Greek tragedy. We suffer in your sufferings, but can do very little to help.[192]

This drew from Robert one of the most bitterly angry letters of his life. 'Clarissa,' he began:

> After making every conceivable indulgence to you on account of the ignorance, supported by spiritual and suppressed physical depravity, shown in your letter, I must nevertheless write to you as a penance of shame to deplore that it should be possible for the most ignorant, blind,

illnatured or filthy-minded person to write of my relations with Laura as you have just done – 'a patriarchal style of living with wife and mistress' – that it was not plain even to such a person that my feeling for Laura was not a human romantic one but an increasingly clear recognition in her of an absolute truth and goodness which answered a knowledge in me that such a thing must somewhere be, a recognition which in spite of herself Nancy finally made before relapsing into dirty humanity. As for my 'sufferings' they do not exist, unless you can characterise as such certain unreasonable regrets that people whom I have loved have proved no better than they have proved.[193]

Clarissa did not bother to reply to this letter; and indeed it was Robert's last attempt to contact any member of his family for some months. As a result of Laura Riding's determination to continue with their development schemes, despite Norman Cameron's having withdrawn his financial support, she and Robert were now facing a most serious financial crisis, and there was no time to continue with family feuds.

CHAPTER 9
The Road to the Sea

Graves and Riding had not been unduly worried by Norman Cameron's departure. It would be troublesome finding alternative financial backing for their road and hotel-building plans, but they felt that they were now 'compromised to the affair', and in any case it should not be impossible. Indeed they had soon managed 'to raise a good deal of money'. Among other things, they persuaded Jonathan Cape, who was shortly to publish *No Decency Left*, to promise them an advance of £500 on the three further books which they had to offer him: Graves's *The Real David Copperfield*, now virtually finished; and two works by Riding: *Everybody's Letters*, a selection of real letters on all kinds of subjects which she was in the process of editing; and a book of stories.

Before long there were two other works in hand: Laura was writing a long poem in French entitled *Le Monde ou vivent les Morts*, to be illustrated with designs suggested by her and executed by John Aldridge; and she had also begun working with Graves and a newcomer to their circle named Jacob (Bruno) Bronowski on what Robert described as 'a joint thing...called *The Critical Vulgate* which will come out every so often and deal in an uncompromisingly authoritative way with the values of things'.[194]

Bronowski, 'a young Polish Jew who is really a geometrician at Cambridge and has a very good mind',[195] had come out to Deyá with his companion Eirlys Roberts, a classicist who had just completed the third of her four years at Cambridge. They had both developed a tremendous admiration for Laura Riding's intellect – Eirlys also thought that she was 'beautiful', and 'a pleasure to look at' – and they had been invited to stay for a few weeks at Canelluñ.[196] Riding had soon fired them with enthusiasm for the *Vulgate*, and it was agreed that they should return the following year and take a house in Deyá. It was also agreed that Laura's part in the *Vulgate* would be 'the general statement of values', Bronowski's 'the glossarian work', Robert's 'the internal interrogation and illustration'; other 'outside disputants' would 'provide material for evaluation', and Eirlys Roberts would have the task of 'collation'.[197]

Neither of these projects seemed likely to make much money; but when *No Decency Left* appeared, and was greeted with 'brilliant reviews ... almost everywhere', the financial future looked bright. However, the sales figures soon turned out to be dreadfully disappointing. Before long Graves was explaining to T.E.Shaw that the book had been 'disgracefully handled by Howard, in Jonathan's absence in the States. . . . I don't suppose it's sold more than 2,500 copies anywhere and there's no American edition.' Cape appears to have taken the contrary view: it was the authors' fault, and not his firm's, that the book was doing so badly; and the result was a quarrel which put the £500 advance on Graves and Riding's further work in jeopardy.

Then, in July 1932, it became necessary to pay some of the money which was due on the land needed for the road to the sea; and Graves and Riding were suddenly in desperate need of £1,500. 'We could easily get it from local business men,' Graves told T.E.Shaw confidently,

> but that would mean interference with our plans. We want to control the whole thing ourselves and without mortgaging anything. So Laura and I are writing to friends who have money or possible access to money in case they would like to invest in Spanish castles at a somewhat higher rate of interest than they would get from war-loan and with greater security than English industrials.

In the meantime, they had 'secured a fortnight's moratorium with the proprietor who has promised in the interval not to do business with the Germans and [we] hope that things will break right'.[198]

With help from T.E. and others, the immediate crisis was surmounted, the land was bought and the building of the road begun. However, Canelluñ had had to be mortgaged, and without a substantial injection of funds during the next two years Graves and Riding would clearly be facing ruin. It was possible but not at all probable that the new road could somehow be made to pay for itself, by the sale of building plots alongside it; and in a personal effort to save the situation Robert had begun work on an idea which he had dismissed from his mind almost exactly three years previously: an historical romance based upon the life of the Roman emperor Claudius.

CHAPTER 10
The Writing of *I, Claudius*

Towards the end of August 1929, with *Good-bye to All That* newly completed, Robert Graves had 'found it hard to stop dead when I unexpectedly noticed that it was finished'[199] – and to fill the sudden gap in his writing life he had begun to keep what he described as a 'Journal of Curiosities'. In the course of his entry for 5 September, he remarked that 'dozens of winning ideas' attacked him:

> in my weaker moments of sleep or day-dream, and are only with difficulty repulsed. It is not long since a complete historical romance or interpretative biography occurred to me – 'The Emperor Pumpkin.' I had been reading Suetonius and Tacitus. It was about Claudius, the emperor who came between Caligula and Nero. . . . Claudius has always been a puzzle to the historians, as indeed he was to his contemporaries.[200]

The puzzle was that Claudius, an apparent buffoon who was satirized by Seneca in *The Pumpkinification of Claudius*, was also responsible for many valuable public works. Graves's solution was that Claudius had been 'an idealistic enemy of Caesardom', who only 'escaped ... assassination ... by a parade of his physical infirmities, an affected lowness of taste and a cultivated weak-mindedness'. Later, when elected emperor, he had deliberately played the fool in order to bring Caesardom into disrepute, and hasten the return of the Republic. After sketching in a few more details, Graves added that he was recording 'all this', only 'to lay the ghost of an idea which otherwise might continue to plead for execution'.[201]

However, the ghost had not been laid; and by October 1932, after an intensive course of background reading, which included (as he told T.E. Shaw) 'Tacitus, Josephus, Dio Cassius, Suetonius, Seneca, Arosius, etc. and the Companion to Latin Studies, and Dictionary of Class. Ant.',[202] Graves was ready to begin work on his historical romance. After reading

Claudius's Aeduan speech to give himself a sense of the appropriate literary style, Graves decided to write his novel in the first person as *I, Claudius*, and he began it with this memorable paragraph:

I, TIBERIUS CLAUDIUS DRUSUS NERO GERMANICUS This-that-and-the-other (for I shall not trouble you yet with all my titles) who was once, and not so long ago either, known to my friends and relatives and associates as 'Claudius the Idiot', or 'That Claudius', or 'Claudius the Stammerer', or 'Clau-Clau-Claudius' or at best as 'Poor Uncle Claudius', am now about to write this strange history of my life; starting from my earliest childhood and continuing year by year until I reach the fateful point of change where, some eight years ago, at the age of fifty-one, I suddenly found myself caught up in what I may call the 'golden predicament' from which I have never since become disentangled.[203]

The first person apart from Robert to read these words was Mary Ellidge, a red-headed English girl with an attractive smile and a stunning figure, who was then in her early twenties. Robert Graves answered a knock at the door of Canelluñ one October morning to find Mary standing there at the side of a young man, George, her husband. The newcomers explained that they were on honeymoon for six months, and that their wanderings in search of a perfect Spanish village had led them to Deyá, where they had heard that Laura Riding had a house to let.

Graves told them that the house had gone – it was a mistake that the particulars were still being advertised in Palma – but he was glad to see some fresh English faces, and he invited them to come in, have a drink and stay for lunch. Soon they were being introduced to Laura Riding, who was wearing one of her picturesque antique Mallorquin dresses; and the four of them struck up an immediate friendship. Laura was badly in need of new disciples: not only had Norman Cameron and the Matthewses gone, but John Aldridge, Jacob Bronowski and Eirlys Roberts were all back in England; and over lunch, as Mary Ellidge later recalled, Robert announced that he was 'desperate': apparently he was just beginning a new book, 'and I haven't anyone to type it for me'. Mary immediately volunteered, on one condition: 'Well, if you'll find us a house,' she said:

'I'll type it for you.' So he found us a house. It was called the 'Vina Vieja', the old vineyard, and we moved in the next day and the day after he arrived with about twenty foolscap pages. He always wrote on foolscap pages without any lines – spiderish handwriting, crosses out and so on – the manuscript was a mess. And he said: 'This is a little

story I'm writing about the Emperor Claudius. Will you type it for me?'
And I said: 'Yes, of course.' That was the understatement of all time.
That little story lasted for two years, two volumes and is still going strong
now fifty years later.[204]

The story of *I, Claudius* begins with the Emperor Augustus firmly in control
both of the Roman Senate and of the Roman Empire. But who will succeed
him? His sister Octavia has a son Marcellus, who is married to Julia, Augustus's only child; so, to begin with, Marcellus appears to be the most likely
candidate for supreme power. However, Augustus is no longer married
to Julia's mother, but to the formidable Livia, who has divorced her own
husband in order to marry him, and who is secretly determined that it
shall be her own elder son, Tiberius, who will become the next Emperor.
An utterly ruthless woman, Livia systematically begins poisoning or otherwise disposing of everyone who stands in her way.

Other members of the Imperial Family have their own ideas about the
succession; and when, in 10 BC, Claudius is born into this family, both
as the great-nephew and the step-grandson of Augustus (since Claudius's
grandmothers are Octavia and Livia), his chances of surviving the ensuing
struggle for power seem remote. However, being a sickly child, as he grows
older he learns to trade upon his physical infirmities, exaggerating for
instance both his stammer and his limp, so that he appears to most people
to be a harmless idiot who can pose no conceivable threat to any other
member of the Imperial circle. The result is that Claudius survives the
reign of his increasingly depraved uncle Tiberius, whom Livia succeeds
in making Emperor on Augustus's death; he also survives the reign of
his monstrous nephew Caligula; and he is then reluctantly compelled to
become Emperor himself.

This is a very strong plot; and Graves's use of the first person, usually
a great risk for a novelist because of the considerable restrictions which
it imposes upon him, succeeds brilliantly as an effective contrast to the
horrors with which the novel is filled. Graves, – as Claudius – writes that
he wishes his 'eventual readers of a hundred generations ahead, or more'
to feel themselves 'directly spoken to, as if by a contemporary'; and he
adopts the same cool, laconic, matter-of-fact, almost conversational
approach which had helped to make *Good-bye to All That* such a success.

T.E.Shaw, having laid his critical finger upon the weakest point of the
novel – that the middle part of it was 'crowded with figures and moves
too slowly' – commented disapprovingly that 'it is a Chamber of Roman
Horrors too. In every direction you take the way of crime, so that your

chronicle becomes more scandalous than the most hostile Roman story....
In so much human nature there would have been some good specimens,
surely?'[205] Indeed there are moments when the novel appears to be a pictorial
catalogue of human vice. At one of these an innocent fourteen-year-old
girl has to be raped by the public executioner before he puts her to death,
'to avoid the ill-luck that would befall the City if they executed her while
still a virgin'.[206] 'It gripped me against my will,' T.E. commented.

> I couldn't help reading at it, long after bed-time. . . . The writing is
> superb: the aloof and cold-blooded narration masterly: the possibility
> of Claudius having written it always borne in mind, and always made
> possible. And yet – and yet – *quo vadis, Domine?* I have an uneasy feeling
> that it will be valued and collected and talked about for its vices, rather
> than for its force. It is not an essential book.

He added that it was 'an extraordinary book, and will raise your publisher-
value, at any rate. The man who can do it can do anything.'[207]

Some of the strength of *I, Claudius* undoubtedly comes from the fact
that Robert Graves subconsciously used it as a vehicle for expressing the
dark side of his feelings for Laura Riding. One of the most powerful scenes
in the book, the one in which Claudius has to recognize that Caligula
has become a God,[208] must be a kind of parody of the scene in which
Graves had to recognize that Riding had become Finality.

It is also evident that there are strong elements of Laura in the fictional
character of Livia, who is described by Claudius as being 'unique in setting
no limit at all to... [her ambitions], and yet remaining perfectly level-headed
and cool in what would be judged in any other woman to be raving madness'.[209] Again, Claudius tells us that the name 'Livia':

> is connected with the Latin word which means Malignity. My grand-
> mother was a consummate actress, and the outward purity of her conduct,
> the sharpness of her wit and the graciousness of her manners deceived
> nearly everybody. But nobody really liked her: malignity commands
> respect, not liking. She had a faculty for making ordinary easy-going
> people feel acutely conscious in her presence of their intellectual and
> moral shortcomings.[210]

Livia, like Laura, not only makes people feel acutely aware of their shortcomings; but also ruthlessly manipulates them to serve her own ends, and
is in general highly successful in so doing.

Numerous other fragments of autobiography intrude, of which two may have special importance. When writing, as Claudius, of a marriage which has failed and which has therefore deprived him of his legitimate sexual activity, Graves comments: 'I do not think that it is natural for an ordinary man to live so long without a woman ... and I do not think that I can be blamed for living with [someone else].'[211] In the light of Riding's well-known sexual rejection of Graves, this may well have been read as an encouraging personal message by his new secretary–typist, Mary Ellidge, who, despite her newly married state, was already falling in love with him.

Robert Graves's subconscious desire for freedom from Laura Riding's tyrannical rule is still more strongly expressed in the conflict of political ideas between Claudius and Livia. Throughout *I, Claudius*, up to and including the moment when he finds himself being acclaimed as the new Emperor, Claudius remains devoted to the restoration of the Republic, while Livia lives and dies as the champion of the supreme power of the Roman emperors.

Consciously, however, Graves was still Riding's adoring disciple. In the autumn of 1932, he described her as the incarnation of the goddess Isis, saying that:

In Egypt she was the holy name of the year of holy months: she was known to her priests as the invisible removed one, and to her people as the manifoldly incomprehensible. Every new moon crowned her with its peculiar head-dress – a rose, a star, an ear of barley, the horns of a goat: and she became the Moon itself, the single head of variety, Hecate by name. And Lilith, the owl of wisdom, because her lodges were held in stealthy darkness.[212]

If Graves's earlier view of poetry is at least partially correct, that is, that its principal function is the resolution of conflicts within the mind of the poet, then the conflict between his conscious and subconscious feelings about Laura Riding must have helped to make this a highly creative period of his life; and *I, Claudius*, as well as being a most remarkable product of that creativity, also provides us with a series of illuminating insights into the mind of its creator.

CHAPTER 11
The Vulgatites

November 1932: in Deyá the figs are over, the oranges and tangerines are just starting, and the olive-picking season is in full swing. Meanwhile, the new road had made seven or eight turns on its way to the sea, and Laura Riding and Gelat were attempting, with a total lack of success, to sell off building plots along its route. So far the only positive benefit of the road was that heaps of olive wood from the felled trees were piling up ready for use on winter fires.

Neither had it been possible to resolve the dispute with Jonathan Cape; and so Graves's and Riding's work was to be published by Arthur Barker, a young publisher with premises in Garrick Street, for whom Robert Graves now continued working on the early chapters of *I, Claudius*, and also completed the revision of a collection of verse, entitled simply *Poems: Nineteen Thirty to Nineteen Thirty Three*.[213] In this poetry Riding's influence as Graves's Muse is everywhere apparent. The new collection includes not only 'On Portents' and Graves's prose-poem to Riding/Isis, but a further poem of dedication to Riding's service which runs:

> To whom else other than
> To whom else not of man
> Yet in human state,
> Standing neither in stead
> Of self nor idle godhead,
> Should I, man in man bounded,
> Myself dedicate?
>
> To whom else momently,
> To whom else endlessly,
> But to you, I?
> To you who only,
> To you who mercilessly,

To you who lovingly
Plucked out the lie?

To whom else less acquaint
To whom else without taint
Of death, death-true?
With great astonishment
Thankfully I consent
To my estrangement
From me in you.[214]

Consciously, Graves believed that it was Laura who had 'Plucked out the lie': or (as they both appear to have understood these words) it was Laura who had removed his inclination to embroider the truth for artistic reasons, and had replaced it with a fixed determination to tell the whole truth as clearly as possible in his poems. Here Graves's almost obsessive reworking of his poems became a virtue, and in 'Devilishly Disturbed' he records with a certain amount of pride how:

Devilishly disturbed
By this unready pen:
For every word I write
I scratch out nine or ten,
And each surviving word
Resentfully I make
Sweat for those nine or ten
I cancelled for its sake.[215]

Despite Graves's obvious devotion to Riding, she now began to show an interest in other men which, though it did not lead to sexual intercourse (for which, despite her 1929 injuries, she could now have been ready), was undoubtedly based upon strong sexual attraction. Graves at once became subject to a new set of intensely emotional pressures, and began to depict himself in an unnaturally humble manner, condemning (for example) what he saw as his 'greed and credulity'; and imagining himself, when retelling the legend of Isis, not as Set, her new young lover, but as 'Osiris yearly drowned'.[216]

It was horribly clear to Graves that he could never live up to the ideals at which he aimed. Sometimes he was almost amused by this. But alongside Graves's humorous 'Down, Wanton, Down!' must be set his nightmarish 'The Succubus',[217] in which sexual frustration leads to orgasmic dreams: and Graves finds that the woman who comes to him in those dreams comes 'never as longed-for beauty/Slender and cool, with limbs lovely to see', but 'with hot face,/With paunched and uddered carcase'; and as she 'Gulp[s] away' his soul, he is forced to ask himself: 'Flesh, is she truly more gross than your lust is gross?' In 'The Commons of Sleep',[218] another poem on this theme, Graves asks himself whether it is shameful 'to lie down in hope to find/Licence for devilishness of mind', and in a powerful concluding verse he describes how:

> ... lamps burn red and glow-worm green
> And naked dancers grin between
>   The rusting bars of love.
> Loud and severe the drunken jokes
> Go clanging out in midnight strokes.
>   I weep: I wake: I move.

Thanks to seeing his own work through Riding's highly critical eyes, Graves did not even have the satisfaction of enjoying the reputation which he had earned as the author of *Good-bye to All That*; so that when, in January 1933, he received proofs of *The Real David Copperfield* he told Arthur Barker that he had no wish to be described on the title page as the author of his own autobiography. 'I can't deny that I wrote it, of course,' he declared, 'but the "success" of the book which my way of writing it invited – by no means ingenuously – is nothing to brag about.'[219]

Nevertheless, living with Laura Riding had drawn Graves into a world beyond the world; and seeing a cloud in the shape of a great dragon with a Jew's head, he asks wonderingly:

> What times are these – to be allowed
> This ancient vision of grey cloud
>   Gone in a casual breath?
> The times of the torn dragon-wing
> Still threatening seaward and the sting
>   Still poised for death.[220]

The times were magical but dangerous, and were severely overshadowed for some months by a mysterious illness which Riding developed. By the end of November 1932, this illness became so unpleasant that rumours reached Amy Graves in North Wales to the effect that Laura was 'seriously ill & dying & that Nancy is hoping Robert will come back to her.... What a solution Laura's death might bring!' Amy wrote to John, though she recognized that the rumour about Nancy wishing to return to Robert was almost certainly untrue.[221] Nancy, after all, was living happily with Geoffrey Phibbs at Poulk, where they had set up a printing press, and were about to receive their first order 'to print a book for £40'.[222]

However, Laura Riding's ill-health was real enough. On Christmas Day (as she wrote to Maisie Somerville, Robert's friend from Islip days, and now working at the BBC, supervising Schools Broadcasting) she was well enough to enjoy an excellent supper at Gelat's, together with Robert, Mary Ellidge (now publicly using her maiden name 'Burtonwood' in deference to Riding's dislike of 'couples', so that hardly anyone knew she was married), and George Ellidge. Within three days, however, Laura was writing gloomily of her ill-health, declaring that she was uncertain whether she was suffering from appendicitis, intestinal trouble, or even some difficulty with her ovaries, but that she shrank from allowing anyone in Majorca to carry out even a simple appendectomy in case further problems arose during the operation.[223] Earlier she had complained to Jacob Bronowski that she alternated between periods of extremely good and extremely poor health, although she sometimes wondered whether the bad times were simply the result of nervous strain. In any case, she could not possibly ease up on her work, for in editing the *Critical Vulgate*, she was weaving a web with so many different strands that to slacken her concentration for a single day would be disastrous.[224]

Riding's letters to Somerville and Bronowski were part of the massive correspondence which she had undertaken with actual or potential 'Vulgatites', in other words all those who, she hoped, would contribute something either to her *Critical Vulgate*, or to one of a series of related projects – though the word 'contributor' was not officially allowed: as she explained in a letter to the poet and artist John Cullen, one was never a contributor, but a collaborator. In practice this meant that one was expected to make the *Critical Vulgate* one's highest priority, and, above all, never to submit *Vulgate* material to any other periodicals or magazines.[225] In Riding's mind the *Vulgate* had become a work of supreme importance. It was to be a final definition of truth, a carefully-arranged study of everything that there was to be studied,[226] in which no writer would speak as merely himself or herself, but with an intimate and therefore unassailable awareness of the truth.[227]

The nature of Maisie Somerville's contribution to the *Vulgate* was never clearly defined. In December 1932 Riding sent her an unusually vague letter asking whether she would be writing anything;[228] and Maisie remained on the fringe of the 'Vulgatites', a valued friend but never a collaborator. Laura did not wish to lose this beautiful and perhaps influential woman from her circle, and turned over various possibilities in her mind. In January 1933, for example, she outlined an ambitious plan for Maisie to help Eirlys Roberts and Jacob Bronowski to devise a scheme of secondary school education along *Vulgate* lines;[229] and later she asked whether Maisie might throw up her career at the BBC and come to live permanently in Deyá to help with editorial work.[230]

Laura Riding hoped to gather around herself in Deyá a permanent group of writers and artists whose activities she would control and direct; and, by the spring of 1933, it had been decided that Jacob Bronowski and Eirlys Roberts should come to Deyá in the summer, to settle down as long-term residents.[231]

The poet James Reeves, a friend of Bronowski's, was also invited to Deyá. He did not come at once, but Riding began a correspondence with him, and gradually drew him in to write about 'The Romantic Habit in English Poets': (Shelley was serious but deluded, wrote Riding early in February after seeing a first draft, while Keats was so light-weight that none of his opinions was even worth considering.[232] Another poet, John Cullen, was to contribute some of his verses, and to collaborate with Laura Riding in a long article on 'Germany', in which the Germans were to be described as 'spiritual liars', ready to 'claim the freedom from moral considerations granted to the artist'.[233] Eirlys Roberts had moved on from collating material to thoughts about the female sex (Laura wrote of her pleasure that these deliberations had begun, and hoped that the first *Critical Vulgate* would define the female sex clearly enough to enable them to begin a more thorough investigation into women's true importance in the second);[234] while Len Lye began drafting an article about 'Film-making'; and John Aldridge was to contribute reproductions of some of his latest paintings.

Robert Graves's role (in the moments that he could snatch from the writing of *I, Claudius*) was to be 'Associate Editor', and also to contribute critical essays on 'Coleridge and Wordsworth', 'Keats and Shelley', and 'A Note on the Pastoral'. In addition, he wrote his highly autobiographical 'A Poem-Sequence', which he dedicated 'To the Sovereign Muse', and in which he chronicled the state of guilt, lust and desire for glory from which, as he saw it, he had been rescued by his worship of Laura.[235]

In the meantime, Tom Matthews, who had recently been promoted within *Time* Magazine (Laura rejoiced that he could now compel every new novel to be judged according to the standards of the *Critical Vulgate*),[236] had prepared some notes for 'The Idea of God', an article which under Riding's supervision gradually developed (as a friend of Matthews's later commented) into a kind of:

manifesto of her crusade against masculinity. Theology for her is man's dodge away from the inevitable admission that the solution to all his problems ... lies in the woman. Woman is God. If one brings this down to the brass tacks of Miss Riding's personal claim, it is that she is God, which in turn means that she is not only a man but a super-man. All her mystifications, her misuse of words, her transparent evasions are designed to conceal the brute fact that she is not a man and senses in man something which she passionately envies and therefore implacably hates.[237]

Besides sending Laura Riding his 'notes on God', Matthews wrote that he hoped to be able to send her fifty dollars: for which promise she was most grateful, commenting that every coin meant a measure of progress with her road-building.[238] However, far more was needed; and as 1933 progressed it became clear that Riding's ambitious schemes for road and hotel were rapidly bringing her and Robert Graves to the brink of ruin.

CHAPTER 12

Financial Crisis

By the end of January 1933, Laura Riding's new road, in its rough unfinished state, was nearly through to the sea. All that remained was to give it a smooth surface.[239] But there were still no buyers for plots of building land beside the road; and towards the end of the previous year Laura had begun writing letters to her friends, suggesting that they should invest in the new hotel which would be built by 'Luna', the notional company run by herself which was now in charge of operations.

This produced a substantial sum of money from John Aldridge, but almost nothing else; though news of Laura's plans reached Robert Graves's half-sister Susan, who commented acidly: 'She is . . . thinking of being manageress of a hotel, but she still has screaming fits. Fun if No. 13 wanted something and the manageress couldn't attend to him 'cos she was rolling on the floor in a fit of hysteria!'[240]

By the time, in late January 1933, that one of Laura Riding's friends, Anna, wrote to say that she was unable to help, Laura had already been compelled to mortgage Canelluñ to half its value to pay for the work which remained to be done on the road. Finding enough money, she told Anna, was fraught with difficulties; but she was full of ideas, and, with Gelat to inspire her, she was confident that everything would turn out well. Her current plan was to persuade the owner of an hotel in Palma to go into partnership with Luna, the name of an imaginary company of Laura's own creation, with herself at its head. Such a partnership would provide Laura with sufficient capital to complete the road and possibly even to build an hotel, while allowing her to retain ultimate authority. She also told Anna of the likelihood that the completed road would be bought by the Spanish Government, and of plans by the tourist authorities to build houses on the land alongside.[241]

This was almost entirely wishful thinking; but Robert, at least, remained supportive, and on the day that Canelluñ was mortgaged he gave Laura a ring which she liked very much; and this gift turned what might have been a dismal occasion into a celebration.[242]

Riding's flow of money-making ideas continued. For example, feeling embarrassed at not being able to give Eirlys Roberts the 'hotel or associated work' for which she had expressed a desire, Riding wrote to Jacob Bronowski telling him of the possibility that she and Gelat would build a house by the end of the road leading to the Cala, with a cafe or shop attached to it. She wondered whether he and Eirlys might run a small business there during the summer months.[243] This, however, was another plan which came to nothing.

At the same time, Laura was keeping an eye on the progress of current literary projects, and busily suggesting new ones. Current projects included her own *The Life of the Dead* and *Everybody's Letters*, together with Robert's *The Real David Copperfield*; while among Riding's new ideas were what she thought of as the first really suitable children's dictionary (based upon a scheme which she and Graves had earlier submitted to Heinemann) and, associated with it, a children's home university library.[244] Riding also began writing what she hoped would be a popular book about Deyá; and, besides sending Arthur Barker several letters about *The Vulgate*, she suggested to him that *No Decency Left*, the unsuccessful collaboration which she and Graves had written for Cape, might be shortened and then republished together with a sequel.

Arthur Barker (or 'Arthurby', as Laura Riding now addressed him) did not jump at the idea of a rewritten *No Decency Left*. Indeed, he frequently found himself not only having to act as a brake upon Riding's over-enthusiasm, but also having to check her unprofessionalism. In January 1933, for instance, he asked her to make sure that she had the goodwill of all those whose letters had been included in *Everybody's Letters*. Apparently the Book Society had been about to recommend the volume in their February list, which would have been a virtual guarantee of a substantial sale, when their reviewer had grown worried about the possible feelings of the letter-writers. This threw Riding into some confusion: not only had she breached copyright by using letters addressed to her or to Robert without the permission of the writers; but a number of the letters had actually been stolen by a friend of Elfriede's. However, after writing an anxious letter on the subject to John Aldridge, now her closest confidant, Riding decided it was unlikely that anyone would take legal action, and she told 'Arthurby' that it was safe for him to proceed with publication. In the event *Everybody's Letters* gained a number of good reviews (some admittedly from friends such as Eirlys Roberts, who reviewed it for the *Granta*), but sales were highly disappointing.

Graves's *The Real David Copperfield* was also published by Barker in March 1933, and was also a commercial failure. At the end of the month Graves sent Barker a long article entitled 'The Two Abbeys' in an attempt to boost sales. In it, he compared the overcrowded state of the monuments in Westminster Abbey with the overcrowded state of:

> another ancient Abbey, built of ink and paper. It is called English Literature. Its aisles are lined with imposing monuments which are known as classics. These too have already seriously encroached upon the space available for the appropriate ritual – namely, the reading of good books.

Graves then suggested that a number of works including Bacon's *Essays*, Burke's *Selected Speeches* and Ruskin's *Seven Lamps of Architecture* could be safely disposed of, and replaced with other works such as Lord Herbert of Cherbury's *Autobiography*, Defoe's *Moll Flanders* and Samuel Butler's *Erewhon*. Dickens, he went on to say, represented a special case; and (not surprisingly in the circumstances) he recommended 'the complete rewriting of certain books, sentence by sentence, as it might be imagined that the authors would have written them in their own day had they been free to write slowly and carefully and economically, and to suit the story, not their public'.[245] It was an article full of interesting ideas, but sadly it seems to have had little or no effect upon sales of *The Real David Copperfield*.

Neither could much be expected from the two hundred printed copies of Riding's *The Life of the Dead*, a joint venture between Arthur Barker and the Seizin Press. The printing costs were far greater than Riding had anticipated; and although the slim volume is notable for a set of outstanding illustrations by John Aldridge (the originals of which were exhibited from mid-March 1933 in the Leicester Galleries), Riding was at her most contrived and least satisfying. Possibly she had hoped for a critical success to match Eliot's *The Waste Land*, for when the engraver, a Mr Beedham, complained about the morbidity of the illustrations, she explained to him that she was writing about people who were spiritually rather than physically dead.

Arthur Barker was prepared to risk money on all these publications; but when, early in March, a pile of material for the first number of *The Critical Vulgate* arrived, he was frankly appalled. Riding had already agreed to pay half the costs of publication, thus reducing Barker's potential losses;[246] but he could see at once that there was no prospect whatever of making any profit. However, he did not wish, by antagonizing Riding, to lose Graves from his list of authors. So, after sending a polite telegram of acknowledgment, he simply kept silent.

By 25 March, Riding was complaining to him in violent language about the creative impotence to which his delays had reduced her;[247] and a few days later she commented in a letter to John Aldridge that, so far as she and Robert were concerned, everything was finished between them and Barker, if he could not do better.[248] But despite her fury she did have the presence of mind to hold out the bait of Graves's first *Claudius* volume to Barker, telling him that it would be ready later in the year;[249] and Barker replied almost by return of post with a conciliatory letter in which he admitted his failure to anticipate fully the size of the *Vulgate* project, but suggested that he should travel out to Deyá to see what could be arranged.[250]

On the day that Riding had written to 'Arthurby', she had written still more fiercely to Norman Cameron, who had sent her an irritatingly cheerful letter, and whom she now blamed entirely for the financial problems caused by her own road-building folly. There were other troubles too: Ca'n Torrent and Ca'n Pa Bo had no tenants, and the present occupants of Casa Salerosa were leaving at the end of the month. But, when it was decided that 'Arthurby' should come out to Deyá at Easter, things looked more promising for a little while.

When the time came, 'Arthurby' was installed in Canelluñ as a most honoured guest, and on Easter Sunday 1933 he took part in the grand opening of the road to the Cala. This was achieved (appropriately enough, since Gelat's influence over Laura was such that not only the road itself but any potential building land alongside it had been registered in his name) by Gelat driving down the new road in his car, with Laura Riding, Robert Graves, Arthur Barker, George Ellidge and Mary Burtonwood as his passengers. For Laura it was a flawless hour; and she wrote to Tom Matthews a few days later saying she had come close to tears.[251]

No wonder: although the building of the road had been financially reckless, it had also been bold and daring, an act of faith in the future, and it was now a solid achievement to be set against numerous disappointments. Arthur Barker explained that both *Everybody's Letters* and *The Real David Copperfield* had been 'a dead loss'; and in the circumstances Riding could not press him so strongly over *The Critical Vulgate*, though he promised to investigate the idea of publishing it as a series of pamphlets. However, Barker must have been pleased by the progress which Graves was making on *I, Claudius*; and he also took away with him the draft of a novel which Riding had written with George Ellidge, and which she described as a work of fiction presented cinematically.[252]

This collaboration, no doubt begun in mid-March after the idea for revising *No Decency Left* had fallen through, was yet another attempt at a bestseller. Entitled *14A*,[253] it was also a *roman-à-clef*, very closely based upon the dramatic events of 1929, and containing unmistakable portraits of Robert Graves (who appears as 'Eric'), his sister Rosaleen (Molly), Nancy Nicholson (Edith), Geoffrey Phibbs (Hugh), Norah McGuinness (Maureen) and many others, together with a self-portrait of Laura Riding herself (under the name of Catherine). As a novel, it is dreadfully tedious, with seemingly interminable passages of the most pretentious dialogue. As a record of Riding's view of people and events, however, and as her substantially rewritten account of episodes in her own life, some of it makes fascinating reading.

Riding's retrospective malevolence against those who in real life had opposed her will, for example, appears to be boundless. Norah McGuinness, for whom Geoffrey Phibbs had once deserted her, is allowed to be 'pretty' but is also described as 'fat' and 'slightly common-looking';[254] while, for good measure, Riding has added a totally unhistorical incident in which Norah is clearly made out to be a thief.[255] Again, Geoffrey Phibbs is associated with the Devil at a very early stage;[256] and Riding has rewritten history to make it clear that she fully understood his 'falsity' from the moment that she met him, and that she also had occult knowledge of the fact that he and Nancy (who has 'at least a dozen [car] crashes a year') would eventually become lovers.[257]

Conversely, Riding's own virtues are shown to have been apparent to everyone. To Hugh (Geoffrey) she is 'sacred'.[258] 'You know very well, Molly [Rosaleen],' says Edith (Nancy), 'that Catherine [Laura] means everything that she says quite literally, and that she's always right.'[259] And in her own eyes Riding is one of the 'real people', after centuries of 'mostly crowds and very dim groups';[260] she is immensely attractive to men, none of whom can resist her;[261] and she is unique: 'Oh, I did die,' she says after her fall from the window. 'But then, I'm not people.'[262]

Most interesting of all is the attitude which Catherine (Laura Riding) displays in *14A* towards Eric (Robert Graves). Introduced as 'large, slightly grey, slow to act and think, but very sure of himself when he does act and think',[263] Eric is seen as touchingly but, in the end, rather tediously devoted to Catherine. Reading the main body of the book must therefore have been hard enough for Robert to bear; but worse was to come. On the final page, in a kind of epilogue, Riding fantasizes that she has finally disposed of him. Eric is made to return to Edith (Nancy); and, when he meets Catherine briefly in London, she explains that their previous close relationship can never be revived; and then, in his presence, she tells another man (of whom she is evidently fond) that 'Eric comes and talks to me sometimes, when I send for him – about once a year. But I must never let it be for more than an hour'; and then she prepares to leave with the other.[264] Consciously or subconsciously, this was the clearest possible warning to Graves that Riding did not see their relationship as a permanent one.

It may also have been a teasing message to her collaborator George Ellidge, whose wife Mary was now in the last stages of pregnancy. Despite her repudiation of sexual activity, Riding clearly liked men to be sexually attracted to her. However, her increasing fondness for George was masked for a while by her still stronger feelings for John Aldridge, who returned to Deyá accompanied by Lucie Brown, and laden with commissions. For Robert there was a good shaving brush; and for Laura there were Cuban cigarettes (of which she was now smoking sixty a day), a bottle of mouthwash, some cold cream from Selfridges, and six yards of Japanese silk from which she could make underclothes. Aldridge had also been asked to bring some records for dancing; but there was little enough cause for merriment.

Money was running out fast; and, by May 1933, Graves decided that he must swallow his pride and write a begging letter to Siegfried Sassoon, with whom he had been out of touch since their acrimonious correspondence following the publication of *Good-bye to All That*. 'I want to know', Graves demanded:

whether you still have money in any quantity, and accessible and if so whether you can lend me some. I need about a thousand pounds, because I have got into a hole... and have nothing left in the bank or mortgageable and have exhausted all possible book advances. The last three books I have written have fallen flat and as I am determined to write no more books of which to be ashamed (like *Goodbye*) and which alone sell, I don't know what to do.[265]

Sassoon was evidently hurt by the fact that Graves's only motive for writing to him appeared to be a financial one; and in his reply he asked how serious things were, and commented: 'I do feel that you are asking a good deal of me.' Graves replied, on 8 June, that it was certainly 'serious enough in its way. If the money does not turn up before the end of the summer it means spectacular financial ruin'; and he added that 'it would be a nice thing if, for a change, money could be the excuse for writing by which broken friendship gets repaired, instead of a signal that a friendship is wearing out.'[266] Siegfried did not reply until almost the end of the month, when he wrote that he could do nothing for Robert because Robert had told him 'nothing definite'; and he feared that, because of his inability to help, their friendship would once again lapse.[267] Further letters were exchanged; but as in 1930 they became increasingly acrimonious, and on 7 July 1933 Graves wrote an angry letter which he must have assumed would bring the correspondence to an end.[268]

News on most other fronts continued to be bleak. Graves had enjoyed helping Frank Richards, who had been in his platoon in France, to prepare his war memoirs for publication. But although *Old Soldiers Never Die* was a fine piece of work, and sold well when Faber and Faber published it later in 1933, Graves could expect only a small fee for the substantial revisions which he had made. *I, Claudius* was not yet completed, so no money was available from that source; and Laura Riding was unable to make any financial contribution. Indeed, on 8 July, she was infuriated to discover that Jonathan Cape, who had already ordered the pulping of her *Contemporaries and Snobs*, her *Anarchism is Not Enough* and her collaboration with Robert Graves entitled *A Pamphlet Against Anthologies*, had now allowed the remaining unbound stock of her *Poems: A Joking Word* to be sold as pulp.

By mid-July, in Graves's own words, he and Riding were 'nearly sunk': they faced the prospect of losing 'all our money and some £1,000 more that isn't our own'.[269] And then, at what must have seemed to be the last possible moment, Bernardo, the former owner of the land which had been used for the road, agreed to take only the interest which was due, and to let the capital repayment go by for a year. The immediate financial crisis was over; but it left both Robert and Laura feeling emotionally drained and unusually irritable with each other.

CHAPTER 13
Cross-Currents

Towards the end of 1933 Robert Graves wrote that it had been 'a rotten year in almost every way'.[270] Even the long-awaited visit from John Aldridge and Lucie Brown had not been a great success. For the time being Graves and Riding could not pay Maria to do the cooking and found visitors to Canelluñ more of a burden than a pleasure. Lucie made matters worse in the eyes of her hosts by being unable to 'stand onions or oil in her food'.[271] The best thing to come out of their visit was the extraordinary portrait which John Aldridge painted of Laura Riding. Wearing one of her embroidered Mallorquin costumes, together with earrings and a heavy necklace, Riding clearly wishes to be attractive; and Aldridge has captured the superficial sexual sheen which had once dazzled Geoffrey Phibbs and infuriated Norah McGuinness. But Aldridge sees beyond that sheen to the intensely powerful and yet tormented spirit beneath. So much striving, so much sorrow are visible. It is easy on looking at this portrait to hear Laura saying, as she did to John Aldridge when the first disappointing reviews of their *Life of the Dead* were published that year, how exhausted she was, and how she constantly asked herself whether there was any point in continuing.[272]

Even the birth of Mary Ellidge's child, which should have been a joyful event, was another difficult and exhausting experience. There were complications, the village midwife was unable to cope; and Laura Riding, who was present, had to use desperate measures such as immersing it in icy water, and pushing a finger down the back of its mouth, before she succeeded in reviving the new-born baby.[273]

Four years previously, in 1929, Robert Graves and Laura Riding had been drawn very closely together in their common struggle against the difficulties which faced them; but the continual struggle to survive had worn them down, and new pressures served only to drive them further and further apart. There was no open quarrel: how could there be, when

Graves was always prepared to put Riding first? But Riding began writing cross letters about Graves in one of which – for instance – she attacked him most unkindly first for having lost his wallet, and then for having dropped the butter down the well. It was due to his being so feminine and so emotional, she complained, and because his most sensitive area was between his legs, she had ordered some extra-long night-shirts for him to wear in bed.[274] And at about the same time Graves was writing to Julie Matthews in less than wholly respectful terms about Laura's 'comic accident . . . [she] sat on a Ca's Pintat chamber pot which split neatly in two and cut her bottom right across like the sign of the cross – scars she will wear to her dying day'.[275]

Their life together was only really tolerable for Laura Riding when there were other people besides Graves to be dominated; and with 'darling' John Aldridge's departure early in July she appears to have been socially at something of a loose end. It was easy enough to resume her mild flirtation with George Ellidge; but he was busily occupied for most of the day in doing the housework and looking after his young child. This responsibility fell to him because Mary Ellidge had resumed her secretarial duties at the earliest possible moment after child-birth. Officially, of course, her principal task was to assist Laura; but as time went by she spent more and more time with Robert, whose eyesight had deteriorated alarmingly during the final stages of his work on *I, Claudius*, and who therefore began to need her not merely for typing his completed manuscript, but for dictation also. Later Mary was to recall how she and Robert had enjoyed:

> a very pleasant life. . . . we used to work in the morning and go to the beach in the afternoon. . . . But George didn't like the sun or the beach and Laura didn't like the sun or the beach so Robert and I used to go alone. And then we all used to meet in the café . . . at 5.30 for coffee or vermouth or wine and the post used to arrive at that time. . . . We lived practically in each other's pockets. . . .[276]

By the middle of August, Graves had completed *I, Claudius*. It was impossible to post a parcel in Deyá, so he hired the village taxi, and Gelat drove him and Laura and George and Mary into Palma with the precious type-script. Laura, according to Mary Ellidge,

> was in a bad mood because she'd been up half the night reading the typescript. . . . So she was tired of course and she was cross and she was *jealous* because she knew that this was going to be a successful book

and she could never write a successful book. And so, sitting moodily in the taxi she suddenly said: 'All I can say is, it's a very boring book.' And poor Robert was like a pricked balloon because he'd been on top of the world you see, so happy that he'd finished the wretched thing.[277]

It was at about this time that their small circle was suddenly increased by the return of Jacob Bronowski and Eirlys Roberts, who were now to spend almost a year living in rented accommodation in the village. Bronowski at once began working on *The Critical Vulgate* with Laura Riding, for whose mind he had a tremendous admiration; while Roberts, who had studied Classics at Cambridge, was asked by Graves to look over a copy of the text of *I, Claudius*, and to check the accuracy of its classical references.[278]

Eirlys Roberts's task was an easy one: the only error she was able to discover was that Graves had ascribed the wrong colour to the hem of the prostitutes' gowns; and in any case when she pointed this out Robert 'politely took no notice'.[279] Another friend who read through the text was T. E. Shaw; and, besides his general rather adverse comments about it being 'a Chamber of Roman Horrors', he made a few detailed criticisms: suggesting, for example, that Graves had made 'too much use of paper, to the entire exclusion of parchment and papyrus'; and also that the word 'assegai', Bantu for a stabbing spear, seemed an odd way to describe a German throwing-spear.[280] Robert made no alterations as a result of these criticisms; but he thought them important enough to be answered in an explanatory 'Author's Note' as a foreword to the book.[281]

In the meantime, there was a further bitter exchange of letters between Graves and Sassoon, in the course of which they quarrelled afresh over the extent of Riding's influence upon Robert's life and work. Laura, predictably, was interested rather than embarrassed by this. She even put out a tentative feeler in Siegfried's direction, enjoining Robert to send him the photograph of a portrait of herself by the academician Arnold Mason, and to tell him that: 'she recommends you her next book of poems (Arthur Barker. November. Title *Poet – A Lying Word*) to be read intrinsically. She noticed in one of the poems you sent the word "mindsight", which also occurs in a poem in her book: perhaps that may be a tie that binds.'[282] It was not, and Laura Riding took no further steps to make it so. After another brief correspondence later in the year in which Graves successfully recommended an unemployed ex-fellow-officer to Sassoon's charity, Robert and Siegfried both felt that there was nothing more for them to say to each other; and apart from a letter of congratulation which Graves sent to Sassoon on his marriage to Hester Gatty in December 1933, there was no further contact between them for more than twenty years.

Riding's general sense of irritation with Graves had now been significantly fuelled by her belief that *I, Claudius* would be a bestseller, and this had an unexpected and notable consequence. On 18 September 1933, Amy Graves wrote to her son John telling him that she had just been astonished to receive:

> a very nice letter from Laura Riding, admitting her former relationship with Robert to have been wrong, but all that has ended & Robert agrees that it was wrong. Now she wants to bring me & Robert together again, as she sees how much I love him. – I answered back in the same spirit & said that though I could not afford a trip to Deyá, yet my thoughts would be much happier now for her letter & I signed myself 'Yrs. gratefully & sincerely Amy Graves.' Robert's eyes have prevented his reading a word or writing for weeks. . . . He sent me his affectionate greetings but could not write himself. Please tell Clarissa, she will be so pleased about this change of heart in both.[283]

It was certainly a major change of attitude. Back in March, for example, when Rosaleen had tried to make the birth of her first child, Dan, the occasion for a reconciliation with Robert and Laura, the only response from Deyá had been a thoroughly hostile letter from Laura. Still earlier in the year, Robert had not even written to his daughter Jenny to congratulate her when, as a young actress of only fourteen, she received glowing notices for her appearance before a West End audience in Richard (Diccon) Hughes's play *A Comedy of Good and Evil*.

Clarissa was as pleased as Amy had guessed she would be; and, with her usual insight, she told John of her 'shrewd suspicion' of what this new attitude betokened. 'It probably means', she wrote, 'that Laura intends to leave him & that she is determined to see him reconciled to you before she goes in order to soften the blow. In her horoscope it was written some years ago that at about this period she would enter into new and fruitful alliances.'[284]

Two weeks later, there was 'a really affectionate letter' for Amy from Robert himself, in which he told her about *I, Claudius*, about his new glasses, and about his resolve to 'work . . . hard to make money for his children'.[285] The optimistic tone of this letter is surprising, in view of a recent disaster: on the night of 29 September, a tropical downpour had washed away the lower section of the road to the Cala, putting an end for the foreseeable future to any hope of recouping the vast sums which had already been lavished upon it. Robert did not even mention this disaster to his mother; and, a week later, he followed up his cheerful letter with a photograph on which he had signed himself 'Ever your loving son'. 'Wonders,' Amy wrote happily to John, 'Wonders will not cease!'[286]

Amy, at seventy-six, had become accustomed to the thought that she would never be reconciled with Robert in this life; and she was so excited by the friendly tone of his letters that, when John offered to take her on a cruise of the Greek islands the following summer, she replied as diplomatically as she could:

> What flashed through my mind was: Would you take me to Mallorca? We might spend a day or two with Robert, but chiefly at the village Inn, vine-covered & explore. As Robert & Laura are quite apart now & sorry for the past & want me to come I should simply love to go. Should you mind? The less we stay with them the better, as I know you would not want to, but it would be generous & kind to share your loving Mother with Robert for a few days, who is evidently hungry and thirsty for a little of the past.[287]

When John agreed to this plan, Amy wrote at once to Canelluñ, and was soon delighted to hear that Robert welcomed their proposed visit. The prospect was so pleasurable to both mother and son that it made their various anxieties easier to bear.[288]

CHAPTER 14
Visitors from England

The New Year of 1934 opened very cheerfully for Robert Graves and Laura Riding and their circle, with what Robert described as 'a lovely New Year's Party, what with gramophone, guitar, sherry, sandwiches and our best dresses. Jacob sang a rousing Russian song & I danced the Dance of the Seven Veils & George was a clown & Laura danced & danced & danced all night & is still alive and well.'[289] Dancing, when she was well enough, was Laura's only form of recreation. On many evenings she joined Robert to hold court in the less popular of the two village cafés; but her handsome and vigorous partner was pitied for being attached to someone who was 'practically an invalid';[290] and it was with Mary Burtonwood or one of his other friends that Graves went walking or swimming. Other diversions, as he told John Aldridge, now included 'deck-tennis played outside Ca'n Torrent [with] Jacob, Eirlys, Mary [and] George';[291] and on special occasions Robert would involve everyone in party games, some of which he remembered from his childhood, others of which he had invented. 'Shooting the Ensaimada', for example, involved pegging ten of these Mallorquin pastries onto a clothes-line slung between two trees, and shooting at them with bows and arrows which Robert himself had made especially for the game.

Early in the New Year the 'inner circle' (which Laura had begun to regard as a kind of embryo university) was enlarged by the addition of two more visitors from England: a couple of young freelance journalists named Honor Wyatt and Gordon Glover. Deciding that they were getting into a rut, and that they wished to travel a little before beginning a family, they had arrived in Deyá the previous October and, through an intermediary, they had been renting Ca'n Pa Bo from Laura Riding for six shillings a week ever since. Sometimes Honor and Gordon saw Robert and Laura in the café, and overheard bits and pieces of their conversation; but there was no formal contact between them until Gordon put his toe through one of the Ca'n Pa Bo sheets, which gave Honor an excuse for sending Laura a note of apology.

In return, Honor and Gordon were invited to tea at Canelluñ, where they were shown into Robert's library. It was immediately clear to both that they were being inspected; and a turning-point in the conversation came when Robert asked them: 'What's your philosophy?' 'I make do with my own,' replied Honor. This showed that they were people of independent thought, and from that moment the four of them became friends. Laura liked Gordon Glover, a skeletally thin and yet handsome man who carried off wearing pink linen trousers and a Mallorquin shirt with a pink-and-white check; but she seems to have been still more attracted to Honor Wyatt, a warm-hearted young woman who was not as tall as she, but who bubbled over with wit and good humour. Feeling that Riding's sympathetic interest in her was a great honour, Honor Wyatt came to 'love her and to admire her tremendously: I put her in the place of Christ when I was young, and behaved as I hoped she would like'.[292]

No such sentiments would ever animate the spirited old lady who lived in her draughty fastness on the road above Harlech, and who was even now preparing for her own visit to Majorca by teaching herself Spanish with the aid of a dictionary and an elementary school primer. But, by the beginning of March, bronchitis had led to heart-trouble, Amy was in bed, being dosed with digitalis and strychnine, and the prospect of her being fit enough for foreign travel seemed utterly remote. However, as the month progressed the digitalis was replaced on her doctor's orders by a small wine-glass of champagne after dinner; and on 4 April 1934, although she was still an invalid, Amy Graves began her journey southward by setting out with John for London. The doctor had not actually given his permission for her to travel; but he had thought it wisest not to oppose her; and, as Amy later recounted to some of her Harlech friends, it was she who finally 'decided to take the risk; though my good maid had tears in her eyes as we drove off. I fancy she thought I might not live to come back, and I thought the same, but I wanted to see my son Robert, who lives in Majorca, and one can but die anywhere.'[293] After breaking their journey for a few days at Barcelona, the travellers took the night ferry to Palma, where they arrived at 7 a.m. on the morning of 10 April. Soon after they had berthed, John saw Robert and Laura among the crowd waiting on the quayside. His critical eye noted that Robert had 'a dirty brown hat pulled over his eyes and a green Burberry'. that he had grown long side-whiskers, and that his face looked dirty, while Laura by contrast sported 'a white hat & coat ... & looked remarkably well'.[294] When Amy came up on deck a few minutes later, her maternal gaze noticed principally that Robert 'looked sad and had some grey in his black curls'.[295] John, watching from a slight distance, saw that when Amy first appeared Robert's face 'quite lit up & he waved & kissed his hands while Laura also waved, but with the palm of her left hand – an eerie movement'.[296]

Breakfast followed on shore at the Alhambra. Robert and John had already agreed to avoid 'debatable points';[297] and John appreciated the way in which Laura 'made great efforts to be friendly', though he felt perhaps a little unkindly that they came from the head rather than the heart. Later in the morning, after Robert and Laura had done some shopping, they were all driven to Canelluñ, where Laura took Amy up to her room to unpack; and that afternoon Robert and Amy went for a walk together while John relaxed in the grotto, 'a scooped-out, sheltered garden at the north end of the property', which was entered down steps through the rock.[298]

Here John began reading *14*(A), which had recently been published by Arthur Barker; and he found it as unsatisfactory as most of the critics had done. Even Robert's friend Tom Matthews had written at some length about the novel's evident weaknesses. At one time this would have meant immediate ostracism; but although Robert still respected and admired Laura, and showed his devotion to her in all kinds of ways (for example, giving her breakfast in bed each day, rolling her cigarettes, and doing all the shopping and all the fetching and carrying), he was no longer passionately in love with her, and he contented himself with an indulgent reprimand. 'You say in so many words', he wrote to Matthews,

> that Laura has no dramatic sense, that she can't write, and that she has failed to convey any clear impression of characters or events. When you reached this conclusion I wonder you didn't reach the secondary conclusion that school-children do when in an arithetic problem they get the answer '$5\frac{1}{2}$ sheep and $4\frac{3}{4}$ cows grazing in the field' – namely that something is wrong with their reasoning.[299]

The opinion of the general public about *14A* was hardly to be tested: a friend of Norah McGuinness's drew her attention to 'an easily recognisable portrait of me – and an incident suggesting I was a thief. I sued [Laura Riding] for libel. The book was withdrawn.'[300]

Graves was still playing down the significance of his own forthcoming novel, whose publication had mistakenly been postponed 'on the chance of its being made a Book Society choice'.[301] In March, Robert had told his brother John that 'There's no saying about *I, Claudius*. It's not an inspiring, accurate or important book but A.B. ought to be able to sell it. It would have been a Book of the Month, I think, if I hadn't an enemy on the committee – Blunden.'[302] And now, when there was a discussion one evening about writing,

> Robert said that Laura's work was much finer than his – it had a permanent value, while his was only forming. Laura did not deny this, but said: 'Of course we are engaged on different work' – as much as to say that Robert was not really in her class. When she was not there, Robert said that her work had first attracted him, and that she was the only poet who had reached all the historical levels – whatever that means. I [John] said: 'Do you mean that she is greater than Homer, Dante, Virgil, and Sophocles?'

But Robert somehow managed to side-track this awkward question, 'saying that wasn't the point, but that she brought something new and permanent that had not been there before'.[303]

During the early part of their stay at Canelluñ, Amy and John were gradually introduced to the inner circle. On their very first afternoon they went into the village where they met Gordon Glover, 'a tall, thin, stammering Englishman, with honest brown eyes and a sincere way of speaking'; and his 'buxom, cheerful wife, Honor', together with Glover's father, 'a fine, big man, with good brown eyes who looks like an actor'. Then after dinner they were visited by Eirlys Roberts, described by John Graves as 'a tall, well-made girl in glasses.... With her came a short, black-bearded man of 26, Jacob Bronowski, who cannot pronounce his "R"s.... They form part of the "group" and are used as collaborators and proof-readers.'[304] Currently, John learned, Laura was writing 'a book about Woman' with Eirlys Roberts, and 'a dictionary' with Jacob Bronowski;[305] but the two of them also wrote independently,

> though Laura looks through all their work. The 'group' form Laura's idea of a University. They meet from time to time to discuss some subject or other, with Laura in the chair. She said one day that it would be very good discipline for me to attend – implying that I talked off the point. Heaven preserve me![306]

On the following day, 11 April, John and Amy met Mary Burtonwood for the first time, when she came to tea, pushing her son Anthony[307] in a pram. Behind her trailed George Ellidge, 'a small man with a small, well-shaped head, a pipe, an old khaki-coloured coat, & white, baggy trousers with a thin blue stripe. He wears an old pair of sandals, [and] seems friendly but highly strung. . . .' Mary herself was described as 'tall, with brown, reddish hair done in coils over her ears. She has a fine forehead, fine eyes & nose – but her face trails off into a large, disconsolate mouth, with a large number of large, clean, but irregular teeth. She speaks quite well, but without parting her teeth. . . .'[308] The most recent addition to the group, twenty-two-year-old Karl Goldschmidt, arrived on 12 April with a beautiful bunch of pink geraniums for Laura.

It was Robert who had first met Karl one afternoon the previous August, when, walking past Gelat's house in the village, he had stopped to explain to an angry young man, who was denouncing Gelat's bus service, that it was pointless waiting for the next bus to Palma: it would not leave until the following morning! But it was Honor and Gordon who had first talked to Karl at any length. Early in 1934, hearing about a beautiful house in Lluch Alcari, a hamlet above the sea about a mile to the north of Deyá, they had walked over to look for it; and, when they knocked on the door of one of the Lluch Alcari houses, it was opened by a very frightened-looking young man, behind whom stood a most beautiful girl with golden hair. The man was Karl, a graphic artist and a highly sensitive and highly intelligent Jew who had fled from Hitler's Germany in order to continue his liaison with an Aryan girl.

When, some weeks later, the girl deserted him for a German painter, Karl went to live in Palma, hoping to make his living as a graphic artist; but this was impossible as he had no labour permit, and he thought gloomily that when his money ran out he might as well commit suicide. However, by this time he had been befriended by other members of Robert and Laura's inner circle, including Jacob Bronowski, who spoke German and sympathized with his plight; and he began to be invited to Canelluñ for weekends. During these visits Robert and Laura struck up a friendship with Karl, which was to be of immense importance to all three of them for the next five years; and then to Robert and Karl alone for a further quarter of a century after that.

The combination of such stimulating company, of dry sunny weather, and of a complete absence of domestic worries was now improving Amy's health from day to day. Above all, these days saw the healing of the terrible wound which she had suffered when Robert withdrew his love from her. On the very first evening at Canelluñ he had expressly told Amy how much her visit meant to him; and for part of each day thereafter, while she sat and read in a shady spot at the edge of the piazza, Robert would 'bring any work he was at, such as preparing vegetables, so as to be near me'.[309] One afternoon Robert took Amy and John on an expedition to the little harbour at Sóller, some miles to the north; and one evening, when Eirlys and Jacob came in for a game of bridge, Amy surprised them by persuading Robert to play; but the highlight of Amy's and John's visit probably came on 17 April, two days before their departure, when it was decided to have a grand picnic.

Laura, 'pleading the fear of fatigue', stayed behind at Canelluñ; and Jacob and George also remained in the village, saying that they intended 'to play chess and work'.[310] But Robert, Amy, John, Eirlys and Mary (who was carrying her son Anthony) crowded into a car driven by Gelat's son, and set off down the new road to the Cala. It was from the point where it began to run alongside the Torrente that all the surface of the road had been washed away, and in places most of the foundations had gone as well: so that the picnickers had to leave their car and make their way carefully along a rocky path towards the sea.

Robert and Eirlys went swimming while the others talked; and later, when Gordon and Honor had arrived, the food which each person had brought was added to the communal spread, and they all settled down to an unusual but delicious feast of bread, butter, lettuce, radishes, dried figs, bully beef, biscuits, cabbage, raisin pies, omelet sandwiches, oranges, bananas, wine and lemonade.

As they lay back contentedly after their meal, their heads protected from the blazing sun by large straw sun-hats, there was a moment when it seemed that the happiness of the occasion might be destroyed, as Amy suddenly began putting pressure on Robert to do as she wished: displaying in minia-ture the very kind of social tyranny which he had come to Majorca to escape. First she wanted him to read out one of his poems from a volume which she had persuaded him to bring; but he resisted by saying that 'he could find nothing suitable'. Then she suggested a recitation; but 'he said he knew almost nothing. "Not even of your own?" she asked. "No!" he replied.'[311]

An instant later, however, and Robert had relented. After all, he must have reflected, he had already fought and won all the essential battles. Why not allow a minor victory to this frail old lady who loved him so much that she had risked her life to come and visit him? It would cost him very little, and would give her a great deal of pleasure. So he admitted to knowing 'some amusing verses and said he would sing them if John [who had brought a guitar down to the beach] would accompany him'. John, as requested, struck a chord; and there was an almost magical change in the atmosphere.[312]

John had already been asked by Robert to translate one of Claudius's edicts into English for use in a sequel to *I, Claudius*; and that evening John was allowed to read what his brother had so far written of *Claudius the God*, 'leaving him in Britain, preparing to fight a conclusive battle [at Brentwood], aided by camels, a thunder and lightning apparatus, Indian elephants, Moors, and trip-wire to upset the British chariots under Caractacus'.[313] The following morning Robert and John talked at length about how the battle might develop; and John promised that on his return to England he would seek out large-scale maps of the Brentwood area so that Robert could make his account as geographically plausible as possible.

On 19 April, the day of their departure from Canellun, Amy and John 'talked all the way to Palma about Robert and Laura'. Laura herself had made a series of indelible impressions upon them. They recalled her striking Mallorquin skirts, above which she habitually wore light-coloured blouses surmounted by a tight bodice; the haze of cigarette smoke in which she worked; the way she had of dominating a group simply by settling back in her chair and staring intently at whoever was speaking; the ring she wore on her left hand, with its 'enormous, irregular pale sapphire ... all the more noticeable,' John recorded, 'as she uses a pointed forefinger frequently in conversation, wagging it at someone in mild reproof, or to emphasise a point'; and her way of talking: on the whole very clearly, and sounding her final t's and d's with particular precision; but at times she had 'a lisping way of speaking', she said 'blee-oo' when she meant 'blue', and put an accent on the second syllable of Ro*bert* that sounded very odd to Amy and John.[314]

But what of Robert and Laura's value to each other? That seemed difficult to assess. Financially it seemed likely that Robert's contributions to the household would always be larger than Laura's; and yet it was evident both that she worked very hard and that she provided the environment in which Robert had done much of his best writing. Most important, perhaps, as John noted, was the fact that 'They both read over everything the other writes, and Robert has always needed someone like that.'[315]

Other observers describe the links between Graves and Riding in a manner which shows that they were considerably less strong than they had been a year or two earlier. Graves still felt that there was 'something holy' about Riding;[316] but Eirlys Roberts, for example, says that although Graves 'superficially ... did all that [Riding] wanted', he 'never lost his own personality', but 'lived as he wanted in his head and in his writings';[317] while Mary Ellidge believed that he 'respected' Riding and 'thought that she was good for his writing', but had long ago 'stopped *loving* her'.[318]

The difference had its inevitable effect upon Graves's poetry, whose force depended to a large extent upon the quality of his relationship with the woman with whom he was currently in love. For several years he was to produce little that was memorable, and many of his verses read as though they were written to a formula rather than the product of genuine inspiration. The total dedication of a poem like 'To Whom Else' has been replaced with hollow protestations of 'A POEM-SEQUENCE to the Sovereign Muse',[319] in which Graves declares:

> You in woman's beauty
> I shall love till I die
> As living green, earthily
> The immortal sky.

And, before long, Graves's enormous success with *I, Claudius* and *Claudius the God* had the joint effect of considerably increasing Riding's financial dependence upon Graves, while considerably widening the emotional gap which had opened between them.

CHAPTER 15

Publication of the Claudius Novels

When in May 1934 Robert Graves's *I, Claudius* was published by Arthur Barker, it was immediately recognized as an outstanding achievement. When writing to his brother John to thank him for some research for *Claudius the God*, Robert added that:

> Claudius has had a practically unanimous good press: I don't know yet about sales, though. Only two critics have ventured to question me on points of scholarship: neither however knows his stuff so I have been able to stamp on them. E.g. one said that Dares was a mediaeval invention: he wasn't. His *Iliad* was extant during the third century B.C. to the first A.D and accepted as genuine by the best critics.[320]

The arrival of so many excellent reviews at the village post office in Deyá infuriated Laura, and was therefore something of an embarrassment to Robert. After glancing rapidly over his latest batch of press-cuttings in the café, he would stuff them hastily into a pocket, remarking that they were 'a lot of nonsense'. Laura, when asked on one of these occasions whether she would consider writing an historical novel herself, replied with barely concealed rage that she 'didn't think she could sink so low'.[321]

I, Claudius could only be mentioned in Riding's presence in a scornful tone of voice; and so it was all right when Graves and his friends arranged an informal entertainment at a little theatre which they had created in the grotto, and George Ellidge appeared in a kind of toga as 'Claudius – the choice of the Emperor of the Month Society'. George also appeared with his wife Mary as one of the 'Canny Loons' – the others were Gordon Glover and Honor Wyatt; but there was little remaining sympathy between George and Mary, who made a dramatic solo appearance singing Marlene Dietrich's 'Falling in Love Again', while seductively peeling off clothes to reveal transparent, pale-green silk camiknickers.

Eirlys Roberts, watching Mary with Gordon Glover, could not help but assume that the two of them would soon run away together;[322] while Honor Wyatt wondered whether Mary Ellidge, with Riding's connivance, was in the middle of a passionate affair with Graves.[323] Laura Riding may have been prepared to pardon any 'brutal lapses'[324] as she called them (if indeed they occurred) provided that he remained under her control in other ways. She liked, for example, to mention that she had woken up one day and told him (at a time when they were out of season) that she 'must have the taste of strawberries'. Robert had had to spend hours mixing up peaches, vanilla and other ingredients until at last the taste was pronounced to be satisfactory; and Laura recounted the story 'in a slightly boastful manner, in which the sentiment "Wasn't he sweet?" was far outweighed by the unspoken declaration: "Look what power I have!"' Certainly there was a memorable occasion on which Riding pointedly declared that she was opposed to sexual intercourse as a matter of principle, and Mary Ellidge boldly commented: 'But we're doing it all the time!' Riding then made it clear that despite her views she did not think that who was sleeping with whom was a matter of great significance.[325]

Mary herself, asked many years later about her relationship with Robert Graves, wrote very movingly that:

> my two years working with Robert on the Claudius books were the happiest years of my life. I was 26 when we met & he 38. He became something of a father figure to me – my own father died when I was 9. The first time he kissed me I said 'I have waited a long time for that'.[326]
> Yes, I loved him.[327]

Graves was happier and livelier than he had been since the summer of 1931: his letters reflect his more cheerful frame of mind; and one day he even arranged a 'Canelluñ sports day', which, in his own words,

> included a contest for making coffee in the open, tramp-fashion, with no implements but coffee beans and one empty tomato tin. It was very funny and all the results were undrinkable. Also we had shooting the ensaimada (suger bun) with bow & arrow. It was clothes-pegged to a line. Nobody could hit it. So I showed them how (I was a judge) and twang! pierced it to the heart at the first pull. Pure faith.[328]

During the summer of 1934, there were occasional fresh recruits to the inner circle: some of them quite unexpected. For example there were the Ward Hutchinsons. He was an American photographer, and Laura Riding had always despised photography. But when they met at the café the Ward Hutchinsons 'made a fuss of Laura'. The result was that Riding declared that photography *in the right hands* could be thoroughly respectable,[329] and Ward was invited to write an article on photography for the *Critical Vulgate* – for which, incidentally, there was still no publisher, Arthur Barker having finally washed his hands of the project.

However, the continuing success of *I, Claudius* placed fresh strains not only upon the relationship between Graves and Riding, but also upon the relationship between Riding and the inner circle centred upon Canelluñ. The sales figures had been highly satisfactory both in England and in America, where it was published in June 1934 by Harrison Smith. August saw the completion of *Claudius the God*, which Arthur Barker published only three months later; and that too (though a much patchier work than *I, Claudius*) was both a critical and a commercial success.

As the disparity between Riding's actual achievements and her position of authority at Canelluñ became more and more evident in the light of Graves's success, a number of the group, including Jacob Bronowski, Eirlys Roberts and George and Mary Ellidge began talking critically about Laura when they met for private conversations in the village. Bronowski, or 'Bruno' as he was usually called, had never been afraid to take a different point of view from Laura Riding, much as he admired her intellect; and, by the end of the summer, he had begun to feel that the demands which she made upon him could not be reconciled with his maintaining any kind of intellectual integrity. Besides, he felt that it was time for both him and Eirlys to begin proper careers; and in September 1934, when it became clear that Riding was unhappy to let him go, Bronowski reluctantly decided that the only way to effect his escape was to pick a quarrel with her. The ensuing row is said to have been a memorable one, in which Riding denounced Bronowski as a bad character, and he retaliated by telling her that she herself 'was no lily-white angel'.[330] Within hours Jacob and Eirlys were on their way: he to become a lecturer in mathematics at Hull University, and she to teach classics at a mixed grammar-school. For both Jacob Bronowski and Eirlys Roberts the brief association with Laura Riding had been a formative one. It led them totally to reject the kind of elitism which she represented: so it is not altogether surprising that, in later years, Roberts became well known as the moving force behind the Consumer's Association, which aimed to protect ordinary people from exploitation by big business; while Bronowski achieved fame for his ability to communicate scientific truths to the layman; and in his much acclaimed television series, *The Ascent of Man*, there is a highly autobiographical passage in which he talks

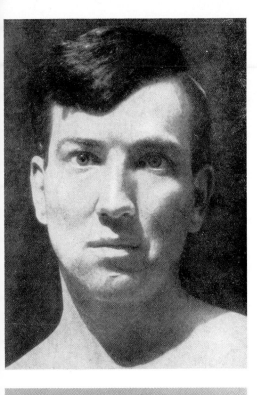

ABOVE LEFT Robert Graves in 1929 as he appeared in the frontispiece of *Good-bye to All That*.

ABOVE RIGHT Laura Riding, Robert's lover, in 1928 or 1929, when T. E. Lawrence found her as glamorous as a movie star and decided that, given the opportunity, she had all the qualifications for an imperial role in real life.

LEFT Nancy Nicholson, Robert's wife, in the mid-1920s.

ABOVE LEFT Alfred Perceval Graves, Robert's father.

ABOVE RIGHT Amy Graves, Robert's mother.

LEFT Rosaleen Graves, Robert's sister, in the 1920s when she was training as a doctor at Charing Cross Hospital in London.

ABOVE RIGHT Geoffrey Phibbs drawn by Nancy's father, William Nicholson.

BELOW RIGHT Nancy Nicholson, Robert's wife, on the *Avoca* in 1929 with their children, Catherine, Sam, Jenny and David.

Laura Riding when she was living with Robert in Majorca during the 1930s.

Alice in the Grotto painted by John Aldridge.

Robert Graves, accompanied by a peasant and a donkey, bringing up stones from the beach in 1934.

Gelat (with Robert's dog Solomon), Gordon Glover, Laura Riding, Honor Wyatt, Mary Phillips, Karl Goldschmidt and Robert Graves in Deyá.

Canelluñ in 1934, photographed by Robert's brother John. Laura and Robert are both faintly visible in the doorway.

ABOVE A picnic at Cala on Sunday 17 April
1934, photographed by John Graves. (*From
left to right*) Honor Wyatt, Gordon Glover,
Mary Ellidge, Robert Graves, Eirlys Roberts
and Amy Graves.

RIGHT Robert Graves rock climbing above
the Cala, Deyá in April 1934, photographed
by John Graves.

LEFT Robert Graves, Karl Goldschmidt and Laura Riding in Deyá in the 1930s.

BELOW Juan Marroig [Gelat] and his wife, known as the Medora, with their grandson.

LEFT This powerful portrait of Laura Riding was painted by her friend, confidant and collaborator John Aldridge, with whom, it was rumoured, she was in love.

BELOW John Aldridge, Robert and Laura's friend, in his studio.

ABOVE LEFT Karl Goldschmidt, Robert and Laura's secretary, with Robert's dog Solomon.

ABOVE RIGHT Francisca, the village girl befriended by Laura.

LEFT Maisie Somerville the broadcaster, a friend of Robert's from the 1920s, who came out to visit Robert and Laura in Deyá and saw much of them on their return to England in 1936.

RIGHT A photograph of Robert Graves inscribed on the back, 'with best love from Robert, Feb. 1936'.

BELOW Jenny Nicholson, Robert's daughter, in 1936, when she was dancing in Cochran's revue, *Follow the Sun*.

LEFT Clarissa Graves, Robert's sister, in the 1920s when she was in charge of children's broadcasting in Palestine.

BELOW Robert's friend, Alan Hodge, with Beryl Pritchard to whom Alan was briefly married, but who later became Robert's wife.

Harry Kemp, the young poet, who from 1936–9 was one of Robert and Laura's closest associates.

Tom Matthews of *Time* magazine, who stayed in Deyá in 1932. He contributed to *Epilogue*, and welcomed Robert and Laura to America in 1939.

Robert Graves

Robert Graves at his desk after the break with Laura.

about the dangers of becoming caught up in an intellectually arrogant view of the universe.

Not long after Graves and Riding had broken with Bronowski – a break which, according to Riding, left them both feeling 'worn out and full of tears', there was an equally decisive and still more painful break with Mary Burtonwood and George Ellidge. In this case there was no open quarrel; but two Americans[331] came to Canelluñ with a detailed account of the predominantly anti-Riding conversations in which Mary, George and others had apparently been indulging at the café. As Riding reported in one of the two bitterly unhappy letters which she subsequently wrote to John Aldridge, it seemed that there had been talk about members of the inner circle not daring to take a different point of view from hers, because she could never be wrong, Indeed they thought she considered herself the Supreme Being. Apparently they had described her as a person of no importance, who brutally dominated Robert. They had also said that she always wanted to control others, except where sex was involved, and then she liked to be controlled. They believed she was strongly attracted both to Gelat and to John Aldridge himself, and felt that Robert's dedication to Laura made him worthy of contempt, since he could only stay with her in return for constant and constantly desired flattery.[332]

There is an obvious element in this description of the kind of short-hand or caricature in which people indulge when gossiping, but it was too close to the truth not to hurt most painfully. In her second letter to John Aldridge, Laura told him how difficult it was to forget that Mary, George and others whom she had once thought of as close friends should have discussed her so unkindly.[333] And although it was a relief for her to tell John what had happened (in letters at least partially calculated to arouse his sympathy or even his sexual interest in her), Laura could not bring herself directly to confront Mary and George with what she had heard.

There was another element in all this: Riding, who appears to have imagined that George Ellidge was securely under her control, heard stories that he had been involved in a sexual liaison with an American woman, and did not really believe him when he denied it. This incident may have aroused Laura's jealousy over Robert's relationship with Mary; and it is more than likely that when Riding heard about the stories which had been circulating about her, she embellished their anti-Graves aspects (talking for example of vicious remarks about Robert's sexual behaviour), so as to drive a wedge between Robert and Mary. This would have been another reason for avoiding the kind of direct confrontation in which these embellishments might have been exposed for what they were. In any case, with

Robert now feeling doubly betrayed, both on her behalf and on his own, Laura persuaded him to join with her in telling Mary that they could no longer afford her services as a typist, but that they were prepared to pay for her and George to return to England.

When this offer was accepted, Graves and Riding suddenly felt too unhappy to remain in Deyá (or so Riding said), and left for a night at the Alhambra in Palma. While Laura sat in their hotel room writing to John Aldridge about what had just occurred, Robert went out to arrange about Mary and George's boat; and then he wandered round the shops, indulging himself in one of his favourite pursuits: hunting round for small objects of interest, usually antique or classical in origin, and often associated with his current work, with which he decorated his study at Canelluñ. Robert also bought a ring for Laura, which she received with unusual pleasure.[334]

CHAPTER 16
Prosperity and Burning Coaches

Robert Graves was now working on a new novel, *Antigua, Penny, Puce* which (as he explained in the diary which he began to keep in February 1935) he had started chiefly 'as a means of extracting higher royalties from Harrison Smith [his American publisher] for *Claudius the God*'.[335] By the last week of February, Graves reckoned that he had written about a third of *Antigua, Penny, Puce*; and he had also outlined the remainder of the plot. Since he was no longer in any great need of money, he was seriously wondering whether to abandon the novel. He had already described it in a letter to John as 'a silly story which may come to nothing';[336] and at the beginning of April, having taken a completed draft of the sixth chapter to be typed by Karl Goldschmidt – who was now living in Deyá and doing secretarial work for him and Laura – he laid the novel to one side.

Superficially, at least, life had become far more relaxed both for Graves and for Riding; but there seems to have been no attempt to reserve for future use any of the royalty money which was now flooding in to Canelluñ. On the contrary, it was poured out again almost as fast as it poured in. Much of it was well spent: for example, during the course of 1935, Robert sent Nancy several considerable sums of money both as his current contribution towards their children's upkeep, and to make up for two years of non-payment. No longer did Robert have to cook all the meals and do much of the housework: besides Sebastian, the eighty-year-old gardener, they could now afford a resident maid called Isabel, and were soon to employ Isabel's sister Josefa as well, 'to help her, and do the washing'. The gardens at Canelluñ were improved with a great number of shrubs and trees, including mimosa, tamarisk, oleanders and nectarines; and Graves also bought The Posada, a beautiful but somewhat dilapidated old house at the back of the church, which they wished to become 'a permanent guest-house for Canelluñ'.[337] Their purchase was complicated for some weeks by the fact that the village priest, from whose house there was a way through to the church *via* The Posada, refused to allow this to be closed up. At one time it looked as though court action would be necessary to dislodge him; but Gelat had the idea of interviewing his bishop; after which the ecclesiastical authorities, scenting a scandal, applied the necessary pressure. The Cura withdrew; and by mid-July, after extensive alterations and repairs, The Posada had been transformed into a fine property.[338]

However, Riding needed a constant stream of money to finance her various projects; and not even the substantial *Claudius* royalties could possibly satisfy her needs for long. Graves had been forced by her to break with Arthur Barker over his refusal to publish *The Critical Vulgate*, now renamed *Epilogue*; but no other publisher could be found who would accept *Epilogue* on normal terms; and at last, in what amounted to a massive exercise in 'vanity publishing', Graves paid the firm of Constable a large sum of money, in return for which it was agreed that *Epilogue* should appear under the joint Seizin Press/Constable imprint, and that Constable would handle its distribution.

At the end of 1934, Graves had sold the film rights for *I, Claudius* to Alexander Korda; and for much of the spring and early summer of 1935 he was busy with the comparatively tedious task of preparing *The Fool of Rome*,[339] a heavily condensed version of his Roman epic which could later be sold as the book of Korda's film. In the meantime, the seal of critical acclaim was set upon Graves's original *I, Claudius* and *Claudius the God* when he was awarded two major literary prizes: the James Tait Black Memorial and the Hawthornden. This must have infuriated Riding who, having declared that she would never stoop so low as to write an historical novel, had recently decided to show her literary partner how it should be done by producing a 'proper' historical novel about the siege of Troy.[340]

Graves (who had to tell family and friends that he was pleased with his literary prizes, but was *not* to be congratulated on them),[341] had already spent some time thinking about his recent successes, and two poems in particular stem from his reflections. In the first, 'The Devil's Advice to Storytellers', he somewhat ironically advises would-be novelists not to keep probability too closely in view, but to:

> Do conscientiously what liars do –
> Born liars, not the lesser sort that raid
> The mouths of others for their stock-in-trade:
> Assemble, first, all casual bits and scraps
> That may shake down into a world perhaps;
> People this world, by chance created so,

With random persons whom you do not know ...
Let the erratic course they steer surprise
Their own and your own and your reader's eyes;
Sigh then, or frown, but leave (as in despair)
Motive and end and moral in the air;
Nice contradiction between fact and fact
Will make the whole read human and exact.[342]

'To Bring the Dead to Life'[343] is a more deeply felt poem, in which Graves answers in a most sinister fashion one of the more uncomfortable questions at the back of a novelist's or biographer's mind. While writing about someone else's life, to what extent can he be said to be living his own?

> To bring the dead to life
> Is no great magic.
> Few are wholly dead:
> Blow on a dead man's embers
> And a live flame will start.
>
> Let his forgotten griefs be now,
> And now his withered hopes;
> Subdue your pen to his handwriting
> Until it prove as natural
> To sign his name as yours.
>
> Limp as he limped,
> Swear by the oaths he swore;
> If he wore black, affect the same;
> If he had gouty fingers,
> Be yours gouty too.
>
> Assemble tokens intimate of him –
> A ring, a hood, a chair:
> Around these elements then build
> A home familiar to
> The greedy revenant.
>
> So grant him life, but reckon
> That the grave which housed him
> May not be empty now:

You in his spotty garments
Shall yourself lie wrapped,

These were among several poems which (with only two emendations) passed
Laura's inspection one day early in March: for Graves still depended upon
Riding's critical surveillance of his work – or, as Amy expressed it 'How
humble Laura keeps him. He believes in her still.'[344] But his relationship
with her remained profoundly unsatisfactory, and from far beneath the
surface of Robert's mind disturbing images continually bubbled up.

On 8 March, for instance, when both he and Laura were suffering from
influenza, Robert 'thought of Lewis Carroll's way of converting one word
into another by overlapping words', and tried changing 'Graves' into 'Riding' in this manner. The resultant whole word read as follows:

GRAVESTIGERMANEATERRIBLEARIDING

from which one can pick out GRAVES, VESTIGE, GERMANE, MANEATER,
TERRIBLE, BLEAR, ARID, RIDING; and the words TIGER, ATE and RIB
also stand out clearly. Graves's converse experiment ran:

RIDINGRATEDENGRAVES

from which there emerges a similarly powerful set of words:
RIDING, INGRATE, GRATED, EDEN, ENGRAVES, GRAVES. [345]

Dreams conveyed further messages both about Robert's current difficulties and about the ultimate hopelessness of his situation. In one sequence,
on the night of 25–26 March, it seemed to him that he had been given
the task of:

> saving people from a burning house, a very tall building in the process
> of construction in the middle of a university or public school: somewhat
> Charterhouse. 100 prisoners and 120 workmen in danger. Had to go
> and get a ladder: leaving my lieutenant in charge with fire brigade of
> 20. Could get no outside cooperation, ladder too short too heavy to move
> & one leg broken off. . . . When finally got it to building it was collapsing.
> I dodged falling bits of roof. My lieutenant, a mixture of a 2nd lieutenant
> I knew in Wales in the war, and Karl, had done his best. Only eleven
> dead bodies. . . .[346]

Three nights later Robert had what he described as 'Another fire-dream.

This time I was a subordinate set a futile task by stupid superiors. I was in the front compartment of a train going 70 miles an hour. The fire was in the rear coaches but the authorities wouldn't stop the train.'[347]

Those coaches were to go on burning at the back of Graves's mind for another four and a half years before the crash came; but then his injuries were mental, and he survived them. By contrast his old friend T.E.Shaw, recently retired from the Royal Air Force, was very shortly to receive serious physical injuries in a motor-cycling accident; and when the news reached Deyá on the morning of 14 May 1935, it was reported that the great Lawrence of Arabia was almost certainly lying on his death-bed.

CHAPTER 17
The Death of a Hero

Many of Robert Graves's friendships had been injured by his association with Laura Riding: even that with T.E.Lawrence, who had remained loyal to Robert when other friends fell away in the late 1920s and early 1930s. The problem was, Lawrence felt that Riding's work was not merely obscure, but of secondary importance to Graves's; and he made the mistake, during 1934, of allowing Graves to become aware of his feelings. This led to a break in their correspondence; and when after some months had passed they independently began writing to each other again in January 1935, Graves could not forget what had occurred, and was soon taking Lawrence to task for the 'error' of having written as though Laura were:

> a sort of intellectual freak and worse than that, of Laura having no status of her own but as being some sort of appendage of mine.... Granted you and I are very old friends, and that you have not been able so far to see Laura more than occasionally and as a friend of mine, and you have not felt capable of the concentration that reading her more concentrated work demands, you should not have made such a graceless error; which I feel very much more strongly than Laura who merely dismisses from her mind people who attempt to treat her as you have done....[348]

However, Graves had been upset to learn that, on T.E.'s retirement from the RAF at the end of February 1935, his income would fall dramatically to around twenty shillings a week; and in an effort to repay his old friend for some of his past kindnesses, Graves generously offered to 'bring your income back to £2.2/– for a year or so: may I? I could find the money in March when I begin to cash in on *Claudius*.' And since Graves had recently been asked by *The Times* to write an obituary of T.E. for their files, he added: 'Would you like to earn a few pounds by writing your own obituary? No-one need know. 2000 words.'[349]

T.E. politely declined Robert's offer of financial support, saying that it was 'needless. I can easily make that. Easier still I could make ten times that; it's the stopping short that is skilful. I blame not circumstances but my own bad calculating.' As for his relationship with Laura, he declared diplomatically that there were no faults on either side, 'but common sense, the recognition of a difficulty too arduous to be worth the effort of surmounting, when there are so many other more rewarding activities within reach'. On the question of the obituary, or 'epitaph' as he called it, T.E. wrote at greater length. He made it clear that he had no intention of writing it himself, and that if it was to be written, then,: 'Rather you than Liddell Hart' (the military historian who, in 1934, had published *T.E.Lawrence: In Arabia and After*) 'who seems to have no critical sense in my regard.'[350]

T.E. also gave Robert an outline of what he would like to be written about himself. He begged him, for example, not to attach too much importance to:

> what I did in Arabia during the war. I feel that the Middle Eastern settlement put through by Winston Churchill and Young and me in 1921...should weigh more than fighting. And I feel too that this settlement should weigh less than my life since 1922, for the conquest of the last element, the air, seems to me the only major task of our generation; and I have convinced myself that progress to-day is made not by the single genius, but by the common effort....

'That for eight years', T.E. concluded; 'and now for the last four I have been so curiously fortunate as to share in a little revolution we have made in boat design', of which he gave some interesting details.[351] Graves still had this letter to hand three months later, when news came of T.E.'s accident.

It had happened on the morning of 13 May, when T.E. was returning on his motor-bike from Bovington Camp to Clouds Hill, the lovely Dorset cottage to which he had retired. Very much upset by leaving the RAF and suffering at times from a premonition that his life's work was over, T.E. was nevertheless making plans to fulfil his undergraduate ambition of setting up a printing press; and to close friends he talked seriously about preparing himself for an important role in what he had come to believe was an inevitable conflict with Hitler's Germany.[352]

But, when riding at speed over a crest of the narrow road, probably with a car approaching him on the off-side, T.E. suddenly came up behind two boys on bicycles. Braking sharply, he changed down into second gear, and tried to swerve out of the way. Too late to avoid colliding with one of the bicycles – fortunately the boy was thrown clear and escaped serious injury – T.E. had crashed into the road, fractured his skull and immediately lost consciousness. Taken to the army hospital at Bovington Camp, he clung to life for a few days, while newspapers throughout the western world reminded their readers of the daring wartime exploits of Lawrence of Arabia, the man whom they called the uncrowned King of the East; and radio news bulletins carried regular reports about his physical condition, as though he were indeed some dying potentate.

Robert Graves, asked by one of the London news agencies for an article on Lawrence, accepted their offer, and worked through the night of 14–15 May writing an obituary based largely upon extracts from T.E.'s February letter. Two days later, having received a wire from Eddie Marsh with the news that there was 'Almost no hope', and that T.E. was 'sinking', Graves posted what he had written to his agent Pinker, telling him that it must only be used in the event of T.E.'s death.[353]

T.E. held on for a further two days, and then died without every having regained consciousness. King George V sent a personal telegram of condolences to the Lawrence family; and Winston Churchill wrote sadly of his own hope, now thwarted, that T.E. should 'quit his retirement and take a leading part in facing the dangers which now threaten the country'.[354] A number of books about T.E. were republished, including Graves's *Lawrence and the Arabs*; and Graves's obituary notice rapidly became a bestseller. After appearing in the *Evening Standard*, on 20 May, under the slightly misleading heading 'Myself, by Lawrence', it had soon been sold to so many other English and American papers that within a few weeks it had earned Graves almost £200. Unfortunately he had used quotations from T.E.'s letters without clearing the copyright, and it was some time before he was able to settle the consequent dispute with the Lawrence estate; but from the original appearance of his article in the *Standard* came first a correspondence with Basil Liddell-Hart, then a friendship, and finally a collaboration.

Both Graves and Liddell-Hart had some reservations about Lawrence, but both of them had found him one of the most remarkable men whom they had ever met; and at one point Graves was even comparing him in some respects with Jesus Christ: 'No room for the whole thing here,' he wrote to Liddell-Hart,

but anyhow the Devil was (you agree) constantly leading T.E. up to an exceeding high place and showing him all the kingdoms of the earth, etc., and they both had the same proud humility, and logical–witty mastery of evasion, and *both had mothers*, and both tried to manage without women (with as little offence to women as possible) and both had fanatic disciples, and both were profoundly mistrustful of themselves, and both believed in being all things to all men, and after both their deaths it is impossible to rise at a dinner to mention them in any but hushed awed tones, for fear of blaspheming.[355]

The high esteem in which Lawrence was held not only by Graves but by so many who had known him, from the most humble aircraftman to men of the stature of Winston Churchill or George Bernard Shaw, is a remarkable tribute to the way in which Lawrence acted throughout his adult life as an enabler, inspiring others with a vision of what they might achieve. Lawrence had certainly helped to sustain Graves's belief in himself during the early 1920s when his reputation as a poet was ebbing away; and he had also helped him financially out of more than one crisis. More important, for the longer term, was the way in which Lawrence had inspired Graves with what was to be of central importance in his dealings with others: namely the ability (which Graves had recognized in Lawrence, and portrayed in the character of Germanicus)[356] always to be ready to assume the best of those whom he met, and in this way (though constantly in danger of appearing naive in his judgement of human nature) to bring out the best of which they were capable.

As the summer of 1935 wore on, Graves became increasingly fascinated by his correspondence with Liddell-Hart; and towards the end of August, while 'abstractedly' swimming at the Cala, he had the idea that he and Liddell-Hart should use the Lawrence material at their disposal to prepare 'a joint book of *materia historica*'.[357] It was in the course of this collaboration, somewhat reluctantly sanctioned by the Lawrence estate, that Graves would finally set his feelings about T.E.Lawrence in order.

CHAPTER 18
Arrogance and Wasp Waists

When Robert Graves had been suffering from nightmares in March 1935, his worries about his future had surfaced in his writing, and he had written several drafts of 'And should I fail?', a poem about whether he would have a place in history.[358] Laura Riding, whose own health had been poor (they were both of them affected most at that time by what Robert described in his diary as 'nervous voices'),[359] had noticed how ill Robert looked, and it had seemed to Karl Goldschmidt as though Graves had become an old man.[360] One of the factors in Robert's recovery was almost certainly the daily walk which he now began taking with Salamo, later called Solomon, his ten-month-old cross between a Mallorquin and an English bull-dog. Together with this new companion, located for him by Gelat at a cost of 125 pesetas, Graves spent part of each day happily roaming through the countryside around Deyá, enjoying the healthy exercise, and forgetting more serious worries as he concentrated upon such things as making Solomon walk to heel, finding sheeps' heads for him, or deciding whether or not to buy him a muzzle. And when they returned to Canelluñ Solomon would curl up and sleep contentedly on a sheepskin rug in Graves's workroom.

By mid-April, within three weeks of Solomon's arrival, Laura noticed that Robert was looking much better as a result of his walks; and Karl agreed with her that he 'looked young again'.[361] Karl incidentally was now doing so much work at Canelluñ (on more than one occasion even stopping the night after typing into the early hours), and so much time and energy were being wasted by what he himself called 'a lot of running about between us', that towards the end of April he accepted an invitation to move into next-door C'an Torrent.[362]

But although Graves was now in a more cheerful frame of mind, much of his time was being spent on ill-fated or comparatively minor projects. While writing *The Fool of Rome*, for example, which took him until the beginning of July, and was never published, Graves also worked for Korda on a screenplay of *I, Claudius*, which was never used; corresponded with Korda and others about a possible screenplay based on the life of T.E. Lawrence which came to nothing; and worked for Riding on a volume entitled *Poets* for a hypothetical Child's University Library which never found a publisher. There was also work on the first volume of *Epilogue*, on a novel written by Tom Matthews called *The Moon's No Fool*, and on *Focus*,[363] a newsletter financed by Graves and edited by Riding, each of whose four issues was longer than the last, and more grossly over-burdened with utterly trivial matters such as Gordon Glover's sentiments on having a novel rejected,[364] or Laura Riding's thoughts about Karl Goldschmidt always making her the first cup of tea.[365]

The principal visitors during the summer were Honor Wyatt, her three-month-old son Julian, her husband Gordon Glover, and her friend Mary Phillips, a cheerful and competent young women who was soon assisting Karl with his huge workload of typing. She and the others stayed in Deyá for two months, from the end of May to the end of July. They joined in the usual round of Canelluñ activities, with most afternoons ending in the café; and they all went with Robert, Karl and Laura on two expeditions to bullfights in Palma: once to see Laura's 'special hero', the bullfighter Domingo Ortega.[366] Laura had developed a morbid fascination for what she though of as the beauty of cut flesh, and had even written in one of her *Focus* articles how much she had enjoyed seeing the interior of a man's leg when it had been cut open in a motor-car accident near the gates of Canelluñ.[367]

Soon after Honor and her party had arrived from England, Robert received some surprising news from his mother. It appeared that 'The Devil', as Graves and Riding still called Geoffrey Phibbs, had decided to leave Nancy, and was shortly to get married to Mary, an attractive young woman with whom he remained for the rest of his life. Susan, Robert's half-sister, commented acidly: 'I never thought much of Geoffrey, but I did hope he'd have the decency to stick to Nancy. But perhaps she doesn't mind.'[368] The truth is that Nancy *did* mind, and so did her children; but knowing how much Geoffrey wanted a family of his own (which she felt unable to provide), Nancy had generously released him; and even agreed that the two of them should continue printing together after Geoffrey's marriage. Robert was highly delighted, almost immediately sent a large sum of money to Nancy, and told Amy that Geoffrey's going was all to the good: he had been Nancy's evil genius, and had warped her sense of justice.[369] Now, perhaps, the way would be open for him to re-establish better relations with his four children.

In the meantime, Graves's working life continued to be busy. He was immersed in two new projects: the general editing for Frank Richards of *Old Soldier Sahib*, a 'prequel' to his successful *Old Soldiers Never Die*; and the translation of a work which had been written in German by Georg Schwarz, a next-door neighbour and former art-dealer who was also on the fringes of the Graves/Riding inner circle. *Almost Forgotten Times*, published by Seizin/Constable in 1936 as *Almost Forgotten Germany*, tells of tranquil pre-Great War days; and Robert worked from a literal translation begun by Karl and completed by a Frau Thelen from Palma.

Laura turned occasionally from wrestling with her historical novel about Troy (Graves noted wryly that she drank a good deal of whisky when it was going particularly badly)[370] to advise Graves and others about their work or conduct.[371] More important to her, the first *Epilogue* was published later in the year. Laura's outrageous arrogance appeared on page after page, both in her own major contributions (so numerous that she adopted the pseudonym of Madeleine Vara for some of them) and in the editorial footnotes which she scattered liberally throughout the volume. There were indeed a number of highly interesting essays: Robert Graves's 'A Note on the Pastoral' was worth reading, as were his pieces on 'Coleridge and Wordsworth' and on 'Keats and Shelley'; while James Reeves contributed a penetrating study of 'The Romantic Habit in English Poets'; and Len Lye's article on 'Film-Making' was also included. But the good things were submerged by the bad.[372]

Graves, however, continued to believe steadfastly in Riding and in her dictats; but one of his dreams shows how he secretly longed for a more pliable woman partner. In it, he imagined that he was in the 'strange hall of a house in 1900-ish London'. Above one of the doors he could see 'a faded print called "In the Gay Old Days. The Duke of Westminster celebrates his Coming of Age in the company of 10,000 Ladies of the Town."' The print showed the Duke, 'a long-faced fair-haired young man in evening dress, elbows on knees staring greedily forward: in the middle of an auditorium full of girls with doll faces and wasp waists[373].'

CHAPTER 19

Denounced as Spies

By the autumn of 1935, two and a half years after Adolf Hitler had come to power in Germany, both Robert Graves and Laura Riding were well aware that they were living in the shadow of another major European war. Hitler had already suppressed the trade unions, purged his political opponents, and begun both a massive and illegal rearmament and the steady elaboration of a totalitarian police state; while his anti-Jewish policies had met with so little resistance that by September 1935, not content with having effectively banned Jews from any public office, he felt secure enough to decree that there should be no further marriages between Jews and Germans. Internationally he had formed an alliance with that other dictator, Benito Mussolini of Italy; and it was clear both from Hitler's writings and from his speeches that he intended to carve out for the German people a vast empire in eastern Europe. Graves's fire-dreams could be interpreted in a wider context as worries about the inevitability of war; and, in the summer of 1935, Riding herself had 'several persistent [dreams] about Hitler, in which he sweated to assure me that he had no secret purposes. Alas, no' she wrote ironically for the third *Focus*. 'And indeed all the secret purposes grow in Italy nowadays.'[374]

This perceptive comment was followed shortly afterwards by the Italian invasion of Abyssinia, from which it became evident to clear-sighted observers that Mussolini intended to establish a new Roman Empire in Africa to parallel Hitler's proposed conquests in Europe; and not only did Mussolini's invasion heighten international tension: it also sharpened the contrast within other European countries between those forces working for democracy, and those which favoured an approach to the totalitarianism of the German or Italian model. Graves and Riding themselves were soon to be personally affected both by the increased international tension and (more profoundly) by the internal politics of Spain, where a microcosm of the coming European conflict was already in preparation.

It was four years since, in 1931, King Alfonso XIII of Spain had gone into exile, leaving the way clear for the foundation of a more democratic regime, the Second Republic, dominated by an alliance of moderate Republicans and Socialists. But then, in the elections of November 1933 the moderates had been swept from office, to be replaced by a Conservative Government in which the Catholic right played a major part. In October 1934 the Socialists, fearing that the new Government was operating according to a kind of Catholic Fascism, and that they would be purged just as their fellow-Socialists in Germany had been purged by Hitler earlier in the year, launched an unsuccessful revolution which was suppressed by the army.

From then on, political opinion in Spain had become increasingly polarized. The very fact of the rebellion against what was, after all, a legally elected Government gave those on the political right (and many of those in the centre) profound fears about a future Communist or neo-Communist uprising; while the way in which military force had been used to bring the rebellion to an end confirmed the fears of those on the political left (and many of those in the centre) about the Fascist or neo-Fascist leanings of the Government.

Deyá, although utterly remote from the centre of political life, was on an island which might have strategic importance in the event of war. All foreigners were therefore suspect: Riding's road to the Cala had been viewed by the authorities as a possible invasion route, and they had sent along a secret agent to examine the situation.[375] Now, towards the end of September 1935, Graves and Riding heard from Gelat that they and several of their friends had actually been denounced to the authorities as spies. It was a complicated story, clearly involving a doctor against whom Gelat was battling for water-rights; and Gelat told Robert and Laura not to worry: one of the accused, a Mallorquin named Castañer, had a son-in-law who was 'bosom pals' with the adjutant of an influential army officer named Franco, and this connection would ensure that the truth came out. So it did: though Graves and Riding were both interrogated about their new road, and it was not until mid-November that they were officially cleared.

Under the pressure of these events, both Graves and Riding continued to live as though their future in Deyá were secure. Besides all their existing projects[376] Riding embarked upon *Schools*, a comparative study of educational systems from all over the world which she hoped would appear alongside *Poets* in her projected 'Subjects of Knowledge' series; while Graves had once again taken up his *Antigua, Penny, Puce*. This novel was now developing into a story of the most venomous sibling rivalry, in which

Robert combines a satirical attack upon English education and family life[377] with an intriguing series of ideas about possible developments both in the arts and in social behaviour. [378] So ingenious were some of these ideas that Philip Larkin would one day praise *Antigua, Penny, Puce* as 'unique among novels' for 'its variety of original invention, not to mention its humour'.[379]

All this labour must have been a welcome distraction from the risky political situation; but Robert and Laura (joined for the Christmas vacation by Alan Hodge, an Oxford undergraduate who was an admirer of Riding's poetry) were driving themselves so hard that their health was affected. Robert had a series of digestive illnesses which meant that for five months he never felt really well; while Laura 'half-fainted' one day at the gates of C'an Torrent, and took to her bed with increasing frequency suffering from all kinds of mysterious aches and pains.[380] There would be a comparatively brief period during the spring and early summer of 1936 when the political situation appeared to ease, and health improved; but it would be no more than a prelude to the long-awaited political explosion.

CHAPTER 20

One Suitcase Each

In the Spanish elections of February 1936, much to the delight of both Robert Graves and Laura Riding, there had been a left-wing landslide. 'If this new Spanish government lasts,' Robert wrote to his brother John, 'it will be a great benefit to Spain, and not least to the Balearics. Personally, owing to a funny business connected with secret police-spies and our local enemy the doctor, we were greatly relieved that the Lefts got in.'[381] Gelat, who had helped to turn out the left-wing vote, was also very pleased with the result of the election: when rather merry one evening, he declared that he was 'more than a socialist, he was a communist';[382] and after a successful series of political intrigues he managed to have himself elected Mayor of Deyá in the spring local elections.[383]

Graves and Riding continued to work hard through the spring and early summer;[384] and although a number of projects were either curtailed or failed altogether,[385] reducing 'expectations of about £2–3,000' to 'a deficit of £200. . . . Who the hell cares?' Robert asked his brother John. 'Money's always gettable if really needed.'[386] As if to reward him for his philosophic calm, on 18 July a telegram arrived from Constable announcing that they would be 'very glad to publish *Antigua*'; and both Robert and Laura felt more cheerful and optimistic than they had done all year. But that evening came news, over the radio, of 'a military insurrection at Melilla & Seville and the degradation of Franco and 5 generals'.[387]

The military rising against the 'Government of the Popular Front against Fascism' had begun on the previous day, Friday 17 July 1936, with simultaneous insurrections both in Morocco and in a number of garrisons in metropolitan Spain. At its outset, the trouble seemed utterly remote; and yet the Fascists had immediately taken control in Palma, where they imposed martial law; postal communications were cut with the outside world; and by Sunday evening there were disturbing rumours 'of fighting in Barcelona & air-bombing in Valencia'.[388]

On the evening of Monday 20 July, Robert, Karl and Alan Hodge (who was staying with Karl at C'an Torrent) went to the village to listen to the radio (which Robert and Laura had bought some time ago as a present for Gelat) and heard that the Fascists had now seized power not only in the Balearic Islands, but in twelve other provinces; and that Gelat and other 'Popular Front' mayors had been instructed to hand over power 'to some non-political'. As yet there was no local Fascist chief in Deyá itself, but Graves noted that the village doctor and a number of his right-wing cronies were 'strutting about' in high spirits.[389]

By Tuesday, Graves felt that Majorca was thoroughly isolated. Orders arrived from Palma 'to close radios'; and that night he had the sinister experience of watching troops drive through Deyá 'in *camions* with cannon, shouting '*Viva el Fascismo!*' Menorca, the fleet and the air force were thought to be loyal to the Government, and some radio news bulletins from the Continent announced on Wednesday that the revolt was being broken. Graves, busily occupying himself with some painting at The Posada, did not know what to believe.

Apart from the Fascist convoy passing through Deyá, Robert had personally witnessed no more than a British warship steaming by on some unknown mission, and an unidentified aeroplane flying low overhead. Then at three o'clock on Thursday morning all the electric lights in the village suddenly came on and, later in the day, Graves learned that eighteen Fascist youths in five cars had arrived in the village during the night. Telling Gelat that, although none of them was more than seventeen years old, they had already shot and killed eight men, they ordered him to switch on the lights. Then, under the false impression that the doctor (one of their own party) was harbouring the Mayor of Inca, a prominent Socialist, they banged on his door demanding entry. When there was no reply they poured a volley of rifle-fire into the door and broke it down; but the doctor, fearing that they were Communists sent to kill him by Gelat, had already escaped through the back door in his underclothes and a pair of rope-sandals; and soon afterwards the Fascists drove away. No one in Deyá had been hurt; but news of the incident helped to create panic in the village, which was already filling up with frightened refugees from Palma. One woman, fearing that Deyá would be bombed, took her entire family down to the Cala for safety; and Graves watched another, out of her mind with terror, rush shrieking down the road.[390]

That evening Robert and Laura sat quietly on the terrace of C'an Torrent with Karl and Alan, wondering whether they would hear any firing or explosions above the tinkling of the sheep-bells. Then they played gramophone records and danced, before venturing into the village which was now 'divided into two camps, the rights talking hard at *Ayuntamiento*, the lefts silent outside the *Sala* [Gelat's café]'.[391]

Elsewhere in Spain open fighting continued; but in Majorca, though it seemed reasonable to suppose that the Government might soon begin a full-scale assault upon the Fascist-controlled island, there was a lull in military activity. Robert's forty-first birthday fell on Friday; and he woke to find that the panic in Deyá had subsided, and that everyone in the village was working normally. He himself returned to his researches for *Schools*, while Laura Riding worked on the last part of *A Trojan Ending*; and it began to seem that Government control of the sea would be the decisive factor in this theatre of war. 'Apparently', Graves wrote in his diary on Saturday evening, 'Mallorca is being left to fall by itself without bombardments, being cut off from the outside world.'[392]

On Tuesday 28 July, the lull was abruptly ended at mid-day when two Government aeroplanes flew over Palma and dropped bombs. Graves learned that they were '"canisters" like the sort the Germans used at Fricourt filled with scrap metal: great moral effect, kill many, do little harm to property.' At once everyone began fleeing Palma again;[393] and the following day a Fascist captain arrived in Deyá to conscript Fascist 'volunteers', and to post an anti-aircraft machine-gun on the heights above the village.[394]

At first, Graves and Riding had no fears about their personal safety, though they wondered whether they would be compelled to leave the island 'because of interrupted communications'; but the seriousness of their situation grew more evident from day to day and, by Friday, they had decided that they would only stay on Majorca for a week – long enough, they hoped, to 'get *Troy* and *Epilogue* done'; and Graves noted in his diary that Palma would be 'a dangerous gauntlet to run'.[395] On Saturday, when the first grapes were ready to be picked, it seemed for a moment as though Robert and Laura would be able to stay at Canelluñ after all: there was an encouraging postcard from Short, the British Agent in Palma, telling them that he expected the 'all clear' to be sounded within a week.[396]

But at two o'clock in the afternoon of Sunday 2 August 1936 there was an altogether unexpected visit from a British ex-Consul who told Graves, Riding, Goldschmidt and Hodge that their:

last chance to go was this evening by a destroyer from Los Pinos, Palma. One suitcase each. We had just had lunch. Packed hurriedly and at random. Gelat came and undertook to do everything. He said '*Sinvergüen-*

zas' and wept.... Gelat took keys, will keep everything for us, 'don't worry', will take Solomon for walks. Everyone weeping as we went off.[397]

On their way to the docks they skirted Palma and 'saw broken windows, no other damage', though they were told that sixty bombs had been dropped earlier in the day. Everywhere they could see Fascist soldiers, whom Graves described scornfully as 'lounging about. Growing beards already,' though when they met Short they found him 'confident' that the Fascists would soon win. Then their passports were examined by a British naval officer at the English tearoom.[398]

This was a dangerous moment for Karl Goldschmidt. All refugees were to be returned to their own countries, and in his case this would have meant being compelled to board the *Graf Spee*, a German pocket-battleship in Palma harbour, en route for Germany and a concentration camp. However Robert pleaded strongly on his behalf, with the happy result that Karl was allowed to stay with them when, that evening, Robert, Laura and Alan went aboard 'the *Grenville*, a brand-new [British] destroyer, by tender'.[399]

At the time, Graves, Riding and Goldschmidt must all have hoped that they would be able to return to Deyá in a matter of months, if not weeks; but it was to be almost ten years before Robert set foot once again upon Majorcan soil; and although Karl Goldschmidt remained as Graves's assistant, and eventually followed him out to Deyá, Laura Riding had long before departed from the scene.

BOOK FIVE

WANDERERS IN EXILE
1936–1940

CHAPTER 1

Landfall

Escaping from the dangers of the Spanish Civil War, Robert Graves and his companions – Laura Riding, Karl Goldschmidt and Alan Hodge – were relieved to join the refugees already aboard HMS *Grenville* on the evening of Sunday 2 August 1936, and they received a particularly warm welcome: no doubt it helped that Lieutenant-Commander Evans admired Graves's work, and even had a copy of *I, Claudius*, which he asked Graves to sign. Robert 'made an exception' in this case to his general rule of refusing autograph-hunters; and in return Evans invited him to the ship's bridge, where Graves noted with some satisfaction that, despite a number of the most up-to-date gadgets, the course still had to be set using an 'Old-fashioned chart and sliding rule'.[1]

Later that evening, Graves shared with the other refugees a simple meal of bully beef, ship's biscuit and lime juice; and then, while the women found spaces in the officer's cabins, he and the men spent the night on deck 'on collision mats with 1 blanket apiece'. The following morning HMS *Grenville* carried them on to the island of Ibiza, where they stayed on board all day while more foreign nationals were rounded up and rescued;[2] and then, on Tuesday, they crossed over to the port of Valencia on mainland Spain. Here they were transferred by tender to the British hospital ship *Maine*, which had come on from Malaga with more refugees. Once again there was a period of anxiety about Karl's future; but, as Robert noted, the surgeon commander of the *Maine* who took the passports 'carried on the generous trad[ition] of [the] *Grenville*'[3] in allowing Karl to remain with his friends. The *Maine* sailed at dusk on Wednesday; and by eight o'clock on Thursday 6 August (after calling in at Barcelona to collect more refugees), it had reached Marseilles, where Graves, Riding, Goldschmidt and Hodge were safely landed on French soil.

An irritating day followed: they had no money, but the British Consul, on hearing that it might be possible for Graves and his companions to obtain money through a local bank, refused at first to lend them even the price of four third-class tickets to England; Laura needed a new passport as her old one had expired, but was treated with such little courtesy by the American Consul that she came out crying; and Karl needed a special stamp which took three hours to obtain. However, by the evening they had secured everything but an English visa for Laura; and that night they travelled northward by train, arriving in Paris early on Friday morning.

Graves, for once, was firmly in charge. The British Consulate did not open until 10.00 a.m.; but by 10.06 he had obtained Riding's visa, found a taxi and bundled everyone into it; and by 10.19, just as it was about to leave, he had somehow managed to buy tickets and hurry them all '(Laura protesting)' into the boat-train for Dieppe. From there, he sent a wire to Maisie Somerville announcing their imminent arrival in England; and by six o'clock that evening, when Maisie met their train in London, 4 she was able to tell them that she had secured the loan from Kitty West, a mutual acquaintance, of 32 York Terrace, Regent's Park: a house which Robert described in a letter to his children as 'palatial ... with hot baths & two Welsh maids & a telephone & every comfort'.5

Robert noticed that their flight from Majorca had given Laura 'a lot of grey hairs';6 and for several days he himself felt not merely tired but in a state of emotional shock, in which he was chiefly conscious of 'sherry, hot baths, [and repeating] our story over and over to different people'.7 Telling their story had begun on Friday afternoon, on the boat from Dieppe, when they had met the black-caped poet Roy Campbell (to whom they took a strong dislike after he apologized to them for 'a libel on us in Georgiad or something'8 of which they had previously been quite unaware); then, on Saturday, Kyllmann of Constable's came to see them at 32 York Terrace; and his visit was followed by telephone conversations with Arthur Baker, Jonathan Cape and others; by the arrival in London of an over-excited Amy Graves (who was politely rebuffed when she announced that she wanted to whisk her son away to Harlech for a week); and by supper with their old photographer friends Ward and Dorothy Hutchinson.

For day after day there seemed to be no chance to recover from their exhaustion: on Sunday 9 August, for instance, Robert first lunched with Amy and his half-brother Philip at Prada's (in Euston Road, and a favourite haunt of the Graveses); and then, no doubt surfeited with family news, he agreed to travel with Amy by taxi out to Halstead to see his sister Rosaleen, now living there with her husband Jim Cooper and their son Roger, and looking 'unchanged' after an interval of seven years.9 On Monday and Tuesday, besides work on the proofs of *Antigua, Penny, Puce,* there were meetings first with Graves's new literary agent A.S.Watt (recommended to him by Liddell-Hart), and then with Honor Wyatt and Gordon Glover; and so it continued.

On first arriving in England, it had been Robert Graves's firm intention that he and Laura Riding would 'return to Spain the moment we can';[10] and after the comparatively tranquil pace of his existence as the inhabitant of a remote village on a remote island, he found the rush of London life both oppressive and (at first) disorientating: but it had several important advantages. For the first time since 1929, Graves was living at the heart of things; and having established himself financially by the sale of some Lawrence MSS for the vast sum of '£1,000 (£884 clear)'[11] he was able to take a more active role in promoting his own interests both with publishers and with the film world. He was also able to re-establish contact with his children at a time when sixteen-year-old David had severely tested his patience by saying that he wished to go in due course not to Oxford but to Cambridge, a university for which Robert had an abiding hatred;[12] and when seventeen-year-old Jenny, who had trained as a dancer and appeared in revue as one of 'Cochran's Young Ladies',[13] was found in a considerably troubled state, and in need of much more than the occasional holiday at Canelluñ. Equally important, freed of the customary psychological and intellectual constraints of living so exclusively under Laura Riding's influence, and thrown suddenly (after a vivid reminder of his wartime experiences) into a much larger world, Graves was soon to experience a sudden and dramatic renaissance in his literary powers.

CHAPTER 2
Midnight Laughter

The difficulties with the Lawrence Trustees were still unresolved, and on 12 August, less than a week after his return to England, Robert Graves spent much of the day with Basil Liddell-Hart, who was established in grand style at an hotel in Guildford with his son, his secretary and his wife Jessie, whom Robert described as 'masterful'. It was Graves's first meeting with Liddell-Hart, who impressed him by alluding to the vast income of some £3,400 a year which he earned by combining the roles of military correspondent to *The Times* and of personal adviser to the Minister of War. The two men agreed that the Trustees were asking them to accept impossible terms, and Liddell-Hart promised to try one more personal appeal to A.W.Lawrence (T.E.'s brother, Arnold) 'before declaring war'.[14]

The following day, Graves had another taste of high living when Alexander Korda sent a car to fetch him to Denham Studios to discuss the filming of *I, Claudius*, in which it had been arranged that Charles Laughton would play the title role. Korda was then directing Laughton in the title role of *Rembrandt*, and Graves watched the shooting of a scene between him and his co-star Elsa Lanchester. For Graves the day had a surreal quality, especially when they all lunched together in a restaurant 'filled with costumes of Elizabethan film, Swedish police & Russian refugees, English waiters etc. Vivien Leigh supplying dirty rhymes'; but he was able to have a serious talk with Laughton about playing the part of Claudius, while Korda did everything he could to make Graves feel thoroughly welcome: promising him money, offering to send the car for Laura, and saying that he would like to give Robert's daughter, Jenny Nicholson, some film work.[15]

Robert and Laura had recently had supper with James and Mary Reeves; and Graves returned from his 'mad day at Denham Studios' to find that Laura had arranged for a meeting with Harry Kemp,[16] one of James's friends, and a poet in his early twenties who was (in his own words) 'being inspected by LR as a possible *Epilogue* recruit'. Earlier in the year he had sent a batch of his poems out to Deyá, from where Laura Riding had returned them 'with many detailed suggestions for improvement'; and in the correspondence that ensued he had sent Riding 'some pages of notes on poetry'. These related to the fact that Kemp had been 'a Communist at Cambridge ... but had defected and was now working things out again from scratch', and Laura had found them thought-provoking.[17] In August 1936, Harry Kemp had resigned from a teaching post in Peterborough, and he was now living with his new wife, Alix, a German refugee, in a flat off Baker Street. On first meeting Graves and Riding, Kemp made only one *faux pas*, when he praised a poem by John Cullen which had been published in *Epilogue I*. He was not to know that Cullen had fallen out of favour (perhaps because of his continued friendship with Bronowski), and an 'ominous silence' followed. However, Kemp was 'much too shy to inquire the cause', and the rest of the evening was a great success. Not only did he get on well with Graves, having read and admired both his autobiography and all his recent poetry; but also it became clear that he was very well acquainted with Riding's work, and that he would make a willing and intelligent collaborator.

The next day, Friday 14 August, Robert, Laura, Karl and Alan had been invited to travel northwards out of London into the heart of the Essex countryside to spend just over a week with John Aldridge and Lucie Brown at The Place, their beautiful sixteenth-century home in the village of Great Bardfield. While they were still packing their things, Jenny Nicholson arrived, on her way to Korda's to see whether he would keep his promise to her father and offer her a job. Robert found his seventeen-year-old daughter, whom he had last seen as a child of eleven, 'very sweet', and took her out to lunch. However, circumstances had forced Jenny into learning how to survive by whatever means came to hand, and Robert did not realize at this stage how clever she was at manipulating other people for her own ends. For example, Jenny had been receiving a great deal of help and encouragement in her career both from her Uncle Charles, who lent her money, attended her first nights and put her name in his newspaper column; and from her Aunt Peggy, who advised her on clothes, make-up and social etiquette, and listened thoughtfully to her problems. Jenny knew, however, how much Robert disliked Charles, and so while they were having lunch together on this occasion she told her father: 'I like clothes and I like jewellery and I'm not ashamed. The only thing I'm ashamed of is keeping up with your brother Charles.' Robert found this point of view thoroughly satisfactory; and, in the after-glow of his meeting with Jenny, he wrote to Nancy sending her a cheque for £100, and no doubt congratulating her on having brought up their eldest daughter so well; and then he and his companions set out for Great Bardfield: Robert, Karl and Alan by train as far as Bishop's Stortford, where they were picked up by John Aldridge; and Riding by car, chauffeur-driven from door to door by Gordon Glover.[18]

The Place was a peaceful house with an early-Victorian interior in which Graves soon felt at home. He was a useful and generous guest, not only helping with the washing-up, but giving Lucie Brown a silver skewer and a silver necklace, and buying two of John Aldridge's pictures. He also went mushrooming with Alan Hodge and played ball-games in the large garden with both Alan and John. In the evenings they all went out together to the local public house, The Bell; and, within a few days, Graves was feeling more cheerful than he had done for weeks. On Sunday he wrote up his diary, which had lapsed since the day when he and Riding had been forced to leave Canelluñ; and on Monday he enjoyed what he described as his 'first real day of work' since arriving in England. Besides going over a good deal of *A Trojan Ending* with Laura, he completed checking the galley proofs of *Antigua, Penny, Puce*; and, before returning to London on 21 August, he was delighted to have a letter from Jenny in which she announced that Korda had indeed given her some film work.[19]

Graves found it displeasing to be back in the metropolis, walking along the streets at night-time 'under [the] unhealthy glare of Neon lights'[20] instead of under the stars; but after going to an hotel for two nights (while Laura stayed briefly with Maisie Somerville), he and his literary partner settled comfortably enough into a tiny flat which they rented from John Aldridge's mother at 25, Marlborough House in Osnaburgh Street, not far from Regent's Park. One compensation for their return to London was a chance encounter with their old friend Len Lye, whom they met out walking in St James's Square; and then on the evening of 24 August they 'saw Norman [Cameron] for the first time since 1932'.[21]

Norman's partner, the beautiful Elfriede, whose bad treatment at Laura's hands had been a principal cause of Norman Cameron's estrangement from Graves and Riding, had died of tuberculosis in the spring of 1936; and Norman, now working in advertising, found it easy to pick up the threads of his former friendship, meeting Robert and Laura for supper from time to time, and allowing Laura to look over his poems. However, Laura never regained her former hold on his affections; and perhaps, as her extreme feminism reached its height, she had no wish to do so.[22]

Jenny was a regular caller at Marlborough House and, on 25 August, she arrived with the excellent news that she had secured a three-month dancing engagement at the prestigious Dorchester Hotel, starting on the 17th of the following month. Nor was it long before Robert saw his other children. On 26 August, Sam and David arrived to spend five days in London on their way to Harlech, and Robert was delighted by them both: not only was Sam astonishingly handsome, and talking much better than Robert had expected from Nancy's letters; but he also found an easy sympathy with David, later writing to him that it had been 'such a pleasure to me to have got to know you again and to like you quite as much at 16 as at 9: more in fact'.[23] Then, at the beginning of September, Robert telephoned Catherine, who was with her grandmother at Harlech, and arranged for her to visit him on her way back to Nancy's house in Wiltshire.

Catherine was terribly excited to hear Robert's voice 'for the first time since you went to Spain';[24] and, on 10 September, she arrived in London where for five days she shared a flat with her twenty-year-old half-cousin Diana (Dick Graves's daughter), but saw her father each day, helping with the cooking, accompanying him to see his publishers, or to the cinema (in which he had developed a great interest since the possibility of *I, Claudius* becoming a film had first been mooted), and going with him on one of his regular visits to the Caledonian market. Robert's passion for collecting small objects (many of which he gave away almost at once) was being indulged to the full; and on this occasion he bought no fewer than fifteen items, including a carbuncle and moonstone necklace later given to Honor, two Staffordshire zebras, an ivory fan, a George IV constable's truncheon, a blue Bristol glass vase, some pinchbeck green earrings, a Venetian glass necklace & ivory paper-cutter for Catherine, star earrings for Laura, and a blue Bristol bowl.

Graves remained unhappy about living in London, but hopes of a speedy return to Deyá looked increasingly unrealistic; and earlier in the month, when he and Laura had spent a few days on the south coast with the MacCormacks (who had rented C'an Torrent two years running) at their home in Old Bursledon not far from Southampton Water, there had been some talk about 'buying or renting a house-boat' in the area.[25] In the meantime, work had continued on *A Trojan Ending* and on the page proofs of *Antigua, Penny, Puce*; while there were more discussions about the Lawrence Trustees with Liddell Hart; Riding's idea for a novel kind of dictionary was being eagerly examined by Kyllmann at Constable's; and on the day of Catherine's arrival Robert had made a second tip to Denham Studios (this time accompanied by Laura), and over lunch with Korda they had discussed not only *I, Claudius*, but the possibility of making a film based on *A Trojan Ending*. They also talked about Jenny Nicholson; and Korda had offered to join them at Jenny's Dorchester opening on the 17th.

So far Graves's newly re-established relationship with his elder daughter had given him almost nothing but pleasure; though she always seemed to be short of money, and had already persuaded him to settle one of her hotel bills. Then, on 14 September, Robert heard that Jenny had telephoned Laura, asking her if she would help her out by buying 'a wedding present for Sarah Churchill [daughter of Winston Churchill, then Member of Parliament for Epping] who is running off with Olivier [*sic*] the Cochrane [*sic*] *Follow the Sun* humorist'.[26] Laura complied; but three days later Robert was told by Jenny that she was 'in trouble with the Churchills about her part in the Sarah business'.[27]

What had happened was this: early in 1936, C.B. Cochran had engaged the Austrian-born entertainer Vic Oliver as the comic lead in his West End revue *Follow the Sun*. Liking to have the daughters of famous men among his 'Young Ladies' for the sake of the extra publicity which they would attract, Cochran had in his cast not only Robert Graves's daughter Jenny Nicholson, but Winston Churchill's daughter Sarah. Jenny and Sarah rapidly became close friends; and Vic Oliver, thirty-eight years old, whose marriage had broken up several years previously, soon noticed these two 'young beaut[ies] of the chorus'[28] who were always in each other's company, and struck up a friendship with them. Later he recalled that 'Jenny...was the brilliant type, who wanted success to reach her quickly, I think she thought the world owed her a living';[29] and he was much more strongly attracted to Sarah, who was then living on a chorus girl's wages, and seemed 'humbly willing to make a slow climb, starting at the bottom of the so-called ladder'.[30]

Before long Vic Oliver and Sarah Churchill were talking of marriage; and in October, when Vic opened in a show of his own in America, he proposed to Sarah that she should come over and join him. Sarah discussed things with Jenny before sending Vic Oliver a telegram which read 'Am sailing tomorrow on the Aquitania'.[31] She left with a wedding-present from Jenny in her baggage; and then Jenny, thinking it all highly romantic, could not resist giving away the news of Sarah's departure to one Conway of the *Daily Mail*. Within days the newspapers on both sides of the Atlantic were full of excited headlines such as 'Sarah Churchill flees Country to join Prospective Husband', and 'Sarah Churchill defies Wishes of Family'.[32] The Churchill parents were inclined to be angry with Jenny for having allowed the news to break in such a sensational manner; but when Jenny had told Robert her own version of events, in which she had been at fault only through her lack of experience at fending off awkward questions from determined reporters, Robert helped her to write an apologetic letter to Mrs Churchill. He also penned a covering letter to Winston Churchill, in which no doubt he made much of Jenny's youth and innocence; and a few days later he received a 'nice note' from Mrs Churchill in reply.[33]

Jenny had successfully used Robert's influence to extricate herself from a difficult situation, and had given him no idea of the rather seedy kind of life to which, as mere chorus-girls, she and Sarah had both been reduced, which Charles and Peggy later described as 'moral ruin' ('i.e.', Robert commented, 'prostitution'),[34] and which before long was to land Jenny in far more serious trouble than her friend. In the meantime, however, Jenny's life appeared to be both glamorous and comparatively care-free; and on the night of 17 September, she opened in Cochran's *Midnight Laughter* at the Dorchester. Robert Graves was in the audience together with Laura Riding, Basil Liddell-Hart (with whom Laura had stupidly quarrelled at the dinner-table over what she called his 'drawing-out tactics') and Maisie Somerville. Jenny danced well; and then after the show, as Amy Graves heard a few days later, there was an unexpected meeting:

> While talking to Jenny in the Restaurant … Jenny wearing a beautiful Grecian dress given her by Peggy, she said to Robert: by the way, this is one of your brothers & he & Charles shook hands, also with Peggy, but no word was spoken. The brothers had not recognised each other. Both give the praises of Jenny, who looked so pretty on the stage (Robert says) & who is the pet of the show, so Charles says.[35]

Robert was delighted by Jenny's success, and three days later he wrote the first few drafts of 'Parent to Children', which begins:

> When you grow up, are no more children,
> Nor am I then your parent:
> The day of settlement falls.
>
> 'Parent', mortality's reminder,
> In each son's mouth or daughter's
> A word of shame or rage!
>
> I who begot you ask no pardon of you;
> Nor may the soldier ask
> Pardon of the strewn dead.

The procreative act was blind:
It was not you I sired then –
For who sires friends, as you are mine now? [36]

Graves may have hoped that 'the day of settlement' had now arrived between himself and Jenny, who was henceforward to be regarded as his friend rather than his daughter. However, Jenny made certain that his parental responsibilities could not be so easily shrugged off. On the very next day, Monday 21 September, she came to borrow money from him, explaining, much to Robert's exasperation, that her shortage was 'due to letting a broke boy-friend off paying for night-club on the Thursday';[37] later that week she asked Robert to help her write an outline of her life-story for the *Daily Sketch*, who had made her an offer of £10; and before the end of the year she had involved her father in an unpleasant saga of blackmail, venereal disease and a threatened abortion.

CHAPTER 3
The Woman Question

Living in Deyá, it had been almost possible for Robert Graves to believe that, to most of those who really counted, sexual intercourse was not only somewhat *passé*, but slightly degenerate and best avoided for the sake of one's spiritual health. Now that he was in London this mental conjuring trick was more difficult, and Robert's peace of mind was not improved by the appearance on the scene of the attractive and outspoken young woman Robin Hale, some of whose work was to be published in *Epilogue III*.[38]

Robert first met Robin Hale on the first Friday in October 1936 when she brought some of her poems to the flat to be examined by Laura. He only saw her briefly (though he described her in his diary that evening as 'a big handsome girl') because she spent most of her visit sitting in the living-room listening to Laura's comments, while Robert was resting next door on Laura's bed, suffering from a sore throat and an incipient boil: his first for more than six years.

Five days later, Robin made another visit to Marlborough House. Robert's boil, after giving him several days of intense pain, was now slowly healing; but he was once again immured in Laura's bedroom, this time because – at her request – he was trying to pick up the threads of the *Schools* project. However, he could not help overhearing the two women's voices, and found their 'conflict on values' far more interesting than his work. Strongly opposing Riding's views about bodies having had their day, Robin Hale 'uph[e]ld ... sex as necessary and delightful'.[39]

During the next few weeks Graves's life became increasingly difficult. In particular, there was trouble with the film-script of *I, Claudius*, which Graves saw for the first time when he visited Denham Studios immediately after a celebratory lunch at Prada's to mark the publication of *Antigua, Penny, Puce*. He was accompanied to Denham by Dr Ian Richmond, a Professor of Archaeology who had made a particular study of the Roman Empire, and who had therefore been called in by Korda to advise on

historical authenticity. Graves took an immediate liking to Richmond –
another Oxford man; and by the time that they had returned to Graves's
flat – where a considerable group of friends was now gathered, including
not only Tom and Julie (over in London for a month), but also Vyvyan
Richards, John Graves and Len and Jane Lye – they were united in their
indignation at a number of gross anachronisms in the script. 'Claudius,
for instance,' John Graves reported to another member of the family:

> hands his horse a LUMP OF SUGAR! And he has a dramatic dialogue
> with Cymbeline of England (long dead!). The film people want the Roman
> soldiers to get bad colds from the damp cold climate, but as they were
> drafted from the Rhine, even this is hardly correct. I can see Robert
> having a battle Royal before he is finished.[41]

Robert himself 'wrote angrily to Korda', after reading the complete film-
script and finding it to be 'absolutely cheap nonsense, strong on historical
absurdities'.[42] Korda was impressed by the strength of Graves's feelings;
and, on the evening of 18 October, Graves was invited to his house to
talk things over. Graves once again told him 'how awful' the scenario was,
and 'Persuaded him to recast [it] entirely.' They went over it together,
from the moment Graves arrived at 6 p.m. until 11.30 p.m., 'with an hour
off for [a] very special dinner (champagne etc.)'.[43] The sequel to this meeting
was that Graves had to work extremely hard on a complete rewrite, which
he presented to Korda on the evening of the 23rd. Korda and one of his
associates went over it, but would only 'pronounce ... it as a useful second
stage', and agree to 'stew over it for 10 days'.[44]

Negotiations with the Lawrence Trustees had also continued to be
unsatisfactory; and things were further complicated by Laura's attempt
to destroy Graves's friendship with Liddell-Hart. At their first meeting
she had recognized Liddell-Hart as someone with a mind of his own,
who would never consent to becoming her acolyte, and she moved swiftly.[45]
First (as Liddell-Hart records) she began by 'twisting my casual remarks
in a way that astonished me';[46] and then – when that failed to do enough
damage – she engineered a ridiculous quarrel between the two men over
Liddell-Hart's prose style. Fortunately, thanks to Liddell-Hart's fundamental good sense, they emerged relatively unscathed from this ordeal.
However, though Laura retained sufficient power to prevent Robert from
renewing his friendship with his former mentor Basanta Mallik, who was
himself returning to England after an absence of some twelve years, against
Liddell-Hart she could not prevail.

Tom and Julie Matthews had already noticed that Laura drove Robert 'with a looser rein',[47] and that, although she 'held court in London very much as she did in Deyá ... she was not quite so much the absolute monarch: her rule was more extensive but less sharply defined. Certain relaxations were not only permitted but encouraged.'[48] For example, on 5 November, Tom and Julie's last day in London, they accompanied Robert and Laura to the night-club at the Dorchester. Laura was wearing a white gold-brocaded jacket, a red velvet skirt, a red and gold cap, a gold chain, a black mantilla,

> and her golden-wire [head-band] that spelled LAURA [in Greek letters]; Robert wore a kind of eighteenth-century evening dress, with a ruffled shirt and a stock. Jenny had just been given a promotion in the show: she came on stage by herself, doing a cartwheel. This was considered [Tom Matthews records] next-best to being given a line to speak.[49]

Earlier, in mid-October, Tom and Julie had gone with Robert and Laura to spend a night in Oxford, where Riding had been invited by Alan Hodge (then in his final undergraduate year at Oriel College) to give an address to the English Club at the Taylorian on 'The End of The World'. When the formal part of her address was over, Riding spoke for a few minutes on politics – an earlier speech had stressed the importance of the English Club as an anti-Fascist organization – and this led to a prolonged discussion which was continued by a select few in the lounge of the Randolph Hotel just across the way.

It was through her role as editor of *Epilogue* that, in her own mind, Laura Riding had been extending her sway from the realm of poetry and criticism to that of national and international political morality. At this time she was very much concerned with the Spanish Civil War – saying to Robert one day: 'I haven't done much work lately, but then I've been fighting so hard in Spain'[50] –, with the threat to European peace posed by the rise of the dictators; and with the role of women in society.

The role of women usually aroused the most interest; at a dinner-party given by Maisie Somerville on 14 October, Graves and Riding had been introduced to Rebecca West and her husband Henry Andrews, and had talked a good deal from a feminist point of view about 'education, early environment and tenderness towards "population"'.[51] Such tenderness was no doubt roundly condemned; and in the course of the debate Riding seems to have come to believe that Rebecca West might be induced to cooperate with her on 'the woman question' – which later became 'woman power' – because, a week later (on Graves's and Riding's return from Oxford) 'Rebecca West and her Henry' were invited to a sherry party at which the other guests included Maisie, Tom, Julie, Kyllmann (back in favour after a brief lapse during which Graves and Riding had agreed that there was 'not sufficient enthusiasm' at Constables over *A Trojan Ending*),[52] and Sally Graves, Philip's daughter, a brilliant young Oxford graduate of twenty-two who 'surprised [Kyllmann] by knowing everything',[53] and gradually became one of Robert's most trusted confidantes.

By this time the conflict in Robert between his conscious adoration of Laura and his subconscious hatred of her for rejecting and even despising his sexual desires was acute; and it was a considerable shock for him when, on 25 October, suffering from another boil and with talk of 'woman power' and hostility towards 'population activities' still ringing in his ears, he chanced to meet his former secretary, Mary Ellidge, to whom he had been very dear. The meeting happened at Arkesden in Essex where Robert was accompanying Laura on a visit to Honor Wyatt, and where he learned that Mary's own 'population activities' with the landlord of The Green Man public house had apparently 'been creating a local scandal'. Afterwards Robert and Laura drove on to Great Bardfield which now seemed to Robert to be full of 'Ghostliness', with John looking 'haggard', and 'No real talk'.[54]

Back in London at Marlborough Street, Laura was going over Robin Hale's poems with her when, for Robert, the tension suddenly became almost unbearable. He was eating an apple (of obvious erotic symbolism), when he complained of feeling 'poisoned'.[55] For some days it seemed to Robert that he faced a descent into mental disintegration, perhaps even into madness; and, on 8 November, he began writing 'Before Bedlam'[56] (later 'The Halls of Bedlam'), one of his most chilling poems, in which a man comes face to face with the knowledge of impending insanity:

> Forewarned of madness:
> In three days' time at dusk
> The fit masters him.
>
> How to endure those days?
> (Forewarned is foremad)
> '– Normally, normally.'
>
> He will gossip with children,
> Argue with elders,
> Check the cash account.

'I shall go mad that day –'
The gossip, the argument,
The neat marginal entry.

His case is not uncommon,
The doctors pronounce;
But prescribe no cure.

To be mad is not easy,
Will earn him no money,
But a niche in the news.

Then to-morrow, children,
To-morrow, or the next day
He resigns from the firm.

His boyhood's ambition
Was to become an artist –
Like any City man's.

To the walls and halls of Bedlam
The artist is welcome –
Bold brush and full palette.

Through the cell's grating
He will watch his children
To and from school.

'Suffer the little children
To come unto me
With their Florentine hair!'

A very special story
For their very special friends –
They burst in the telling:

Of an evil thing, armed,
Tap-tapping on the door,
Tap-tapping on the floor,
'On the third day at dusk.'

Father in his shirt-sleeves,
Flourishing a hatchet –
Run, children, run!

No one could stop him,
No one understood;
And in the evening papers ...

(Imminent genius,
Troubles at the office,
Normally, normally,
As if already mad.)[57]

Graves spent several days working on this psychologically accurate account of a descent into depression-induced mental illness, in which, typically, the victim suffers from anxiety and even from hallucinations while, to all outward appearance, he continues to function normally right up to the moment of complete breakdown. He had already written on this theme in his 1924 poem 'From Our Ghostly Enemy'; but in the earlier poem, despite the unhappiness and uncertainties at that stage of his life, he could imagine a happy ending to his troubles; while in the later poem there is no such hope.

Three days later, on 11 November, came Armistice Day, the eighteenth anniversary of the end of the Great War. Graves and Riding were up at 7.30 packing all their belongings[58] for a move to 10, Dorset Street (just off Baker Street), where they had taken the flat immediately beneath that of Harry Kemp (now definitely approved as one of the inner circle) and his wife Alix. At 11 a.m. they paused during the loading of the removal-van for the traditional two-minute silence. It was the first time for eight years that Robert had been in England on Armistice Day. It made a great impression upon him: not so much because it revived old memories of his ordeal in the trenches on the Western Front; but because in the heart of the silence he found an echo of his present predicament, in which he seemed to be trapped in a kind of emotional limbo, unheeded by those around him even when he was desperately crying out for change. That evening he recorded in his diary how he had heard a trumpeter on the roof of a nearby church sound the Last Post; and how, apart from one loud, angry voice in the distance, everything was 'frozen still'.[59]

CHAPTER 4

The Mark of a Devil

At the end of October 1936, Jenny Nicholson had been given another small film part at Denham Studios by Korda (who was still having work done on her father's version of the *I, Claudius* scenario), but her normal life remained that of a chorus-girl in the cabaret at the Dorchester, hard-worked, low-paid and finding it difficult not to live beyond her means. In those circumstances many chorus-girls were preyed upon by essentially heartless men, who knew that they were sometimes ready to swap sexual favours for a few good dinners; and soon Jenny had been seduced by one Pat Moran. She fell violently in love with him, and remained loyal to the point of wanting to marry him, even when it appeared that Moran had given her gonorrhoea, by sleeping with her when he knew that he was infectious. Later it became clear that Moran knew Jenny was Robert Graves's daughter, and wanted to get her pregnant. Then he hoped to blackmail Robert into permitting the marriage (and perhaps even into paying off his debts) by threatening a public scandal.[60]

When Jenny discovered that she was ill, she was too frightened at first to tell anyone but her friends in the chorus; but Tom Matthews had noticed, on 5 November, that something was wrong: when he danced with her that evening at the Dorchester, Jenny was 'shaking and distraught, constantly looking over her shoulder to watch for the arrival of someone she either longed or dreaded to see';[61] and her unhappy visit to Dorset Street on Tuesday 17 November must have left her father feeling very apprehensive.

The next Tuesday, Robert arranged to meet Jenny again, this time at her lodgings at Curzon House, in Mayfair. She was so late for this appointment that, by the time they met, Robert had already left her 'an angry note'; but after shopping together (she placated him by persuading him to buy himself an expensive vicuña overcoat)[62] they had lunch at the Spotted Dog in Burton Mews. Here Jenny introduced her father to Pat Moran, and another friend, Tony Wheeler. Still nothing was said by Jenny either about her illness, or about her relationship with Moran; but Tony Wheeler, a married man who struck Robert as 'hard-boiled', spoke against Jenny living alone, and said that 'without a "background" – you'd only get a chap like Pat "if you wanted to marry"'.[63]

Graves noted this advice with some misgiving, but there did not seem to be any immediate crisis, and so he merely invited Jenny to supper the following day. Then he went on to the interview which he had been granted by Winston Churchill, with whom he discussed the possibility of intervention in the Spanish Civil War. Churchill's view was that both sides had their hands stained with innocent blood, and that Great Britain would not stand for intervention. Graves, who had made many visits to news cinemas, and had seen the audience reaction to such events as Franco being proclaimed Dictator, suggested that public feeling was strongly against the Fascists; but when Churchill asked him directly whether he wished for intervention, Graves replied cleverly: 'Not in any sense of taking sides in Spain, but of defending British interests in the Mediterranean.'[64]

The mention of British interests touched a raw nerve, and Churchill, overwrought, began 'rushing up and down the room'. He told Graves that seven French deputies, some of the best brains in their country, had just been making frantic appeals to him to urge intervention; and he lamented British military weakness, which he blamed on Baldwin, then Prime Minister. Churchill added that he was most pessimistic about the future: there would be 'Equal chances of victory or defeat' when it came to a European war; and Parliament, at present, was 'lethargic'. Graves nevertheless suggested that if he spoke out on the Spanish issue, urging intervention, he would have 'an overwhelming popular following'.[65] Churchill still would not believe that intervention was militarily possible; but Graves had persuaded him that public opinion favoured intervention more strongly than he had thought; and a week and a half later, when making a major speech at the Albert Hall, Winston Churchill declared publicly that 'he wished the liberal, free nations of the world had the power and strength to separate the combatants and procure a parley'.[66]

On Wednesday 25 November, the day after Graves's interview with Churchill, Jenny came to Dorset Street for supper with Robert and Laura; and, although protesting in answer to Robert's enquiry that she was happy enough living alone, she knew that sooner or later she must tell him of her predicament. She came to see him every day for the rest of that week;[67] and finally, on Tuesday 1 December, she plucked up the courage to tell Robert about her disease. The news came as an enormous shock. Robert was physically at a low ebb, having just begun a course of injections to clear up another boil; and that night he and Laura stayed up discussing Jenny's future until three in the morning, at which hour they resolved to 'send for N[ancy]. N[icholson].'.[68]

By Thursday morning, Nancy had arrived from Wiltshire, and she and Robert spent most of that day talking to Jenny about her future. By the evening nothing had been decided, except that for the time being Jenny should continue with her dancing, while Nancy should take a flat and stay in London until all could agree on some long-term plan.

On Friday, their discussions continued, totally overshadowing so far as they were concerned the constitutional crisis which had suddenly broken over the King's involvement with the American divorcee Mrs Simpson. When Graves went out, he was amazed to find crowds in the streets chanting slogans on behalf of the beleaguered monarch. The next morning Robert and Nancy agreed finally that Jenny should go down to Wiltshire to stay with her mother while possible cures for her illness were being thoroughly investigated; and after a farewell supper at Prada's Jenny was escorted to the Dorchester for a final night of dancing, and then whisked away to a flat belonging to one of Nancy's friends.[69]

Before seeing Jenny off to Wiltshire, Robert took her to Paddington Station, where he warned her to have nothing more to do with Pat Moran, and as a result they had a violent argument. Graves went to the Dorchester where he had further long discussions about Jenny's difficulties with Sherrick, her manager. Later that day, Robert posted to Nancy an impassioned letter in which, after declaring how good it was that the two of them had been able to 'get together over this', he admitted that 'I *did* boil over at Jenny this morning when she accused me of being a Victorian! My Bloody Christ!' He added that, for Moran to have infected Jenny knowingly was:

the mark of a *devil*.... O Nancy, for Christ's sake get her to see that she has been *bewitched*, and make her vow on her knees to put all that foulness behind her – burn that picture of him with a pair of tongs, give away all his gifts to her, *break* with him irrevocably in a short note....[70]

For the next week, while Jenny remained in Wiltshire, Robert tried to return to work, but without much success. There was no lack of good news to encourage him: Denham Studios had announced that the filming of *I, Claudius* was now to be undertaken by that great director, Josef von Sternberg; and they also told Graves that the contract for another project, known as the 'refugee' film, would soon be ready.[71] In addition, Graves and Liddell-Hart at last agreed with the Lawrence Trustees about a limited edition of 1,000 copies of their work, to be followed by a trade edition once the official *Letters* had appeared in print. However, Graves was understandably preoccupied by worries about his daughter, who for a time was threatened by a possible abortion as well as by the ravages of venereal disease. Graves wrote about Jenny to Mrs Churchill (enclosing a letter to Winston in which he wittily reminded him that in a traditional Fable, 'Baldwin' was the name reserved for the ass).[72] He also wrote to Jenny herself. Furthermore he consulted his doctor and, during the course of one period of thirty-six hours, he not only telephoned Nancy but also wrote to her no fewer than five times.

At this stage Robert was hoping that Nancy could find somewhere for Jenny's treatment in Bath; but she failed, so that, on 14 December, Jenny was brought back to London, where Robert settled her at great expense into a private nursing home called Belleville. There Jenny remained for several weeks. Robert visited her every day, with a constant supply of fruit, flowers and magazines, and at first Jenny seemed grateful, and was 'glad to see me';[73] but after a few days that changed.

The trouble began on 19 December when Jenny, not content with complaining 'about the ward, the nurses, [and] about [Laura] ... sending her the wrong kind of bodice', told Robert that she had written to Pat Moran, and that she wanted to go on seeing him. Later that day, Laura wrote sternly to Jenny saying that she had no right to send Robert home shaking with anger as a result of her cruelly self-centred attitude;[74] and on 20 December, fortified by Laura's advice, Graves returned to Belleville where (as he reported to Nancy) he was:

> dreadfully harsh with [Jenny] and felt bloody, but it was about time I showed her that I was tired of being fooled.... [I] said that naturally one expected a person to put the person they loved before their relatives & friends, so long as that person loved in return and was reasonably decent.... [But if Jenny] made a point of being 'loyal' to [Moran], it meant a complete break with me, and she could go to Hell in her own way....

Robert went on that the problem was Jenny's 'absurd vanity and selfishness. Poor darling'; and that at the end of his speech she had broken down in tears, apologized, and said that she would write contrite letters both to him and to Laura that very evening.[75]

Days of happier visits were regularly interspersed with unpleasant scenes of this kind, but it all had the effect of bringing Robert, Nancy and Laura closer together than they had been since the days before the arrival on the scene of Geoffrey Phibbs back in 1929. As in those days, most members of the Graves clan were kept to some extent in the dark about what was really happening: Amy, for example, heard that Jenny was suffering from 'strain', and would probably give up dancing to become an actress;[76] Charles and Peggy, who had been so kind to Jenny, were not even allowed to know her whereabouts (which led to Charles speaking very angrily to Robert over the telephone); John, who had been back in favour for some months, was also forbidden to 'meddle' in Jenny's affairs;[77] while Laura wrote sympathetic letters to Nancy about Jenny's worst excesses. At Christmas, Nancy sent Laura a friendly card, and gave Robert two little china poodles; and Robert responded by giving Nancy a present of a guillotine for use in her printing work. Early in January 1937 – after taking Sam for a highly successful visit to an ear specialist, as a result of which he was able to hear birdsong for the first time, and to converse with his mother across the width of a room – Nancy lunched with Robert at the Josef; and it was even decided (when Robert, Laura and Nancy had heard the news that Sally was to be married to one Richard Chilver later in the month) that all three would attend the wedding, with the proviso that if one of them could not be present at the last moment – which is what happened – then neither would the others.[78]

Jenny was discharged from Belleville nursing home on 8 January, two days after her eighteenth birthday; but her freedom was strictly limited; and, within four days, she was once again under medical supervision. Complications had set in which made an operation necessary; and on Tuesday 12 January Jenny was admitted to Hammersmith Hospital. On Wednesday she underwent a successful operation; and on Thursday, Robert wrote to Nancy saying that as soon as Jenny was fit to leave hospital, she must once again become Nancy's responsibility.[79]

The reason was that for tax purposes Robert must avoid acquiring an English domicile; and this meant that he and Laura had to leave the country at least two months before the tax-year ended on 5 April.[80]

At the beginning of 1937, Robert had still been hoping that in the near future he and Laura might be able to 'return to Deyá after all, if in any way practicable';[81] but the continuing Civil War in Spain made that impossible. Both Holland, and the Bordeaux region of France, were discussed as alternatives; but eventually it was decided that at the beginning of February they would go to Switzerland and live for a while at Lugano, of which their Deyá neighbours Georg Schwarz and his housekeeper Emmy Strenge, who fled there, had sent glowing reports.

Robert Graves seems to have welcomed the thought of a change from London; but Laura Riding was initially 'depressed at the idea of a 2 months trip out of England, especially with so much work in hand'.[82] With the help of Karl Goldschmidt, who had been living close by, at 7, Dorset Street, Riding had been working hard on preparing for publication both her novel *A Trojan Ending* and the third volume of *Epilogue*; while she was also thinking seriously about her plans for a dictionary.[83] This, as Tom Matthews writes,

> was to be a kind of etymological dictionary, like Skeat's – but with a fundamental difference that would make it unique in its field. Instead of depending on the harmless drudgery of lexicographers to dig up the root definitions of key words, Laura's poetic intelligence would illuminate and irradiate these nuggets of scholarship: she would supply the key definitions, making them not only exact but poetic.[84]

However, Riding's energy was principally directed at this time towards solving a more urgent problem. There were intense discussions with a number of people including Robert, Harry and Alix Kemp, Alan Hodge and Maisie Somerville, during the course of which Laura began drafting a circular 'Letter on International Affairs'.[85] This was to be sent to a representative selection of the men and women on whom she was depending to save the world from the current 'international muddle';[86] and her idea was that their replies would form the basis of an influential book.

On the day after Jenny's operation, Laura was asking Robert for his final words of advice on the existing draft of the 'Letter'; and two days later, on 16 January, she considered that it was ready for publication. 'What shall we do?', she asked her readers:

> Let us first consider who 'we' are – we, the 'inside' people. First of all we are the women. Women are those of us who are most characteristically, most natively, 'inside' people ... with us, on the inside of things, we have had the poets and the painters and all those men who have been able to treat the outer mechanism of life as subsidiary to its inner realities – who have discovered the inside importances.[87]

What had gone wrong, in Riding's view, was that the 'outer' and predominantly 'male' world – which included the world of international affairs – had become 'recklessly disconnected from the world of personal life and thought', and had 'broken its affiliations with those inner realities which are predominantly female in quality'. [88] She concluded her 'Letter' with the plea for answers, which might 'help us all to see with a more united vision what this unhappiness is that surrounds us, and to know better what we may unitedly do about it *from the inside* – if, indeed, there is anything to be done'.[89]

On Tuesday 19 January, while Laura's 'Letter' was still at the printers, Nancy came up to London and had supper with Robert, Laura and Norman Cameron at the Dorset Street flat. Afterwards Laura worked with Norman on a translation of work by Rimbaud, while Robert and Nancy talked; and on Wednesday morning Nancy collected Jenny from Hammersmith Hospital, and took her down to recuperate at Sutton Veny, in the hope that, when Jenny felt strong enough, she might go on to stay with Diccon Hughes and his family at Laugharne Castle in South Wales. After that her future was uncertain; but, when Robert visited Denham on Thursday, Korda told him that Jenny would certainly be given a part in the film of *I, Claudius*, the final scenario for which should be ready in a week.

Earlier in the month, when writing to Julie Matthews, Graves had referred to some extraordinary twists and turns in the saga of the *I, Claudius* scenario, telling her that 'its permutations in and out of German, Hungarian and English as various big-shots take turns at it would make you laugh'; and he commented that 'Films are insane: if they occasionally drop gold on our hats as we pass, that's all right.'[90] Now, however, his future in the film world was suddenly looking very hopeful. Korda told him that in a week's time he would be discussing a contract by which Graves and Riding would jointly write some more scenarios; and that he might very well need Robert's particular help on the script of a film about T.E.Lawrence and the Arab Revolt. A few days later, encouraged by Korda's promises, and perhaps also by the prospect of heavy sales of his 'book-of-the-film' version of *I, Claudius*, Graves turned down the offer of a massive advance of £2,000 for a book with the title *In the Steps of Hannibal*. 'I said I didn't go in anyone's steps,' he confided rather grandly to his diary, 'H.V.Morton's [author of the popular *In the Steps of St Paul*], Christ's or anyone's.'[91]

A further meeting between Korda and Graves on Thursday 4 February, ended with Korda promising 'work in 3 months' time & payment for the *Claudius* scenario';[92] and on Friday afternoon, with this encouraging news to cheer them on their way, Robert Graves, Laura Riding and Karl Goldschmidt set out for Switzerland.

CHAPTER 5
The Villa Guidi

Robert Graves and his companions spent the next four months at Lugano in Italian Switzerland, where they rented a set of furnished rooms in the Villa Guidi, an ex-Milanese palace in the suburb of Paradiso. Laura Riding was at her most demanding; but Harry Kemp had already noticed that Graves often seemed 'at his happiest ... when he was kept busy fulfilling [Riding's] many day-to-day demands of him', and that even when she was at her most high-handed, he could be 'eminently cheerful and resilient';[93] and indeed, Robert seems to have been feeling not only well – despite another boil – but happy. In mid-February 1937 he settled down to his 'first real day's work for weeks ... [an] answer to Laura's "Letter on International Affairs"', copies of which had by then been despatched to some four hundred people.

The world had reached its present unhappy state, Graves explains, because so much of what happened was 'based on a sentimental glorification of paternity. History proper', Graves asserts, reverting to a theme which he had first outlined as long ago as 1924 in his Biblical romance *My Head, My Head!*,

History proper begins everywhere with the suppression of matriarchal culture by patriarchy, of poetic myth by prosaic records of generation – how this hero begat that hero and he another – with notes of the battles and laws which made each hero famous. And all subsequent history has been eloquent of the pride that man has felt in the knowledge that he is the cause of woman's pregnancy – and so the real creator of her children, and so responsible for their behaviour and maintenance, and so to be looked up to by her. The original discovery was so stimulating to his self-pride that he elaborated it into a universal religion; for indeed the Jewish and Christian and Mohammedan and Hindu Gods are all paternity symbols, and the Chinese are paternity fanatics.[94]

Graves offers no blue-print for a new society, though it is clear from what he says that it will somehow come to be dominated by women and 'inside' men;[95] and he makes it clear that, unlike many of his fellow-poets during the 1930s, he is not going to be drawn into any 'societies, leagues, meetings, badges ... because for the inside to inform itself ... by the outside method of propaganda would be to confuse the issue with organized pacifism, social-ism, feminism and so on. These isms', he says, 'are not to the purpose.' Political minorities have no effective power, and the only way forward must be for intelligent 'inside' people to spread their ideas on how to live 'by means of private talk and personal example'.[96]

However, it was one of Graves's most fundamental beliefs that it was not a poet's job to become involved in politics; and in one of his most interesting poems at this time, 'The Fallen Tower of Siloam', there is an implied, though perhaps subconscious, criticism of Riding's determined efforts to bring about social and political change: 'It behoved us indeed, as poets,' Graves wrote,

> To be silent in Siloam, to foretell
> No visible calamity.[97]

He felt happier when Riding concentrated on her literary work: they were both looking over their poems for possible collected editions; and on 13 March Graves noted in his diary with a mixture of relief and sorrow that Laura had written 'her first poem for months: "To Juan Marroig in Pri-son"'.[98]

Graves and Riding had maintained indirect contact with Juan Marroig by corresponding both with Short, the British Agent in Palma, and with Gelat's sister Anita who had been living for some years at Rennes in Brittany. Gelat could have joined Anita and her family at Rennes; but despite his evident loyalty to the Republican side in the Spanish Civil War he had too many financial interests at stake to consider leaving Deyá; and on 1 March a letter from Short reached Lugano with the unsurprising but depressing news that Gelat had been locked up in mid-February. According to his son, 'young Juan', Gelat's imprisonment was the result of further machinations by his old enemy the doctor, and it seemed likely that 'nothing serious' would happen.[99] However, Graves and Riding were both under-standably worried about their old friend. For several weeks they anxiously awaited news, only to hear on 22 March that he was still languishing in gaol, and that, so far, the authorities had not even bothered to bring a formal charge.[100]

Gradually Graves's self confidence was returning. It was a relief not to be too closely involved with Jenny for a while; and, when he heard that his daughter had contracted pleurisy and wanted to come to Switzerland for convalescence, he told Nancy that it would be 'difficult and inappropriate' and refused to have her.[101]

Not even news about the probable collapse of his hopes in the film world could seriously upset him. It was mid-March after a months shooting, when he heard from Denham Studios that Merle Oberon, who had been playing Messalina to Charles Laughton's Claudius, had been 'injured in a car-smash & the *I, Claudius* film is likely to be scrapped'.[102] Writing to Nancy with the news, Robert told her: '"That little bitch Merle Oberon" (Alex Korda in a private moment of spite) seems to have mucked it up. I was hoping to make quite a lot out of the bookstall version (finished today) but if the film isn't finished', he concluded philosophically, 'well, that's that. Something else, then'.[103]

Laura, by contrast, was overwhelmed with anxiety. She wrote to Nancy both about her general sense of powerlessness [104] and about her inability to sleep. When she did sleep she suffered from bad dreams: Robert was informed that her bedroom had 'evidently had a lot to do with death at one time or another'; and one day, early in April, when it was clear that *A Trojan Ending* was never going to be a great popular success (though it had received several complimentary reviews) she bemoaned the 'hopelessness of carrying on a decent writing or publishing business in face of the dark age opposition to anything good'.[105] Later that month, she had depressing news: Oxford University Press had turned down her *Dictionary* as being 'too individual and personal ... words cannot be put into straitjackets'; and on 22 April – the day that *Epilogue III* was published – Laura decided that she would collaborate with Robert upon a popular novel, which they decided to call *The Kind Ghost*.

Graves worked at this novel, later renamed *The Swiss Ghost*, for the remainder of their stay at the Villa Guidi; but the surviving draft shows that it was a dreadfully tedious piece of work, without the slightest imaginative force. Graves's creative energies appear to have been going almost entirely into his poems, of which he was suddenly writing a large number. Many of them, including 'A Wounded Man', 'Tolerance' and 'Pledge to Strangeness', were later discarded; but of those which survived two are of particular interest: 'The Laureate', in which his theme is that of a poet who has committed creative suicide, and yet 'Still turns for comfort to the western flames / That glitter a cold span above the sea';[106] and 'Or to Perish Before Day', in which Graves describes a dreamlike world of poetic magic which contrasts strongly with dull reality.[107]

On the day that Robert completed 'Or to Perish Before Day' he noted in his diary that he was 'feeling the weight of exile more than ever'; and, perhaps in an effort to impose some order upon a life which seemed increasingly directionless, he had a long discussion with Laura about their finances, about the Seizin Press, and about their friends: particularly Maisie Somerville with whom there had been a serious row, as she had written 'accusing Laura of judging by hearsay'.[108]

CHAPTER 6

A Telegram from Anita

Robert and Laura gave notice that they would leave the Villa Guidi at the beginning of June: Harry and Alix Kemp had found a house at Ewhurst in Surrey which it was proposed that the four of them and Karl would share. But soon after returning to England Robert became too unwell to enjoy the company of his old friends. It was discovered that his latest 'boil' was actually a fistula connected with the colon, for which a minor operation was necessary. For a while Robert became extremely gloomy; and on entering hospital he reverted briefly to complete emotional dependence upon Riding, penning the first lines of a self-condemnatory poem about lust and guilt which began:

> Heart with what fearfulness you ached
> How lecherously mused upon
> That horror with which Leda quaked
> Under the spread wings of the swan.[109]

On Monday 21 June, Robert underwent a successful operation, talking to his sister Rosaleen beforehand while he was having his 'intra-venous Twilight sleep injection' (he complained that she spoilt the effect of this by discussing a 'controversial topic'); and later being visited both by Laura and by Nancy. He was not in much pain, thanks to 'opium draughts every four hours', but would be allowed only fluids for the next four days;[110] and so he was in a considerably weakened state when, on Thursday evening, Harry Kemp arrived with a telegram from Gelat's sister Anita which read as follows:

= IOI RENNES 1381 14 24 1645 =
=LAURA RIDUIG 5 NOTTINGHAM STREET LONDON W =
PAPA LIBRE TENGO BUENAS NOTICIAS ABRAZOS
ANITA = = = =[111]

So Gelat had been freed at last! Robert Graves wept with relief for about half an hour on hearing this news;[112] four days later his spirits were still further improved when he heard that Cassells had made an offer for an historical novel which he proposed to write about Belisarius, a general in the service of the Byzantine emperor Justinian; and from then on he made a rapid recovery.

This recovery was aided by a visit from his sister Clarissa, whom he had not seen for almost eight years, and to whom he had written most bitterly back in 1932. However – much to Clarissa's surprise and delight – an extremely friendly letter from Robert had reached her in Palestine, where she was then in charge of children's broadcasting, in the autumn of 1936; and they now resumed a mutually respectful friendship, based on their admiration for each other's writing, which was to endure until Clarissa's death almost forty years later.

Alan Hodge, too, came to visit Robert Graves in hospital on 5 July (the day before Robert was due to leave) bringing his friend, Beryl Pritchard, a young undergraduate of twenty-one, who was to play an increasingly important part first in his life, and then in Robert's.

CHAPTER 7
Beryl Pritchard

On 22 February 1915, twins named Hardinge and Beryl[113] were born in Hampstead as the fourth and fifth children of a prosperous London solicitor named Harry Pritchard, and his wife Amy. Beryl's father was a man of great distinction, well known within his profession as an expert on legislation connected with local government, and during the course of his career he drafted single-handedly numerous Bills for Parliament on behalf of a number of local authorities, including the London County Council. Beryl's mother, on the other hand, was a quiet but charming woman with a somewhat unusual background. As a child, Amy had seen a great deal of her uncle, the well-known naturalist Frank Buckland (an enemy of Darwin's) at whose house – though she was not at all fond of animals – she was often placed in uncomfortably close proximity to cheetahs, monkeys and wild life of all kinds; and where she was also introduced to Siamese twins and to people like 'giants' who were suffering from some genetic or pituitary irregularity.

Fortunately for Beryl, both Harry and Amy believed strongly that boys should not be the only ones in their family to be well educated. Her older brother Wentworth, the third in the family, had certainly had an entirely traditional education, going first to Charterhouse and then to Balliol College, Oxford, before joining the family firm of Sharpe, Pritchard & Co.; but then her eldest sister Evelyn, who was already fifteen when Beryl was born, had preceded him to Oxford, where she was up at St Hilda's College; while her next sister, Enid, had been up at the Home Student's College, Oxford (later St Anne's), before training as a solicitor.

Beryl herself was sent first to the nearest day-school to her home an then, after taking matriculation, to Queen's College, Harley Street: and extremely enlightened institution. Unusually for a girls' school in those days, it was run by a headmaster; and, although there was a relaxed atmosphere, the academic standards were high. Here, during her last two years of schooling, Beryl developed a keen interest in Natural History and Botany; and she had also had an unusually good grounding in both History and Literature, as well as developing a special love of poetry. At school, she studied the work of T.S.Eliot; and through her friends she was introduced to the periodical *New Verse*, which was edited in Hampstead, and featured the work of other contemporary poets such as W.H.Auden and Louis Mac-Neice; while she also knew Harold Monro's Poetry Bookshop, where she came across the work of Robert Graves, whose first volume of poems, *Over the Brazier*, had been published by Monro back in 1916.

It was the strength of her answers to examination papers in History and English Literature, in the autumn of 1932, that led to the Home Student's College, Oxford, offering Beryl a place for the following October; and when she explained that she would prefer to read Politics, Philosophy and Economics, the College readily agreed.

While Beryl was up at Oxford, she poured her energies not only into her course – where she found philosophy 'most fun' – but also into politics. It was the time of the Great Depression, of mass unemployment, and of the Jarrow hunger marches; and where her brother Hardinge and others like him[114] believed in a religious solution to man's troubles, Beryl had a more practical turn of mind. Strongly influenced by G.D.H.Cole's lectures on Socialism,[115] she joined the Oxford University Labour Club, distributed leaflets outside the Morris motor manufacturing works; and, on her twenty-first birthday, in February 1936, during her last year at Oxford, she toasted the coming to power of the new left-wing Government in Spain. Although she never joined the Communist Party, one of her best friends did so; and she remained strongly sympathetic, not only to Socialist regimes but to anyone who had ever suffered (as did the unemployed of her youth) at the hands of an apparently uncaring right-wing establishment.

It was while she was at Oxford that Beryl Pritchard had first become friendly with Alan Hodge; and they kept in touch with each other while Alan was in Deyá during the summer of 1936. By then, Beryl had gone down from Oxford, first taking a job in Yorkshire as a sales-girl with Unilever – which she lost through an understandable lack of enthusiasm in selling an expensive brand of frying fat to people who were too poor to buy it – and then returning to London where a short secretarial course was followed by a variety of jobs, including counter work at Christmas in the Oxford Street branch of Woolworths.

Alan was one of the first to welcome Graves and Riding back from Lugano on 8 June 1937; and ten days later he had brought Beryl to their Nottingham Street flat. Her coming was no surprise: Beryl had first been drawn to

Robert's attention nearly six months earlier, in January 1937, shortly before he and Laura were due to leave for Lugano. Alan had failed to turn up to a 'goodbye party' given for Robert and Laura by James and Mary Reeves; and the following morning he explained to Robert that he had missed the party 'because of Beryl', and talked about her at some length.[116] Beryl found the flat itself 'awful'; and at first she was very much in awe of Laura; but she was amused by the pleased tone of voice in which Robert announced, 'I'm going to have an operation!', and by the end of that first meeting she felt that she liked both of them very much.

Laura seems to have been uncertain about Beryl at first, perhaps wondering whether she might not draw Alan away from his allegiance to their circle; and when Laura visited Robert in hospital on 27 June she told him that Beryl had been 'rather rude' to her the previous evening, and made Robert discuss at some length what he described in his diary entry for that day as 'the Alan–Beryl position'.[117] However, Alan showed no signs of falling away: indeed, on 6 July, the day after taking Beryl to visit Robert in hospital, it was Alan who was deputed to fetch Robert home to 'a frantic scene of packing and telephoning at 5, Nottingham Street';[118] and when Graves and Riding had settled with the Kemps into a rented house at Ewhurst – Harry Kemp had given up teaching for the time being, to write full-time – Alan Hodge and Beryl Pritchard were among their earliest visitors.

CHAPTER 8
Archery and *Count Belisarius*

Robert Graves, Laura Riding, and Harry and Alix Kemp arrived at Ewhurst on the afternoon of Wednesday 7 July 1937. Graves was still weak after his long stay in hospital and 'could not help much'[119] with the initial settling in; but he was extremely pleased to find that their house, Highcroft, which Laura had earlier described as 'rather depressing',[120] was much better than she had made out. Certainly, it was quite ordinary, but it was comfortable, and it had a large garden 'with a good lawn, & [a] rough bit at the end with a huge oak and a lean-to suitable for camping under'.[121] In any case, in Graves's pleasure at being both out of hospital and out of London he had soon forgotten (as he put it) that he was an invalid:[122] on Thursday he walked all the way into the village with Laura to look for a maid; and on Friday he 'carried tables upstairs etc, washed up 2 meals, helped to cook one, unpacked and cleared up'.[123]

Looking around his 'bed-workroom' on Saturday, Robert found it 'pleasant now with all my things'; which included:

[a] work-table lined with brown paper & my Swiss pewter tray-plate & marble ... [a] paper weight and pewter cigarette case, & my refugee toys – ... [a] pin cushion ... [and a] lock & key, the N[ancy] N[icholson] dogs etc. My patchwork quilt (the triangle-cut one) on my bed. My ash chair with the rush bottom.[124]

On the walls there was a map of Spain, to remind him of the country from which he had been exiled; and a drawing of Solomon, the dog which he left behind in Deyá. His pleasure was the limited one of a boy at boarding-school, who decorates his study so as to make it a small corner of the home world from which he has been temporarily exiled; and perhaps it was with something of this in his mind that on the very next day, 11 July, Graves asked Harry Kemp to drive him over to Charterhouse, where many years ago he had felt exiled from his home in North Wales.

Like most returning pupils – and despite his generally hostile account of Charterhouse in *Good-Bye to All That* – Graves felt mildly nostalgic when he revisited his old school. Entering Gownboys, he looked for a few moments at 'pleasant boys spending a rowdy (wet) idle Sunday afternoon';[125] and he also went into the school library where, much to his delight – as he wrote to his mother – he was recognized after more than twenty years by 'the stammering Librarian' Mr Stokes.[126]

Graves's current reading centred around research for the new historical novel. On his second day at Ewhurst, he had completed Mahon's *Belisarius*; and then began reading Procopius, the Byzantine historian, who had accompanied Belisarius on several of his campaigns, and had written both about these and – in his *Historia Arcana* – about the personal lives of members of the Emperor Justinian's court. In the intervals of doing this research, Graves completed preparing his *Collected Poems* for publication, wrote an occasional new poem, and worked with Riding on *The Swiss Ghost*. On 12 July Alan Hodge and Karl Goldschmidt arrived, and were found rooms in Ewhurst by Laura; four days later Beryl came to stay with Alan; and gradually a kind of routine developed.

Robert continued to do a good deal for Laura, and once during their stay at Highcroft, when Alix and Robert were respectively getting breakfast trays for Harry and Laura, Alix joked '*Lives of Wives!*',[127] the title of one of Laura's latest projects; but his mornings were generally devoted to his own work. Laura, meanwhile, was dealing with her 'Letter Book', consisting largely of the answers which she had received to 'The First Protocol', together with her own comments, and later to be published as *The World and Ourselves*; while she also spent the first hour of each day generously 'going over, sentence by sentence', what Harry Kemp had written the previous day for his book *The Left Heresy*,[128] an account of why Kemp – both as a poet and as a former Communist – now believed that poetry should be entirely divorced from politics.

Each day after lunch, Kemp records, there was time for more light-hearted activities. To begin with, he and Graves:

> engaged in a brief game we ourselves invented, on a solitaire marbles board. In the course of these encounters he became Ffyffes-Graves and I Kemp-Hovis. Laura in turn invented the 'Thread Game'. This was played on the sitting-room carpet. Each of two contestants, facing each other about a yard apart placed a number of coloured threads parallel in front of him. Each then in turn tried with one strong puff to blow one of his threads so that it lay across one of his opponent's. Overlapping

threads became the prize of the successful puffer, till there were none left. L[aura] R[iding] enjoyed watching this gentle buffoonery between two of her admiring males; and occasionally got down on hands and knees to play the game herself.[129]

There were also ball-games to be played in the garden: one of them, of Robert's invention, involved 'putting on the lawn, driving a coloured india-rubber ball between opposite goals';[130] and on 24 July 1937, Robert Graves's forty-second birthday, he was given by Alix and Harry 'an old English bow and a quiver of arrows'.[131] Archery became for a number of weeks a consuming interest. To begin with Graves simply shot at a formal target; but he became interested enough to begin fletching his own arrows; and soon he was stalking rabbits and shooting at them in the neighbouring fields, without much success; though once, as he recorded, he missed one 'by a mere paw's breadth'.[132] More work followed; then perhaps a walk through the countryside; and in the evening Robert, Laura, Harry and Alix and anyone who was staying with them would usually walk into the village for a drink at The Crown, much admired by Robert for its 'most beautiful garden, lawn, roses, dovecote and enclosing cypresses'.[133]

Two days before his birthday, Graves had begun writing the novel which he first called simply *Belisarius*; then, at Laura's suggestion, *The Faith of Belisarius*; and finally, on the publisher's insistence, *Count Belisarius*. Unfortunately, although there are many very fine set-pieces in the novel, such as Graves's description of the battle of Daras, *Count Belisarius* is sometimes overloaded with tedious historical details, and also suffers from a serious central flaw. Namely, Belisarius himself. Painted as having been not only a Christian gentleman, but a wholly good and admirable character from his childhood onwards (Laura's proposed title for the novel was well chosen), Belisarius never entirely engages our interest. Later Graves would respond angrily to critics who wrote along these lines, asserting in one instance that it was 'a rather shocking comment on twentieth-century literary taste that when, as a rare case, a really good man is shown actively, patiently, loyally at work in his struggle against the forces of confusion, nobody must admire him whole-heartedly: it must be said that he is wooden, humourless, over-correct, that he '"does not come to life"'.[134] Graves could not see that it was he himself who was at fault, for having failed to show his readers even a glimpse of the darker side of his hero's soul. By contrast, the most striking aspect of *Count Belisarius* is Graves's complex portrayal of Antonina, the shrewd, level-headed prostitute whom Belisarius marries.

In writing about Antonina, Graves consciously records a view of sexual behaviour altogether at variance to that which, under Riding's influence, he had been expressing for the past eight years. We are told, for example, that at the age of fifteen Antonina 'had already lived a promiscuous life for three years'; and Graves adds that 'being a healthy, vivacious girl, she had thoroughly enjoyed herself and suffered no ill-effects'. His rider to this statement is that 'amusement with men is an altogether different thing from love for a man',[135] in which case a different set of principles applies. But he had made his point that sexuality in itself is no cause for shame; and so strongly had Graves become attached to this wholesome idea that when he wrote *Count Belisarius* he had begun by making Antonina the narrator. Not surprisingly Riding did what she could to tone down this aspect of the novel (and probably weakened its emotional force as a result), by persuading Graves to alter his viewpoint, so that in its final version the story is narrated not by Antonina, but by her slave, the eunuch Eugenius.

Riding continued to work energetically upon her own projects, and her remarkable *Collected Poems*, the volume upon which her lasting reputation as a poet depends, was ready for the publishers by 25 August; but she and Graves still relied almost entirely upon Graves's earnings; and, as the summer of 1937 wore on, it became increasingly important that *Count Belisarius* should be a popular success. In mid-July Korda was talking once again about a film of T.E.Lawrence's life, and telephoned Graves, wanting to give him £200 for the film rights of his *Lawrence and the Arabs*, but this project came to nothing; as did a '*Smuggler*' screenplay which had been commissioned by Korda soon after their return to England from Lugano.[136] Meanwhile the premature end of the *I, Claudius* film had meant that Graves's 'book of the film' was worthless, so that by mid-August the prospective American publishers, Random House, were demanding that Graves should return the $1,000 advance which they had paid him, or that the sum should be set off against some other work. In addition, there was disappointing news about the sales of Seizin Press books; and the result of all this was that during the last week in September Graves and Riding became so depressed about their publishing prospects that they decided, once it became safe to return to Majorca, they would 'start a school in Deyá'.[137]

Earlier in the summer their days at Highcroft had been enlivened both by the proximity of Karl Goldschmidt and Alan Hodge and by visits from numerous friends. Karl, besides performing his usual secretarial duties, and joining in with everything from light-hearted ball-games to serious discussions, also fell in love with the cook at Highcroft, Marie, and announced on 7 September that he hoped one day to marry her – 'All right with us', commented Robert Graves laconically.[138] Hodge, who was helping Robert research *Count Belisarius*, occasionally brought Beryl with him to Highcroft, and told Robert that he too was hoping to get married.

In August they were briefly visited by Jenny. As usual she had been running into debt; but recently she had written Robert a long letter in which, after first complaining that 'you won't trust me', she had successfully held out an olive-branch by adding, '(or perhaps you do [trust me] and are a friend and Laura too – how nice that would be)'; then she had declared that she was 'most awfully glad' that Robert had recovered – both from his operation and from a bout of violent toothache which had only been ended by the extraction of an eye-tooth – and she sent Laura her love.[139] This letter smoothed things over between father and daughter, and encouraged Robert to pay Jenny's debts; but, by the end of September, she was at the centre of another family dispute. Charles and Peggy had made some extremely hostile comments to Amy about Robert's treatment of Jenny; and when Amy unwisely retailed these to Robert, the result was a very angry correspondence, in the course of which Robert wrote to Jenny 'ordering her to break with Charles unless he apologised and retracted'.[140]

Further awkwardness was caused during Graves's and Riding's stay at Ewhurst by their association with an Irish Catholic called Mary Lucy, a friend of Nancy Nicholson's family, who had developed a feeling of enormous respect for Riding's literary work. Arriving at Highcroft on Robert's birthday, she stayed there for three days. During this time she impressed Robert so much that after reading some of her work he wrote in his diary: 'Mary Lucy is a poet ... obviously she is a poet. A year ago [she] had had an instinct about Laura: from a chance word about her. Would get to know her.'[141] However, Mary's husband John Lucy disapproved of her having anything to do with Robert and Laura, and they received first 'a quarrelsome letter, self-assertive';[142] then, when they had replied to that, a further letter which Graves described as 'very vulgar';[143] and next a 'mad' letter, accompanied by one from Mary Lucy, from which they learned that her husband had been physically assaulting her.[144]

There was also a difficult meeting on 14 September with James Reeves's sister Ethel, who talked so unceasingly that she was described by Graves as 'the most tiring woman I know'. When he 'took her for a walk to get her at least out of a confined space', he discovered to his surprise that she had come 'as a sort of emissary of [his former friend and mentor] Mallik who is finishing his philosophy book and will then return to the mountains, having done his duty by the race'.[145]

By far the most awkwardness, however, was caused by the unfolding of a variation in a now quite predictable pattern of behaviour on Riding's part, relating to the friendship between herself, Robert Graves and Harry and Alix Kemp. To begin with Riding worked for long hours with Harry Kemp – in a process no doubt chiefly designed to help him with *The Left Heresy*, but also partly aimed at rousing Robert's jealousy – while Alix enjoyed light-hearted banter with Robert: so that, for example, she teased him by renaming his archery 'lechery'.[146]

However, this was nothing. Harry and Alix were devoted to each other, and Robert was no more seriously attracted to Alix than Harry was to Laura. Later Harry Kemp recalled that:

> Although I admired [Laura Riding] and enjoyed working with her at first, she never had occasion (as occurred with Tom Matthews) to accuse me of having fallen in love with her. In fact I found her physically unattractive. Her undershot jaw, primly ascetic lips, rather prominent nose, curvaceous and tobacco-stained fingers and wobbly blue eyes, if anything slightly repelled me: as also did her too-theatrical Mayorquin [*sic*] costumes and gold-wire tiaras spelling LAURA. After three months house-sharing and intensive close contact, I began to resent her nit-picking bossiness; as did my wife. When this became noticeable to her an atmosphere of mounting hysteria was generated (LR was adept at this). The party was over.[147]

The Highcroft lease was not due to expire until the end of December; but by the last few days of September a strange and rather sinister atmosphere had developed. On the evening of Monday 27 September, bats got into both Robert's and Harry's rooms; and not long afterwards, in the early hours of Tuesday morning, everyone woke up and somehow found their way to Laura's bedroom, where they congregated round her bed, drank heather-wine, and worried about burglars. On Wednesday, after breakfast, Laura 'had violent colic pains, & almost sent for a doctor'; and Robert noted that Alix too was 'rather ill: nerves: with repercussions'.[148] Thursday morning was largely spent in talking about 'whether to go to France or stay in England'; and although the upshot was a 'decision to withhold decision for a month',[149] by Monday it had been settled (probably at Laura's instigation) that they would all make an early move to London.

This was not done explicitly on account of Harry and Alix's increasing antipathy for Laura, so that Harry later wondered to what extent Robert had been aware of 'the situation that had evolved primarily between LR and myself';[150] but within a week flat-hunting had begun in earnest; and on 20 October Graves and Riding agreed to rent a small house which would be vacant by the middle of the following month at 31, Alma Square, off the Abbey Road in St John's Wood.

The last few weeks at Highcroft had an uncomfortable feeling about them. Superficially it appeared that nothing much would be changing. Karl soon found rooms in Alma Square which he could share with Marie; while Harry and Alix Kemp took a flat in Abbey Road itself; before long Alan and Beryl would find a flat at 88, Adelaide Road, not far away in Hampstead; and there was every intention that communication between all of them should continue to be frequent and friendly. In addition, Graves was making excellent progress with *Count Belisarius*: before leaving Highcroft he had written a first draft of nineteen of the novel's twenty-four chapters; while Riding was similarly close to completing her work on *The World and Ourselves*.

However, nothing was quite so good as it had been. On Thursday 28 October, Graves wrote in his diary: 'Sunny day; arrows. But no marbles, a chill having fallen athwart things.' That day it was noticed, when they were out walking, that Riding had lost the topaz from one of her rings; and when, on Friday, Graves found it, 'by rationalised search', at the top of the stairs, Laura did not seem very pleased, but commented unkindly: 'You ought to buy a grocery shop & sell jams & pickles & say "I made them all myself." That would be your madness.'[151]

The following day there was a change of mood when Graves and Riding went up to London for a long weekend, partly to arrange things with the owner of the house they were to rent, and partly to see old friends: such as Norman Cameron, who treated them to oysters, pheasant and white Burgundy at Boulestin's; and Len Lye, with his 'Hollywood plans'. There was also great excitement on their first evening in London when Graves was rung up by the *Sunday Express* to be told that he 'was a candidate for the Nobel Prize in Literature'.[152] Graves and Riding 'talked late' after hearing the news: in the enthusiasm of the hour, Graves even 'decided to write a book about [Riding]' – perhaps to even up the balance in the event of his winning the prize – and the following afternoon, when Alan Hodge and Beryl Pritchard joined Robert and Laura for tea, they were busily making out 'a list of 16 good minds and several doubtfuls'.[153]

Once back at Highcroft, on Tuesday 2 November, this more cheerful and self-confident mood soon evaporated. On Thursday, after completing another twenty-one pages of *Count Belisarius*, Graves did write the first half page of his proposed book about Riding; but on the same day, when he was shooting in the garden, his antique yew-bow was broken, which somehow seems the more symbolic event; and he wrote in his diary that evening that he was now left with '10 orphaned arrows'.[154]

After a week of hard packing, putting back the old lampshades, and hanging up the old curtains, Graves noted that Highcroft was 'beginning to return to the sordidness in which we first found it'.[155] Then, three days before they left Ewhurst, there was a major disappointment: they heard on 12 November that the Nobel Prize had gone to the relatively unknown M.Du Gard. Graves's bow had been broken and now, echoing those words of the Psalmist which he had known so well since his childhood, it might be said that his spear had been knapped in sunder.[156] All that remained was for his chariots to be burned in the fire.

CHAPTER 9
The Covenant

London. Late November 1937. Robert Graves and Laura Riding moved into the house at 31, Alma Square in north-west London, while Harry and Alix occupied a Victorian Gothic flat in nearby Abbey Road. This separation, in Harry's words, 'probably saved the situation that had evolved primarily between L[aura] R[iding] and myself'; [157] and the four of them continued to meet frequently both in one another's houses and elsewhere.

For the next two and a half months, Graves was principally occupied with *Count Belisarius*. When he had completed it, Riding made numerous alterations; and almost as soon as those had been dealt with, in mid-February 1938, Graves had to start checking the proofs. He was also turning *A Trojan Ending* into a play; and with Laura just as tired as ever, and at work on her new *Lives of Wives* project, as well as trying to set the world to rights, there was no let-up in the pressure. When, on 5 March, Robert lunched with Amy, Rosaleen and two of Amy's protégés, miners' sons who, in Amy's words, were 'making their way up in the world', he had to leave early to return to his work, and Amy noticed that he was 'highly nervous'.[158] Visitors were continually arriving and interrupting his work, often with long sessions of serious discussion; and on one day, 19 March, after visits not only from his son David but, as Graves records, from 'Harry & Alix (Alan & Beryl [now married][159] & a person called 'Pina?' a German refugee) then David again & Len & Jane & Harry & Alix again', he became 'hysterically over-tired'.[160]

At least by 25 March, Laura Riding was on the last page of *The World and Ourselves*; and, 'Karl having a kold', as Robert writes, Alan and Beryl were helping her with the typing.[161] But Laura had already prepared the ground for another major initiative. The following day, despite having worked until 6 a.m. in the morning on her 'Letter Book', Laura Riding presided over a meeting of twenty-six of her closest associates, 'to decide on moral action to be taken by inside people: for outside disorders'.[162]

When Laura Riding's grand meeting began, soon after lunch on Saturday 26 March 1938, those present included Robert Graves, Alan Hodge and Beryl, Maisie Somerville, Honor Wyatt and Gordon Glover, Norman Cameron, James Reeves, John Aldridge and Lucie Brown, Len Lye, Harry and Alix Kemp, Dorothy and Ward Hutchinson, and two newcomers to the inner circle: Dorothy Simmons, a brilliant young sculptor in her early twenties, and her husband Montague, who wrote poetry and worked in the children's branch of the Home Office.[163]

The proceedings began with a speech from Laura which lasted about half an hour; and then nearly everyone else spoke. At a time of increasing despair among intellectuals about the state of the world and its gradual drift towards a war which, it was feared, would bring about the end of modern civilization, Riding offered her listeners hope; and such was the force of her personality that by the meeting's end (when it was agreed that a 'moral protocol' would be drafted 'on Sunday week') there had not been a single dissentient voice.[164]

Within two days of presiding over this preliminary meeting Riding had finally completed *The World and Ourselves* and was ready to begin work upon the Protocol. The first necessity as she saw it was to find the correct words to describe 'the inside way of doing things'. On the evening of Monday 28 March, she and Graves and Hodge therefore spent 'hours' on this problem, coming only to the conclusion that 'all good words' were 'either stiff or tainted'.[165] For the next few days, however, while Graves continued with his dramatization of *A Trojan Ending* and – with Liddell Hart's assistance – revised the proofs of *T.E.Lawrence to his Biographers*, Riding worked night and day like a woman possessed. By the end of the week she had not only corrected the proofs of her *Collected Poems*, and handed them over to Cassells, but she had also drafted twenty-six articles of a Protocol which could stand as a basis for moral judgement and practice.

On Saturday evening – after some encouragement from Liddell-Hart, who 'was in complete agreement with L.R. about moral war against dis-order', and even made some 'verbal suggestions for amending protocols' – Riding and Graves and Harry Kemp began going through the twenty-six articles word by word; but so important was it to Laura that the meaning should be clear and precise that, by midnight, they had 'only [covered] four articles'.[166] On Sunday 3 April, Graves and Riding together continued the work for a further nine and a half hours, from nine-thirty in the morning until seven at night; and there was then a formal meeting of sixteen 'insiders' at Maisie Somerville's. Laura went over the Protocol, while Beryl took notes, and a number of alterations were suggested, although Graves later observed that the only 'profound' amendment had been 'a Christian one of Maisie's'.[167]

To anyone who was a Christian, Riding's twenty-six articles eventually left a bitter taste in the mouth. 'Conventional religion' was said by her to have failed 'the multitudes';[168] and insiders were admonished both to recognize that it was they who were 'innately appointed to fulfil the most serious responsibilities of existence' and 'to assume that with these responsibilities goes authority for which the current democratic distinctions of prestige do not make allowance'.[169] It was thus hardly surprising that within a few days of hearing the twenty-six articles for the first time, two of Riding's associates withdrew from her Protocol: one of them for undefined 'Christian reasons',[170] and Maisie Somerville more specifically because 'God [is] love.'[171] No doubt Maisie also resented the dictatorial aspects of Laura's message; as did the historian A.J.P.Taylor, a friend of Len and Jane Lye whom Graves and Riding met for the first time on 10 April, and who told them that in his view 'the good should differ'.[172]

One particular problem was to find 'a suitable covering name for the whole activity'. The first search for this name began on the evening of 18 April, and lasted until midnight when Laura 'found *Countermand*', but was understandably 'not sure yet';[173] four days later she and Graves 'rediscovered [the word] "University"' (unaccountably lost for several years)[174] and for a while they thought of calling the protocol: *Transaction – the University of Moral Values*.[175] However even this grandiose title did not satisfy Riding for long. On 26 April, Graves notes that 'The word "literal" has come up. Worked on the problem till 2 a.m.';[176] and finally, two days later, Laura (with a deliberate reference, no doubt, to the Ark of the Covenant which had been for years the home of the Ten Commandments) settled upon *[The] Covenant of Literal Morality*.[177]

Financial problems remained acute, and were not improved either by the directors of Chatto and Windus, who said that they would only print *The World and Ourselves* if Riding paid 'half the production costs, £150';[178] or by Jenny, who had a spell in the London Clinic, and, as usual, asked Robert to foot the bill.[179] Thus, while working on *The Covenant*, Graves and Riding were also compelled to be busy with half-a-dozen other projects: Laura's *Lives of Wives* (for which Robert did a good deal of research); the 'Smuggler' screenplay for Korda; the dramatized version of *A Trojan Ending*; and the Graves/Liddell-Hart collaboration, *T.E.Lawrence to his Biographers*, which continued to cause problems with the Trustees until the middle of June. There were also further efforts to secure a publisher for the *Dictionary*; despite their usual objections to anthologies, Graves and Riding advised the publishers Sidgwick and Jackson on the compilation of a 'wholly "modern"' poetry anthology for schools;[180] and they even worked on another chapter of their uninspired *The Swiss Ghost*.

Not surprisingly, this severe pressure affected their health: by the end of May, Laura was suffering from 'faintness and palpitations'[181] (partly the result of incessant smoking and constant cups of black coffee), and was told by her doctor that her heart was tired and that she must have a holiday; while the morning after a walk with Dorothy Simmons across Regent's Park,[182] Robert woke with 'a chill: which', as he wrote, 'changed to a cramp over my liver which frightened Dr Barber into thinking I might have to be operated on'. Robert had to be injected with morphia to calm the pain;[183] and it was a considerable relief when, a week later, x-rays showed that there was no internal obstruction.

The good news, as Robert had written to his brother John in April, was that *Count Belisarius* was 'do[ing] what I required of it: namely, sell';[184] and this enabled him to indulge what Beryl had described as 'his greatest relaxation from the grind of work':[185] the purchase of many small objects from the Old Caledonian Market in north-east London. But it still seemed absolutely necessary to avoid paying income tax, and Robert had been told that, to achieve this, he must spend no more than three months of the tax year in Great Britain. Various ideas were considered by Robert and Laura, including a visit to the United States; but, by the end of April, it had been decided that they would go to France, and live for a while close to a number of their Majorcan friends in Rennes. Alan Hodge and Beryl would go with them, as would Dorothy Simmons, whose husband Montague would join them whenever possible at weekends.

In the meantime, Alan Hodge had made a preliminary visit to Rennes in mid-June, and had come back with glowing reports of the town, and with a gift of peaches and *chevrie* (the local venison) from Gelat's sister Anita. After staying up until 1.30 a.m. on 11 June, Laura Riding had now put the finishing touches to *The Covenant of Literal Morality* (often referred to more simply as *The First Protocol*); and just eighteen days later, Graves and Riding (who had spent the intervening period both in packing and in tying up all sorts of literary and social loose ends)[186] finished revising proofs of *The Covenant* 'just in time' before their journey to France.[187]

CHAPTER 10
Le Château de la Chevrie

After a rough crossing from Southampton, Robert Graves, Laura Riding, Alan Hodge and his wife Beryl Pritchard all arrived at St Malo in the early morning of Thursday, 30 June 1938. Anita's husband Juan Vives met them in his car and drove them to Rennes, where they put up at the Hôtel Central and where Anita wept to see them. To begin with, each couple made arrangements to take a separate flat in the town; but by Sunday they had decided that, instead, they would live together, and lease 'a proper house in the country'.[188] Nothing was to be had in the immediate vicinity of Rennes; but on Tuesday they found, thirty kilometres away, on the outskirts of the large village of Montauban-de-la-Bretagne, a 'seemingly perfect'[189] eighteenth-century mansion known as the Château de la Chevrie, or 'Venison Castle'. It contained, in Graves's words, '12 main rooms furnished & outside sanitation: no electric light, a deep ivy-coloured well, 10 acres of grounds, including a waterlily lake; parquet floors, sentimental wall-paper, rats until we get a cat. We are leasing it for a year (at about [£40 a year]!) Rates come to [£2 10s.] a year!'[190]

While the lease was being drawn up, Robert, Laura, Alan and Beryl remained in Rennes for another ten days. For Robert Graves (apart from one 'dreadful day' spent failing to secure a temporary *pied-à-terre* in the town;[191] and an unpleasant ride another day on a 'headachy bus' to Nantes where Laura was able to renew her American passport)[192] it was a happy time, and he began feeling better in health. The news from Deyá, as he wrote to Karl, was that 'it is all awful there what with compulsory Mass and compulsory *vivas* – and recently a Government ship shelled Deyá by mistake for Sóller and a shell landed in the [caves below] Canellun!'[193] But it was good to be among people who reminded him of the days before his exile began: as on Sunday 10 July, when he ate not only with his immediate circle, but also with 'Miguel & Francisca Ripoll . . . Gabriel the doctor's son, Miguel of [Son Cortei], Juan, Anita, Juanita, and . . . [a Spanish employee of Miguel's] who made a Majorcan rice; & we had pimientos, sobresada, olives, wine & everything nice'.[194]

Afterwards, they went to the races to watch 'trotting, gallop, curricle, [and] steeplechase'. Robert and Beryl in particular were thoroughly enjoying themselves – both won small sums of money by betting on the results – and Robert only 'came away ... because it was heavy weather (with the milk turning in the cafés)'.[195] That same evening Robert wrote to Nancy Nicholson, to whom he was still married (having failed to give her a divorce when she wanted one,[196] presumably to stop her from marrying Phibbs), to tell her about the château and to add that he had been 'thinking again about the divorce': he would now allow Nancy to charge him with desertion, and promised that, if she did so, he would not make any defence.[197] Robert's primary concern in writing this letter must have been to free himself. It had become most unusual for him to take any interest in Nancy; and indeed the previous November, when she had been so ill with a pontine haemor- rhage that she had been 'given up by two doctors', he had not even heard about it until later, and then seemed more delighted by her subsequent determination to leave Sutton Veney (where Phibbs still lived) than saddened by the severity of her illness.[198]

While Robert and his friends were waiting to move into La Chevrie it was often easier to write letters than to concentrate upon serious work. On the morning after their day at the races, for instance, Laura dictated no fewer than sixteen letters to Beryl who, for the time being, had assumed Karl's secretarial duties. Robert himself managed to make a number of background notes to assist Laura with her *Lives of Wives*, and also to revise some of the material for his forthcoming *Collected Poems*; but many days ended with a sense that little had been achieved.

On Thursday 14 July, Robert Graves and Laura Riding moved together into the Château de la Chevrie. They found that the Comtesse de Kerel- louan, from whom they were leasing La Chevrie, had 'hung it all with pictures and put about marvellous French–Breton ornaments, and furnished it with old-world splendour – but not aired the beds or lit fires or removed rat-dirt'. They began by working 'very hard indeed moving things about: first getting Laura's workroom ready';[199] on Friday morning, after 'an uncomfortable night with a bat about somewhere', they lit huge log fires in the bedrooms to air the bedding; and on Friday afternoon, when Alan and Beryl arrived, they moved more furniture, began 'a custom of [playing] $7\frac{1}{2}$ at night, and another of a stockpot for soup'; and even bought a small grey kitten, named first Shadow, and then Nono, whose presence made their echoing mansion feel more like a home.[200]

There was one moment of horror on Sunday evening, when Laura opened the door of her bedroom, and found that the single 'bat about somewhere' had been the precursor of 'a nightmare of bats'[201] swirling around inside. Immediately a determined campaign was begun to drive them out and keep them out: windows were shuttered, holes patched up in the attic, and one brood of bats was beaten to death by Robert and Alan with wooden boards, in an engagement they laughingly described as 'the battle of Tricameron'.[202] Bees also became a problem, and huge fires of cypress branches were lit in an unsuccessful effort to clear them from the chimney.

Despite these difficulties everyone seemed happy, and Graves noted that he himself had 'lost all my unnecessary weight & feel very well'.[203] Dorothy Simmons arrived from England on 24 July 1938, Robert's forty-third birthday; and when Juan and Anita and some other Spanish friends had come over from Rennes, they all drank champagne, ate almond cakes and 'played $7\frac{1}{2}$ for three or four hours'. Laura was lively and amusing, and that evening there was a magical time when they all sat around a wood fire in her bedroom fireplace, with the mirror candles lit.[204]

In the small enclosed community at La Chevrie, however, Riding could control her companions more fully than had been possible in London; and one day, as Beryl recalls, she 'lashed out' at Robert in a most 'awful' manner for having ordered a table to be made, without consulting her first. Robert took her reprimands in his stride. 'She was his Muse,' Dorothy Simmons comments, 'and he loved her and abandoned himself to her.'[205]

On the surface, everything at La Chevrie proceeded in a smooth, well-organized fashion. The beginning of August had seen the start of 'real work on [the] "Dictionary"';[206] and areas of domestic responsibility had been clearly defined: thus Graves was in charge of the fuel supply, keeping the kitchen clean, making sure that the lamps were in order, looking after the bicycles and seeing to the flowers; Alan was in charge of 'clocks, grounds, lavatory'; Beryl of 'groceries & stores'; and Laura – in a merely supervisory capacity, as they were now employing both a full-time cook and a maid – of 'meals & tidiness of rooms'.[207]

But Robert and Beryl were becoming more and more interested in each other. In Alma Street days, Laura had been very much aware that Robert was uncommonly attracted towards the household at Adelaide Road; and, early in December, there had been a curious occasion on which Laura walked with Robert all the way there: but then, as he records, her influence was such that they 'did not go in, somehow'.[208] Robert continued, however, to be on the best of terms with Alan and Beryl; one day later that month he had become involved in 'a long walk with [them both] – Beryl having abstract doubts' about getting married to Alan;[209] and when the wedding had gone ahead, on 29 January 1938, Robert was absent, and contented himself with recording in his diary that 'Papa Pritchard [had been] very rude to Alan (not a word) & Mama [had] told her she was throwing her life away'.[210]

Later, Laura was to write angrily about Beryl 'shooting intense glances at [Robert] across the Chevrie table';[211] and Robert's diary shows how he in turn began to feel warmly towards Alan's wife: though he was not yet in love with her. 'We are getting very fond of Beryl',[212] he writes on 11 August (rather as he had once written about Laura in the early days of their association); and he became sympathetically involved in Beryl's experiences. One evening, for example, Robert was in the kitchen, preparing a hot-water bottle for Laura, when he found himself answering a ghostly voice. 'This kitchen ghost', he writes in his diary, 'Beryl already knows. It left an old-fashioned poker on the stove; which disappeared when she touched it.'[213]

Riding was immediately aware of this development. But it was one for which she had not bargained; and so although she had so little genuine feeling left for Robert that she was shortly to confide in Dorothy Simmons, 'Robert can't hold me,'[214] the situation did leave her tense and ill. First she suffered from bad headaches; and then, blaming the 'Montague situation' for her ill-health, she had what she described as 'an appendix attack':[215] which gave her a chance to show that she still had sufficient power over Graves to summon him from his bed six times in a single night.

On Sunday 14 August, James Reeves's brother David arrived at La Chevrie (rather irritable 'after a crowded crossing from Southampton'),[216] in order to work with Laura on a book about furniture; and by Monday morning Robert, who never liked it when Laura was about to closet herself for long hours with another man, was himself feeling 'cold and cross'. A series of minor irritations followed. Anita had given them some greengages for jam, and Robert felt that he 'had to make it' as they were going bad. And so, with help from Dorothy, he began boiling the greengages over a wood fire in his bedroom fireplace. But then Laura, who was 'always trying to get [Dorothy] to leave Montague', whom she disliked as he was critical of them all,[217] summoned Dorothy for a discussion about her personal life; and the result was that Dorothy stopped helping, and:

> the jam caught and I didn't put enough sugar & boiled up again with jello & not enough jars: about 17 lbs of it – Then Alan got cross because Laura arranged two chairs as if in consultation with his own in the stair-

case room he is using as a study, with a bolster upright in his ... and
Montague hanging about like a skeleton at a feast...[218]

Later, there was another tiresome scene with 'everyone crossly peeling
mushrooms';[219] and Robert's feelings of annoyance bubbled up into a poem
which he called 'Assumption Day' and which reveals, as one discerning
critic has already noted, that he had much more than these petty difficulties
on his mind:

> What was wrong with the day, doubtless,
> Was less the unseasonable gusty weather
> Than the bells ringing on a Monday morning
> For a church-feast that nobody could welcome –
> Not even the bell-ringers.
>
> The pond had shrunk: its yellow lilies
> Poked rubbery necks out of the water.
> I paused and sat down crossly on a tussock,
> My back turned on the idle water-beetles
> That would not skim, but floated.
>
> A wasp, a humble-bee, a blue-fly
> Uncooperatively at work together
> Were sucking honey from the crowded blossom
> Of a pale flower whose name someone once told me –
> Someone to be mistrusted.
>
> But, not far off, our little cow-herd
> Made mud-cakes, with one eye on the cattle,
> And marked each separate cake with his initials.
> I was half-tempted by the child's example
> To rescue my spoilt morning. [220]

CHAPTER 11

'A Beautiful Insincerity;
& True'

For the next few months, there was a more settled time at La Chevrie. A fruitful autumn, in which the landscape seemed dominated by heavily laden apple-trees, was followed by Christmas with snow lying six inches deep on the ground, and a huge Yule log burning on the kitchen hearth. Inside the château, games and good humour ran alongside hard work; and somehow it seemed unnecessary to face squarely any of the serious personal issues which now divided Graves and Riding.

However, on 3 January 1939, the Christmas issue of *Time* magazine arrived at La Chevrie, with a 'comprehensive report on current poetry'[221] by Schuyler Jackson, an ex-Princeton friend of Tom Matthews's. Five years ago Jackson's powerful intelligence and strength of character had interested Laura Riding so much that she had several times invited him to become a Vulgatite. He had declined in a manner which intrigued her still more, and left him as a kind of rocklike eminence somewhere in the background of her thinking.[222] More recently he had endorsed *The Covenant of Literal Morality*; and his article in *Time* set in train a series of events which brought the relationship between Graves and Riding to what she herself accurately described as the moment of ultimate hopelessness.[223] It was as though, in their world of the unchanging present, everything had begun to move forward once again: slowly at first but with increasing and eventually dangerous speed.

Laura read the review first, and then passed it round the breakfast table at La Chevrie. In dividing the poets whom he was considering into three classes – poets, poetasters and poeticules – Jackson had awarded the title of poet only to Rainer Maria Rilke (dead since 1926) and to Laura Riding; and he had described Riding's *Collected Poems* (published to a very dismissive review from the *Times Literary Supplement* the previous September),[224] as the 'book of books of the mid-twentieth century'.[225] Robert Graves (whose own *Collected Poems*, published in November, had received generally disappointing reviews)[226] read Jackson's comments with a mixture of satisfaction and surprise, and described the review in his diary that evening as 'daring'.[227]

Yet Robert seems to have been more interested just then in a domestic saga, involving a hedgehog which Beryl had found and adopted and was keeping in her attic room. After disturbing Leonie, the cook, in her next-door attic with its scratching, it had been exiled to a grandfather clock in the stable, from which it had escaped; and Graves wrote that 'Beryl's hedgehog, when it wakes up from its interrupted hibernation, will say: "I had the craziest dream – something about bread and milk and a typewriter and a grandfather clock."'[228]

Jackson's review continued its journey round the breakfast table; and when it reached Dorothy Simmons, she read it through so slowly and carefully that Laura snapped at her: 'Don't make a meal of it! What do you think?'

'I think the man's in love with you,' Dorothy answered.

'The vulgarity of your mind', said Laura dismissively, 'staggers me.'[229] Yet secretly she appears to have been pleased with what Dorothy had said. Ten weeks previously she had ordered her to break up a stone portrait head which Dorothy had made of her; but now she told Robert that Dorothy's sculpture was 'a success at last';[230] and the following week she roughed out a letter to all those who had endorsed the *Protocol* (including of course Schuyler), in which she asked for suggestions in drafting some new articles: the intention being (as Graves explained in a separate letter to Liddell Hart) to 'fram[e] an agreement as to another side of the *Covenant*: i.e. friendship. The people who find *Protocol One* rather forbidding in tone will have reassurance in this.'[231]

Montague Simmons had arrived at La Chevrie on 7 January, for a twelve days' holiday; and he was soon caught up in the general excitement of helping Laura with what was already described as *Protocol Two*. On the evening of Saturday 14 January, for example, Montague and Dorothy joined Robert, Alan and Beryl in a 'conference on the subject of common obligations in friendship';[232] and on Sunday morning Montague and Robert wrote out the results of their talk so that they could present Laura with a concise summary of their views.

Monday 16 January 1939 was Laura Riding's thirty-eighth birthday. She had asked for no presents, but her companions gave her an azalea, and white flowers, and chocolate peppermints, and a cake with her name on it, and each of them wrote her a letter. Robert Graves was still acting consciously as though he were entirely devoted to Laura, and he had recently written a poem, 'The Love Beast',[233] in which he advocates what he imagined was still Riding's point of view about sexual relations: so that he describes how two lovers who give way to their sexual desires soon find themselves 'Loathing each other's carrion company'.[234] However, Robert seems to have enclosed with his birthday letter to Laura another new poem which he had previously entitled 'The Hostage', and which later appears as 'Dawn Bombardment', with these opening lines:

> Guns from the sea open against us:
> The smoke rocks bodily in the casemate
> And a yell of doom goes up.
> We count and bless each new, heavy concussion –
> Captives awaiting rescue.[235]

Riding took no less than a month and a half to reply to Graves's letter and poem; and she began her reply by explaining that 1 March seemed right for answering his letter, and that they should therefore call it the world's birthday – and indeed, later that day, she encouraged everyone at La Chevrie to drink champagne in the world's honour. The remainder of her letter contained a kindly written but most surprising suggestion (as plainly phrased as the use of a simple metaphor would allow) that Robert should have his sexual freedom. His poem, she told him, contained a quite erroneous view of his present situation. He should under no circumstances consider himself to be a hostage in some besieged stronghold. In her view, the stronghold only imagined that it was under attack from the sea: the guns were really its own; and Robert's feeling of being imprisoned would disappear as soon as those guns were fired, and the fortress windows could once again be used for looking out. He was not to act as though he had no hidden guns of his own; and now, Laura concluded, he should prepare to fire, both to appease the pagan deities and to put an end to so much repression.[236]

What had happened to enable Laura to write in this manner? Almost certainly she had now decided that she wanted Schuyler Jackson (though she had never even met him), and in the six weeks since her birthday she had made a considerable advance in her campaign to win him over.[237] In particular, she had persuaded Graves early in February that they should arrange to travel 'to [the] USA in the spring to stay in Pennsylvania for a few months near the Jacksons and Tom and Julie'.[238] Tom Matthews had often told Laura that it should have been Schuyler Jackson and not he himself who had visited her in Deyá; and so now Tom was asked to find somewhere for them to stay. At the same time Laura continued her correspondence with Schuyler, to whom she posted a fresh letter on the very day that she effectively offered Graves his sexual freedom.

Riding did not want to lose Graves altogether; but she appears to have believed that, if his sexual desires could be satisfied elsewhere, then he could still be persuaded to remain part of her entourage, and no doubt to provide her with a significant part of his income into the bargain. Laura had therefore been unusually kindly towards Robert for a while: commiserating with him when he hurt his shoulder badly in a bicycle crash, joining in his unholy satisfaction on hearing of Yeats's death, and even leaving the château to go on one or two private walks with him. However, there were times when she made it quite clear how much she preferred Jackson to Graves: for example, when she and the others were playing a word game one evening, choosing new and more appropriate surnames for themselves and for each other, Graves's request to be a 'White' was denied: Schuyler Jackson, said Riding, was a 'White'; Graves only deserved to be a 'Gallagher'[239] – and his status was apparently lowered still further in her eyes the following day (the day on which Laura wrote about reservations on boats to America), when she decided that he was actually a 'Fortaskew'.[240]

However, Graves did not seem to feel at this stage that his special relationship with Laura Riding was in any way threatened. They worked together as normal while she cleared away what he described in a letter to Karl Goldschmidt as an 'enormous' pile of work: by mid-February she had completed not only *Lives of Wives* and her scenario based upon *A Trojan Ending*, but the furniture book which she had been writing with David Reeves. In addition, what had seemed a serious problem with the prospective American publishers of the *Dictionary* had been cleared up. As Graves reported to Karl:

McIntyre of Little, Brown got qualms about the *Dictionary* because he had showed the plan to two linguistic cranks and asked Laura to send objections before proceeding. Laura sent him an 18-page foolscap letter by return, like a mule's kick, demolishing the cranks and giving him only till the 15th to decide about getting ahead. (I contributed two pages on the grammatical and vocabularistic errors occurring in the report by one of the cranks: he had managed to get 14 mistakes on a single sheet!) Yesterday a penitent 34-word cable came from McIntyre admitting that the 'so-called experts' had been answered fully. . . . So that's all steady now.[241]

Robert Graves's equanimity was based upon the fact that his increasing pleasure in Beryl's company made almost anything else seem tolerable. On 27 January, for example, he found that the news of Franco's capture of Barcelona 'has made no difference to us, somehow';[242] on 10 February, following a 'walk with Beryl to the lake after dark', he noted rather to his surprise that he was 'feeling thoroughly happy, somehow';[243] and towards the end of that month, although he and his friends were aware of 'a great political change going on: we all feel something cracking', a letter from Sally Chilver to the effect that war was very near seemed to Graves to make 'no real sense'.[244]

In one part of his mind, Robert was perfectly well aware of what was happening between himself and Laura, and between himself and Beryl. In his poem 'A Love Story', which he completed on 8 February, he clearly states that his relationship with Laura Riding has brought him 'less than luck,' and that he was now once again living in that haunted land of inspiration and moon-magic in which every poet seeks a fresh Muse when the present one has 'turned beldamish'.[245] But Graves was able to keep this knowledge in some separate compartment of his brain; and on 2 March, less than a month after completing 'A Love Story', he was walking with Alan Hodge to the lake, and having a serious talk with him 'about Laura as a focus of love among us'.[246]

Laura herself was now firmly wedded to her new set of plans for the future, and had begun (as usual) to draw universal conclusions from her subjective experiences. She even called Robert into her bedroom at 4 a.m. one morning simply to inform him of her sudden revelation that 'Love is a beautiful insincerity; & true.'[247] By this time, Laura was determined to prepare herself physically as well as mentally for her meeting with Schuyler Jackson. After years of chain-smoking cigarettes, she had recently given up tobacco altogether; and, within ten days of her early-morning conversation with Robert, she suddenly cut down from an unhealthy fifteen cups of coffee a day to just one or two.

Schuyler Jackson knew nothing of these efforts on his behalf; but already, as Dorothy Simmons had guessed, he was more than half in love with Laura Riding. Not only did he admire her poetry, but she wrote to him very warmly at a time when he had come to regard his own wife, Katharine (usually known as Kit), with what Tom Matthews describes as 'a strange mixture of contempt and reverence':[248] indeed he had almost left her the previous year for a figure-skating champion. Now Schuyler willingly helped Tom to 'scour... the countryside' in their joint neighbourhood to find a house for Robert and Laura; and, as Tom recalls, when nothing at all suitable turned up:

> Schuyler had an idea. On his farm stood the ruin of an eighteenth-century farmhouse; why not rebuild it? It would be quite a job, as nothing remained but a stone shell; the builder's estimate for the reconstruction was $25,000. I took out a note at the bank for that amount and Schuyler and the builder between them drew up the plans.[249]

By the end of March, packing began at La Chevrie, and it had been decided who would accompany Graves and Riding to America, and who would stay behind. Norman Cameron, for instance, who had been asked to join them, 'counted himself out';[250] while Karl Goldschmidt, who had recently visited them at La Chevrie, bringing with him such welcome delicacies as Earl Grey tea, Patum Peperium and Oxford marmalade, could not contemplate such a move as it was impossible to have his German passport renewed; and Dorothy Simmons, officially out of favour with Laura after her ill-timed comments about Schuyler Jackson, had no option but to go back to Beckenham for the time being. However, David Reeves decided that he would like to join them; and it was understood that Alan Hodge and Beryl would also come to America, after first spending a few weeks in England.

Separate cabins were therefore booked for Robert Graves and Laura Riding on the *Paris*, due to sail from Le Havre on 19 April; and it was arranged that David Reeves would board the ship when it called at Southampton, and would share Robert's cabin for the rest of the voyage to New York.

In the meantime, the weather in Brittany had become, in Graves's words, 'suddenly marvellous';[251] Robert's spirits were further improved by the news that *Count Belisarius* had been awarded the prestigious Prix Femina Vie Heureuse; his friendship with Beryl continued to prosper; and his final ten days at the château were almost wholly idyllic. There were apple and plum blossom in the garden, the chestnuts were in leaf, and the hazels just beginning; there were beds of violets, primroses, celandines and spotted orchids; and in the air a variety of butterflies, jays and magpies; the tapping of a wood-pecker could be heard, and the calls of cuckoos. One night, making his customary connection between love and apples, Robert dreamed that Hercules had come not only to Lyons, but also to Montauban to plant apple-trees;[252] and the only 'miserable' day was apparently redeemed the following morning by the knowledge that a letter had been on its way all the time from Schuyler Jackson.

In the early hours of Wednesday 19 April, Robert and Laura made their farewells to Alan, Beryl and Dorothy (who were themselves shortly to set out together for England), and were collected from the Château de la Chevrie by the taxi hired to take them to Le Havre. Later that day, they had almost completed their journey across Brittany and Normandy when, stopping for coffee, they bought a paper and read that the *Paris* had been burned out. Their baggage was safe; but the destruction of this ship was an unlucky omen; and, instead of sailing that evening, they spent the night in an hotel in Le Havre, a place which, for Robert, had many unhappy associations. The old army camp, as he noticed, had gone from the hill above the town; but during the Great War it had been from Le Havre that he had several times set out for the trenches on the Western Front. The following evening, when Graves sailed with Riding in the *Champlain*, he did not know that he was once again travelling towards a place of horror.[253]

CHAPTER 12
Into a Darkness

After an uneventful voyage across the Atlantic – Robert Graves passed some of the time writing a 'long chronicle letter to Beryl and Alan'[254] – the *Champlain* docked at New York on the morning of Friday 28 April 1939; and Graves and his companions were met on the quayside by Tom and Julie Matthews, together with Schuyler and Kit Jackson. The voyagers had already learned that work was well under way at Schuyler's farm, near the township of Brownsburg, on the rebuilding of Nimrod's Rise, as the ruin had now been christened; but that it could not possibly be ready for occupation until at the earliest the beginning of June. So Schuyler drove them in his truck to Princeton, where it had been arranged that Robert and Laura would stay in Tom and Julie's house for the time being: Laura in the spare room, while Robert made do with a cot in Tom's study. Lodgings had been found nearby for David: only five doors away, as Graves noted with interest, from where Albert Einstein was living.

That Friday evening, Schuyler and Kit came over to Tom and Julie's house for supper, and Robert and Laura handed over a few presents such as a silver cloak clasp which they had bought from an antique shop in Le Havre. Not much was said; but on Saturday – which, Graves realized, was the tenth anniversary of Laura's fall from a high window in Hammersmith – Schuyler collected Robert, Laura and Julie and her three boys (Tom had left that morning for work in New York, to which he commuted almost daily) and drove them over to Brownsburg.

There they saw Schuyler Jackson's farmhouse, which was white, with 'green shutters & pines & large barns'. Then Schuyler walked them the hundred yards or so down into the bottom of a valley and up again to the place where Nimrod's Rise was being built: a substantial dwelling, which (besides kitchen, bathroom and store-room) would have an imposing porch, a large L-shaped living-room, and four bedrooms.[255]

After admiring the work that had been done so far, the newcomers celebrated their first visit to the site by helping Schuyler to plant a Carpathian walnut-tree nearby. They also met Schuyler's hired man, 'David Owl the Indian & his brood of children'; and Kit's four young children: from twelve-year-old Griselda Jackson down through Maria and Kathy to five-year-old Ben. Kit herself was more talkative than the previous day, but Schuyler was still saying little: his entire history of 'the Ruin', as Graves still called it, consisted in the laconic remark that 'A nigger once lived there & the roof caved in.'[256]

There were further meetings between Robert, Laura, Schuyler and Kit on Sunday and Monday, and a number of practical details were sorted out: for example, Laura and David bought a 'Ford 1936 black sedan 4 door car' for $365; Robert had his back treated by a chiropractor at Trenton, the State Capital (a few days later he went again, and felt better after the chiropractor claimed that he had 'pushed my sacrum into place');[257] and at some stage Laura and Schuyler had a long talk, and, in Graves's words, 'got things clear'.[258]

On Tuesday 2 May, Tom Matthews joined Robert, Laura, David and Julie on a picnic at Schuyler's farm, where they sat outdoors 'in chairs and on rugs on the ragged lawn'. Tom found that the atmosphere was already 'tense with subdued response'. It seemed to him that Laura had taken charge already, and that:

> Schuyler seemed to accept that: he said very little but his lowered eyelids and continual slight smile looked receptive. Kit was friendly and open, as she was with everybody except the few people who put her teeth on edge. I wished Laura would stop calling her 'Katharine'; it sounded all wrong: it was like putting a stiff, unbecoming hat on Kit and made Laura seem governessy. Robert gambolled awkwardly about Laura, like a benignant bear, on the watch for something to fetch or carry, and getting the kind of reward from Laura he often did: 'Robert, stop *fussing*!'[259]

After a while, Laura 'made an announcement, almost a kind of speech'. She told her audience that she and her assistants (among whom Schuyler was now to be numbered) would be working from day to day on the *Dictionary*; but there would also be:

> other work to do in which we would all have a hand; and it was this work which had been the primary cause for their coming to America. The *First Protocol*, to which we had all … subscribed, declared our soli-

darity as 'inside' people and our general purposes. The new *Protocol* would be more specific: it would in effect be a program for inside action ... by declaring ourselves with effective intensity, [we would attempt] to save the world from war.[260]

That evening, Robert Graves wrote in his diary that Laura was 'happy but thinner and not sleeping well'.[261] There were good reasons for Riding's happiness. Newly returned to her homeland, she had already established an ascendancy over Schuyler, the man she was determined to make her own. That she was thinner, and not sleeping well, may have had something to do with the intense mental effort which she was making to bend certain people to her will.

In his celebrated poem 'On Portents',[262] Graves had once written about Riding's ability to cause 'strange things' to happen, by the 'strong pulling of her bladed mind'; and, when Laura Riding was exerting the full force of her personality, it had often seemed to those around her that she was possessed of paranormal powers. Both to Robert Graves in the early years of his relationship with Riding, and to other observers such as Honor Wyatt, it appeared that if Laura was in this sense a 'witch', then she was a 'white witch', who used her remarkable powers only for good.[263] Dorothy Simmons, on the other hand, describes with great sadness the darker side of Riding's influence:

> Laura undoubtedly had power: and it was not a very pleasant power at times. Dressed in a black cape, with something round her head, she could look truly sinister: she then became tight and ugly and horrible. That was when she used her will for wrong ends: there is something genuinely evil about that.[264]

It was on the morning of Wednesday 3 May that Kit Jackson came over to Princeton for what Graves describes as 'her first talk alone with Laura'. At the time there seemed nothing remarkable about this; and that evening Kit and Schuyler came over to supper, and everyone talked about the 'friendship' *Protocol*.[265] Yet in retrospect it appears that something very sinister was happening. If Laura was to have Schuyler completely to herself, then Kit must be removed from the scene; and now she was probing into Kit's mind, to discover how best this might be achieved.[266]

It now seemed strange to Robert when a day passed without seeing Kit or Schuyler;[267] and Schuyler evidently began to feel that it was abnormal for a day to pass without seeing Laura. Early on 5 May, for instance, he seems to have driven to Princeton for no better reason than to wish Robert and Laura an enjoyable outing to New York.[268]

After visiting Bloomingdales – where Laura recalled that she had once been lost as a child – Graves and Riding met their old friend Robin Hale for tea. The flicker of attraction that had once existed between Robert and Robin had completely died: although he found her 'very sweet', he noted with exasperation that she kept on bringing 'wrong names' into the conversation: names such as 'Faulkner, Auden [particularly detested by both Graves and Riding, who alleged that he had plagiarized Riding's work]' and '*Grapes of Wrath* Steinbeck'. However, a thoroughly cheerful supper followed at a Spanish restaurant, where they met Tom and Julie Matthews and David Reeves;[269] and that evening Graves wrote in the best of spirits to Karl Goldschmidt, that:

> I cannot tell you how happy we all are here; the important thing being that Schuyler and Katharine Jackson, whom Tom and Julie have known for years and to whom before we came we felt close in a predestined sort of way, are exactly the people we knew, counted on them being, and that means an innumerability of old problems cleared up – like a game that cannot properly begin until all the players are present: now we all are.

Robert went on that they were hoping to start work soon; and then in a corner of a page he appended the following message from his Muse: 'Laura says "You know all will be done that needs to be done for all." '[270]

The exalted state of mind in which Graves had written to Karl depended partly upon a belief that he and his companions had once again succeeded in slipping out of history and time into an eternal and timeless present in which, under Laura's direction, great things would be possible; but it also depended upon the tension created by his efforts to hide both from himself and from others the growing awareness that his relationship with Riding was about to change for the worse. At the end of the following day, therefore, he wrote a message in his diary which he consciously intended to be an acknowledgement of the unimportance of the recent historical past; but which reads more like a bitter farewell to his partnership with Riding: 'At this point the diary seems graveyard; so I stop it.'[271]

Work on the *Dictionary* was suspended for the time being while, under Riding's direction, there was a series of meetings (mostly at Tom and Julie's house but sometimes at the Farm) in order to work out the details of the *Second Protocol*. Tom had arranged to take a couple of weeks of his vacation early, and thus:

> was able to be there the whole time. Laura kept us all busy: running errands, writing letters, protecting her privacy, re-arranging our daily lives to conform to her pattern. There was no time for tennis or the movies, or seeing our friends, or any such nonsense.... I remember seemingly interminable meetings ... when we sat around the sides of the room in a brooding circle, trying to discuss – or keeping silent: and the silences were the worst. They not only weighed more than they should have but they stopped the clock.[272]

After a while, Tom felt that the house was no longer his: it had become Laura's headquarters. Visiting friends were soon discouraged by 'stony stares and monosyllabic replies'; and 'word got about that something was going on at our house – something that felt like sitting up with a dead body'.[273] When his vacation was over Tom was able to escape daily to his work in New York; and returned 'with dragging steps'. After a while it dawned on him:

> that this long-drawn-out torture, which had brought everything to a standstill and all of us to the tautness of hysteria, was for a purpose: we were being put to the question, and one of us must sooner or later break. I think that we all knew that the pressure was coming from Laura; but who would be the one to go under?
>
> In a stab of unreasoning fear I thought: it might be Julie! Without stopping to think, I burst out: 'If it's Julie you're after, it's me as well, because we're together!' It must have been funny, for they all laughed, and the tension was temporarily broken. But soon it tightened down again.

In that tense silence, imposed by Laura, it seemed to Tom that he and the others 'sank down through sunless levels into darkness where we were each alone, isolated in the blind dark ...'.[274]

The process was still continuing in the third week of May, when Alan and Beryl Hodge arrived in Princeton. A room was found for them: perhaps in the same boarding-house as David Reeves's; and for the next week or two, like the others, they did no proper work, but took part in endless discussions.

Early in June, with Nimrod's Rise still incomplete, it was decided that

Robert, Laura, David, Alan and Beryl would move out to Brownsburg and stay at Schuyler and Kit's farmhouse for the time being. However, there were frequent return visits to the Matthewses' house by some or all of the Brownsburg contingent; and it was on one of these occasions when someone finally began to crack. They were sitting at dinner, when Kit Jackson suddenly 'leaned forward and laid her head on the table. If she was weeping', writes Tom Matthews, 'it was very quietly; but there was something dreadful, hopeless, defeated in her gesture. I think Schuyler and Laura took her back to the farm. It was the last I saw of her for months.'[275]

From now on Tom and Julie (whom Beryl remembers as 'the most normal people' then part of the Graves/Riding circle) remained on the fringe of things; while all kinds of dramatic changes were taking place in the relationships between those who lived at Schuyler and Kit's 'White House'. David Reeves was probably least affected by these changes: he had undergone a period of mild depression soon after first arriving in the USA, when he realized how minor a role he had been allotted in Laura's drama; but he had now begun seeing Robin Hale regularly in New York, and would later marry her. For the others, however, and especially for Kit Jackson, the changes were devastating. She had to watch while, in Tom Matthews's words, her husband Schuyler and her supposed friend Laura:

> were falling in love. What a way to do it! – in front of our fascinated, wincing but unseeing eyes. I thought of two basilisks, motionless and staring, the rest of us like little lizards, waiting, immobilized into cramped stone until the predetermined affair was ready.[276]

The climax arrived one June evening, when the entire colony were having dinner at Schuyler and Kit's farm. Kit left the table, saying that she was going for a walk with the children. Laura (from her seat at the head of the table):

> said that Robert would go along too. Kit flared up: they were her children and she would not have Robert with her, or anyone. And off they went down the marsh path to 'Nimrod's Rise' and the woods beyond. Robert came running along after them; Kit screamed at him to go back. Laura dispatched other messenger-guardians – David, Beryl, finally Schuyler. Just before Schuyler appeared Griselda had been quizzing her mother: 'Something is wrong with you. What's the matter with you?' and Kit had persisted in denying that anything was wrong. Griselda kept after her, plaguing her for the answer. Kit lost the last of her control; as Schuyler came racing up she had Griselda by the throat.[277]

Kit was brought back to the farmhouse, and 'terrible scenes'[278] followed. Several years later, viewing what had happened to Kit Jackson as a 'nervous breakdown of sexual origin', Robert Graves would describe how Kit had 'instinctively reproduce[d] in faithful and disgusting detail much of the ancient Dionysiac ritual', and how he had witnessed this 'in helpless terror'.[279]

Riding then insisted upon interrogating the poor demented creature to which Kit had been reduced until she 'finally dropped her mask and confessed her evil practices'.[280] Laura could now confidently assert to her acolytes that Kit Jackson was a witch: a grimly ironic assertion to anyone who recalls that it was Riding herself who, ten years previously, had employed black magic in her efforts to secure the return of Geoffrey Phibbs. On the present occasion, presumably, it was Riding again who was responsible for the introduction of black magic, either directly or by suggestion, and for the 'evidence' of Kit's 'cabalistic relics' which were soon being found in the farmhouse.[281]

Next morning, Tom Matthews returned to Princeton from a stint of work in New York, to be told by his wife Julie and by David Reeves that 'Kit had been taken to hospital; Laura was rearranging the farm. And "they wanted to see me". No one had to tell me that "they" no longer meant Laura and Robert; "they" were now Laura and Schuyler.' Tom drove over to Brownsburg alone, and found the farm:

> seething with activity and the kind of fussy bustle that Laura induced when she was directing household work; Robert, Alan and Beryl were running up and down stairs, carrying small pieces of furniture, calling to each other and asking Laura for instructions. It looked like a spring cleaning. The Jackson children were nowhere to be seen, neither was Schuyler. Laura summoned me to the study.
>
> In the first three minutes, although I don't think that on that occasion she ever used the word 'witch', I understood what it was she wanted me to agree to. She was telling me that 'Katharine' was a witch, that she had been unmasked and her sorceries brought to nothing: that the house was now being purified of her cabalistic rites and of all her associations with it.[282]

Tom was asked whether he would show his 'solidarity' with the others by doing his share of the 'purifying chores. . . . Everything [Kit] had touched or might have used for her spells, all her private possessions were being burnt, destroyed or otherwise got rid of.' Tom, feeling certain that Laura was wrong about Kit being a witch, refused to stay on to take part in this; but to get away from Laura and, in order to avoid seeing Schuyler, agreed to take with him an ornament that belonged to Kit; and on the last bridge before Princeton he stopped his car and 'flung the little china figure into the creek'.[283]

For Tom Matthews, this had been a nightmarish day: for a while he had been close to the centre of a terrible darkness (Griselda Jackson, with a child's vivid awareness, had for some time felt 'wrongness in the house, like bad air that everyone had to breathe – a wrongness not concentrated on Laura but surrounding her');[284] however, as soon as Tom was at home and could talk to Julie, he 'felt reassured of my sanity'.[285] For Robert, on the other hand, the nightmare not only continued, but intensified. Later, in 1939, he confided in Liddell-Hart that while in America he had 'stayed night and day with ... a mad woman', and that he had started 'seeing things and "going bugs"' himself.[286]

To the dreadful strain of living at close quarters with someone who was going mad had been added the almost equally dreadful strain, for Robert, of seeing himself displaced by Schuyler in Laura's affections. Robert's devotion to Laura was still such that, with one part of his mind, he attempted to remould himself to fit in with any changes that she ordained; but it was very hard, and he wrote a letter to Karl telling him that he had 'done no writing work and practically no letters for 3 months: and this is not laziness but a sense of strangeness here'. Robert could always escape to his 'small, hot, very sweet bed-room' which had 'all my familiar things ... arranged on the table'; or he could go down to 'the pool in the creek where Alan, Beryl and I swim under the shade of very tall birch trees';[287] but at last the moment came when he could no longer hide from what was happening.

On Kit's departure to the hospital, Laura had taken over the running of the household: which she did in some style, having breakfast in bed brought to the guest room in which she slept alone, and hissing at Griselda never to call her 'Laura' in front of the servants. But before long she and Schuyler had become lovers. After so many years of condemning sexual intercourse, Laura disappeared with Schuyler into a bedroom for two days, emerging to announce (for the benefit of anyone who was uncertain about her present views on the subject) that 'Schuyler and I do'.[288] From this moment on, as Tom Matthews records:

Schuyler had supplanted Robert but he had not taken Robert's subordinate place: he was to be not Laura's servant but her equal, and the

signs of this dual monarchy were soon evident to us all. The orders
and manifestos, written and verbal, no longer issued from Laura but
from the two of them: I'm not sure that in the signatures Schuyler's
name didn't precede hers.[289] Robert Graves found this change devastating: it brought him to what he later regarded as a minor (nervous) breakdown;[290] and the final entry in his diary is a poem, in which he records
just how badly he was affected by his sudden and final realization of
the truth – that his own relationship with Laura could never be the same
again:

THE MOON ENDS IN NIGHTMARE

I had once boasted my acquaintance
With the Moon's phases: I had seen her, even,
Endure and emerge from full eclipse.
Yet as she stood in the West, that summer night,
The fireflies dipping insanely about me,
So that the foggy air quivered and winked
And the sure eye was cheated,
In horror I cried aloud: for the same Moon
Whom I had held a living power, though changeless,
Split open in my sight, a bright egg shell,
And a double-headed Nothing grinned
All-wisely from the gap.

At this I found my earth no more substantial
Tha[n] the lower air, or the upper,
And ran to plunge in the cool flowing creek,
My eyes and ears pressed under water.
And did I drown, leaving my corpse in mud?
Yet still the thing was so.

I crept to where my window beckoned warm
Between the white oak and the tulip tree
And rapped – but was denied, as who returns
After a one-hour-seeming century
To a house not his own.[291]

Luckily for Robert's sanity he still retained the ability which he had learned
in the Great War, and which since then had often served him well: to
endure somehow, from day to day. Still more luckily, he had Beryl's loving
companionship to sustain him through this period of darkness.

CHAPTER 13
A Grin of Triumph

Instead of making a clean break with Laura Riding in June 1939, Robert Graves remained at Brownsburg in an effort to hold on to as much as he could of their relationship. He still regarded Laura as a kind of deity. He still wanted to walk in the shining light of her presence.[292] He still wanted to work, knowing that everything he wrote could be submitted to the critical scrutiny of her brilliant mind.

Certainly, it was now evident that Laura shared a bed with Schuyler; but need that impair the purity of the loving concern which Robert hoped that she still felt for him? Here Robert's thinking became muddled. Riding had so often stated her contempt for sexuality that on an intellectual level Graves still believed that love and sexual desire had very little to do with each other; and when he asked Laura to explain the new situation to him 'in human terms', she was unable to do so: which left him puzzled and wretched.[293] The trouble was that Laura's sexual relations with Schuyler were not merely the satisfaction of a physical appetite, but the expression of a deep-seated and abiding love; which meant that Laura could no longer offer Robert the special interest which had made it tolerable for that naturally passionate man to remain at her side despite her sexual coolness towards him.

It was something of a relief when Nimrod's Rise was finally ready for occupation. Robert moved into it in mid-June with Alan, Beryl and David; and in Beryl's company Robert began to find periods of what he described later that year as a 'lovely calmness'. The two of them began to spend more and more time together, and (in Robert's words) to 'do things like keepsakes and camel-chesterfield smokings'.[294] They were now evidently in love with each other; and Robert's efforts to believe that his relationship with Beryl was still of less importance that his relationship with Laura may have temporarily deceived him; but they deceived no one else, least of all his sister Clarissa, who received a letter from him about this time, and knew instantly that all was over between him and Laura, and that 'his affections were otherwise engaged'.[295]

Laura Riding could not help observing that Robert and Beryl were becoming very close, and she commented on their friendship most unfavourably. Laura, Robert and their circle had developed earlier in the year at La Chevrie[296] an 'inside' analysis of character originally invented by Lucie Aldridge and based on the belief that, although a few people had a single consistent nature, most had a ruling and a secondary nature. The two chief categories for women were 'two-in-hand' (which seems to have denoted a kind of intellectual grace combined with wisdom and self control) and 'one-in-the-bush' (the quality of being a home-maker); while men could be 'swingering swine' (hard work and controlled determination) or 'joulting pigs' (those with an element of romantic wildness).[297] Laura herself was considered to be 'pure two-in-hand', and Schuyler 'pure ... swingerer'. Robert on the other hand was perceived to be 'swingering swine faintly crossed with joulting pig', while Beryl was 'two-in-hand faintly crossed with bush'. This meant that there was a discrepancy in the characters of both Robert and Beryl; and Laura named that discrepancy in Robert, 'Oscar', and in Beryl, 'Lake Bottom'. Then she told Robert that he and Beryl were 'in danger of letting the secondary nature rule us and getting mixed in a merely sentimental Oscar–Lake Bottom way'.[298]

Laura was clearly worried by the possibility that, if Beryl proved too attractive to Robert, she herself might lose her influence over him altogether; and, rather than allow that to happen, she decided that she would give Robert a gentle nudge in the direction of someone who seemed less threatening to her own position than Beryl: namely Nancy Nicholson. Once before, when Riding had been in love with Geoffrey Phibbs, she had hoped that Graves would be content to remain her literary partner and financial support, while staying with a wife whom he loved, but to whom he was not absolutely devoted. Geoffrey's desertion meant that the experiment had yet to be given a fair trial: perhaps now was the time.

Robert had also been thinking about this wife, though not in the same terms. For years he had closed his conscious mind to the truth about Laura's disenchantment with him, so that her love-affair with Schuyler seemed like a kind of betrayal; and it had made Robert think very hard about his own treatment of Nancy back in 1929, and about the suffering which he now realized that he must have caused her. 'I have been thinking of you a great deal lately', he wrote to Nancy from Nimrod's Rise on 25 June, 'and wishing you well';[299] and by 18 July, under pressure from Laura, Robert had decided that he would travel over to England for 'about a month ... and if you would like to see me', he told Nancy, 'to clear up anything between us that may need clearing up, I would like it too, & feel cleaner for it'.[300] Robert would be accompanied across the Atlantic by Alan Hodge, who was on his way to Poland;[301] and in the meantime Beryl and David Reeves would remain behind with Laura and Schuyler at Brownsburg, where Laura had recently won another round in the battle against her lover's wife.

In mid-July, after only a few weeks in hospital, Kit Jackson had persuaded the specialists that she was well enough to return home, and had been allowed to set out for Brownsburg. When news of her imminent return reached the farm (as Tom Matthews heard later from Griselda Jackson), Laura immediately 'made the children tidy up the lawn, under Robert's direction, to a ridiculously immaculate degree'. Kit arrived, looking 'ghastly and obviously far from well' to find that everything (including the lawn) was the same, and yet somehow different; and the unnerving contrast between the home to which she had expected to return, and what she actually found, rapidly overwhelmed the frail degree of sanity which she had attained. To begin with there were 'strained greetings and a few stilted exchanges'; but very soon the children were being sent to their rooms and Kit, after a 'horrible struggle' which Griselda watched from an upstairs window, was 'taken back to hospital in a straitjacket'.[302]

Before setting out for England Graves wrote again to Nancy Nicholson, this time telling her that his ship, the *Georgia*, would be arriving at Southampton on 13 August, and that at some stage he would like 'to spend a day with you at Boar's Hill'. He added that:

> I don't expect you to greet me feeling 'Poor' (but the years have certainly made strangers of us) nor to think of me as 'Poor', which many do: knowing the confusions into which I have often brought myself.
>
> What happened long ago is finished with except as history, and if we were to go into it and apportion blame, I would claim a good share – not to make you feel better, but in honesty. I don't want, either, to start anything old up again: only to see whether we can be friends in a true way, though at a distance – not 'for the sake of the children' but for the sake of the element of good that was in our confused love once, and that got lost. I think that this is a debt we owe each other; and it is perhaps my chief reason for coming over.[303]

This letter reads calmly enough; but by the time he left America Graves had been reduced to a state of complete misery. It was bad enough to be leaving Beryl behind; but on the eve of his departure from Brownsburg there was a scene at the Farm which Graves found very hard to bear. Summoned very late in the day to Riding's room, he opened her door to find that she was with Schuyler Jackson. Schuyler looked at him with a curious smile which Robert interpreted as a grin of triumph. It felt as though he had been invited to Laura's room simply in order to be humiliated;[304] and so deeply was he wounded that the following day, at the dockside in New York, he seemed to Tom Matthews to be 'desperate and wretched, near the end of his tether'. As they said goodbye to each other, Tom could not help wondering whether he and Robert 'would ever meet again'.[305]

CHAPTER 14
'Rose-Bud'

When Robert Graves and Alan Hodge arrived in England on 13 August 1939, they spent a night with the MacCormacks near Southampton;[306] and then Alan set out on the next stage of his journey to Poland, while Robert went on to Boar's Hill to see his wife.

Their last meeting, back in January 1937, had been over supper in the flat which Robert had then been sharing with Laura Riding in London. At that time Nancy was quite free, having already been living apart from Geoffrey Phibbs for eighteen months; but Robert had still been unquestionably Laura's partner. Now, however (as Nancy had learned from family gossip), it seemed likely that there had been a permanent break between Robert and Laura;[307] and in the circumstances Nancy did not take very seriously her husband's assertion that he did not want 'to start anything old up again'. Why else should he come all the way from America chiefly (as he had told her in a recent letter) to see her? Talking about this with her brother-in-law John Graves (now working for the Oxford Education Authority), she told him privately that if Robert asked her to take him back, she would do so.[308]

However, Robert's visit was a brief one – a matter of an hour or two on the morning of 16 August – and any frank communication between him and Nancy was hampered by the presence both of their eldest son David and of Nancy's father Sir William Nicholson. Robert made it clear that there had been a great change in his relationship with Laura; but much to Nancy's disappointment he said nothing about the possibility of returning to live with his family; and, indeed, in conversation with Sir William, he talked chiefly about 'Laura and her literary projects'. When he added that he was on his way to London to see Jenny, and would then be travelling up to Erinfa, where Catherine and Sam were staying with Amy, David agreed to accompany him, but Nancy said that she could not go; and she remained behind, thoroughly dispirited.[309]

Jenny, by contrast, was in excellent form. After a successful season with the Liverpool Repertory Company (for whom she had undertaken a number of major roles), her acting career seemed well established; and, when Robert and David arrived at Harlech at ten o'clock that night, they brought with them the news that she was 'playing the principal part in the BBC drama' the next day.[310]

Returning after an absence of fifteen years to that timeless land where, in his memorable words, 'The rocks jut, the streams flow singing on either hand, / Careless if the season be early or late', Robert found that it worked its familiar enchantment upon him. For a while, as Amy noticed, he still had 'a haunted look';[311] but before long she was writing to John that 'Robert's visit is turning out better than I could have hoped. He even sits close to me for family prayers & the children come also.'[312] Robert spent a great deal of time on the beach or in the hills with his children; and it was a time of reconciliation with several other members of the family, including Clarissa (who was helping Amy to look after Catherine and Sam), Charles, who wrote a letter saying that he was ready to forget their past differences,[313] and their half-brother Dick, who was also at Erinfa.

As the days passed, it seemed to Amy that Robert had begun to look more and more like 'his old, young self';[314] but she did not realize the extent to which this transformation was the result of a renewed confidence in the future of his relationship with Laura Riding. Hardly had he set out for England, before Laura was writing him the most charming letter, in which she asked Robert to purchase some red roses as a present from her and Schuyler;[315] and when this message reached him at Erinfa, Robert immediately asked about a flower-shop, explaining why he needed one. Told that there was no such shop in Harlech, he seemed to have dismissed Laura's request from his mind; and Amy soon felt that it was safe to write to Nancy in a most encouraging manner about the possibility of Robert coming back to her. But then, on 23 August, the day before Robert was due to leave Erinfa, he was returning with his mother from their final stroll together, when she was touched to see him pick her best red rose-bud. For one happy moment she expected that he would give it to her; but then, without a word, he stuck it into his own buttonhole. At once, Amy recalled Laura's request, and realized with a shock of dismay how wrong she had been to raise Nancy's hopes.

Still more dismaying was the rapid approach of another European war. Chamberlain's appeasement of Hitler the previous year had bought time for a measure of rearmament; but the situation was near-desperate. Liddell-Hart had suffered a nervous breakdown from overwork, in his efforts to

alert the British people to the dangers which they faced; and everyone
at Erinfa had recently learned at first hand about the extreme views now
held by quite ordinary people in Germany. For the first part of Robert's
visit, one of his fellow-guests had been a German cousin, a woman who
was deeply imbued with the most offensive Nazi propaganda. On the out-
break of the First World War, Amy had declared that her race had 'gone
mad'; and Robert would soon take the same line, writing in a long article
for the *Sunday Graphic* that the Germans were:

> a nation suffering from what morbid psychologists call schizophrenia
> or 'split personality'.... when things go a little wrong with them and
> the worse nature, the Boche, gets the upper hand they forget who they
> are and what they are saying and doing....
>
> The only way that one can think of Germans now, as a nation, is
> as one thinks of a violent mental case struggling with ambulance men
> on the way to a padded cell and strait-jacket.[316]

The first member of the family to be directly affected by the coming conflict
was Dick Graves. During the night of 23 August, he received a telegram
from the War Office ordering him to report to London at once, and to
have a suitcase packed so that he could fly out to Cairo by the weekend.
In the morning, over breakfast, Robert talked about his own plans; and
his first impulse, despite the horrors which he had endured in the Great
War, was that he should once again volunteer to join the army and, as
he told Amy, to 'do whatever is most useful, training officers, or helping
in Spain'.[317] Robert travelled south on the same train as Dick; and then
settled for the time being at The Place, Great Bardfield, with his friends
John Aldridge and Lucie Brown. It was from there that he wrote to the
War Office offering his services; and it was there that he was staying when,
on 3 September 1939, Hitler's invasion of Poland led to Great Britain declaring war on Germany.

At first, as Robert wrote to Beryl, it seemed likely that Alan Hodge had
been caught up in the invasion, and might be trapped in Poland for the
duration of the war. Robert had been corresponding warmly with Beryl
several times a week since arriving in England, even though nothing that
he wrote to her remained private for long. Laura insisted upon reading
all his correspondence with any member of her household, and had already
expressed her irritation when she felt that one of his letters to Beryl had
contained items of information which were of special interest to herself.

Her own letters to Robert were usually full of the most loving solicitude.

Writing on 1 September, for example, Laura seemed genuinely pleased to learn that he was in a much calmer frame of mind: she felt that once more he was in charge of his own life, and that was one of the principal benefits which she had hoped he would gain from his journeying. She added a note of her own difficulties: Schuyler had been ill, and Kit (whom she persisted in calling Katharine) was back at the Farm, where a psychiatrist was keeping a watch on her. According to Laura the psychiatrist's opinion was that a legal separation from Schuyler might make Kit well, but it was also possible that she would have to return to a mental institution.[318]

A few days later, Laura wrote again to Robert, this time in an effort to set recent events into an intelligible context, and in so doing to offer him an acceptable way of returning to America as her literary assistant. Stating that it had been a joint desire for the survival of ancient truths which had enabled them to work together, she declared that many of those truths had been incorporated within their chosen way of life, and that through loving each other so honestly they had been able to achieve much. Sadly, however, the more widespread renewal for which they had striven had never occurred. Despite that, they had persevered bravely, but (in her view) the common feeling which had united them had degenerated from mutual aspiration to mutual need. Now, in their new circumstances, it was a time for the strength of their original purpose to be tested. She herself was certain that they could work together, and that there could be a new beginning. She now liked to think of herself, she concluded, as already living within the world of that new beginning, from where she sent Robert both her deep affection, and the assurance that he was constantly being remembered.[319]

Warm touches like these (one of her letters began: 'Dear Robert (dear means dear here)',[320] encouraged Robert to feel that there could indeed be a new beginning between him and Laura. And if she could love him in a purely spiritual manner, then perhaps her more worldly love for Schuyler might be balanced by his own love for Beryl. Where Alan fitted into the picture was obscure at this stage; but, in any case, Robert had already been told by Laura that whether or not Alan Hodge returned had nothing at all to do with the relationship between Robert and Beryl. So far as Laura was concerned, all that was important in this matter was the relationship between Alan and herself.[321] So, when he wrote to Laura, Robert did so with the intention of establishing as precisely as possible where he himself stood with her; and he wrote openly and honestly in a way which made it clear that Beryl was constantly in his mind.[322]

Laura, not liking so much emphasis upon Robert's relationship with

Beryl, but fairly certain that she could still bring him back to Brownsburg on her own terms, began her next letter in the most affectionate manner, but went on to say that, in her view, Beryl had become an over-large figure in his mind. Beryl had been someone whose company had kept his depression at bay, wrote Laura, but long-term dependence upon her undoubted goodness would eventually result in an even greater depression.[323]

Laura went on to say that Beryl was not truly serious and that she could show no emotion of any kind for Schuyler. Beryl often disliked Laura intensely, and she had no real remedy for Alan's similar bouts of rebellion. Robert, Laura insisted, was wrong to make a mistress out of her, and should treat her merely as a companion for light-hearted moments. His feelings for Beryl, Laura explained, had temporarily diminished him. That was why Robert had misinterpreted Schuyler's smile on his last night at the Farm – it had actually been expressing not triumph, but the hope that Robert could once again become his former self, and be wholly true both to his own better nature and to those who loved him.[324]

Robert's reply to this audacious rewriting of what had actually happened was so satisfactory in Laura's eyes that she addressed him in her next letter as a truth-seeker, and told him that she and Schuyler had both been heartened by his recent communications. She herself had been particularly aware of the change in his attitude, and loved him all the more.[325] Robert felt that he could now begin to make plans for returning to America, especially as his efforts to return to active service had foundered: his letter to the War Office had finally produced a medical board for the Officer's Emergency Reserve, but he had only been 'passed Grade 2 which means', he told Liddell-Hart, 'that I can only be accepted for non-combatant and very dull corps'.[326] In those circumstances, and now that he appeared to have secured a new understanding with Laura Riding, he had:

> decided that with so many people unemployed because of the war it was altogether unnecessary for me to do-my-bit in the Educational Corps or Army Pay Corps just in order to be in uniform – so am calling it off and returning to America which I am free to do because of my age and disability pension. Laura is short-handed over there and I have to work in order to support my family and various war-stranded semi-dependants.[327]

Robert was certainly very short of money at this time; and he felt under a great moral obligation not only to provide Nancy and their children with financial support, but also to look after the interests both of Karl Gold-schmidt and of Alan Hodge: who had now turned up safe and well in Sweden, and was hoping to return to London as soon as possible. Robert's solution to these financial difficulties was to begin work on what he hoped would be another *I, Claudius*, which not only would provide him with money, but would mean that he could offer secretarial and research work to his friends. The idea seems to have come from Methuen, who expressed interest in an historical novel on the subject of the American War of Independence; and Robert found a hero in the person of Sergeant Roger Lamb, who had served with the 9th and 29th companies of the Royal Welsh Fusiliers, and had left behind a *Journal* and *Memoir*, published in Dublin in 1809 and 1811, which would provide the bones of an excellent yarn. 'It will not be really fiction', he told Liddell-Hart, 'but the real stuff enlarged by con-temporary evidences of the sort of things that happened. I hate this sort of writing; but it can be justified as making readable what is not readable at all.'[328]

Going back to America would also relieve the pain of separation from Beryl, which, as Robert told her, expressed itself in a 'tightness in the solar-plexus which means that I am away from home and can't really relax until we are together again'.[329] Robert was still confused about their feelings for each other, and began one letter very tentatively:

I do hope it's all right my coming back without Alan but really I have no alternative on practical grounds – no possibility of really working here and income tax is 7/6 in the £. . . . It will be all right, though, if when I do come back there is a work atmosphere again.

I know it seems funny – me, as it were, preparing to go into the war with a flourish and then coming back the same as usual. But really there *is* no war here – yet – and I am very relieved not to feel obliged to pretend there is. . . . If the war did change for the worse so that they really needed me, I would of course go back again. . . .

It all seems so dreamlike my coming back after all. You are so much with me in this chapel [rented by Robert from John Aldridge and Lucie Brown]. . . . It is just like talking to you. I will never speak ill of aeroplanes again – so grateful to those mail clippers![330]

While Robert was writing this letter, a telegram arrived from Alan Hodge with news that he would shortly be setting out from Bergen on a ship bound for Newcastle; and in passing on this information Robert told Beryl that he would ask Alan 'to do research work for me until he can find some job or is called up'.[331]

A few days later, after long conversation with John and Lucie, Robert began to feel (quite wrongly) that he could to some extent accept Laura's view of his love for Beryl. The attraction which they felt for each other had been characterized by their circle as the product of their secondary natures: described as 'joult' in Robert, and 'bush' in Beryl; and Robert wrote to Beryl in late September that this attraction was:

> only a sweet and harmless and joking part of us and [we] rightly do not cut it out. – On the other hand, we know that the other sense of love such as we breathe at the Rise in *now*ness, is the really important thing. We could never go back to joult and bush seriously; and I could never fail Laura and Schuyler while they continue to love us.

They could be 'fast friends', he told her, but there could be no '*grande passion*' between them. But then, having sounded so decisive, Robert asked rather plaintively whether or not Beryl agreed with him.[332] The truth is that he was still highly uncertain about his future; and, on the day that he wrote this letter which appeared to put an end to any thoughts of a closer union between himself and Beryl, he was nevertheless preparing the ground for such a union by writing to Nancy to suggest that 'Since there cannot any longer be any misunderstanding between you and me about L and me, don't you think that now a divorce for us would be the cleanest thing?'[333]

Robert had now decisively rejected Nancy (who was both upset and furious when his letter reached her),[334] and in his muddled state of mind he had even attempted to push Beryl further away from him. It was at this moment, when he was more isolated and vulnerable than ever, that letters arrived from Laura which showed that his current plans were quite unworkable, and once again he was brought to the edge of a nervous breakdown.

CHAPTER 15
A Really Good Person

In her letter to Robert of 26 September 1939, Laura Riding at last made it absolutely clear that she would not tolerate any kind of relationship with Robert which involved Beryl, too, playing an important role in his life. Robert had been discussing Beryl and himself, she wrote angrily, in the light of his entirely mistaken notion that there were problems in her own relationship with Schuyler Jackson. He seemed to think that if he took a friendly view of those problems, she and Schuyler would respond gratefully by taking a friendly view of his relationship with Beryl, a relationship in which the only problems, according to Robert, were caused by Laura's and Schuyler's hostility.

Perhaps, she continued, he could try to grasp the elementary fact that his relationship with Beryl was completely irrelevant to the matter in hand. If, and when, Robert returned to America, he would be doing so as Laura's long-standing associate, sharing Laura's wish to make progress in whatever manner possible. If, however, he insisted upon building up Beryl's importance so that she came to occupy the place in his life once occupied by Laura, then any kind of future co-operation between Laura, Schuyler and Robert would be out of the question.

Laura added that Robert's idea that he was protecting Beryl from the combined forces of herself and Schuyler was wholly unreal. Beryl needed no such protection, and if only Robert would leave her alone, it would give Laura and Schuyler the chance to become her friends. Then, perhaps, they could help her to free herself from the knots she had been tied in ever since she had started looking lovingly at Robert during their stay at La Chevrie.[335]

Receiving this letter plunged Robert into a state of acute misery, which was painfully evident to all around him. In the company of close friends, such as John and Lucie, or James and Mary Reeves,[336] he burst into tears as he told them how bad things had become between him and Laura. To

Basil Liddell-Hart, he wrote more calmly on 2 October:

> I am undecided about my plans: from the news that has just reached
> me from America, Laura has changed her entire way of life since she
> went there.... I can't jeopardise the love that is between us by going
> back now and risking finding the differences between us still insurmoun-
> table.... It will be all right in the end but there is a lot of suffering
> in which all our friends are involved, to the extent that they really love
> us.[337]

He had, however, written a further letter to Laura in which, besides telling
her that he was very short of money, he mentioned the excellent offer
which Methuen were prepared to make for his Sergeant Lamb novels, and
asked her whether he should accept it. At the same time, he stated that
it was still his intention to return to America 'unless you say "definitely
not"'.[338]

It was at this moment that Beryl made a decisive intervention. Although
she may have been saddened by the letter in which Robert had emphasized
his primary loyalty to Laura and Schuyler, she must have noticed that
it was in that very letter that he had moved for the first time from the
quite ordinary 'Dear Beryl' to the much more intimate 'Beryl dearest'.[339]
She knew that she and Robert could have a future together: but not in
a place dominated by Laura and Schuyler. She therefore decided, on 4
or 5 October, that rather than wait for Robert at Brownsburg, she would
sail for England at once on the *Mauretania*. 'Beryl went, honourably', Robert
told Montague Simmons:

> because she knew I was coming and felt that our love for each other
> would not be given a chance at The Rise; and she thought that Laura
> needed me. She expected to cross me on the Atlantic. She says she is
> going to Alan if he wants her. But the tone of her letter says that she
> is dreadfully unhappy and wants me.[340]

At the same time, Robert received a letter from Laura, in which she told
him that she and Schuyler did not wish actively to discourage him from
joining them in America, but nor could they go so far as to summon him
to their side. Something might happen to change this problematical state
of affairs, but in the meantime, she concluded, perhaps it was better for
him to remain where he was.[341]

In the light of these letters from Beryl and Laura, Robert immediately cancelled his own sailing, and determined to meet Beryl at Liverpool. There was still the problem of Alan; but, as Robert wrote to Montague Simmons:

> If he and Beryl continue together good. If not: it is Beryl and me – he would, I believe, not want a triple relationship ... in which Beryl felt for me as she does. I was very ill and unhappy yesterday, but Beryl's letter using the same language of despair, made me know that it was not a private sorrow.[342]

Then, on Wednesday 11 October 1939, Robert met Beryl in Liverpool at the end of her voyage across the Atlantic. The conversation which followed utterly changed the course of their lives. It became finally clear to both of them that they wished to remain permanently together. There was no longer any question of Beryl offering to remain with Alan, though she knew that she must go to London to explain things to him; and Robert also had some explaining to do. That night, back at Great Bardfield, he penned this apologetic and moving letter:

Dearest Nancy:

Please forgive me for my clumsiness & misunderstanding. I never quite wholly understood you, or you me – something Scotch in you and perhaps something (??) Irish in me. What was good was very good; but we could never go back to anything more than the good that there was: which was not enough for permanent togetherness. It made four good children: and that is a fact & a good one.

When I wrote about the divorce I was being honest in meaning it as a practical closing of a practical account; I had no other intentions.

But things have happened very quickly since I wrote. I have decided not to return to America, at any rate for some time, and there is someone whom you would recognise as a really good person who will soon be permanently with me. This is not a sex-romance, and she is not even a writer or anything: but it is serious to the point of there being a child intended and this being so, it might be convenient, for travelling and so on, for us to marry one day. You do not know her and if you want to meet her, I should be glad. She is what you would call ... a 'lady' and when I was in America she was the person who saved me from a nervous breakdown when Laura and I changed our relationship. But I never knew until she came over from America ... that it could be like this between us. If you love me Nancy you will be kind to me in this; and I will truly love you for it.

Love: Robert

Laura doesn't approve of the relationship: & has done her best to end it. But fact is fact.[343]

Nancy replied that she was profoundly shocked by Robert's letter, and told him crossly: 'Your affairs do not concern me personally. But they affect the children and your family and I owe them more consideration than I owe you.' She therefore suggested that Robert should 'deal with the situation' through one of his family: perhaps John.[344] This infuriated Robert, who told Nancy to 'forget it', and said that he was 'perfectly well able to manage my affairs without further interference by muddle-headed hot-handed (albeit kind-hearted) John'.[345]

Beryl's effort to reach an understanding with Alan met with a much more friendly response. After a brief period of hostility, he accepted the new situation with good grace. In mid-October he received a letter from Robert which began: 'I am asking Beryl to come here on Saturday unless you two have pressing business together. I hope she will be able to come.' Robert went on to offer Alan research work on his Sergeant Lamb novel, and concluded: 'Dear Alan – I think that since this has had to be, it will end happily for us all; you know how I have always felt towards you. And how to me the only painful thing has been when it seemed that you were fighting me. Yours ever affy. Robert.'[346] Instead of tearing up this letter in a rage, as many less remarkable men might have done, Alan allowed Beryl to leave him without rancour; began working first (for a brief period) as Robert's literary assistant, researching for his *Sergeant Lamb* novels, and then as his collaborator on *The Long Weekend*, a social history of Britain between the wars; and all the while he remained Beryl's good friend.[347]

For some weeks, it seemed that Laura was capable of a similar graciousness. On 1 November, she began a letter to Robert with an affectionate greeting, and referred in a friendly manner to those times of quiet hope that they had spent together. She suggested that now, released from the difficulties of their former relationship, they could begin to enjoy a true friendship based upon their mutual and deeply-felt desire for what was best. Not only was she prepared to admit her own human fallibility, saying that she had been wrong to assume sole responsibility for knowing what was necessary, not only did she seem less insanely confident about her ability to influence international affairs, but she made the generous suggestion that she should transfer all the Deyá property[348] to Robert, telling him that with his new plans for the future he might feel differently about going back to Majorca.[349]

Robert and Beryl were now living together at Great Bardfield in the chapel rented from John and Lucie where they had found a personal happiness which is reflected back to us in one of Graves's most tender poems:

THROUGH NIGHTMARE

Never be disenchanted of
That place you sometimes dream yourself into,
Lying at large remove beyond all dream,
Or those you find there, though but seldom
In their company seated –

The untameable, the live, the gentle.
Have you not known them? Whom? They carry
Time looped so river-wise about their house
There's no way in by history's road
To name or number them.

In your sleepy eyes I read the journey
Of which disjointedly you tell; which stirs
My loving admiration, that you should travel
Through nightmare to a lost and moated land
Who are timorous by nature.[350]

Robert was working hard and happily on his historical novel, for which Random House as well as Methuen had now offered him a substantial advance; and in the light of some very friendly letters both from Laura and from Schuyler it began to seem possible that he and Beryl might return to Brownsburg in the spring of 1940. Robert explained it to Liddell-Hart:

Laura and I (you know, I think) were colleagues and inseparables, but not what is called 'lovers'[351] though there was/is great love between us. She now has a very close intimacy with an American (poet and also farmer – very good farmer) of whom I am very fond: his name is Schuyler Jackson – we were staying on his farm – and I am really very happy indeed that she is happy with him. And as Laura is also very fond of Beryl, it is all right all round: though confusing to people at first. Beryl and I will be going back to live with Laura and Schuyler Jackson in the spring, if there are no worse sea-warfare menaces to prevent us.[352]

Amicable correspondence continued with Laura, who wrote about a number of literary projects including the *Dictionary*, *The Swiss Ghost* and a new book to be called *The World Has Changed*; and who also passed on the news that Kit Jackson's brother[353] had visited them, and that, although Kit was now apparently well, her family had agreed that it would be best for her to be legally separated from Schuyler.[354]

Robert now felt so secure in his new understanding (or, more accurately, misunderstanding) with Laura that when he met Basil Liddell-Hart accompanied by Kathleen Norris, the woman who was to become Basil's second wife, he invited them to join him and Beryl on their voyage to America the following March.

Christmas came, and the future still looked settled. As part of the festivities at Great Bardfield Robert, and Beryl (who was now expecting a child the following summer), took part in a play which Robert had written, and in which (as he told Karl):

> John & Lucie were the King and Queen of Essex, Beryl a princess (in a long old-fashioned night gown & coronet, a blue sash and a heavy cold) our two Spanish refugees were princes – dressed in English Guardsmen's uniforms – who had killed a dragon, & I was a Lord in Waiting dressed in a lot of red curtains and a red cap made of a hot water bottle cover. It was the first time I had ever seen a play of mine acted![355]

It was not long, however, before Robert became aware of further changes at Brownsburg, which filled him once more with doubts about the wisdom of returning to America.

After years of being the dominant figure in her circle, Laura Riding had found in Schuyler Jackson someone who would not bend to her will; and, instead, she began to bend to his. The note of humility which had entered her writing in November was entirely the result of Schuyler's influence; and perhaps after so many years she was glad enough to be relieved of her burden of authority and responsibility. However, the new role which she had to learn was very different from the one to which she had become accustomed, and for a while everything must have felt very strange. Soon after Christmas, Robert told Karl that he had received a letter in which Laura had:

> mentioned casually that she & S intend to marry – odd! It was not really a happy letter and I don't quite see how I can work with her & him on the *Dictionary* because the method they are using seems to be a very

personal one – anyone who wasn't constantly with them, night & day, would be an intruder if he tried to help: or if not an intruder, then a bottle washer. And anyhow I think they want to be alone. Laura's general condition makes me very anxious.[356]

Schuyler certainly had no wish for any of Laura's former circle to return to Brownsburg, or for Laura to continue with any literary activities which might make that necessary; and so, on 31 December, Laura wrote Robert a further letter telling him she could not go on with *The Swiss Ghost*, and that he was to publish it as his. She sent good wishes to him and Beryl and to their unborn child. She told Robert that she and Schuyler hoped for a spring wedding, and could not make any other arrangements for that time. She added once again that Robert must take possession of the property at Deyá.[357]

Then, in January 1940, Robert received two very contradictory letters from Laura. In the first of them she was perfectly friendly, and ended by saying that she hoped to see Robert in March, and once again wished him and Beryl a happy life together with their child. However, as Robert reported to Karl, Laura had written:

another[358] to say that she doesn't want to see me in March and that there is no possibility of my helping in the *Dictionary*, which is being done in an entirely different way, except by helping her financially with the *Sergeant Lamb* money; and that because of extraordinary expenses she cannot repay me the £450 paid to her in error last November from Random House, which Random House will now recover from my *Lamb* advance. She also will do all in her power to break the power of the *Ist Protocol*, that 'infected' document, wherever it raises its head.[359]

Before allowing Laura to post these letters, Schuyler had enclosed a further missive of his own, in which he wrote that he had not answered Robert's last letter because it had made him feel bad: it contained no warmth at all, he complained. He then rudely described Beryl as suffering from Robert's desire, adding for good measure that Laura had ruined her health in her efforts to procure Robert's salvation (admittedly, Schuyler commented, an unwise thing to have attempted). Laura had now recovered to such an extent that she could not possibly hold any interest for Robert in his present degenerate condition. He went on to accuse Robert of having been, like Kit, an unworthy beneficiary of Laura's divinely-inspired words. In Schuyler's view, Robert had somehow used those words to his own advantage, preying upon their truth in order to counteract his own degeneration. He had done this so effectively that virtually none of the words survived unsullied to greet the dawning of a new age in which mankind could be truly innocent.[360]

Robert, having read over this sorry nonsense, retailed it to Karl with the comment: 'Don't let all this sadden you. Be happy in what good Laura bequeathed to us before she left us.'[361] To Basil Liddell-Hart he wrote at about the same time that the common ground between him and Laura was now:

> shrinking to postage-stamp size.
>
> The most astonishing thing is her withdrawal from the *Covenant of Literal Morality* as "superseded by events"; just at a time when most of us were feeling its value most strongly and feeling most anxious for a second protocol on the subject of the recognition of good (i.e. friendship – love) to reinforce the first protocol on the judgement of evil....
>
> ... I feel that my chief object in going to America is now removed, and that my place is really with the friends whom I love who are still here. Beryl, who was very anxious to go to America, thinks the same. Instead, we think of taking a house before long in S.Devon, near where my sister [Rosaleen] is established, and in the hope of you two also perhaps remaining in the same neighbourhood.[362]

Despite further efforts by Robert to secure a *rapprochement* with Laura (mid-February found him writing to Karl that his 'only wish' was 'for Laura's happiness, but it seems a very long time in coming'),[363] Laura had now set her face firmly against him; and in a letter dated 17 February 1940, she wrote a final letter of dismissal.

Addressing Robert with sudden formality by his surname as well as his first name, Laura referred coldly to having received from him two communications which could not possibly be answered. In addition, she had received three more which she intended to answer only insofar as they dealt with a business-like separation of their interests. Her letter, she told him, would terminate their correspondence. Robert could have everything that had been stored in London, and everything that had been waiting for them in Majorca. Her only proviso was that he should burn all her private papers at Canelluñ.

Under Schuyler's influence Laura had now rewritten the entire fourteen years of her association with Robert, and she concluded her letter with some extraordinarily bitter words for the man who had been devoted to her for so long. She now believed, she told Robert, that by joining him in England in January 1926 she had made a serious error of judgement. This had resulted in Robert becoming very much indebted to her, while at the same time she had allowed him to become her protector. Long before their flight from Deyá, however, Robert had fully discharged his debt by turning much of his life into a lengthy atonement for the sin of having summoned her as though she were truly necessary to him, when, in actual fact, that was clearly not the case. Laura ended cruelly by saying that she had only allowed Robert to act as her protector because she had accepted his need to atone. With her current understanding of the true nature of their time together, it was now impossible for her to feel the slightest gratitude for a single thing that he had done.[364]

It was all over; and no doubt in a way it was a profound relief for both of them. Laura no longer had to carry the burden of Robert's dependence upon her; and Robert, after the depressing years during which Laura had been gradually drifting away from him, and after all the emotional turbulence of the past ten months, found himself, with 'a really good person' at his side, in an unexpected oasis of settled happiness.

AFTERWORD

When Robert Graves first met Laura Riding in January 1926, he was in a fundamentally unhappy state: with a failing marriage, a fading literary career, and the alarming conviction that his personality was fragmenting. Although he thought of himself as a radical he remained in part a prisoner of his conventional past, and at times felt trapped by the moral weight of the wider family which had saved him once too often from destitution.

Within three years, Laura had rescued Robert both from his marriage and from his wider family and all that they represented; and had acted as intellectual and spiritual midwife not only to a kind of personal rebirth but also to Robert's writing of *Good-bye to All That*, a work of genius which made him famous and in which he offered up a heavily rewritten version of his past life upon the altar of his present love.

The quality of Robert's literary work was dramatically improved by Laura's detailed criticisms in which her chief principle was that Robert should be precise and say exactly what he meant. However, Laura soon became sexually disenchanted with someone whom she could so easily control; and, although for all kinds of reasons she wished to continue living with Graves, she was soon doing so in the light of her new philosophy that 'bodies have had their day'. This set up new conflicts in Graves's mind between his devotion to Riding, whom he came to regard as a source of ultimate or 'final wisdom', and his steadily increasing, but largely subconscious, resentment of her manipulative treatment. Where this conflict surfaced in his dreams, it produced terrifying visions of blazing buildings and burning railway coaches. Where it surfaced in his literary work, as in his *Claudius* novels, and as in much of his most interesting poetry, its emotional force had a powerfully beneficial effect upon the quality of what he produced.

Robert's final break with Laura was as difficult as it was inevitable; but it was made much easier not only by his good fortune in being already settled with a new partner – 'With Beryl here,' he had written to Liddell-Hart on 30 November 1939, 'everything is very simple and sensible'[1] – but by the fact that, within a few months of meeting Schuyler Jackson, Laura had so completely altered her way of life. Writing again to Liddell Hart in February 1940, Graves asked himself, 'What can I say about Laura?' and answered, 'She reached (for me) a point of shall we say poetic (i.e. hyper-moral) excellence that nobody has ever attained before.' Now, however, she had 'admitted into her scope so many foreign elements' that it was 'difficult to regard her as the same person.'.[2]

Robert remained, at first, most faithful to the memory of the source of inspiration that Laura had once been; and within a year of their parting he wrote this tribute to her:

It was in 1927 that Laura Riding, a young American who had recently come to Europe, first published her poems and critical work in England. Wiping her slate clean of literary and domestic affiliations with America, she became for the next twelve years the best of 'good Europeans'; the Americans only knew her as 'the highest apple on the British intellectual tree'. In England she was assailed as a 'leg-puller', 'crossword puzzle setter', 'Futurist', 'tiresome intellectualist', and so on: none of her books sold more than a few dozen copies, nor did she ever (as Gertrude Stein did after the Wall Street crash, in her chatty *Autobiography of Alice B. Toklas* and during her American lecture tour) consent to give the larger public what it really wanted. She was the one poet of the time who spun, like Arachne, from her own vitals without any discoverable literary or philosophical derivations: and the only one who achieved an unshakeable synthesis. Unshakeable, that is, if the premiss of her unique personal authority were granted, and another more startling one – that historic Time had effectively come to an end. In her *Preliminaries* to *Epilogue* I she wrote:

'All the Chinese bandits having chopped off all the foreign ears, we have time to consider not only the subject *Atrocity*, but the subject *Bandits*, and the subject *Missionaries*, and the subject *Foreigners* and the subject *Chinese*. All the politicians who are going to be elected have been elected; and all the artificial excitement in events which no one really regards as either very important or very interesting has been exhausted. All the historical events have happened.'

This left the poets the pleasant if arduous duty of reporting 'the single event possible after everything has happened: a determination of values'. The literary *avant-gardistes* could do nothing with her: she was interested in value, not in post-temporal fashion, she had a better head than any of them and a better heart than most, she was accessible but not clubbable, and she resented the constant unacknowledged borrowing from her work by the ambitious and insincere. This made everyone uncomfortable: they would have liked to make a Great Woman out of her, but to do so would have meant changing their own unsynthesized habits. They did their best to ignore her. Laura Riding was remarkable as being in the period but not of the period, and the only woman who spoke with authority in the name of Woman (as so many men in the name of Man) without either deference to the male tradition or feministic equalitarianism: a perfect original. At the very end of the period she returned to the United States, surprisingly rediscovered her American self, and wiped the slate clean once again.[3]

Later he would feel less kindly towards her: so that (for example) she was entirely eliminated from his 1957 version of *Good-bye to All That*. However, the image of Riding as she had been, especially in the earlier years of their relationship, had rapidly sunk down into Graves's subconscious, from where it had an important effect upon much of his work, and in particular re-emerged as one of the principal constituents of *The White Goddess*, that 'historical grammar of poetic myth' which was first published by Faber and Faber in 1948, and which remains essential reading for anyone with an interest in poetry.

Robert and Beryl spent the Second World War years at Galmpton in South Devon, where three children were born to them, my cousins William, Lucia and Juan; and they then went out to Majorca, where everything at Canelluñ had remained untouched since Robert and Laura had fled from the island in the summer of 1936; and where Robert's eighth child Tomas was born in 1953.

With Karl Goldschmidt's editorial eye replacing that of Laura Riding until the mid-1960s, Robert remained a prolific professional author of all kinds of work, from historical novels such as *Wife to Mr Milton* or *The Golden Fleece*; to essays and short stories and a rewriting of the Greek myths; and to *The Nazarene Gospel Restored*, a brave attempt (with Joshua Podro) to discover the truth behind the authorized version of the life of Jesus.

Poetry (which Laura Riding abandoned in 1939 as an inadequate means of telling the final truth about things) remained Robert's principal calling; and in his middle and later years he was inspired to produce some of the finest love poems of the twentieth century. The key to the remainder of his life (which may one day be the subject of a third and final volume of the present biography) lies in this highly memorable poem which he wrote 'In Dedication' to the poetic Muse:

> All saints revile her, and all sober men
> Ruled by the God Apollo's golden mean –

In scorn of which I sailed to find her
In distant regions likeliest to hold her
Whom I desired above all things to know,
Sister of the mirage and echo.

It was a virtue not to stay,
To go my headstrong and heroic way
Seeking her out at the volcano's head,
Among pack ice, or where the track had faded
Beyond the cavern of the seven sleepers:
Whose broad high brow was white as any leper's,
Whose eyes were blue, with rowan-berry lips,
With hair curled honey-coloured to white hips.

Green sap of spring in the young wood a-stir
Will celebrate the Mountain Mother,
And every song-bird shout awhile for her;
But I am gifted, even in November
Rawest of seasons, with so huge a sense
Of her nakedly worn magnificence
I forget cruelty and past betrayal,
Careless of where the next bright bolt may fall.

Although his devotion to the Muse sometimes led him and his close family into the most extraordinarily complicated and difficult situations, it was indeed a devotion on an heroic scale; and Graves was fortunate that for the rest of his long life he retained the support and companionship of a woman whom he had once called 'timorous by nature', but who proved to be not only constantly dependable but fiercely loyal.

ABBREVIATIONS

1 UNPUBLISHED SOURCES

ALDRIDGE From the private collection once owned by Robert Graves's friend John Aldridge Esq., and now held by the solicitors Messrs Thompson Quarrell on behalf of the present owners.

AUTHOR The vast collection of family papers built up by Robert Graves's brother John Graves (1903–80) and now owned by John's son Richard, the present author (RPG). This collection has never been worked over before, except by John Graves (JTRG), who made use of some items for his unpublished biography 'My Brother Robert'.

BODLEIAN Letters owned by the Bodleian Library, Oxford.

BROTHER The incomplete typescript of 'My Brother Robert' by his brother John Graves, now owned by John's widow Mary.

DIARY The 1911–31 diaries of Robert's father Alfred Perceval Graves (1846–1931), now owned by APG's grandson Richard, the present author. These diaries have for the most part been seen by no one but RPG and his father John Graves, who made some use of them for his 'My Brother Robert'. However, APG published some extracts from the July to December 1914 entries, on pages 294–301 of his autobiography (see ALFRED below); and in letters to Martin Seymour-Smith JTRG passed on a handful of extracts, some of which were used by MS-S in *Robert Graves: His Life and Works* (Hutchinson 1982).

INDIANA Two collections of papers in the Lilly Library, Indiana University, at Bloomington, Indiana: (i) Nicholson MSS 1929–1973 which contains correspondence between Robert Graves and his first wife Nancy Nicholson; and (ii) Gay MSS which contains correspon-

dence between Robert Graves and his friend and secretary Karl Gay (formerly Goldschmidt).

LETTERS Letters from Robert Graves to his brother John, together with handwritten commentaries by JTRG, now owned by JTRG's widow Mary.

MAJORCA The collection of family papers held by Robert's widow Beryl Graves at her house in Deyá. These were studied previously by Martin Seymour-Smith for his biography (see MS-S below).

MATTHEWS–PC From the private collection of Robert Graves's friend T.S.Matthews Esq.

NYPL Papers from the New York Public Library (chiefly from the Berg Collection), copies of which were seen by the present author at MAJORCA as above.

RG DIARY The diary kept by Robert Graves from February 1935 to May 1939, which is now owned by the University of Victoria, British Columbia; and of which Beryl Graves kindly loaned the present author a photocopy. Studied by MS-S (below).

WILSON Papers from the T.E.Lawrence collection built up by his biographer Jeremy Wilson.

2 PRINCIPAL PUBLISHED SOURCES

ALFRED Alfred Perceval Graves, *To Return to All That* (Jonathan Cape 1930).

BISGO Robert Graves, *But It Still Goes On* (Jonathan Cape 1930).

CHARLES Charles Graves, *The Bad Old Days* (Faber & Faber 1951).

GTAT29 Robert Graves, *Good-bye to All That* (Jonathan Cape 1929). I have quoted from this version wherever possible, believing it vastly superior to the 1957 revised edition (GTAT57).

MATTHEWS T.S.Matthews, *Under the Influence* (Cassell 1977).

MS-S Martin Seymour-Smith, *Robert Graves: His Life and Works* (Hutchinson 1982).

O'PREY(I) Ed. Paul O'Prey, *In Broken Images: Selected Letters of Robert Graves* *1914–1946* (Hutchinson 1982).

SASSOON(3) Ed. Sir Rupert Hart-Davis, *Siegfried Sassoon Diaries, 1923–1925* (Faber & Faber 1985).

WEXLER Joyce Wexler, *Laura Riding's Pursuit of Truth* (Ohio University Press 1979).

NOTE ON THE POEMS

During his working life Robert Graves made many alterations to his poems. But when I am writing about his life in 1926, and decide to quote from a poem written in that year, then I believe that it is biographically more correct to quote from the version published in 1927 than from the slightly altered version published in 1948, or the substantially altered version published in 1959 or later. So I have tried always to quote from the version of a poem which is most contemporary to the context in which it appears.

A FURTHER NOTE ON SOURCES

Since this biography was delivered to the Publishers, much of the material listed under AUTHOR, BROTHER, DIARY and LETTERS relating to the 1895–1940 period of Robert Graves's life has been acquired by the New York Public Library for the Berg Collection.

REFERENCE NOTES

BOOK ONE
A PASSAGE TO EGYPT 1926

CHAPTER 1
A BACKWARD GLANCE

1 AUTHOR: Amy Graves to her son J.T.R.Graves (JTRG) 8 January 1926.

2 O'PREY(I) Robert Graves (RG) to Siegfried Sassoon 20 February 1930 p. 203.

CHAPTER 2
LAURA

3 NYPL, in reply to an enquiry from the present author dated 25 July 1986, gives a report from the US Local History & Genealogy Division to the effect that The Federal Census for New York of 1900 shows Nathan S. Reichenthal living at 161 East 52nd Street. He was born in July 1869 in Austria, migrated to the US in 1884; married as his second wife Sadie in 1897 or 1898; was naturalized, Sadie's parents were born in Germany. Isabella (Bella) was born on 3 March 1894, birth cert. no. 11297. Also *Trow's Directory of the City of New York* for 1900 shows Nathan S. Reichenthal, a tailor, living in Manhattan at 112E 102nd Street.

4 MS-S p. 122, quoting from Laura (Riding) Jackson's own entry in *Twentieth Century Authors* for 1942, has 'down-town Manhattan', names her father 'Nathaniel' and describes her parents as 'Jewish (but not religiously so)'.

5 Tom Matthews, in conversation with RPG August 1988.

6 WEXLER p. 6. Karl Goldschmidt in conversation with RPG March 1989

heard of further pressure from a brother who was an infant prodigy until the age of fourteen when he became schizophrenic.

7 Ibid. pp. 6–7.

8 AUTHOR James Tyler, Rare Books Senior Assistant in the Department of Rare Books at Cornell University to RPG, 25 July 1986. The date is from the *Cornell University Register* of 1918.

9 Laura (Riding) Jackson in *Cornell Alumni News* October 1983.

10 Ibid. pp. 14–16.

11 AUTHOR James Tyler to RPG as note 8 above, from 'Records in the University Archives'.

12 Ibid.

13 Laura did not complete her studies at Cornell, but in 1921 followed her husband to the University of Illinois (where she enrolled in a few courses); and in 1923 the Gottschalks moved on to the University of Louisville in Kentucky, where Louis had been appointed as an assistant professor.

14 As note 9 above.

15 Alan Clark, 'Laura (Riding) Jackson: A Check List' in *Chelsea 35* (1976) pp. 228–39.

16 *The Fugitive* has the poem in vol. 2 no. 8 August/September 1923 p. 124; and the comments in vol. 2 no. 10 December 1923 p. 163.

17 *The Fugitive* vol. 3 no. 1 February 1924 pp. 9–14 ('To An Unborn Child', 'The Quids', 'Initiation', 'Starved').

18 WEXLER p. 8.

19 MS-S pp. 127–8. MS-S writes of 'the repercussions of her brief affair with

Tate', which may allude to this rumour.

20 MATTHEWS p. 121. However, it is difficult to establish the truth; and Laura Riding declared in AUTHOR Laura (Riding) Jackson to RPG 19 May 1987 that she had documentary proof (although she did not supply it) that she had been invited to Nashville.

21 MS-S pp. 126–7. It is only fair to mention that in AUTHOR Laura (Riding) Jackson to RPG 19 May 1987, Riding rejects this account completely, and especially denies having quarrelled with Hirsch.

22 *The Fugitive* vol. 3 no. 5/6 December 1924 p. 130. The April 1924 issue contains 'Improprieties' and 'For One Who Will Dust a Shadow'; August 1924 has 'For One Who Will Bless the Devil'; and December 1924, 'Mortal', 'Forms', 'Saturday Night' and 'Lying Spying'. Other poems appeared in *Poetry, Poet Lore, Contemporary Verse* and *Sewanee Review*.

23 *The Fugitive* vol. 4 no. 1 March 1925 p. 31. This issue contained her 'Summary for Alastor', 'The Sad Boy' and 'The Higher Order'.

24 MS-S p. 127 (but see note 20 above).

25 Ibid. pp. 126–7. Further publications appeared in *The Fugitive*: June 1925, 'Druida', 'The Circus'; September 1925, 'Marey Carey', 'The Only Daughter', 'Virgin Of The Hills'; December 1925, 'Sonnets in Memory of Samuel', 'The Fourth Wall'. In 1925 her poems also appeared in *Sewanee Review, The Lyric, The Guardian* (Philadelphia), *The Calendar of Modern Letters, The Reviewer, The Nation* (New York) and *Poetry*.

CHAPTER 3
ROBERT

26 Robert Graves, *Poems 1914–1926* (William Heinemann 1927) p. 61.

CHAPTER 4
THE VOYAGE

27 AUTHOR Amy to JTRG 8 January 1926.

28 AUTHOR Sally Chilver (Philip Graves's daughter) to the present author 1985.

29 Ibid.

30 Doris Ellitt to RPG 8 March 1986. Sally Chilver comments (1985) that her mother Millicent said to her father Philip, 'Well, one of the party has a head for housekeeping.'

31 Laura (Riding) Jackson to RPG 23 May 1987.

32 Laura (Riding) Jackson to RPG 8 June 1985.

33 MAJORCA has a picture of Laura at this time showing her short hair. When she grew it longer, its luxuriance may have notably contrasted with the sad appearance of Nancy's hair, much of which had fallen out as the result of her illness.

34 GTAT29 C. 242.

35 AUTHOR Amy to JTRG 10 January 1926.

36 AUTHOR Amy to JTRG 16 January 1926.

37 GTAT57 p. 277 adds the story that 'Luckily a P.&.O. Director, who happened to be aboard, persuaded the captain to take the ship within half a mile of Stromboli, then in eruption; by dusk in a hailstorm, with the lava hissing into the sea.'

38 GTAT29 pp. 412–13.

CHAPTER 5
HELIOPOLIS

39 NYPL, Berg Collection (copy seen at MAJORCA) has RG to Sassoon 'Dec 10 or so 1925 Islip' in which Robert asks for a loan of £100–£150 to cover the purchase and export of a 1921 Morris-Oxford motor-car. The Special Collection in the Morris Library at Southern Illinois University at

Carbondale has Sassoon to RG telling him that he has told J.G.Lousada (Sassoon's solicitor) to send him £150.

40 AUTHOR Amy to JTRG 8 January 1926.

41 Laura (Riding) Jackson to RPG 29 May 1987. It is only fair to mention that in this letter LRJ denies Doris Ellitt's assertion that she declared the flat to be haunted though she admits that there were peculiarities sensed or noticed by everybody.

42 AUTHOR Ellitt to RPG as note 30 above.

43 DIARY 9 January 1926.

44 Ibid. 4 February 1926.

45 AUTHOR Ellitt to RPG as note 30 above.

46 GTAT29 p. 434.

47 AUTHOR Ellitt to RPG as note 30 above.

48 GTAT29 p. 413.

49 AUTHOR Ellitt to RPG as note 30 above. AUTHOR Laura (Riding) Jackson to RPG 10 July 1986 comments that she certainly required all her gifts as a communicator to exercise effective authority over her hired help.

50 GTAT29 p. 413.

51 AUTHOR Ellitt to RPG as note 30 above.

52 O'PREY(I) p. 163 RG to Sassoon p.c. pmk 3 February 1926.

53 Ibid. RG to T.S.Eliot 16 February 1926.

CHAPTER 6
CAIRO

54 O'PREY(I) p. 163 RG to Sassoon p.c. pmk 3 February 1926.

55 GTAT29 p. 414.

56 Ibid.

57 DIARY 23 February 1926.

58 GTAT29 p. 415.

59 DIARY 23 February 1926.

60 GTAT29 p. 415. RG was later (ibid. p. 422) pleased to have 'ordered a library of standard textbooks of Eng-

lish literature for the Faculty Library at the University'.

61 Ibid. p. 411.

62 Ibid. pp. 417–19.

63 Ibid. pp. 436 and 432–4. The quotation beginning 'had no intention' was cut from GTAT57.

CHAPTER 7
SEEING GHOSTS

64 GTAT29 p. 437 (cut from GTAT57).

65 BROTHER.

66 DIARY 23 February 1926.

67 O'PREY(I) pp. 161–2 RG to Eliot n.d. November/December 1925.

68 Ibid. pp. 163–4 16 February 1926 from 6 rue Sabbagh Heliopolis.

69 DIARY 2 April 1926.

70 O'PREY(I) p. 165 RG to Sassoon n.d. pmk 31 March 1926.

71 GTAT29 p. 437.

72 Ibid. p. 446. This is taken from the 'Dedicatory Epilogue To Laura Riding' pp. 445–8 which was deleted from GTAT57.

73 Robert Graves, *The Shout* (Matthews & Marrot 1929). The library copy at MAJORCA has in RG's hand: 'Written at Hammersmith. First draft at Cairo; March 1926'. Page references are from the more easily accessible Robert Graves, *But It Still Goes On: An Accumulation* (BISGO) (Jonathan Cape 1930) pp. 79–104. On p. 79 there is an introductory paragraph between square brackets in which RG describes the genesis of the story.

74 BISGO p. 79.

75 Ibid. p. 82.

76 GTAT29 p. 437.

77 AUTHOR Ellitt to RPG as note 30 above.

78 Ibid.

79 O'PREY(I) pp. 164–5 RG to Sassoon n.d. pmk 31 March 1926.

80 AUTHOR Amy to JTRG 6 April 1926 shows RG selling his car: something indispensable to his way of life in Egypt.

81 Ibid.
82 DIARY 12 April 1926.

83 O'PREY(I) pp. 165–6 RG to Sassoon n.d. (May 1926).
84 Ibid.

BOOK TWO
STRANGE TRINITY 1926–1929

CHAPTER 1
RESIGNATION

1 GTAT29 p. 439.
2 DIARY 1 July 1926. RG had told APG he would be 'Glad to come for my birthday [his seventieth on 22 July] but must be back for his own [his thirty-first on 24 July]'.
3 GTAT29 pp. 431–2.
4 DIARY 10 July 1926.
5 Ibid. 14 July 1926.
6 AUTHOR Clarissa Graves to Amy n.d.

CHAPTER 2
MOODS OF DESPAIR

7 O'PREY(I) p. 166 RG to Eliot 24 June 1926.
8 Ibid. p. 167 RG to Sassoon 13 July 1926 and p. 168 n.d. (early August 1926).
9 Ibid. p. 168 RG to Sassoon n.d. (early August 1926).
10 As note 9 above.
11 DIARY 3 August 1926.
12 Ibid. 1 August 1926.
13 Ibid. 9 August 1926.
14 WEXLER p. 8.
15 AUTHOR Amy to JTRG (then tutoring at the Manor House, Hinton St Mary) 25 August 1926.
16 O'PREY(I) p. 169 RG to Sassoon 18 September 1926.
17 See Volume (*The Assault Heroic*) 1 p. 281.
18 AUTHOR Amy to JTRG 17 October 1926.
19 Ibid.

CHAPTER 3
WHITE HEAT

20 As note 18 above.
21 As note 16 above.
22 DIARY 21 September 1926 and AUTHOR Amy to JTRG 27 September 1926.
23 AUTHOR Clarissa to Amy and APG 30 September 1926.
24 AUTHOR Amy to JTRG n.d. (sheet 2 of letter).
25 Ibid.
26 AUTHOR Amy to JTRG n.d. from 9, Northwick Terrace (London).
27 DIARY Sunday 10 October 1926 (other entries show that Amy and APG left England on 4 October, and arrived at Hof Gastein on 6 October).
28 Ibid. Wednesday 13 October 1926.
29 AUTHOR Amy to JTRG 17 October 1926 from Friedrichsburg Hof Gastein.
30 As note 28 above.
31 As note 29 above.
32 O'PREY(I) RG to Sassoon n.d. pp. 170–1.
33 Ibid. n.d. p. 172. NYPL, Berg Collection (copy seen at MAJORCA) has a letter from RG to Eliot dated 9 November 1926 in which RG thanks Eliot for the offer (which may have arrived too late) of some review work for the January *Criterion*.
34 AUTHOR Amy to JTRG 25 October 1926.
35 Laura Riding and Robert Graves, *A Survey of Modernist Poetry* (William Heinemann, 1927). The introductory 'Note' explains that the book is a word-by-word collaboration 'except for the last chapter, which is a

revision by both authors for the purposes of this volume of an essay separately written and printed by one of them'.

CHAPTER 4
A SURVEY OF MODERNIST POETRY

36 As note 35 above. The quotations are taken from pages 10, 84, 137, 118, 282, 58, 47, 117, 121–3, 118–19, 176, 75, 176, 177, 49–55, 58, 170–1, 172, 178, 158, 187 and 158 again.

CHAPTER 5
A SICK HOUSEHOLD

37 DIARY 19 November 1926 APG and Amy, back from Hof Gastein, had found the children exuberant and Nancy in good form: 'I never knew her more forthcoming.'
38 DIARY 10 January 1927 (for the drawing) and as note 37 above.
39 DIARY 13 January 1927.
40 AUTHOR Clarissa to Amy n.d. January 1927.
41 AUTHOR Amy to JTRG 10 March 1927.
42 NYPL, Berg Collection (copy seen at MAJORCA) RG to Sassoon (?) 1 March 1927. He also told Sassoon that he wanted to hear from him.
43 AUTHOR Amy to APG 12 March 1927.
44 AUTHOR Amy to JTRG 16 March 1926. (To add to RG's troubles, the dog was sick.)
45 AUTHOR Amy to APG 19 March 1927.
46 DIARY 27 April 1927; and see AUTHOR Doris Ellitt to RPG 23 November 1986: 'When I returned to World's End Nancy had taken the children to Cumberland. From there she wrote asking me to join her. Robert & Laura visited us once or twice during the summer.'

CHAPTER 6
ST PETER'S SQUARE

47 AUTHOR Clarissa to JTRG 5 December n.d. (1926).
48 Clarissa to Amy 28 April 1927.
49 NYPL, Berg Collection (copy seen at MAJORCA) RG to Sassoon 6 May 1927. He added that he hoped to see something of him soon.
50 O'PREY(I) p. 174 RG to Sassoon 30 May 1927.
51 Mary Lago and P.N.Furbank (eds), *Selected Letters of E.M.Forster*, vol. 2: *1921–1970* (Collins 1985) p. 78.

CHAPTER 7
LAWRENCE AND THE ARABS

52 O'PREY(I) p. 175 RG to Sassoon 5 June 1927.
53 WILSON collection: TE to Hogarth 1 June 1927; also see John E. Mack, *A Prince of Our Disorder: The Life of T.E.Lawrence* (Weidenfeld & Nicolson 1976) p. 367: 'a conspiracy of my friends'.
54 Robert Graves, *Lawrence and the Arabs* (Jonathan Cape 1927) p. 5.
55 Ibid. pp. 6–7: RG's informants included Mrs Thomas Hardy, Mrs Lawrence (TE's mother), Field-Marshal Viscount Allenby, Colonel John Buchan, Mr E.M.Forster, Sir Robert Graves, Mr Siegfried Sassoon, Mr Vyvyan Richards, Mr Leonard Woolley, Dr D.G.Hogarth, Mr Arnold Lawrence (TE's brother) and many others.
56 GTAT29 p. 439.
57 As note 54 above p. 50.
58 O'PREY(I) p. 180 RG to Sassoon 31 October 1927. In the same letter RG refers to a warning from George Bernard Shaw that Cape would 'crash' on it – he had advised Robert that it was 'A great mistake. You might as well try to write a funny book about Mark Twain', and implied that if RG wanted to become a serious biographer he should 'Write a book (if you must) about the dullest person you know; clerical if possible. Give your-

self a chance.' (See GTAT29 p. 440.) Later RG claimed that Shaw had mistaken him for his brother Charles – but no doubt he would have given the same warning to either of them.

59 O'PREY(I) p. 175 RG to Sassoon n.d. (September 1927).

60 Ibid. p. 179 RG to Eddie Marsh n.d. (late October 1927).

61 DIARY 1 August 1927.

62 O'PREY(I) p. 176.

63 Ibid. pp. 176–7.

64 Ibid. p. 177 RG to Eliot n.d.

65 Ibid. pp. 177–8.

66 Ibid. pp. 178–9.

67 Ibid. pp. 170–1 RG to Sassoon n.d.

68 As note 65 above.

69 Robert Graves, *Poems 1914–1926* (William Heinemann 1927) p. 210.

70 As note 51 above, Forster to RG 26 September 1927 p. 81.

71 AUTHOR Dick (in Cairo) to Clarissa 10 November 1927.

72 DIARY 16 November 1927.

CHAPTER 8
THE AVOCA

73 LETTERS 7 January 1928.

74 AUTHOR Clarissa to Amy and APG 14 January 1928, misdated by her 14 December 1927.

75 DIARY 9 January 1928.

76 Quoted in AUTHOR Amy to JTRG n.d. (January 1928). Despite RG's letter to his parents, he did not withdraw an invitation made to JTRG on 7 January to come to lunch on 10 January. When JTRG saw RG on 7 January, incidentally (AUTHOR JTRG to Amy 7 January), RG had 'spent all the morning helping the poor flooded-out folk on the Thames'.

77 DIARY 9 January 1928.

78 AUTHOR A journal kept by JTRG from 6 to 20 January 1928 in an exercise book.

79 AUTHOR Laura Riding to JTRG n.d. (January 1928).

80 AUTHOR Clarissa to Amy 17 January 1928.

81 AUTHOR Clarissa to JTRG 31 January 1928.

82 Ibid.

83 AUTHOR JTRG to Amy 6 January 1928 has RG 'getting things ready for the children in a week's time'. Incidentally MS-S pp. 155 and 159 believes that the *Ringrose* was RG's first barge, and that he later bought the *Avoca*. This is contradicted by e.g. AUTHOR Rosaleen to JTRG 22 March 1929: 'You know he's bought a lovely new one – the *Ringrose* – should be even nicer than the *Avoca*.' The move into the *Avoca* took longer than planned: AUTHOR Doris Ellitt to RPG 23 November 1986 has: 'Nancy asked me to take the children to visit their father in Hammersmith. The *Avoca* barge was being converted for our occupation. However it was not ready when we arrived & we spent a few uncomfortable weeks sleeping on the floor in the flat in St Peter's Square, finally moving into the *Avoca* before it was finished.'

84 AUTHOR Clarissa to John February (1928).

85 AUTHOR Amy to JTRG 23 February 1928. See also AUTHOR Ellitt to RPG as note 83 above, in which Doris Ellitt recalls: '[The children] had all developed severe colds. I complained to Robert that living in an unfinished barge on the Thames in February was not good for their health. Robert did not agree & passed on my complaint to Laura. It was obvious to me that neither of them really wanted to accept responsibility for the children but expected me to do so under any circumstances uncomplaining. The following day Laura accused me of behaving like Nancy. This really upset me because I had never … taken sides.'

86 AUTHOR Amy to JTRG 24 February 1928.

CHAPTER 9
THE SEIZIN PRESS

87 See Volume 1 (*The Assault Heroic*) pp. 103–4.
88 O'PREY(I) pp. 108–82.
89 Ibid. pp. 182–3 RG to Sassoon 20 January 1928.
90 Ibid. pp. 197–201, 19 Sassoon to RG 7 February 1930.
91 AUTHOR Clarissa to JTRG mid-February n.d. (1928).
92 AUTHOR Clarissa to Amy 11 May 1928.
93 As note 78 above.
94 MS-S p. 147.
95 Ibid.
96 GTAT29 p. 441.
97 MS-S p. 148.
98 O'PREY(I) p. 190.
99 Ibid. pp. 190–1 Stein to RG n.d. (1929).
100 This was *An Acquaintance with Description*, written in 1926, and to be published by LR and RG as their second Seizin in 1929.
101 AUTHOR Clarissa to Amy 3 July 1928 (written at ten past one in the morning).
102 AUTHOR Clarissa to JTRG 7 July 1928.
103 AUTHOR Laura Riding to Clarissa n.d. (1928).
104 AUTHOR Clarissa to Laura Riding 12 July 1928 (a copy in CG's own hand).
105 AUTHOR Rosaleen (from Remuera, Skegness) to Clarissa 18 July 1928.
106 Wystan Curnow and Roger Horrocks (eds), *Figures of Motion: Len Lye/Selected Writings* (Auckland University Press, Oxford University Press 1974), Introduction.
107 AUTHOR Roger Horrocks (the biographer of Len Lye) to RPG n.d. (1987).
108 DIARY 27 September 1928.
109 AUTHOR Amy to JTRG 28 September 1928.
110 DIARY 1 October 1928.
111 These included: Laura Riding, *Contemporaries and Snobs* (Jonathan Cape 1928); Laura Riding, *Anarchism Is Not Enough* (Jonathan Cape 1928, Doubleday 1928); and Laura Riding and Robert Graves, *A Pamphlet [Against Anthologies]*' (Jonathan Cape [and Doubleday] 1928).
112 AUTHOR Amy to JTRG 2 November 1928 reports this news from a letter from Charles.
113 DIARY 2 January 1929.

BOOK THREE
THE SHOUT 1929

CHAPTER I
GEOFFREY PHIBBS

1 MATTHEWS–PC Norah McGuinness to T.S.Matthews 6 March 1978.
2 AUTHOR Susan Macaulay (née Graves) to JTRG 28 March 1929.
3 Mary Taylor (who later became Geoffrey Phibbs's second wife) in conversation with RPG in 1986.
4 Terence Brown, *Geoffrey Taylor: A Portrait 1900–1956* (an unpublished monograph written when TB was a young Trinity College, Dublin lecturer).
5 Ibid.
6 Ibid.
7 Ibid.
8 Quoted in ibid., from p. 24 of Frank O'Connor, *My Father's Son* (Macmillan 1968). This description is by a friend; but Mary Taylor writes to RPG 16 December 1986: 'Geoffrey let *one* lock of hair grow on his forehead & he used to toss it back when talking. When indignant or sarcastic, he used to tighten his lips & make them into a narrow line. He had a fairly full well-shaped mouth –

"thick lips" gives quite a wrong impression.'

9 AUTHOR Mary Taylor to RPG n.d. also describes Norah as 'a fairly hard-headed Northerner ... naturally & understandably full of ambition'.

10 As 1 above. AUTHOR Mary Taylor to RPG n.d. comments that Norah 'liked going to Yeats, who made a fuss of her & may have been useful to know'.

11 As 1 above.

12 As 3 above. In a written note AUTHOR Mary Taylor to RPG n.d., MT comments that she never heard Geoffrey actually *'complain* because Norah refused to have children'. In a subsequent conversation with RPG, MT said that sex was 'the sun, the moon and the stars' to Geoffrey; and that Norah was 'very inhibited', and would 'never let [Geoffrey] look at her'.

13 As 4 above.

14 DIARY 6, 10 July 1928. In the first place it was APG who noticed the article, and sent a sympathetic letter to Miss Alexander..

15 DIARY 27 July 1928.

16 MS-S pp. 155–6 believes that Phibbs visited Robert and Laura in October 1928 before being visited by Robert later that year. I can find no proof of this first meeting, and it seems unlikely in the light of Norah's belief that Geoffrey and Laura did not meet until 1929. Nor does *14*(A) suggest an earlier meeting.

17 As 3 above. All the contemporary material suggests that RG and Phibbs were good friends at first – as Phibbs himself later told his second wife MT.

18 MS-S p. 156 has a letter from Phibbs to RG dated October 1928 from The Bungalow, Wicklow, Ireland.

19 Ibid.

20 As 1 above.

21 Ibid. Norah was not 'living intermittently with David Garnett' as stated in MS-S p. 155. AUTHOR MT to RPG

as 9 above comments that 'D.G. had the reputation of being good at sex & perhaps Norah genuinely wanted to find out if he cd. make it work for her. But I do admit I also wondered if the fact that he was part of the Bloomsbury set & knew influential people in London also influenced her.'

CHAPTER 2
THREE INTO FOUR

22 MATTHEWS–PC Norah McGuinness to T.S.Matthews 6 March 1978.

23 Ibid.

24 MS-S p. 157. The suggestion that he turned up 'in rags', although immediately modified, is typical of what appears to be MS-S's humorous prejudice against Phibbs.

25 AUTHOR Rosaleen to JTRG 19 June 1929 reports this form of words. It is incidentally interesting to note the extent to which the relationship between Riding, Graves and Phibbs at this time mirrors that of the three main characters in Truffaut's *Jules et Jim.*

26 LETTERS pmk Hammersmith 31 March 1929.

27 AUTHOR Rosaleen to JTRG 22 March 1929.

28 Ibid. 25 February 1929.

29 Ibid. 22 March 1929.

30 DIARY 26 March 1929.

31 Ibid. 2 April 1929.

32 AUTHOR Rosaleen to JTRG 2 April 1929.

33 As note 22 above.

34 Ibid.

35 MS-S p. 160.

36 Ibid.

37 Ibid. p. 163.

CHAPTER 3
THE SHOUT

38 Laura Riding and George Ellidge, *14*(A) (Arthur Barker 1934) p. 137.

39 GTAT29 pp. 446–7 gives an account

of this journey; also RG's 'Return Fare' in his *Poems 1926–1930* (William Heinemann 1931) pp. 80–1, concluding: 'And so I found the place near Sligo, not the place / So back to England on the Easter Thursday.' It appears he was back in London on 4 April 1929, and left the next day for France with Laura and Nancy.

40 As note 22 above.

41 MS-S p. 163; confirmed by AUTHOR Mary Taylor to RPG n.d. 'I particularly remember [Geoffrey] telling me that when [he and Norah] were together & alone again how absolutely impossible it had become for him.'

42 MS-S p. 162 suggests that this letter did not arrive until their return from France.

43 As note 22 above.

44 Ibid.

45 Ibid.

46 Ibid.

47 Ibid.

48 GTAT29 p. 447.

49 Ibid. DIARY Sunday 7 April 1929. DIARY entries for the next few days show that RG was invited to supper on 11 April, and 'said he'd try to come ... but failed to do so being in a very broken down state'. The next day he 'again failed to turn up'; and on 15 April, back at Erinfa, APG and Amy received a package in which RG returned his Great-Uncle Robert Perceval Graves's ring, saying that he no longer wished to wear it.

50 As note 22 above.

51 MS-S pp. 163–4.

52 As 22 above.

53 MS-S pp. 163–4.

54 As note 22 above.

55 Ibid.

56 MS-S p. 165.

57 As note 22 above.

58 GTAT29 p. 447.

59 As note 22 above.

60 WEXLER p. 53 has: 'Laura remembered a moment of extreme clarity, when she looked into each of them and realised not one truly shared her

concerns ... [she was] feeling utterly alone.' And ibid. p. 54 notes that LR had written in 'Free' in 1926 of death as an escape route from a merely unpleasant life. AUTHOR MT to RPG 16 December 1986 comments: 'The account I had from G. was that Laura, when she was on the window sill, threatened to jump out if Geoffrey wd. not remain with her ... seeing this as emotional blackmail & not expecting Laura to actually do it, Geoffrey refused. I certainly received the impression from Geoffrey that this was the moment of truth when he made it clear to Laura that he cd. no longer accept her domination.'

61 GTAT29 p. 447.

62 As note 38 above, p. 271.

63 Taken from 'The Terraced Valley' in Robert Graves, *Poems 1926–1930* (as note 39 above) pp. 86–7.

CHAPTER 4
CLOSE IN THE SUNSHINE

64 This story first reached RPG in late 1974 or early 1975 in a conversation with Lady Liddell Hart and others. It was suggested that RG had cannily rushed down a floor before flinging himself out, so as to ensure his own survival. I prefer my own equally speculative interpretation which seems more in character, given the overwhelming nature of RG's feelings for LR.

65 O'PREY(1) p. 188 RG to Eddie Marsh 16 June 1929.

66 GTAT29 p. 447.

67 Date and time speculative, *but* O'PREY(1) as note 65 above says G talked to the police when 'He thought Laura must have died.'

68 AUTHOR Rosaleen to JTRG 19 June 1929 shows that this was how Nancy and Geoffrey viewed that episode.

69 As note 65 above.

70 Summary partly speculative but based on note 65 above.

71 As note 65 above.

72 This speculative passage about how

the police viewed events is based upon GTAT29 p. 442: 'been examined by the police on a suspicion of attempted murder'.

73 DIARY 1 May 1929 and AUTHOR Amy to JTRG 2 May 1929.

74 DIARY 3 and 6 May 1929; and AUTHOR Amy to JTRG 6 May 1929.

75 DIARY 7 May 1929.

76 Dating tentative: it is possible that Nancy's and Geoffrey's visits to both Robert and Laura took place on Saturday 4 May 1929.

77 MAJORCA document from which MS-S quotes extensively and which he describes as the 'Précis' (written by RG not earlier than mid-September 1929).

78 Ibid.; partly quoted in MS-S p. 171.

79 AUTHOR Rosaleen to JTRG 7 May 1929.

80 INDIANA Nicholson MSS 1929–1973; Robert Graves to Nancy Nicholson misdated 5 May (RG heads the letter 'I wrote this on Saturday night', i.e. on Saturday 4 May).

81 Ibid., headed '*Sunday Night*', with the further explanation: 'I wrote this without consulting the other letter, to send instead, but now send both. The first was the hot immediate reaction the second the calmer one.'

82 MS-S p. 172 quoting from MAJORCA 'Précis'.

83 See the Preface to Laura Riding, *Poems: A Joking Word* (Jonathan Cape 1930).

84 As note 39 above, pp. 86–7.

CHAPTER 5
BREAKING WITH NANCY

85 The date is taken from the MAJORCA 'Précis', where the details of a meeting said to have taken place on 12 May tie up with the details of MAJORCA 'Report' as note 86 below.

86 MAJORCA. This note, which we shall refer to as 'Report', is undated; but see note 85 above. I have added some words of tentative explanation as

some of the meaning is obscure; my additions are qualified by words such as 'seems', 'no doubt', 'must have' etc. It appears that MS-S pp. 174–7, not content with a few words of explanation, has gone in for substantial 'fleshing out' at this point. He expands the original 320 words of the 'Report' to several times that length, by such devices as (a) adding to reported dialogue, and (b) adding new lines of dialogue and new details for which his authority appears uncertain. Thus:

(a) 'you were being possessive (vulgarly speaking) of him' becomes 'She's just bloody well what she's calling everyone else: *vulgar*. She's jealous of Nancy. She wants me, she wants to possess me, have me, fuck me. Isn't that just *vulgar*? Besides: she thinks she's God. She's sick.'

(b) Additional lines of dialogue include: 'Graves: "You're a liar and a sponger. You're a liar, you know." The verdict sounded like a court-martial finding not subject to higher review.'

Other additions show Geoffrey Phibbs in a somewhat comical light: e.g. 'Phibbs now stood up and sneered petulantly,' or 'abruptly switching from abuse to mawkishness, he sat down again and started a self-pitying monologue, tears rolling down his cheeks'.

87 MAJORCA 'Report'.

88 Ibid.

89 MS-S p. 178.

90 AUTHOR Rosaleen to JTRG 19 June 1929.

91 MAJORCA Phibbs to RG 15 May 1929.

92 As note 89 above.

93 As note 91 above.

94 MAJORCA Nancy Nicholson to RG n.d.

95 MAJORCA 'Précis'.

96 MAJORCA Phibbs to RG 16 May 1929.

97 MS-S p. 179.

98 Dr Rosaleen Cooper (née Graves) in conversation with RPG 11 September 1982.

99 GTAT29 p. 447.
100 MS-S p. 179.
101 Ibid. Date deduced by working back from Nancy's letter of 20 May.
102 MAJORCA Nancy to RG n.d.
103 MAJORCA Nancy to RG 20 May 1929.
104 MAJORCA 'Précis'.
105 Deduced by working back from subsequent letters.
106 MAJORCA Nancy to RG Monday 20 May 1929.
107 MAJORCA Horoscope of Geoffrey Phibbs.
108 MAJORCA Phibbs to RG Monday 20 May 1929; partly quoted in MS-S p. 180.
109 AUTHOR Clarissa to Amy 22 May 1929.
110 DIARY 18 May 1929.
111 DIARY 23 May 1929 and see Volume I pp. 123–33.
112 AUTHOR RG to Amy and APG 25 May 1929.
113 GTAT29 pp. 13–14 has 'irrelevant' and 'proper chaps' (cut from GTAT57).

CHAPTER 6
THE WRITING OF
GOOD-BYE TO ALL THAT

114 GTAT29 p. 13 (cut from GTAT57).
115 GTAT29 pp. 13–14 (cut from GTAT57).
116 GTAT29 p. 14 (cut from GTAT57).
117 BISGO pp. 13–15.
118 GTAT29 p. 10.
119 Ibid. p. 445.
120 Volume I (*The Assault Heroic*) p. 288.
121 ALFRED p. 333.
122 BISGO p. 14.
123 ALFRED p. 333.
124 Volume I (*The Assault Heroic*) e.g. p. 239. It is notoriously difficult for people to like those who have helped them a great deal, and RG could never again view his father quite sanely. AUTHOR Laura Riding to RPG 8 June 1985 describes how at that time RG would frequently declare that APG was the least honest of all the men he knew.
125 GTAT29 p. 75.
126 Ibid. p. 33.

127 Ibid. p. 241.
128 Ibid. p. 99.
129 Ibid. p. 174.
130 Volume I (*The Assault Heroic*), pp. 117, 138 for RG's original attitude; 161 for the change.
131 Volume I (*The Assault Heroic*) p. 177 and GTAT29 p. 322.
132 GTAT29 p. 131.

CHAPTER 7
DISTRACTIONS FROM WORSHIP

133 AUTHOR Rosaleen to JTRG 19 June 1929.
134 Dr Rosaleen Cooper (née Graves) in conversation with RPG 1982.
135 As note 133 above.
136 MAJORCA Nancy to RG n.d. (from Islip).
137 MAJORCA Phibbs to RG 5 June 1929; partly quoted in MS-S pp. 181–2. Phibbs declared that from his reading of the *Encyclopaedia Britannica* venereal disease might indeed be a predisposing cause for the type of paralysis from which Laura had been suffering. But he had never accused her of that. What he had said was that Laura was suffering from delusional insanity of a kind which frequently leads to general paralysis; but if RG felt that a court action would clear things up, he would happily provide him with a libel. MS-S pp. 181–2 seems unsatisfactory in supporting the notion that Phibbs had been maligning Laura. True, RPG has not seen the medical notes on Riding to which MS-S refers; but he has seen the 'worried, cryptic letters to Graves from Nancy'. MS-S states that these 'letters don't say in so many words that Riding had venereal disease' – but to RPG it appears that they do not even hint at such a thing. The only *cryptic* passage seems much more likely to refer to Laura Riding's possible lesbian tendencies. MS-S on p. 181 then mistakenly replaces the words 'delusional insanity' in Phibbs's letter with '[the

disorder referred to above]' – which was 'Venerial [*sic*] disease'.

138 DIARY 10 June 1929.

139 MAJORCA Nancy to RG Islip 14 June 1929.

140 Ibid.

141 AUTHOR Rosaleen to JTRG 14 June 1929.

142 AUTHOR Amy to JTRG 13 June 1929.

143 AUTHOR Rosaleen to JTRG 19 June 1929.

144 NYPL, Berg Collection (copy seen at MAJORCA) RG to March 13 May 1929.

145 Quoted in MS-S pp. 166–7, the source is: King's College London: TE to Mrs George Bernard Shaw 22 May 1929.

146 O'PREY(I) pp. 188–90 RG to Marsh 16 June 1929.

147 MAJORCA Marsh to RG Monday n.d.

148 O'PREY(I) p. 191 RG to Stein 18 June 1929. NYPL, Berg Collection (copy seen at MAJORCA) RG to Marsh n.d. has 'I am very grateful and so is Laura. To know that she is free of the vulgarity of a police enquiry will make her get well much quicker.'

149 MAJORCA Phibbs to RG 15 July 1929 from the *Ringrose*.

150 MS-S p. 182.

151 MAJORCA RG to Nancy 20 August (1929).

152 MAJORCA Nancy to RG n.d.

153 MAJORCA Note signed by Nancy Nicholson, 3 September (1929) from the *Ringrose*.

154 MAJORCA receipt signed NN dated 15 September 1929 gives a 4 September date.

155 MAJORCA 'Précis'.

156 Ibid.; partly quoted in MS-S p. 183.

157 Ibid.

158 Ibid.; partly quoted in MS-S p. 184.

CHAPTER 8
GONE ABROAD

159 O'PREY(I) p. 192 RG to Stein n.d.

160 O'PREY(I) p. 191 RG to Stein 18 June 1929.

161 MS-S p. 190 very slightly misquotes MAJORCA Stein to Graves n.d.

162 MS-S p. 189 (from the MAJORCA collection).

163 Ibid.; but the last forty-one words come from a section of the letter apparently overlooked by MS-S.

164 AUTHOR Amy to JTRG 18 July 1929.

165 DIARY 5 July 1929.

166 Ibid. 29 August 1929.

167 AUTHOR Amy to Clarissa 23 August 1929.

168 AUTHOR Amy to Clarissa 21 September 1929.

169 AUTHOR Amy to Clarissa 25 September 1929.

170 DIARY 29 August 1929.

171 Ibid. 26 September 1929.

172 Ibid.

173 Ibid. 1 and 4 October 1929; and AUTHOR Amy to JTRG 5 October 1929.

174 AUTHOR Amy to JTRG 5 and 21 October 1929.

175 Ibid. 21 October 1929.

176 Ibid. 5 October 1929.

BOOK FOUR
ROBERT GRAVES AND LAURA RIDING
IN MAJORCA 1929–1936

CHAPTER I
CASA SALEROSA

1 MS-S p. 190; though LR would later declare [as in AUTHOR Laura Riding to RPG 15 August 1986] that she and Robert had fixed upon MAJORCA *in advance* of their visit to Gertrude Stein.

2 Or they could have travelled by steamer from Marseilles.

3 Charles Graves, who visited the island some five and a half years later, in the summer of 1935, gives his impressions in *Trip-tyque* (Ivor Nicholson & Watson, 1936) pp. 218–37, and I have drawn heavily on these.

4 Ibid. p. 218.

5 Ibid. p. 234.

6 See Volume 1 (*The Assault Heroic*) pp. 146–7.

7 Maria in conversation with RPG (Beryl Graves interpreting) November 1986.

8 Robert Graves, *Poems 1926–1930* (William Heinemann 1931) p. 89.

CHAPTER 2
THE PUBLICATION OF GOODBYE
TO ALL THAT

9 AUTHOR Amy to JTRG 5 November 1929.

10 Ibid. 7 November 1929.

11 AUTHOR Susan Macaulay (née Graves) to JTRG 17 September 1929.

12 DIARY 8 November 1929.

13 O'PREY(I) pp. 194–5 Marsh to RG 6 November 1929.

14 Ibid. p. 196 RG to Marsh 12 November 1929.

15 Ibid.

16 MS-S pp. 195–7.

17 NYPL has the volume annotated by Blunden and Sassoon. Most of the annotations are plainly factual, but some are witty: for example, when-ever RG begins a passage with the words: 'Another caricature scene. Myself...', every word after 'Myself' is crossed out. Dr Dunn also annotated a copy of GTAT29 which now belongs to the Royal Welch Fusiliers Museum at Caernarvon.

18 Rupert Hart-Davis (ed.), *Siegfried Sassoon: Letters to Max Beebohm & a Few Answers* (Faber & Faber 1986) p. 4.

19 DIARY 18 November 1929.

20 Ibid. 24 November 1929.

21 AUTHOR Amy to Clarissa 19 November 1929.

22 AUTHOR Amy to JTRG 20 November 1929.

23 As note 21 above.

24 GTAT29 pp. 23–4.

25 Ibid. p. 21.

26 Ibid. p. 43.

27 MAJORCA Charles to RG 25 November 1929 (GTAT quotations pp. 90 and 357). Charles added: 'I know quite well that you were getting at Dick. But I wish you had said so. That's his affair.'

28 AUTHOR Amy to JTRG n.d. (from int. evidence 28/29 January 1930).

29 AUTHOR Bernard Rendall to JTRG 2 January 1930.

30 BISGO 'PS to Good-bye to All That' (pp. 13–56) pp. 18–31.

31 DIARY 16 December 1929.

32 As note 30 above p. 17.

33 The Library of the Royal Welch Fusiliers at Caernarvon has a collection of letters written by Dr Dunn to RG.

34 As note 30 above pp. 40–3. RG was writing with particular reference to a review of Brigadier-General Crozier's *A Brass Hat in No Man's Land*.

35 DIARY 16 December 1929.

CHAPTER 3
BUT IT STILL GOES ON

36 'The Seizin Press' by Hugh Ford pp. 121–47 in *The Private Library* Second Series Volume 5:3 Autumn 1972. Len Lye also collaborated with Laura Riding on a collection of his own letters to be published as *No Trouble*, the fourth Seizin Press publication. They were concerned with his ideas for a film to be called *Tusalava*.

37 Laura Riding, *Poems: A Joking Word* (Jonathan Cape 1930).

38 Ibid. p. 91.

39 Ibid. p. 135.

40 Ibid. p. 148.

41 Ibid. p. 170.

42 Robert Graves, *Poems 1926–1930* (William Heinemann 1931).

43 AUTHOR Amy to JTRG 3 December 1929 and n.d. (January 1930) shows that Phibbs had caused enormous offence to the Egyptian authorities by making 'pro-native' speeches, and had been asked to leave the country. Returning to Nancy he had renounced his inheritance 'for a safe £100 a year for life' – for which William Nicholson, who had been trying to find him work, condemned him as a 'young fool'.

44 AUTHOR Amy to Clarissa *and* Amy to John, both March 1930.

45 AUTHOR Amy to JTRG 14 May 1930.

46 AUTHOR Amy to Clarissa 10 March 1930.

47 Laura Riding, *Four Unposted Letters to Catherine* (Paris, Hours Press [1930]) p. 6.

48 Ibid. pp. 12–13.

49 Ibid. p. 18.

50 Ibid. pp. 35–9.

51 Ibid. p. 39.

52 *Authors Today and Yesterday* (New York, Wilson 1933) p. 565.

53 Laura Riding, 'The Damned Thing', on pp. 187–208 of *Anarchism Is Not Enough* (Jonathan Cape 1928).

54 Ibid. p. 193.

55 Ibid. p. 208.

56 Ibid. p. 193.

57 As note 52 above.

58 Robert Graves, 'But It Still Goes On', Part three of BISGO.

59 Ibid. p. 215.

60 Ibid. p. 218.

61 Ibid. p. 293.

62 Ibid. p. 217.

63 Ibid.

64 Ibid. pp. 258–9.

65 Ibid. p. 245.

66 Ibid. p. 229.

67 O'PREY(I) pp. 197–201 Sassoon to RG 7 February 1930.

68 Ibid. p. 199.

69 Ibid. pp. 199–201.

70 Ibid. pp. 201–3 RG to Sassoon 20 February 1930.

71 Ibid. pp. 204–9 Sassoon to RG 2 March 1930.

72 Ibid. pp. 212–13 RG to Len and Jane Lye 8 June 1930.

73 BISGO p. 134.

74 Ibid. p. 136.

75 Ibid. p. 163.

76 GTAT29 p. 445.

77 BISGO p. 206.

78 O'PREY(I) p. 210 RG to Len and Jane Lye 1 June 1930.

79 BISGO p. 9.

80 As note 42 above.

81 As note 72 above.

CHAPTER 4
TO RETURN TO ALL THAT

82 DIARY 23 January 1930.

83 AUTHOR APG to JTRG 27 January 1930.

84 Ibid. n.d. January 1930.

85 AUTHOR Amy to JTRG n.d. 1930.

86 AUTHOR JTRG to APG and Amy 2 February 1930.

87 MAJORCA APG to RG 21 July 1930.

88 Ibid.

89 BISGO p. 22.

90 Ibid. 'Note'.

91 AUTHOR Amy to JTRG 20 October 1930.

92 O'PREY(I) pp. 336–41; and see ibid. p. 337 RG to Stein 28 January 1946 about LR breaking with Stein 'in a

fit of spleen: I think because you always mentioned the weather, and that seemed unworthy': and ibid. p. 339 Stein to RG 4 February 1946 on LR having been 'the materialistic Jew camouflaging her materialism by intellectualism'.

93 AUTHOR Rosaleen to Clarissa 4 August 1930.

94 Ibid.

95 DIARY 2 September 1930.

96 AUTHOR Amy to JTRG 16 September 1930 and Amy to Susan 19 September 1930. RG said he could only afford £270 p.a.: Nancy said that she needed a minimum of £330.

97 DIARY 4 November 1930.

98 Ibid. 7 November 1930.

99 See Volume I (*The Assault Heroic*) pp. 302–3.

100 BISGO pp. 130–2.

101 DIARY 12 November 1930.

102 AUTHOR Amy to JTRG 12 November 1930.

103 Ibid. 15 November 1930.

104 DIARY 17 November 1930.

105 MAJORCA APG to RG 17 November 1930.

CHAPTER 5
NEW BEGINNINGS

106 ALDRIDGE RG to Aldridge 29 March 1931.

107 AUTHOR Laura (Riding) Jackson to RPG 5 January 1987. The house remained Canelluñ throughout Robert's working life, but latterly it was renamed Ca N'Alluny, the correct Mallorquin for 'the far house'.

108 This visit is speculative: though ALDRIDGE RG to Aldridge 15 November 1930 says that Norman is counting the days to March. Ibid. 29 March 1931 has 'Would you mind you & Norman bringing David out when you next come?'

109 'Barbara Rich' (actually Graves and Riding, though Riding has never admitted authorship), *No Decency Left* (Jonathan Cape 1932).

110 ALDRIDGE proof copy of *No Decency Left* dated 1931.

111 Robert Graves, *Poems 1930–1933* (Arthur Barker 1933) p. 33.

112 As note 110 above.

113 As note 42 above.

114 Ibid. pp. 61–2.

115 Ibid. p. 59 ('Anagrammatic').

116 Ibid. pp. 32–3 ('Pavement').

117 Ibid. p. 60 ('Midway').

118 Ibid. p. 14.

119 Ibid. pp. 24–5.

120 See Amy's inscription dated 17 March 1931 in her copy of the book, now owned by RPG.

121 AUTHOR Amy to JTRG 12 February 1931 (from Worthing, where she was staying with APG).

122 AUTHOR Amy to JTRG 17 March 1931 (date from a part of the letter copied out by JTRG).

123 MAJORCA The *Daily Palma Post* Thursday 23 June 1932 has a letter from RG in which, referring to their article of 19 June 1932, he points out that the incident was 'over a year ago'.

124 ALDRIDGE RG to Aldridge 1931 n.d.; and, for Gelat meeting the police, Beryl Graves in conversation with RPG spring 1988.

125 This culminated in an article in the *Daily Palma Post* of Sunday 19 June 1932 headed 'Graves Would Become Deyá Dictator: Alcalde Scolds'.

126 MATTHEWS p. 129.

127 O'PREY(I) p. 215 RG to John Aldridge n.d.

128 ALDRIDGE RG to Aldridge n.d. (1931).

129 Tom Matthews comments to RPG (1988), 'And don't forget the chapter Robert *added* and why: because David Copperfield was such a snob he didn't marry little Emily, so RG gave them a one-night affair in London. The chapter stuck out like a sore thumb – but I believe was not generally noticed!'

130 Francisca talking to RPG 1986, Beryl Graves interpreting.

131 Laura (Riding) Jackson, 'Laura and Francisca' in *The Poems of Laura Rid-*

ing (Carcanet 1980) pp. 345–359. Laura Riding, *Laura and Francisca* was first published by the Seizin Press in 1931.

132 ALDRIDGE RG to Aldridge n.d. (? July 1931 [pre-October, post June]). Karl Gay (formerly Goldschmidt) in conversation with RPG March 1989 was surprised to hear about the canoeing, as by the time he knew Robert there were no canoes: and Robert in any case would not use a double paddle, as he felt that it put pressure on the lung through which he had been shot in the Great War.

133 MATTHEWS-PC Typewritten copy of a Journal by Lucie Brown p. 51.

134 MS-S p. 233.

135 As note 111 above, p. 5.

136 MATTHEWS-PC as note 133 above, pp. 51–2. This account provides the first solid evidence in an area of Robert's life about which much has been rumoured and little has been known. One story, widely circulated for many years, had Elfriede recovering from her abortion at Salerosa, until Laura declared that she was possessed of a devil, and advanced up the stairs, whip in hand, intending to drive her from the house. A similar incident did happen: but later.

137 As note 132 above. In this context, there is an interesting letter: AUTHOR Rosaleen to JTRG 20 August (n.d.) which includes: 'Robert said to me, once, that all a child needed was to be taught to read. The rest of its education it could do for itself.' And when she argued that children needed continuity, 'he instanced Laura's 20 different schools (about).'

CHAPTER 6
THE PASSING OF
ALFRED PERCEVAL GRAVES

138 DIARY 3 July 1931.

139 AUTHOR Molly (in Cairo) to JTRG 12 January 1932.

140 AUTHOR Amy to JTRG 1 August 1931.

141 DIARY 29 November 1931.

142 Ibid. 2 December 1931.

143 MAJORCA JTRG to RG 21 February 1932.

144 DIARY 25 December 1931.

145 Ibid. 26 December 1931.

146 As note 139 above.

147 AUTHOR Susan to JTRG 15 January 1932.

148 AUTHOR Amy to JTRG 26 January 1932.

CHAPTER 7
A HORROR OF LAURA RIDING

149 MATTHEWS-PC As note 133 above pp. 52–53.

150 MATTHEWS p. 133.

151 Tom Matthews; a note to RPG, 1988.

152 MATTHEWS p. 126.

153 Ibid. p. 128.

154 Ibid. p. 127.

155 Ibid. p. 138.

156 Ibid. pp. 129–30.

157 Ibid. p. 127.

158 Ibid. pp. 127–8.

159 Ibid. p. 138.

160 Ibid. p. 140.

161 Ibid. p. 141.

162 Ibid. pp. 141–2.

163 Ibid. pp. 143–4.

164 Ibid. p. 134.

165 Ibid. pp. 134–5.

166 Ibid. p. 134.

167 Norman Cameron, *The Collected Poems of Norman Cameron* (Hogarth Press 1957).

168 MATTHEWS p. 132.

169 Ibid. pp. 132–3.

170 Ibid. p. 148.

171 Ibid. pp. 148–9

172 Ibid. pp. 144–5.

173 Ibid. pp. 149–50. Karl Gay, in conversation with RPG March 1989, regards this interpretation as implausible but Lucie Brown [as note 33 above, p. 54] supports it.

174 MATTHEWS p. 151.

CHAPTER 8
FAMILY MATTERS

175 John Graves, *The Boy's Book of Association Football* (G.Bell & Sons 1931).
176 AUTHOR A document in Clarissa's hand, with details including: Hon. President Mrs A.P.Graves, Secretary Miss C.Graves, Subscription 2/6 per quarter including teas and postage; overseas members 1/– per quarter. Meetings on Fridays between 4 p.m. and 6 p.m. on 5 February, 4 March, 1 April, 6 May, 3 June, 1 July; hosted by Clarissa and Rosaleen, John, Susan, Perceval, Philip and Charles.
177 AUTHOR Amy to JTRG (16?) February 1932.
178 MAJORCA JTRG to RG 21 February 1932.
179 Ibid.
180 LETTERS n.d. (envelope pmk 1 March 1932).
181 LETTERS p.c. pmk 8 March 1932.
182 MAJORCA Amy to RG 18 January 1932.
183 MAJORCA Amy to RG 18 April 1932.
184 MAJORCA Rosaleen to Laura Riding 1 March 1932.
185 LETTERS 1 March 1932.
186 As note 184 above.
187 Ibid.
188 AUTHOR RG to Clarissa n.d. (August 1932).
189 MAJORCA Notes of a meeting in the drawing-rooms Erinfa 8 August 1932.
190 MAJORCA Amy to RG 8 August 1932.
191 As note 188 above.
192 AUTHOR (Carbon copy of) Clarissa (from Erinfa) to RG 19 August 1932.
193 AUTHOR RG to Clarissa 30 August 1932.

CHAPTER 9
THE ROAD TO THE SEA

194 WILSON RG to TE n.d. (July/August 1932).
195 Ibid. Karl Gay in conversation with the author March 1989 points out that

Bronowski was a fine mathematician, and believes that RG is demeaning him by calling him a geometrician.
196 Eirlys Roberts in conversation with RPG 1986.
197 As note 194 above.
198 Ibid.

CHAPTER 10
THE WRITING OF I, CLAUDIUS

199 BISGO 'A Journal of Curiosities' p. 161.
200 Ibid. p. 134.
201 Ibid. pp. 134–6.
202 WILSON RG to TE n.d. (October 1933).
203 Robert Graves, *I, Claudius* (Arthur Barker 1934) p. 13.
204 AUTHOR RPG's transcript of a tape-recording sent by Mary Ellidge to accompany her letter to RPG of 1 June 1986.
205 WILSON TE to RG 12 November 1933 (from a letter partially published elsewhere).
206 As note 203 above p. 388.
207 As note 205 above.
208 As note 203 above pp. 415–20.
209 Ibid. p. 38.
210 Ibid. p. 41. Beryl Graves points out that, despite this passage, some people really *did* like Laura!
211 Ibid. p. 252.
212 As note 111 above, 'As It Were Poems III' pp. 37–8.

CHAPTER 11
THE VULGATITES

213 As note 111 above.
214 Ibid. p. 32.
215 Ibid. p. 21.
216 Ibid. 'As It Were Poems' pp. 34–8.
217 Ibid. p. 7.
218 Ibid. pp. 23–4.
219 MAJORCA RG to Arthur Barker 12 January 1933.
220 As note 111 above, from 'What Times are These' pp. 26–7.

221 AUTHOR Amy to JTRG 30 November 1932.

222 AUTHOR Rosaleen to Clarissa 28 December 1932.

223 MAJORCA Laura Riding to Maisie Somerville 28 December 1932.

224 MAJORCA Laura Riding to Jacob Bronowski 20 December 1932.

225 MAJORCA Laura Riding to John Cullen 7 January 1933. Cullen was a friend of Eirlys Roberts.

226 MAJORCA Laura Riding to James Reeves 7 January 1933.

227 MAJORCA Laura Riding to 'Memory' (about music) 14 January 1933.

228 MAJORCA Laura Riding to Maisie Somerville 28 December 1932.

229 MAJORCA Laura Riding to Eirlys Roberts 4 January 1933.

230 MAJORCA Laura Riding to Maisie Somerville 1 February 1933.

231 MAJORCA Laura Riding to Julie Matthews n.d. (spring 1933).

232 MAJORCA Laura Riding to James Reeves 7 February 1933.

233 *Epilogue* 1 'Germany' by Laura Riding, John Cullen and Madeleine Vara (LR's pseudonym), p. 98.

234 MAJORCA Laura Riding to Eirlys Roberts 9 January 1933.

235 *Epilogue* 1 pp. 87–92.

236 MAJORCA Laura Riding to Tom Matthews 24 January 1933.

237 MATTHEWS–PC: Extract from a three-page comment on 'The Idea of God' by Bob Casey.

238 As note 236 above.

CHAPTER 12
FINANCIAL CRISIS

239 Ibid.

240 AUTHOR Susan Macaulay (née Graves) to JTRG 2 January 1933.

241 MAJORCA Laura Riding to 'Anna' 7 January 1933.

242 MAJORCA Laura Riding to Julie Matthews n.d. (spring 1933).

243 MAJORCA Laura Riding to Jacob Bronowski 14 February 1933.

244 MAJORCA Laura Riding to Eirlys Roberts 16 January 1933.

245 MAJORCA Copy of the article.

246 MAJORCA Laura Riding to Eirlys Roberts 19 February 1933.

247 MAJORCA Laura Riding to Arthur Barker 25 March 1933.

248 MAJORCA Laura Riding to John Aldridge 28 March 1933.

249 As note 247 above.

250 MAJORCA Laura Riding to Tom Matthews 30 March 1933.

251 MAJORCA Laura Riding to Tom Matthews 19 April 1933.

252 Ibid.

253 Laura Riding and George Ellidge, *14*(A) (Arthur Barker 1934).

254 Ibid. p. 8.

255 Ibid. pp. 104–12.

256 Ibid. pp. 20–1.

257 Ibid. pp. 29–30.

258 Ibid. p. 67.

259 Ibid. p. 30.

260 Ibid. pp. 118–19.

261 Ibid. e.g. p. 284.

262 Ibid. p. 293.

263 Ibid. p. 26.

264 Ibid. p. 302.

265 O'PREY(1) p. 220 RG to Sassoon May 1933.

266 Ibid. pp. 220–1 8 June 1933.

267 Ibid. pp. 221–2 26 June 1933.

268 Ibid. pp. 222–3 7 July 1933.

269 WILSON RG to TE n.d. 1933.

CHAPTER 13
CROSS-CURRENTS

270 O'PREY(1) p. 233 RG to Julie and Tom Matthews 22 n.d. 1933.

271 Ibid. p. 224 RG to Julie Matthews 22 July 1933.

272 ALDRIDGE Laura Riding to John Aldridge n.d. (1933).

273 Ibid.

274 Ibid. but a different letter.

275 As note 271 above.

276 AUTHOR RPG's transcript of a tape-recording sent by Mary Ellidge to accompany her letter to RPG of 1 June 1986.

277 Ibid.
278 Eirlys Roberts in conversation with RPG 1986.
279 Ibid.
280 WILSON TE to RG 12 November 1933.
281 As note 203 above. pp. 9–10.
282 O'PREY(I) pp. 230–2 RG to Sassoon n.d.
283 AUTHOR Amy to JTRG 18 September 1933.
284 AUTHOR Clarissa to JTRG 1 October 1933.
285 AUTHOR Amy to JTRG 3 October 1933.
286 AUTHOR Amy to JTRG 10 October 1933.
287 Ibid. 28 October 1933.
288 RG asked for Sam to be allowed to come out with John and Amy. Amy passed on this request to Nancy, who replied in a letter which Amy did not dare to pass on to RG as it was 'rude' and 'in such bad taste'. RG then asked if David could come out; but nothing could be agreed. See AUTHOR Amy to JTRG 18, 24, 26 and 28 November and 9 December 1933.

CHAPTER 14
VISITORS FROM ENGLAND

289 ALDRIDGE RG to John Aldridge 26 December 1933; continued (n.d.) 1934.
290 AUTHOR Amy to JTRG 28 February 1934; information from Susan, one of whose friends had visited Deyà.
291 As note 289 above.
292 Honor Wyatt in conversation with RPG 1986.
293 AUTHOR Amy's contemporary account, written on her return to Harlech to give as a talk in the locality.
294 AUTHOR JTRG's diary 10 April 1934.
295 As note 293 above.
296 As note 294 above.
297 LETTERS n.d. (March 1934).
298 As note 294 above.

299 O'PREY(I) pp. 234–6 RG to Matthews n.d.
300 MATTHEWS–PC Nora McGuinness to T.S.Matthews 6 March 1978.
301 WILSON RG to TE n.d. January 1934.
302 LETTERS n.d. March 1934.
303 AUTHOR JTRG's diary 12 April 1934.
304 Ibid. 10 April 1934.
305 Ibid. 16 April 1934.
306 Ibid. 10 April 1934.
307 AUTHOR Honor Wyatt to RPG 25 October 1988; HW tells that John Anthony 'later known as John, but we all called Tony' tragically died at the age of ten.
308 AUTHOR JTRG's diary 11 April 1934.
309 As note 293 above.
310 AUTHOR JTRG's diary 17 April 1934.
311 Ibid.
312 As note 293 above.
313 AUTHOR JTRG's diary 17 April 1934.
314 Ibid. 18/19 April 1934; and JTRG in conversation with RPG 1975.
315 Ibid.
316 Honor Wyatt in conversation with RPG 1986.
317 Eirlys Roberts in conversation with RPG 1986.
318 AUTHOR RPG's transcript of a tape-recording sent by Mary Elledge to accompany her letter to RPG of 1 June 1986.
319 Robert Graves in *Epilogue* 1 pp. 87–92.

CHAPTER 15
PUBLICATION OF THE
CLAUDIUS NOVELS

320 LETTERS n.d. (pmk 29 May 1934).
321 Honor Wyatt in conversation with RPG 1986.
322 Eirlys Roberts in conversation with RPG 1986. AUTHOR Honor Wyatt to RPG 25 October 1988 comments: 'Strange that Eirlys thought there was "something" between Gordon and Mary. She was one of the few women who never attracted him – much to Mary's annoyance.'
323 As note 321 above modified by

AUTHOR Honor Wyatt to RPG 25 October 1988.

324 MS-S p. 233.

325 As note 321 above.

326 AUTHOR Honor Wyatt to RPG 25 October 1988 comments that Robert 'told me himself that she said, "I have waited a long time for that" when he kissed and he certainly wasn't reporting the reaction of a "daughter"!'

327 AUTHOR Mary Ellidge to RPG 1 August 1986.

328 LETTERS n.d. but pmk 29 May 1934.

329 As note 321 above. Karl Gay in conversation with RPG March 1989 states that Dorothy Hutchinson had been a salesgirl at the Times Book Club.

330 MS-S pp. 225–6.

331 Possibly the Ward Hutchinsons – though Dorothy was English. Beryl Graves in conversation with RPG 1988 recalls them as 'very boring people who lived at Long Melford in England and went to America when the war broke out'.

332 ALDRIDGE Laura Riding to John Aldridge (letter 'a').

333 Ibid. (letter 'b').

334 Ibid. After this, RG's and LR's remaining friends meant more to them. They gave a very warm welcome to Honor Wyatt, who was pregnant, and who stayed with them for several months during the winter of 1934/5, becoming a particular favourite of Laura's. They also launched *Focus*, a curiously trivial twelve-page newsletter financed by Graves and edited by Riding to which members of the inner circle were invited to contribute, and of which the first number appeared early in 1935.

CHAPTER 16
PROSPERITY AND BURNING COACHES

335 Robert Graves's dairy (henceforward 'RG DIARY') 25 February 1935. Beryl Graves kindly loaned RPG a photocopy of this diary, which runs from February 1935 to May 1939, and is owned by the University of Victoria.

336 LETTERS 10 October 1934.

337 O'PREY(1) pp. 242–3 RG to Julie and Tom Matthews.

338 RG DIARY See e.g. 14, 19 and 25 June and 6 July 1935. Gelat's help was far from altruistic: a good deal of the money for the purchase and repair work passed through his hands; and he was also extracting money from RG in connection with several more dubious ventures.

339 Usually referred to in RG DIARY as C[laudius] F[ilm] V[ersion], this title appears on 13 June 1935.

340 RG DIARY e.g. 9 March 1935.

341 E.g. AUTHOR Amy to JTRG pmk 2 April 1935; also NYPL, Berg Collection (copy seen at MAJORCA) RG to Leonard A.G. Strong 29 November 1934 has: 'to me poetry is still the only thing that matters, but my definition of poetry is very much more exclusive ... the books ... which have given me a vulgar reputation have been absolute sidelines – this includes *Claudius*, though of course I tried to do it decently'.

342 Robert Graves, *Collected Poems 1914–1947* (Cassell 1948) p. 98.

343 Ibid. p. 128.

344 AUTHOR Amy to JTRG pmk 2 April 1935.

345 RG DIARY 8 March 1935.

346 Ibid. 26 March 1935.

347 Ibid. 29 March 1935.

CHAPTER 17
THE DEATH OF A HERO

348 MS-S pp. 257–8 has a larger extract (with some misquotations: e.g. 'not' left out after 'literally' at 4e) from this letter, a copy of which has been seen by RPG at WILSON.

349 Ibid., in part unquoted by MS-S.

350 WILSON TE to RG 4 February 1935. Later it transpired that TE had been playing one of his elaborate games

with his own legend; and despite writing to RG 'rather you than Liddell Hart', he had been 'rather emphatic' to LH in contradicting some of the things in Graves's book, though there had been nothing in it which he himself had not both seen and passed.

351 Ibid.

352 Richard Perceval Graves, *Lawrence of Arabia and His World* (Thames & Hudson 1976) pp. 110–13.

353 RG DIARY 17 May 1935.

354 As note 352 above.

355 O'PREY(I) pp. 254–5 RG to LH 18 June 1935.

356 As note 203 above, p. 190.

357 RG DIARY 30 August 1935.

CHAPTER 18
ARROGANCE AND WASP WAISTS

358 RG DIARY 22 March 1935.

359 Ibid. 21 March 1935.

360 Ibid. 13 April 1935.

361 Ibid.

362 *Focus* 3, Karl Goldschmidt p. 20.

363 *Focus* 1, *Focus* 2, *Focus* 3 and *Focus* 4.

364 *Focus* 2 p. 2.

365 *Focus* 3 p. 7.

366 RG DIARY 2 June and 7 July 1935 give the dates of the two bullfights, in the first of which Ortega appeared; and in the second of which they saw the bullfighter Belmonte get badly tossed.

367 *Focus* 3 pp. 12–13.

368 AUTHOR Susan Macaulay (née Graves) to JTRG 5 June 1935. LETTERS 2 June has: 'that fibs fellow. Naturally it is very good news to me: it means a violent break (sooner or later) between N.N. & him, and therefore a removal of his evil influence from my children & a chance of their remembering me again. It seems odd to me that David & Catherine can visit munitions profiteers in Austria & are not allowed here, by apparently the united good-feeling of my supposedly affectionate family in support

of my faithful & understanding wife.' To balance all this, on 22 July 1956, after Geoffrey's death, Jenny Nicholson wrote to Mary Taylor: 'Geoffrey was for me (for all of us) far more important and influential in our own lives than our own father. ... I don't suppose you know quite how marvellous he was to us as children. The endless patience – listening to our plans, suffering our endless nonsense constructively. It was a much bigger blow when he left us than anybody considered at the time.'

369 AUTHOR Amy to JTRG 1 June 1935.

370 RG DIARY 29 August 1935.

371 Sometimes useful, e.g. helping Honor Wyatt with her novel *The Heathen*; sometimes merely arrogant, e.g. telling Michael Roberts, then editing *The Faber Book of Modern Verse*, that he could only include poems by Graves and Riding if he also included poems by James Reeves.

372 Examples of the bad, or merely silly: 'All the historical events have happened' (p. 2); 'She [Woman] is the answer to the question "Does God exist?"' (p. 7); 'Woman constitutes for man complete experience' (p. 15).

373 RG DIARY 5 August 1935; see also *Focus* 4 p. 31.

CHAPTER 19
DENOUNCED AS SPIES

374 *Focus* 3 p. 14.

375 RG DIARY 11 August 1935.

376 Projects included: for Riding her novel on Troy, the next issues of *Focus* and *Epilogue*, editorial work on a novel by James Reeves (who visited in November/December 1935), and on RG's *Lars Porsena*; and for Graves *Lars Porsena*, *Focus*, *Epilogue*, *Schools*, *Almost Forgotten Germany*, *Old Soldier Sahib*, a filmscript on T.E.Lawrence, and *T.E.Lawrence to His Biographers*.

377 RG included a caricature of APG

(as a country vicar, the father of the chief protagonists in the novel); and also held up to obvious ridicule some aspects of the life of his brother John Graves, who was privately very hurt and confused by this, since not only had he helped RG with the research, but RG had been writing to him in the most friendly manner as 'Dearest John' – and even gave him a copy of the novel inscribed 'John with love from Robert 1936'.

378 These ranged from prophetic ideas about women's fashions to ideas about peopling a stage with life-size robots, each able to give a perfect performance.

379 AUTHOR Philip Larkin to RPG 1 June 1983.

380 RG DIARY e.g. 25 November and 9 December 1935 and 14 April 1936.

CHAPTER 20
ONE SUITCASE EACH

381 LETTERS Saturday 21 (March 1936).

382 RG DIARY 31 March 1936.

383 Ibid. (1936) 16 March reveals that Gelat had been to Madrid to see the Governor, the Mallorquin deputies and the Minister of War; 19 March shows him outlining political schemes; 25 March more schemes for the 12 April elections; 2 April Gelat to be Mayor, the Rights to withdraw; 4 April, elections postponed, and the doctor, frightened, retires from politics; and on 11 May Gelat is officially made Mayor.

384 January 1936 saw the publication (delayed from 1935) of LR's *Progress of Stories*, and of *Epilogue* I (which had

hostile notices apart from a warm review by Rebecca West in the *Sunday Times*); February, of the TSM/LR whimsical collaboration *The Moon's No Fool*; and RG and LR were working on *Antigua, Penny, Puce, A Trojan Ending, Epilogue* II, *Epilogue* III, LR's *Convalescent Conversations*, the proofs of *Lars Porsena* and *Almost Forgotten Germany*; and they also spent much time on *Poets* and *Schools*.

385 LETTERS 4 July 1936: 'the Lawrence book will only be allowed to appear in a limited edition, just about paying typing expenses & a few shillings a thousand words ... [and] the Claudius film-book-of-words can't be written until Korda does the film, which may be never'.

386 Ibid.

387 MS-S p. 262 and RG DIARY 18 July 1936.

388 RG DIARY 19 July 1936.

389 MS-S p. 262 and RG DIARY 20 July 1936.

390 RG DIARY 23 July 1936 supplemented by Beryl Graves in conversation with RPG 1988, who adds that the Mayor of Inca was later found by the Fascists in the Costa d'Or hotel – and shot.

391 Ibid.

392 Ibid. 25 July 1936.

393 Ibid. 28 July 1936.

394 Ibid. 29 July 1936.

395 Ibid. 31 July 1936.

396 Ibid. 1 August 1936.

397 MS-S p. 264 and RG DIARY 2 August 1936.

398 Ibid.

399 RG DIARY 3 and 4 August 1936.

BOOK FIVE
WANDERERS IN EXILE 1936–1940

CHAPTER 1
LANDFALL

1 RG DIARY 3 August 1936.
2 Ibid.
3 MS-S p. 265 and RG DIARY 4 August 1936.
4 RG DIARY 7 August 1936.
5 INDIANA Nicholson MSS 1929–1973 RG to Jenny, David, Catherine and Sam from 32, York Terrace Saturday n.d. (8 August 1936).
6 MS-S p. 266, from RG DIARY 10 August 1936.
7 RG DIARY 11 August 1936.
8 MS-S p. 266, from RG DIARY 7 August 1936; and Karl Gay in conversation with RPG March 1989.
9 RG DIARY 9 August 1936.
10 O'PREY(I) p. 272 RG to LH 8 August 1936.
11 RG DIARY 13 August 1936.
12 AUTHOR Amy to JTRG 28 October 1935 is pleased that RG will after all allow David to go to Cambridge – even if he does not wholly approve.
13 RG DIARY 4 February 1936 'Jenny's first night' on the London stage in the Cochran revue *Follow The Sun*; and see AUTHOR Susan to JTRG 24 February 1936.

CHAPTER 2
MIDNIGHT LAUGHTER

14 RG DIARY 12 August 1936.
15 MS-S pp. 266–7, from RG DIARY 13 August 1936.
16 MS-S p. 266 and RG DIARY 13 August 1936.
17 AUTHOR Harry Kemp to RPG 6 December 1986: 'These notes, somewhat expanded by LR, became section 2 of the study of *Poetry & Politics* in *Epilogue* III.'
18 MS-S p. 267 and RG DIARY 14 August 1936.
19 RG DIARY Monday 17 to Friday 21 August 1936.

20 Ibid. 23 August 1936.
21 Ibid. 21–24 August 1936.
22 The only person to whom LR is alleged to have made sexual overtures during this period was a woman, who did not reciprocate.
23 INDIANA Nicholson MSS 1929–1973 RG to David 24 February (1937).
24 RG DIARY enclosure: Catherine to RG 2 September 1936.
25 Ibid. 7 September 1936.
26 MS-S p. 268 and RG DIARY 14 September 1936.
27 MS-S p. 268, from RG DIARY 17 September 1936.
28 Vic Oliver, *Mr Showbusiness: The Autobiography of Vic Oliver* (George G. Harrap 1954) p. 96.
29 Ibid. p. 97.
30 Ibid.
31 Ibid. pp. 99–100.
32 Ibid. p. 100.
33 RG DIARY 22 September 1936.
34 INDIANA Nicholson MSS 1929–1973 RG to Nancy Nicholson 27 September 1937.
35 AUTHOR Amy to JTRG 22 September 1936.
36 *Epilogue* III pp. 164–5.
37 RG DIARY 21 September 1936.

CHAPTER 3
THE WOMAN QUESTION

38 *Epilogue* III pp. 161–3.
39 RG DIARY 7 October 1936.
40 Ibid. 15 October 1936.
41 AUTHOR JTRG to Amy 18 October 1936. BROTHER notes that the script-writer 'had given all the Romans in Britain pocket handkerchiefs, as evidence of the unpleasant climate in which they were serving'.
42 MS-S p. 273, from RG DIARY 16 October 1936.
43 RG DIARY 18 October 1936.
44 Ibid. 23 October 1936.
45 Ibid. 17 October 1936.

46 O'PREY(I) p. 274 LH to RG 10 October 1936.

47 MATTHEWS p. 154.

48 Ibid. pp. 152–3.

49 Ibid. p. 153.

50 RG DIARY 13 November 1936.

51 Ibid. 14 October 1936.

52 Ibid. 7 October 1936.

53 MS-S p. 277, from RG DIARY 21 October 1936.

54 RG DIARY 25 October 1936.

55 MS-S p. 271 and RG DIARY 27 October 1936. That evening RG and Laura had supper with Robin at Prada's; and on 18 November Robin came to tea at Dorset Street; but thereafter she faded from view for several years.

56 RG DIARY 8 November 1936.

57 Robert Graves, *Collected Poems* (Cassell 1938) pp. 160–2.

58 RG DIARY 11 November 1936.

59 MS-S p. 276, from RG DIARY 11 November 1936.

CHAPTER 4
THE MARK OF A DEVIL

60 INDIANA Nicholson MSS 1929–1973 RG to NN 10, Dorset Street Saturday afternoon. See also RG DIARY 5 December 1936: 'Wrote to NN a long letter indicating that PM had deliberately tried to force a marriage by blackmail.'

61 MATTHEWS p. 153.

62 Beryl Graves comments that this coat cost him £35, and RG prized it highly for the rest of his life.

63 RG DIARY 24 November 1936.

64 Ibid., and MS-S p. 272.

65 MS-S p. 272, from RG DIARY 24 November 1936.

66 *The Times* 4, December 1936, p. 18.

67 MS-S p. 271 and RG DIARY 25–28 November 1936.

68 RG DIARY 1–2 December 1936.

69 Ibid. 4 December 1936.

70 INDIANA Nicholson MSS 1929–1973 RG (from 10, Dorset Street) to Nancy Nicholson Sat. afternoon

(Saturday 5 December 1936); see also RG DIARY 5 December 1936.

71 RG DIARY 7 December 1936.

72 Ibid. 6 December 1936.

73 Ibid. 15 December 1936.

74 INDIANA Nicholson MSS 1929–1973 Laura Riding (from 10, Dorset Street) to Nancy Nicholson n.d. (19 December 1936: see RG DIARY).

75 INDIANA Nicholson MSS 1929–1973 Laura Riding and Robert Graves to Nancy Nicholson n.d. (RG DIARY 20 December has: 'To Belleville: row and ultimatum').

76 AUTHOR Amy to JTRG 8 December 1936.

77 INDIANA Nicholson MSS 1929–1973 RG to his children (excluding Jenny) n.d.

78 AUTHOR Amy to JTRG 30 December 1936, 14 January 1937 and 24 January 1937 (the day after the wedding).

79 RG DIARY 14 January 1937.

80 O'PREY(I) p. 275 RG to Julie Matthews 18 January 1937.

81 MS-S p. 277, from RG DIARY 1 January 1937.

82 RG DIARY 10 January 1937.

83 Ibid. 27 January 1937 has Laura discussing the *Dictionary* with Watt on the telephone; and O'PREY(I) as note 80 above has 'Alan [Hodge] ... we hope he will come to Deyá and work on the Dictionary with us.'

84 MATTHEWS p. 157.

85 AUTHOR Harry Kemp to RPG 6 December 1986.

86 As note 80 above.

87 Laura Riding and sixty-five others, *The World and Ourselves* (Chatto & Windus 1938) p. 16.

88 Ibid. p. 17.

89 Ibid. p. 19.

90 As note 80 above.

91 MS-S p. 279, from RG DIARY 26 January 1937.

92 RG DIARY 4 February 1937.

CHAPTER 5
THE VILLA GUIDI

93 AUTHOR Harry Kemp to RPG 6 December 1986.
94 As note 87 above, p. 122.
95 Ibid. pp. 125–6.
96 Ibid. pp. 120–2.
97 As note 57 above, p. 186.
98 RG DIARY 13 March 1937.
99 Ibid. 1 March 1937.
100 Ibid. 22 March 1937; NYPL, Berg Collection (copy seen at MAJORCA) Leonard Strong shows RG's feeling that Gelat's dangerous position tied his own hands: 'we cannot write anything about the Spanish business for fear of retaliation on our surviving friends there'.
101 Ibid. 2 March 1937.
102 Ibid. 18 March 1939.
103 INDIANA Nicholson MSS 1929–1973 RG to Nancy Nicholson 20 March 1937.
104 INDIANA Nicholson MSS 1929–1973 Laura Riding to Nancy Nicholson 23 March 1937.
105 RG DIARY 2 April 1937.
106 As note 57 above, p. 136.
107 Ibid. p. 162. RG DIARY shows that the poem was passed by Riding 'with one or two small corrections' on 19 May.
108 RG DIARY 10 May 1937.

CHAPTER 6
A TELEGRAM FROM ANITA

109 As note 57 above. See p. 122 for *Leda*, a revised version of this.
110 RG DIARY 21 June 1937.
111 MS-S p. 293 and RG DIARY which has this telegram as an enclosure.
112 RG DIARY 24 June 1937. Robert had been so worried about Gelat that (see AUTHOR Amy to JTRG 29 June 1937) he had asked Amy to pray for him.

CHAPTER 7
BERYL PRITCHARD

113 This chapter (except where otherwise stated) is based upon an interview with Beryl Graves (née Pritchard) conducted by RPG on 11 November 1986 in RG's study at Canelluñ; supplemented by Beryl in conversation with RPG after reading over a draft of the chapter in the spring of 1988.
114 Hardinge Pritchard was up at Worcester College, Oxford; but became caught up in the 'Group movement', often known as the 'Oxford Group', a religious movement founded by the American evangelist Frank Buchman, which later rallied under the slogan 'Moral Rearmament'; and from then on Beryl saw little of him.
115 Cole was the author of *Everyman's Guide to Socialism*.
116 RG DIARY 30–31 January 1937.
117 MS-S p. 293, from RG DIARY 27 June 1937.
118 MS-S p. 294 and RG DIARY 6 July 1937.

CHAPTER 8
ARCHERY AND COUNT BELISARIUS

119 RG DIARY 7 July 1937.
120 Ibid. 30 June 1937.
121 Ibid. 7 July 1937.
122 Ibid. 9 July 1937.
123 Ibid. 9 July 1937.
124 Ibid. 10 July 1937. On this day RG, who had been overdoing things, spent the day in bed on Laura's insistence.
125 Ibid. 11 July 1937.
126 AUTHOR Amy to JTRG 20 July 1937.
127 RG DIARY 17 October 1937.
128 AUTHOR Harry Kemp to RPG 6 December 1986; MS-S p. 252 writes: 'By 1936 yet another project was under way. First called *Poetry and Politics*, it developed into *The Left Heresy in Literature and Life*, which was published by Methuen in 1939 as by "Harry Kemp, Laura Riding and Others".' Harry Kemp comments:
'This account is very misleading. S-S, muddled by hindsight, is here conflating two quite separate

pieces of work, in the second of which RG had practically no hand.

The project 'first called' *Poetry & Politics* concerns a study for *Epilogue*, which appeared (still so-called) in *Epilogue* III, Spring 1937. In the conception and execution of this work there was never any inkling of *The Left Heresy*, which was conceived and written by me (with LR's help) between 7 July and 14 November, 1937, at Ewhurst, where its title was first thought of.'

Kemp adds that RG wrote part IV of the *Epilogue* study at LR's request, but contributed nothing to *Left Heresy*, 'until, while reading the finished work, he made suggestions for last-minute changes and additions.... RG wrote part of an *Epilogue* study, which was incorporated in my text to give the book extra weight.'

129 Ibid.
130 RG DIARY 2 August 1937.
131 RG DIARY 24 July 1937.
132 Ibid. 3 August 1937.
133 Ibid. 14 July 1937.
134 RG, letter in the *Sunday Times*, 17 April 1938.
135 Robert Graves, *Count Belisarius* (Cassell [1st edition 1938] 4th edition January 1962) p. 30.
136 RG DIARY June 1937. Serious work on the project began on 28 August 1937.
137 RG DIARY 24 September 1937.
138 7 September 1937.
139 Jenny Nicholson to RG Bank Holiday Sunday (? 1 August 1937); interpolated in RG DIARY.
140 RG DIARY 27 September 1937; and see AUTHOR Amy to JTRG 9, 12, 13 October 1937; and see also AUTHOR Peggy Graves to JTRG 18 October 1937: 'We haven't time for people we don't like & we don't like Robert. As long as he can be made to do his job over Jenny that is all that is required of him. If he feels that he must write me letters I would prefer them rude because then I don't have to answer them.'

141 RG DIARY 26 July 1937.
142 Ibid. 16 August 1937.
143 Ibid. 20 August 1937.
144 Ibid. 1 October 1937. Mary Lucy visited again from 30 November to 9 December 1937, telling RG that her husband remained 'violent and homicidal'. By mid-December John Lucy was threatening to kill not only Mary and their children (who had decamped from Ireland to Cumberland) but Robert and Laura, and RG called in a local police inspector for advice. By April 1938 however Mary was on her way back to Ireland and an eventual reconciliation with John.
145 Ibid. 14 September 1937.
146 Ibid. 12 September 1937.
147 AUTHOR Harry Kemp to RPG 6 December 1986.
148 RG DIARY 29 September 1937.
149 Ibid. 30 September 1937.
150 As note 147 above. See also AUTHOR Harry Kemp to RPG 19 October 1988: 'He [RG] must have been aware of the general atmosphere of hysteria that LR generated, but I still doubt whether he was aware of my, & Alix's, antipathies. As soon as we got to London, & separated, relations improved.'
151 RG DIARY 29 October 1937.
152 Ibid. 30 October 1937.
153 Ibid. 31 October 1937.
154 Ibid. 4 November 1937.
155 Ibid. 10 November 1937.
156 Psalms xlvi 9.

CHAPTER 9
THE COVENANT

157 AUTHOR Harry Kemp to RPG 6 December 1986.
158 AUTHOR Amy to JTRG 6 March 1938. Amy had previously seen RG on 15 December 1937 when she celebrated her eightieth birthday at a grand family gathering at Prada's. It was also a farewell party for Clarissa, shortly to return to her beloved Palestine.

159 RG DIARY 29 January 1938 records Beryl Pritchard married to Alan Hodge on that day. It was at the Hampstead Registry Office. Laura was present but not RG.

160 Ibid. 19 March 1938.

161 Ibid. 25 March 1938.

162 MS-S p. 304, from RG DIARY 26 March 1938.

163 Dorothy and Montague had replied to a copy of LR's 'Letter on International Affairs' which they had received from their mutual friend the printer Vyvyan Richards. Once RG and LR were settled at 31, Alma Square, the Simmonses were invited to supper, and made a favourable impression. Riding appeared to Dorothy to have important messages for mankind.

164 As note 162 above.

165 MS-S p. 305, from RG DIARY 28 April 1938.

166 RG DIARY 2 April 1938.

167 Ibid. 3 April 1938.

168 As note 87 above. Resolutions pp. 519–29: no. 20 p. 256.

169 Ibid. no. 24 p. 257.

170 RG DIARY 6 April 1938 (Tanny Brown).

171 MS-S p. 306, from RG DIARY 8 April 1938.

172 MS-S p. 306, and RG DIARY 10 April 1938.

173 RG DIARY 18 April 1938.

174 Ibid. 22 April 1938: 'rediscovered "University" from five years ago at Deyá'.

175 Ibid. 23 April 1938.

176 Ibid. 26 April 1938.

177 Ibid. 28 April 1938.

178 Ibid. 28 June 1938.

179 Ibid. 9, 11, 13, 15 May 1938. This time it was for tonsillitis.

180 LETTERS n.d. (6 May 1938).

181 RG DIARY 21 May 1938.

182 Ibid. 26 May 1938.

183 Ibid. 27 May 1938.

184 LETTERS 4 April 1938.

185 AUTHOR Beryl Graves to RPG summer 1988, a series of annotations to the first draft of the present work.

186 E.g. clearing up points in LH's TE proofs; finishing the *Smuggler* scenario; seeing Amy, Jenny, David, Len, Jane and others. The previous month RG had devoted some time to Karl, who could not accompany them to France because travelling on a German passport was dangerous for him. There was some idea that he might go to Canada (and RG visited Mike Pearson at Canada House on 21 April on this matter); but in the end he stayed in London, where with RG's help he found work with a bookseller off the Charing Cross Road.

187 RG DIARY 29 June 1938.

CHAPTER 10
LE CHÂTEAU DE LA CHEVRIE

188 RG DIARY 2 July 1938.

189 MS-S p. 311, from RG DIARY 5 July 1938.

190 INDIANA Nicholson MSS 1929–1973 RG to Nancy Nicholson 10 July 1938.

191 RG DIARY 7 July 1938.

192 Ibid. 13 July 1938.

193 O'PREY(I) p. 279 RG to Karl '6 July, I think, 1938'. RG says the shell landed in the grotto, but Beryl Graves as in note 185 above declares that 'it can't have been the grotto', and suggests this emendation.

194 RG DIARY 10 July 1938.

195 Ibid.

196 MAJORCA Nancy Nicholson to RG n.d.

197 As note 190 above.

198 RG DIARY 17 November 1937; and AUTHOR Amy to JTRG 7 December 1937.

199 RG DIARY 14 July 1938.

200 Ibid. 15 July 1938.

201 Ibid. 17 July 1938.

202 INDIANA Gay MSS RG to Karl Goldschmidt 3 August 1938.

203 RG DIARY 21 July 1938.

204 Ibid. 24 July 1938. For LR's behaviour, Dorothy Simmons in conversation with RPG 6–7 January 1986.

205 Dorothy Simmons in conversation

with RPG 6–7 January 1986, modified by a further conversation in late 1988.

206 RG DIARY 4 August 1938.

207 Ibid. 7 August 1938.

208 Ibid. 9 December 1937.

209 MS-S p. 301, from RG DIARY 27 December 1937.

210 MS-S p. 302, from RG DIARY 29 January 1938. Beryl comments in spring 1988, 'I don't believe my Father was rude to Alan.... my mother didn't come but some nice cousins did. I didn't hold it against my mother one bit.' Karl Gay in conversation with RPG March 1989 recalls LR trying to persuade people to play the 'thread' game at the reception. He also believes that the marriage was to some extent 'engineered' by LR.

211 MS-S p. 342, from MAJORCA 26 September 1939 LR to RG.

212 MS-S p. 312, from RG DIARY 11 August 1938.

213 MS-S p. 312, from RG DIARY 12 August 1938. AUTHOR Beryl Graves as note 185 above comments: '"Marthe" it said, "Oui madame," he replied, not knowing if he or the other was the ghost.'

214 As note 205 above.

215 RG DIARY 13 August 1938.

216 Ibid. 14 August 1938.

217 Dorothy Simmons in conversation with RG late 1988. She comments further that Robert and Montague 'did not have a rapport: Montague was a bit traditional and conventional. A gentle man, he was ridiculed, but was too good to take exception.'

218 RG DIARY 15 August 1938.

219 Ibid.

220 MS-S p. 315; the poem was written on 16, 18 August 1938, and there is a typed version loose in RG DIARY.

CHAPTER II
'A BEAUTIFUL INSINCERITY; & TRUE'

221 MATTHEWS pp. 179–80.

222 MAJORCA Laura Riding to Tom Matthews 14 January 1933 and Laura Riding to Schuyler Jackson 17 February 1933.

223 MAJORCA LR to RG 26 September 1939.

224 RG DIARY 9, 15 and 22 October 1938. Graves wrote two letters of rebuttal, neither of which was published; and Riding subsequently cancelled their subscription to the TLS.

225 See letter from RG in *Time & Tide* for 21 January 1939.

226 See e.g. *Time & Tide* 24 December 1938 in which Rayner Heppenstall asserted that all Graves's best work was concentrated into one thin book of *Poems 1930–1933*, and that he had written nothing so good either before or since.

227 RG DIARY 3 January 1939.

228 MS-S p. 322, from RG DIARY 3 January 1939.

229 As note 205 above.

230 RG DIARY 3 January 1939.

231 King's College London (copy seen at MAJORCA) RG to LH 16 February 1939.

232 RG DIARY 14 January 1939.

233 Ibid. 10, 11 January 1939. The poem became 'The Beast'.

234 Robert Graves, *Collected Poems 1914–1947* (Cassell 1948) p. 174.

235 Ibid. p. 172.

236 Enclosed in pages of RG DIARY: LR to RG 1 March 1939.

237 However, take into account: AUTHOR Beryl Graves to RPG, which comments on this section of the first draft of the text (summer 1988), 'I don't believe Laura was a schemer like that. I suppose you could get that impression from the material you have but it is not my view of the situation.'

238 RG DIARY 6 February 1939.

239 Ibid. 26 February 1939.

240 Ibid. 27 February 1939.

241 O'PREY(I) p. 280 RG to Karl 10 February 1939.

242 RG DIARY 27 January 1939.

243 Ibid. 10 February 1939.

244 MS-S p. 324 and RG DIARY 27 February 1939.

245 As note 234 above p. 171.

246 RG DIARY 2 March 1939.

247 MS-S p. 325 from RG DIARY 7 March 1939.

248 MATTHEWS p. 189.

249 Ibid. p. 201.

250 RG DIARY 28 March 1939.

251 Ibid. 31 March 1939.

252 Ibid. 16 April 1939.

253 AUTHOR Beryl Graves to RPG (summer 1988) comments on RG noting in his diary 'March 24th "Madrid surrendered – this was a premature report." March 28th "Madrid surrendered." March 29th. "Valencia surrendered – End of Spanish War."' She adds that: 'In his usual wishful thinking way he must have had a return to Deyá in his mind as he leaves one of the cats "en pension" with Leonie "waiting for us to take him to Deyá" as well as the trunk to keep in store for Deyá.'

CHAPTER 12
INTO A DARKNESS

254 MS-S p. 329, from RG DIARY 22 April 1939.

255 RG DIARY 29 April 1989 and see also O'PREY(I) pp. 281–2 RG to Karl 5 May 1939.

256 MS-S p. 329 and RG DIARY 29 April 1939.

257 RG DIARY I May 1939.

258 MS-S p. 329, from RG DIARY 30 April 1939.

259 MATTHEWS p. 203.

260 Ibid. p. 204.

261 MS-S p. 329, from RG DIARY 2 April 1939.

262 As note 234 above, p. 153.

263 Honor Wyatt in conversation with RPG spring 1986.

264 Dorothy Simmons in conversation with RPG 6–7 January 1986. Karl Gay in a conversation with RPG March 1989 which cannot be ignored makes it clear that he totally mistrusts DS's view of LR's character.

265 MS-S p. 329, from RG DIARY 3 May 1989.

266 AUTHOR Laura Riding to RPG 5 April 1985 defends herself from these charges by declaring that because Kit liked her, she was drawn into Kit's inner world, and failed at first to realize the dangerous direction in which Kit's thoughts were leading.

267 RG DIARY 4 May 1939.

268 Ibid. 5 May 1939.

269 Ibid.

270 O'PREY(I) pp. 281–2 RG to Karl 5 May 1939.

271 MS-S p. 330, from RG DIARY 6 May 1939.

272 MATTHEWS pp. 204–5.

273 Ibid. p. 205.

274 Ibid. p. 206.

275 Ibid. p. 207.

276 Ibid. p. 209.

277 Ibid. pp. 211–12.

278 Ibid. p. 208.

279 Robert Graves, *The White Goddess* (Faber & Faber 1948) p. 399.

280 MATTHEWS p. 208.

281 Beryl Graves writes to RPG (summer 1988): 'I remember Laura asking (telling) me to pack for Kit "as though I were her mother" (why?) She also pointed out to me, when we went into her room, the contents of a packet of Tampax arranged in some sort of triangle which she found very sinister though I didn't understand why. I don't remember any other "evidence of witchcraft".'

282 MATTHEWS pp. 207–8.

283 Ibid. p. 208.

284 Ibid. p. 211.

285 Ibid. p. 208.

286 King's College London (copy seen at MAJORCA) RG to LH 2 October 1939.

287 INDIANA Gay MSS RG to Karl n.d.

288 MS-S p. 336. Curiously, in her *Convalescent Conversations* (Seizin/Constable 1936) LR, under her pseudonym of Madeleine Vara, had included this conversation:

ADAM: ... I think it's very important to establish a strong domestic climate, against the insinuations you meet at every turn that you're like everybody else.

ELEANOR: By doing what everybody else does behind locked doors and coming out with an air of triumphant mystery?

ADAM: That's right. Because some time or other you have to face the fact that you have bodies like everybody else.

289 MATTHEWS p. 209.

290 As note 286 above.

291 RG never published this poem. It remained at the end of RG DIARY which was then sold to the University of Victoria, British Columbia; who included it in 1975 in the *Malahat Review*'s special RG's Eightieth Birthday number.

CHAPTER 13
A GRIN OF TRIUMPH

292 MAJORCA (the inference of RG to Beryl, 25 September 1939).

293 As note 286 above.

294 MAJORCA RG to Beryl 25 September 1939.

295 AUTHOR Clarissa Graves to JTRG 21 February 1940.

296 RG DIARY 16 March 1939 has 'Talked most of night with Laura and AT LAST got the thing right about joulting and swingering.'

297 Beryl Graves in conversation with RPG 11 November 1986; with further information from Beryl Graves to RPG summer 1988.

298 MAJORCA RG to Beryl 25 September (1939).

299 INDIANA Nicholson MSS 1929–1973 RG to Nancy Nicholson 25 June 1939.

300 Ibid. 18 July 1939.

301 The original plan was for RG and Alan to take Griselda Jackson with them, and for her to stay with friends in Buckinghamshire. But Griselda remained in the USA.

302 MATTHEWS p. 213.

303 INDIANA Nicholson MSS 1929–1973 RG to Nancy Nicholson n.d.

304 MAJORCA LR to RG 15 September 1939.

305 MATTHEWS p. 209.

CHAPTER 14
'ROSE-BUD'

306 As note 303 above. RG had hoped to spend a day or two with Dorothy Simmons at Beckenham in Kent; but a week after war was declared she and Montague crossed the Atlantic in the other direction, thus passing Robert and Alan somewhere on the high seas.

307 AUTHOR Amy to JTRG 28 July 1939. Robert had told Rosaleen (as Amy reported to John) 'everything is changed'.

308 AUTHOR Amy to JTRG 15 January 1940.

309 AUTHOR JTRG to Amy 26 August 1939. At this stage Mallik, RG's old Nepalese philosopher friend, reappeared briefly on the scene. In Oxford he talked on 30 September 1939 to JTRG and Clarissa – convinced that his theories would crush those of Laura – but JTRG and C found him 'far too dogmatic', and Robert refused to have anything to do with him.

310 AUTHOR Amy to JTRG 17 August 1939.

311 Ibid.

312 Ibid. 19 August 1939.

313 As note 310 above.

314 AUTHOR Amy to JTRG 24 August 1939.

315 MS-S p. 342 and MAJORCA LR to RG 8 August 1939.

316 RG in *Sunday Graphic* 8 October 1939.

317 As note 314 above.

318 MAJORCA LR to RG 1 September 1939. This was Kit Jackson's third visit back to the Farm. At some stage after RG had left for England, and after Dorothy Simmons had arrived

at Brownsburg, there had been a second unexpected and very brief visit. Beryl Graves writes (summer 1988): 'I remember we were all (Laura, Schuyler, Dorothy, David and me) in Nimrod's Rise having supper when we heard outside "Yoo-hoo, yoo-hoo" in a very excited but cheerful voice, and there was Kit running across from the Farm having arrived unexpectedly from hospital.' It was after this that a curious incident took place: 'Laura was planning to send her back ... and ... Kit herself had to be encouraged to play the piano ... so that she wouldn't hear Laura phoning for the doctor.'

319 Ibid. 4 September 1939.
320 MS-S p. 342 from MAJORCA LR to RG n.d.
321 MAJORCA LR to RG 24 August 1939.
322 Ibid. 15 September 1939.
323 MS-S p. 342 and MAJORCA LR to RG 15 September 1939.
324 MS-S p. 342 and MAJORCA LR to RG 22 September 1939.
325 Ibid.
326 O'PREY(I) p. 286 RG to LH 25 September 1939.
327 Ibid.
328 King's College London (copy seen at MAJORCA) RG to LH n.d.
329 MAJORCA RG to Beryl 25 September 1939 (letter 'A').
330 Ibid. n.d.
331 Ibid.
332 As note 329 above (letter 'B').
333 INDIANA Nicholson MSS 1929–1973 RG to Nancy Nicholson n.d.
334 Ibid. 11 October 1939.

CHAPTER 15
A REALLY GOOD PERSON

335 MAJORCA LR to RG 26 September 1939 (2nd letter).
336 MS-S pp. 343–4.
337 King's College London (copy seen at MAJORCA) RG to LH 2 October 1939.
338 MAJORCA LR to RG (RG quoted in), 5 October 1939.
339 MAJORCA RG to Beryl 25 September 1939 (letter 'B').
340 MAJORCA RG to Montague Simmons n.d.
341 MAJORCA LR to RG 5 October 1939.
342 As note 340 above.
343 INDIANA Nicholson MSS 1929–1973 RG to Nancy 11 October (1939).
344 Ibid. Nancy Nicholson to RG 14 October (1939).
345 Ibid. RG to Nancy 16 October (1939).
346 MAJORCA RG to Alan Hodge n.d. and MS-S p. 346.
347 Alan Hodge very soon secured employment as the private secretary of Brendan Bracken MP (Minister of Information 1941–5).
348 Most of this property, it is true, had been paid for by Robert; so Laura Riding may have felt under a moral obligation to make it over to him. But her generosity was real: her gift included Ca'n Torrent, the house next door to Canelluñ which had been given to her by Norman Cameron, and which now belongs to Robert and Beryl's daughter Lucia.
349 MAJORCA Laura Riding to RG 1 November 1939.
350 As note 234 above, p. 193.
351 Despite this disclaimer, there seems no doubt that RG and LR had been lovers during the late-1926 to early-1929 period of their relationship.
352 O'PREY(I) pp. 288–9 RG to LH 21 November 1939.
353 Tom Matthews comments (1988), 'Jimmy Townsend – a pity we can't have a glimpse of this rollicking character.'
354 MAJORCA LR to RG 16 December 1939.
355 INDIANA Gay MSS RG to Karl Xmas Day 1939.
356 Ibid. 28 December 1939.
357 MAJORCA Laura to RG 31 December (1939) (misdated 1931).
358 MAJORCA has the second 4 January LR to RG letter, in which LR declares her inability to repay a single

penny since doing so would lead to her and Schuyler becoming insolvent.

359 O'PREY(I) pp. 290–1 RG to Karl 26 January 1940.

360 MAJORCA Schuyler Jackson to RG 6 January 1940.

361 As 359 above.

362 King's College London (copy seen at MAJORCA) RG to LH n.d.

363 INDIANA Gay MSS RG to Karl 17 February 1940.

364 MAJORCA LR to RG 17 February 1940.

AFTERWORD

1 King's College London (copy seen at MAJORCA) RG to LH 30 November 1939.

2 O'PREY(I) p. 292 RG to LH 19 February 1940.

3 Robert Graves and Alan Hodge, *The Long Weekend* (Faber & Faber 1940), pp. 200–1.

SELECT BIBLIOGRAPHY

For a full bibliography the reader should turn to F.H.Higginson's *Robert Graves: A Bibliography* (St Paul's Bibliographies 1987); and to Alan Clark, 'Laura Riding Jackson: A Check-list' in *Chelsea 35* (Chelsea Associates Inc., 1976). What follows is a guide to the more important published sources relevant to the period covered by this volume.

1 RELATING TO ROBERT AND LAURA'S LIVES BETWEEN 1926 AND 1940

Graves, Alfred Perceval (Robert's father), *To Return to All That* (Jonathan Cape 1930). The bulk of this work is a straightforward and consistently entertaining autobiography, which had been written though not fully revised long before Robert began writing his *Good-bye to All That*. However, after the publication of Robert's book a new chapter was added in which APG replied to some of his son's criticisms and corrected some of his inaccuracies, and the present title was decided upon. Unfortunately it is a title which has given many people the misleading impression that the entire book was simply an attempt to fight back at Robert.

Graves, Charles (Robert's brother), *The Bad Old Days* (Faber & Faber 1951). This book is chiefly interesting as a somewhat impressionistic account of life in Fleet Street in the 1920s, 1930s and 1940s; but it also contains details which do not appear elsewhere about the troubled relationship between Robert and Charles.

Graves, Robert, *Good-bye to All That* (Jonathan Cape 1929; revised edition 1957). For the writing of this superb autobiography see Book Three, Chapter 6, of this volume.

Graves, Robert, *But It Still Goes On* (Jonathan Cape 1930). This contains some interesting but not always very reliable autobiographical information on the years from 1926 to 1929.

Matthews, T.S., *Under the Influence* (Cassell 1977); contains many detailed recollections of Robert Graves and Laura Riding in the 1930s, including a chilling account of the deterioration in their relationship following their journey to the USA in 1939.

O'Prey, Paul (ed.), *In Broken Images: Selected Letters of Robert Graves 1914–1946* (Hutchinson 1982). The first volume of two. O'Prey gives a very thorough account of some correspondences, but the drawback of his method is that some individual letters of considerable biographical importance slip through his net.

Seymour-Smith, Martin, *Robert Graves: His Life and Works* (Hutchinson 1982). The pioneering critical biography: good on criticism, but factually unreliable.

Wexler, Joyce, *Laura Riding's Pursuit of Truth* (Ohio University Press 1979). The most complete book about Laura Riding: begun with LR's approval; but JW's independence of mind led (predictably enough) to that approval being withdrawn before the book was completed.

2 PRINCIPAL PUBLICATIONS BY ROBERT GRAVES BETWEEN JANUARY 1926 AND JANUARY 1940

1926 *Another Future of Poetry* (Hogarth Press) (critical).

Impenetrability; or, The Proper Habit of English (Hogarth Press) (critical).

1927 *Poems 1914–1926* (London: William Heinemann; New York: Doubleday 1929) (poems).

Poems 1914–1927 (William Heinemann) (poems).

The English Ballad: A Short Critical Survey (Benn) (critical).

Lars Porsena: or, the Future of Swearing and Improper Language (London: Kegan Paul Trench Trubner [and 1936 revised as *The Future of Swearing and Improper Language*]; New York: Dutton) (critical).

A Survey of Modernist Poetry (with LR) (London: William Heinemann; New York: Doubleday 1928) (critical).

Lawrence and the Arabs (London: Jonathan Cape; New York: Doubleday 1928, as *Lawrence and the Arabian Adventure*) (biographical).

John Skelton (*Laureate*) (Benn) (as editor).

The Less Familiar Nursery Rhymes (Benn) (as editor).

1928 *A Pamphlet Against Anthologies* (with LR) (London: Jonathan Cape; New York, Doubleday, as *Against Anthologies*) (critical).

Mrs Fisher; or the Future of Humour (Kegan Paul Trench Trubner) (critical).

1929 *Poems 1928* (Seizin Press) (poems).

The Shout (Matthews & Marrot) (fiction).

Good-bye to All That: An Autobiography (London: Jonathan Cape; New York, Cape & Smith 1930) (autobiographical).

1930 *Ten Poems More* (Paris: Hours Press) (poems).

But It Still Goes On (London: Jonathan Cape; New York, Cape & Smith) (autobiographical, fiction, play, critical).

1931 *To Whom Else?* (Deyá: Seizin Press) (poems).

Poems 1926–1930 (William Heinemann)

1932 *No Decency Left* (with LR, as Barbara Rich) (Jonathan Cape) (fiction).

1933 *Poems 1930–1933* (Arthur Barker) (poems).

The Real David Copperfield (London; Arthur Barker; New York: Harcourt Brace 1934, as M.P.Paine (ed.), *David Copperfield by Charles Dickens, condensed by Robert Graves*) (fiction).

1934 *I, Claudius* (London: Arthur Barker; New York: Smith & Haas) (fiction).

1935 *Claudius the God and His Wife Messalina* (London; Arthur Barker; New York: Smith & Haas 1935) (fiction).

1936 *Antigua, Penny, Puce* (Deyá and London: Seizin Press and Constable; New York: Random House 1938) (fiction).

Almost Forgotten Germany (by Georg Schwarz) (with LR) (London and Deyá: Constable and Seizin Press, New York: Random House) (translator).

1938 *Collected Poems* (London: Cassell; New York: Random House) (poems).

Count Belisarius (London: Cassell; New York: Random House) (fiction).

T.E.Lawrence to His Biographer Robert Graves (New York; Doubleday; London: Faber 1939) (biographical).

3 PRINCIPAL PUBLICATIONS BY
LAURA RIDING BETWEEN
JANUARY 1926
AND JANUARY 1940

1926 *The Close Chaplet* (as Laura Riding Gottschalk) (London; Hogarth Press; New York: Adelphi) (poems).

1927 *Voltaire: A Biographical Fantasy* (Hogarth Press) (poem).

1927 *A Survey of Modernist Poetry* (with RG) (London: William Heinemann; New York, Doubleday 1928) (critical).

1928 *Contemporaries and Snobs* (Jonathan Cape) (critical).

Anarchism Is Not Enough (London: Jonathan Cape; New York: Doubleday) (critical).

A Pamphlet Against Anthologies (with RG) (London: Jonathan Cape; New York: Doubleday, as *Against Anthologies*) (critical).

Love as Love, Death as Death (Deyá; Seizin Press) (poems).

1930 *Experts Are Puzzled* (Jonathan Cape) (chiefly fiction).

Poems: A Joking Word (Jonathan Cape).

Four Unposted Letters to Catherine (Paris: Hours Press) (practical philosophy of life, written for a child).

Twenty Poems Less (Paris: Hours Press) (poems).

Though Gently (Deyá: Seizin Press) (poems and poetic prose).

1931 *Laura and Francisca* (Deyá; Seizin Press) (poem).

1933 *Everybody's Letters* (Arthur Barker) (as editor).

The Life of the Dead (Arthur Barker) (poem).

Poet, A Lying Word (Arthur Barker) (poems).

1934 *14(A)* (with George Ellidge) (Arthur Barker) (fiction).

Americans (Los Angeles: Primavera) (poem).

1935 *Progress of Stories* (Deyá and London; Seizin Press and Constable) (fiction).

Epilogue: A Critical Summary Vol. I (Deyá and London: Seizin Press and Constable) (as editor and contributor, with RG).

1936 *Convalescent Conversations* (as Madeleine Vara) (Deyá and London: Seizin Press and Constable) (fiction).

Almost Forgotten Germany (by Georg Schwarz) (with RG) (Deyá and London: Seizin Press and Constable; New York: Random House) (translator).

Epilogue; A Critical Summary Vol. II (Deyá and London: Seizin Press and Constable) (as editor and contributor, with RG).

1937 *A Trojan Ending* (Deyá and London: Seizin Press and Constable; New York: Random House) (fiction).

Epilogue: A Critical Summary Vol. III (Deyá and London: Seizin Press and Constable) (as editor and contributor with RG).

1938 *Collected Poems* (London: Cassell; New York; Random House) (poems).

The World and Ourselves (Chatto & Windus) (as editor and contributor).

1939 *Lives of Wives* (London: Cassell; New York: Random House) (fiction).

INDEX

RG stands for Robert Graves, APG for Alfred Perceval Graves, NN for Nancy Nicholson, and LR for Laura Riding.